Protecting Your Property

A guide to the law

for landowners

- by-

A. W. Barsby
Barrister
(non-practising)

A. W. & C. BARSBY
LEGAL RESEARCH AND PUBLISHING

A. W. & C. BARSBY
LEGAL RESEARCH AND PUBLISHING

2 Lynwood Avenue, Epsom, Surrey, KT17 4LQ
Tel: +44 (0)1372 742372
Fax: +44 (0)1372 721900

http://www.barsby.com

Published in England

ISBN 0 9521625 6 3

Cover design by Chris Higson. Icons by Ian Tyrrell Graphics.

Preface

Having produced a series of guides to specialised aspects of the law, we were conscious of a need for a book which would explain land law, in some detail, to landowners generally. This book represents our attempt to meet that need. Like our other books, it is accompanied by "Notes and Queries" pages on our Internet site, where we will up-date and add to the printed text, and deal with questions from users of the book.

We are most grateful to all the individuals and organisations who have commented on our work in the past, and particularly to users of our books who have drawn attention to passages which need clarifying or expanding.

A. W. & C. Barsby
Epsom
October 2000

Contents

Cross-references

Cross-references are of particular importance in a book such as this one, because so many explanations depend upon what is said at different places, and readers therefore need to be able to move easily from one part of the book to another. The system used here, which has been specially developed for this book, works as follows:

A signpost means a general cross-reference—usually to a related passage which may be of interest to the reader.

A key means a reference to a definition or explanation which is important to the meaning of the passage in question. Readers may need to refer to the definition or explanation in order to understand the passage.

A treasure-chest means a reference to chapter 12, which lists sources of additional information about the law, and thus serves as a starting point for wider research.

Introduction

The law in perspective

0-0 In thinking about the law, it is easy to make one of two mistakes. The first mistake is to believe that law does not matter at all, and is not worth bothering with; the second to believe that it is all-important.

0-1 People who think that the law doesn't matter may do so because they have no faith in the law itself, regarding it as complicated, obscure and unfair, or in the legal system, on the ground that it is slow, expensive and uncertain. They may make the point that what people want, in their dealings with others, is not legal rights, but patience, tolerance and goodwill—in other words, perhaps, a certain generosity of spirit—since these qualities solve problems far more quickly and efficiently that the law can ever do. In thinking that the law doesn't matter they tend to be encouraged by the fact that it is often ignored; and not just by private persons but by companies and other organisations, big and small, which ought to know better.

0-2 Those who believe the law is all-important tend to feel that so long as they are legally in the right that is the end of the matter, and there is no need to consider the interests or feelings of other people, or to bother with explanations, discussions or compromises.

0-3 In reality the law does matter, but in a way which is subtle rather than obvious. Legal rights can never be a substitute for the friendly settlement of disputes: they are simply the next best thing, which is all the State can provide. They have to be there, so that disputes which cannot be resolved amicably can at least be settled in a relatively civilised way, rather than by violence. In addition, the fact that the law sets out rights and wrongs in a formal way can help people to settle disputes, because they can then see what the court's decision is likely to be if legal proceedings cannot be avoided. This is particularly important when, as is sometimes the case, there is no single, obvious legal solution to a problem.

See further 0-16.

0-4 Both the law and the legal system can indeed be criticised. The law is sometimes complicated, and (like many other subjects) is afflicted by a certain amount of jargon. There is certainly too much of it. On the other hand, it is perfectly possible for non-lawyers to gain a good understanding of the essentials. The legal system is another matter: legal proceedings can be a painful experience, even for the successful party. The best one can say is that it is a human institution, and is frail in the way other human institutions are. But the point is that although criticisms of the law and the legal system are perfectly in order, it is wrong to conclude that the law does not matter—there must be laws and a legal system to make them work in practice. So much for the first mistake mentioned above.

0-5 What about the second? The law has to be relatively precise, so that people can be clear about how it affects them. It is rarely possible for the law to declare simply that people must behave fairly or sensibly. Many laws, in laying down what must or must not be done, look as though they are not concerned at all with what is fair and sensible. But this is deceptive. The law is often very sensitive about such matters and those whose behaviour is unfair or unwise may well find that their attempts to enforce the law are unsatisfactory. The courts can, for example, exercise their discretion to refuse certain remedies to a person whose case is unmeritorious, even though he is legally in the right, and can similarly refuse to order that the successful party's costs be paid by his opponent.

See particularly 3-29 on injunctions.

Aim of the book

0-6 The aim of this book is to provide a practical guide to the law of England and Wales for landowners. "Landowners" is used to include all those who own land, whether the land is a fraction of an acre in a built-up area or a large expanse of countryside, and whether the use is residential or commercial or falls into some other category. In line with what was said under the last heading, the aim of the book is to provide a good working understanding of the legal rights and wrongs of a situation, so that a landowner can:

◆ Discuss and resolve problems with neighbours and others.

◆ Take practical measures where necessary, for example putting up gates or warning notices.

◆ Ask for help from local government staff, or the police, or other official bodies.

◆ Know when to consult a lawyer or other professional in order to obtain advice or assistance on a particular problem, or to set in motion some form of legal procedure.

0-7 Although the book is written from the point of view of the landowner, and deals with the legal problems which he or she may have with neighbours and others, it should be emphasised that the law cuts both ways. Landowners who wish to enjoy their property peacefully must take care to abide by the law themselves.

Understanding the law

0-8 The following paragraphs make some general remarks about how the law works, which should be helpful in understanding later chapters. One general point—the fairness of the law—has already been touched on.

See 0-5.

0-9 *How does the law work?* Although it is natural to speak of laws being about such things as trees, or buildings, they are in reality always about people. Only people can respond to the requirements of the law, although the law can and does impose many rules about how people must behave in relation to trees (for example, by not cutting them down if the tree is subject to a tree preservation order) or buildings (for example, by obtaining planning permission before carrying out development).

See 10-19 for the meaning of "tree preservation order" and 9-13 for the meaning of "development".

0-10 Sometimes the law works on the basis that a right is regarded as being attached to land or some other piece of property. When land is mortgaged, for example, the person lending the money obtains a number of rights, including the right to sue the borrower and also the right to get her money back by selling the land. She has, in other words, a right which is regarded as being attached to the land. But the point made above still applies: the law is still addressed to people, but in this situation is telling them to behave as though the land had a right attached to it.

See 7-52 onwards for mortgages. Land is sometimes said to be "charged" with the payment of money in other situations.

0-11 *Language and the law* The law needs to be clear, but language often has a degree of vagueness and uncertainty. A careful choice of words can help to overcome this problem, and the law very often uses language in a more careful and considered way than is usual in everyday communications. To refer to a plot of land which shares a boundary with another, a word like "adjoining" or "abutting" might be used. But it might be necessary for a particular rule to apply to a plot which was close to another, but did not share a boundary, because the two pieces of land were separated by a narrow strip belonging to someone else—in which case a word like "adjacent" could be used.

See 7-2 onwards for the Access to Neighbouring Land Act 1992, which works in this way.

0-12 In legislation, words are often defined, so as to make their meaning clearer. There is no complete, standard set of definitions, which applies to all legislation. Sometimes, though not particularly often, a definition in one piece of legislation is used in another. Some general rules for interpreting legislation are laid down by the Interpretation Act 1978. For example, and unless the contrary intention appears:

See 1-1 onwards for the meaning of "legislation".

- Masculine words include the feminine—which is why legislation almost always says "he" rather than "he or she"—and the singular includes the plural.

- "Person" includes a private person, a partnership, and company (which is an artificial legal "person"). (The word "individual" is generally used to mean only living persons.)

- Distances are to be measured in a straight line on a horizontal plane.

0-13 The law does not always aim for precision: sometimes an idea is left purposely vague, so that it can take its meaning from the facts of a particular situation. "Reasonable" is the classic example: it means, in effect, what most people would regard as fair or justifiable in the circumstances. A landowner may, for example, be concerned about his neighbour's smoky bonfires. But the law of nuisance, which deals with this sort of problem, does not lay down exactly how smoky a bonfire is allowed to be, how close to the boundary of land it may be, or how long it is allowed to last, before the neighbouring landowner is justified in complaining. Instead, the test is what is reasonable in all the circumstances, bearing in mind that neighbours must put up with a certain amount of disturbance from each other. This allows a simple rule to cover many different situations. The result is rather unsatisfactory in that it is difficult to be sure what "reasonable" actually means without bringing legal proceedings and asking a court to decide. On the other hand, to lay down exactly what factors are relevant, and to what extent, would result in rules which were extremely burdensome because they were so long and complicated.

See chapter 4 on nuisance.

0-14 *Complexity* Sometimes the law can be difficult because it is abstract, and contains artificial concepts which are remote from everyday experience. But the law is often based on an idea which is simple and easily understood. The law of trespass, for example, says that people should not go on to private property without some form of lawful authority such as permission from the owner. This basic idea, however, is too general to be of much use by itself: it has to be fully explained by a whole body of rules which describe what exactly trespass is, who can complain about it, and what action they can take. Such rules can be involved, but the obstacle to understanding is often the volume of the law rather than its complexity. It is a question of working through definitions and exceptions to establish which rules apply in a particular case.

See chapter 3 for trespass.

0-15 What is perhaps more difficult is knowing what legal issues are thrown up by a particular factual situation. There may be no legal implications: the law, for example, does not give a landowner a general right to a view from his property. On the other hand, there may be a range of legal issues. Suppose that a landowner wishes to build an extension close to his boundary with his neighbour's land.

He may need planning permission, so planning law will be relevant. But other legal issues may also arise. If he builds very close to one of his neighbour's windows, he may be infringing her right to light. It may be that there is a restrictive covenant which she can enforce to stop him building. Indeed, if he wishes to build right up to the boundary, he may need to take into account the Party Wall etc Act 1996. All these different parts of the law may be relevant.

See 6-43 for rights to light.

See 7-13 onwards for restrictive covenants

See 2-23 onwards for an explanation of this Act.

0-16 *Solutions to problems* The law has to deal with many problems for which the right legal solution cannot be guessed by someone who does not know what the law is, because there is no single, obvious, predictable solution. Instead, a range of solutions is possible, and one of them has to be chosen by the law and the others rejected. For example, suppose that a landowner is troubled by weeds which grow from seeds blown into her garden from her neighbour's land. She reasons that since the seeds were his, the weeds which grow from them must be his too, and he can hardly object to getting his own weeds back. So she digs up the weeds and throws them over the fence on to his land.

0-17 There may be something to be said for this reasoning. But it happens not to be the way the law approaches the matter, since the law generally regards plants and trees growing in land as belonging to the owner of the land, wherever the seeds came from. The landowner is therefore legally in the wrong in "returning" the weeds, though other action may be open to her.

See 2-46 for more about this rule.

See 4-20 onwards for remedies for nuisance.

0-18 It is common for a problem to be easier to see than the solution to it. Landowners need to be on their guard against jumping to the conclusion that legal wrongs can necessarily be put right in the way which seems right to them. This is especially so where they are thinking of taking direct action themselves.

See 1-25 onwards on "self-help".

0-19 *Enforcing the law* Once the law has imposed a requirement of some kind—for example, that landowners must not carry out development without planning permission, or that they must refrain from disturbing neighbours by excessive noise—the requirement must be enforceable in some way. There are three main sorts of legal procedure by which this can be done. First, the law may give the person affected the right to take proceedings in the civil courts, to obtain compensation or some other remedy, such as an injunction. Secondly, breach of the requirement may be a criminal offence,

See 1-19 for the meaning of "injunction".

See 1-20 onwards for civil and criminal proceedings.

For an example see 10-8.

See 9-84 onwards for enforcement of planning law.

which can lead to a prosecution. Thirdly, a public body of some kind may be given the legal power to take action; for example, the power to enter land and carry out (at the expense of the landowner) work which needs doing, in order to prevent danger or to preserve a building.

0-20 These different ways of enforcing the law are often combined. Planning law, for instance, makes use of all three methods in order to ensure that the rules are obeyed by landowners.

Approach of the book

0-21 *Content* The text summarises the main areas of law which are relevant to landowners, and it covers aspects of the following:

- Land law, sometimes known as the law of real property (hence terms such as "real estate").
- The law of civil wrongs, or "torts".
- Highway law.
- Planning law.
- Environmental law (that is, the law which is concerned with protecting the environment).

See further 1-21 for the meaning of "tort".

See chapter 5 for highway law.

See chapter 9 for planning law.

0-22 The aim has been to deal in some detail with Acts, but less so with delegated legislation. Both Acts and delegated legislation are listed in the Table of Authorities which comes before the Index, and which includes cases and other legal materials. In relation to cases, a lawyers' text-book would cite large numbers of cases—decisions by the courts, which form part of the law—but this book merely gives a small number, as illustrations of how the law works. Most of the cases mentioned are recent, because these show the law in its latest state, and because they very often refer back to earlier decisions, thus

See 1-7 for the meaning of "delegated legislation".

See 1-10 for the meaning of "case law".

allowing researchers to look back and see how the law has developed. We have kept these illustrations separate from the text, in shaded panels. The date given in brackets after the name of the case is the date when the report of the case was prepared. The "v." between the names of the parties stands for *versus*, Latin for "against".

Arrangement Chapter 1 contains some background about the law and deals with some legal concepts which are of general relevance, such as the system of land registration. This chapter is meant as a source of reference, to support the rest of the book with general explanations. 0-23

After that, the aim has been to arrange the material in a practical way, rather than according to legal principles. This is why (for example) liability for animals under the Animals Act 1971 appears in chapter 3, which is mainly about trespassing: if landowners are concerned with animals, it will usually be because animals are straying on to their land. 0-24

See 3-52 onwards.

Where possible, chapters follow a basic pattern, dealing first with the civil law and the rights and obligations it creates, then explaining how this is reinforced by the criminal law and by the powers given to official bodies. The approach is intended to be practical, which means giving more space and emphasis to areas of the law which have a greater practical importance, and less to those which might be interesting to lawyers but which are less relevant in everyday life. It is in any event right to emphasise that the book is only a summary of the law: a full explanation of all of these areas of the law would occupy many thousands rather than a few hundred pages. 0-25

Perhaps the greatest need in a book of this sort is for the reader to be able to see how different areas of the law relate to each other. The system of cross-references explained on page 11 is designed to help here, enabling the reader to see where to look for a definition or explanation, or what other areas of the law may be relevant. Chapter 12, to which some of the cross-references refer, explains where further information about the law can be found. At the end of chapters 2 to 11 are assessments, which try to sum up briefly the impact of the law explained in the chapter—what the problems and areas of difficulty are, and what practical steps a landowner can take in order to avoid legal problems. 0-26

0-27 *Conventions* In the interests of simplicity, the text adopts a number of conventions. First, the functions and responsibilities given by legislation are generally given to government ministers, but in the text are described as though they were given to the relevant government department. The departments mentioned in the text are referred to by their initials, as follows:

Table 1: Government departments

Full name	Abbreviation
Department of Transport, Environment and the Regions	DETR
Department of Culture, Media and Sport (formerly the Department of National Heritage)	DCMS (DNH)
Lord Chancellor's Department	LCD
Department of Trade and Industry	DTI
Ministry of Agriculture, Fisheries and Food	MAFF

0-28 Some of the functions and responsibilities described in the text as belonging to the above departments are in Wales the responsibility of the Welsh Assembly. This includes the power to make delegated legislation; and it should be emphasised that since the Government of Wales Act 1998 delegated legislation for Wales may differ from the delegated legislation which applies in England.

0-29 The position in relation to local government is also simplified. The expression "the local authority" is generally used to cover the various bodies which make up local government; and also the names used in legislation, such as "local planning authority" or "highway authority" which simply mean the relevant part of local government acting in relation to planning or highways. Enquiry will reveal, in a particular case, which part of local government is responsible.

See chapter 5 for highways and chapter 9 for planning.

0-30 Legislation tends to be resolutely masculine in its use of language, relying on the Interpretation Act 1978. But it is becoming increasingly common for books to use "she" sometimes in examples, not just "he", and the present text follows suit.

See 0-12 for the Interpretation Act 1978.

For the technically-minded

The software used to write this book bridges the gap between print and electronic media. A brief explanation may be of interest to the technically-minded. 0-31

While it was being written, the book consisted of a series of files making up the chapters, table of contents, index and other material destined to form the printed version of the text. It also included a set of files dealing with "Notes and Queries", cross-referenced to the relevant paragraphs in the text—including these files meant that the cross-references were automatically synchronised with the text by the software. 0-32

When the work was finished, the files making up the chapters and other parts of the book were split off, processed, and passed to the printers. The Notes and Queries pages remain in use, on computer. They are regularly edited and uploaded to our Internet site. These Notes and Queries pages deal with: 0-33

- Corrections, updates and additions made by us.
- Extra material requested by users of the book, where the printed text is not clear or does not deal with a particular point.

In due course, a further edition of the book will be prepared, and will take into account the material in the Notes and Queries pages.

How to use the book

The detailed Table of Contents should reveal the right starting point for enquiries about a particular point. If not, the Appendix may assist: this sets out to classify different sorts of legal query and to suggest what their main implications may be, and so what parts of the text are relevant. It is unlikely that a complete solution to a problem will be found on a single page; more likely, the reader will need to piece together an answer from different parts of the book. 0-34

For this purpose the system of cross-references explained on page 11 should help, as should the Index. Chapter 12 is devoted to sources of additional information about the legal subjects dealt with in the text, for readers who wish to know more.

How to use the Internet site

0-35 To find the Notes and Queries pages for *Protecting Your Property* either:

- Go to the home page of our Internet site, **http://www.barsby.com**, then click on *Notes and Queries* under *Protecting Your Property.* Or

- Enter **http://www.barsby.com/pypcontents.html**

Then click on a chapter heading to see the Notes and Queries for that chapter. (The contents of each chapter are summarised below the heading.) Material in the Notes and Queries pages is cross-referenced to the paragraph numbers in the printed text.

0-36 Increasingly, legal materials are available on the Internet. This includes Acts of Parliament from 1996, delegated legislation from 1997, and decisions of the House of Lords (the highest court) from November 1996. Government departments and other bodies also make information available on the Internet, for example explanations of new legislation. The Notes and Queries pages contain links to this material.

0-37 All comments about the book and the Notes and Queries pages are welcome. Readers who feel that the text is not clear, or does not cover the point which concerns them, are invited to contact us—by e-mail, if possible, to **mail@barsby.com**. We can then consider whether to add material to the Notes and Queries pages. Please note that under the Data Protection Act 1998 there are important restrictions on the information which businesses can hold. In particular, we cannot generally hold information about people without their agreement.

Topics not dealt with

0-38 Although the coverage of the book is broad, some areas have been omitted, particularly those where there is a need for professional help, including:

- Taxation.
- Conveyancing (i.e. the transfer of land and interests in land).
- Litigation (bringing legal proceedings).

See 1-76 onwards on conveyancing.

0-39 The book doesn't deal fully with the law relating to farming—for example, agricultural tenancies—though much of what is said is of relevance to farmers. Also omitted is the law which regulates many other specialised uses of land, for example cinemas and casinos. Nothing is said about the health and safety at work legislation, which is of course very important to employers; nor about insurance, though many landowners will have insurance against the risk of legal liability relating to their land.

Other points

0-40 This book should not be regarded as a substitute for legal advice, when the need arises. It should be emphasised that the law is constantly changing and evolving, and readers should be alert to the possibility of changes since publication. Changes to the law will be noted in the Internet pages linked to this text, and can also be found in the press and elsewhere.

0-41 The law described is the law of England and, subject to what is said above, Wales (Scotland has its own distinct legal system) as at the end of October 2000.

But note 1-16 on law which does not apply to the whole of England and Wales.

Chapter 1

Basics

Introduction

1-0 This chapter explains some "basics"—aspects of the law and the legal system which are relevant to many other parts of the book, such as where the law comes from, and the way in which the civil law and the criminal law are different. Some important ideas of general relevance are explained, such as "occupying" and "possessing" land. The chapter is for referring back to, rather than reading through: later chapters contain links back to this one.

Sources of the law

1-1 *Acts of Parliament* Acts of Parliament or statutes (the terms mean the same thing) are perhaps the most important source of law. A "Bill" passes through Parliament, and receives the Royal Assent, so becoming an Act. Since 1999, new Acts of Parliament have been published with notes which explain the effect of the new law. These notes are available separately from Her Majesty's Stationery Office ("HMSO"). Acts vary greatly in length—they may contain only one or two sections, or hundreds. They often amend or repeal (cancel) earlier Acts, or parts of them; they may "consolidate" earlier Acts, in order to make the law clearer, meaning that the earlier Acts on a particular subject are repealed and repeated in a single new Act, often with minor changes.

1-2 Acts have in the past often applied to England and Wales, and sometimes to Scotland (which has its own legal system). But they may apply only to a particular area, in which case they are known as "local" Acts. A "private" Act is one which applies only to

See 1-4 for the meaning of "section"

See also 1-16 on devolution.

Few are mentioned in this book but see for an example 10-2.

See for example 10-67.

particular people or interests, as opposed to "public "Acts, which affect the public at large.

1-3 Most of the Acts referred to in this book were passed in the twentieth century. But some nineteenth-century Acts are still relevant; and indeed some older legislation is still in force, though only rarely of practical importance. Property law in England and Wales underwent a major reform in the 1920s, when many ancient features of the law were abolished or simplified. This legislation—including the Law of Property Act 1925 and the Land Registration Act 1925—remains extremely important.

1-4 Acts are divided into sections ("s." is short for "section") and sections may be grouped into Parts or Chapters if the Act is a long one. It is common for less important provisions to be put into one or more Schedules at the end of an Act. When Acts amend earlier Acts, they sometimes replace particular sections, and sometimes add new ones (hence sections with a capital "A", "B", "C" etc added to the number).

1-5 If nothing is said in an Act about the date when it starts to operate—its "commencement", or "coming into force"—then it does so on the date when Royal Assent is given. This may be the case with short and simple Acts. The commencement of longer Acts is often much more complicated. They are often brought into force bit by bit, over a period of time, by delegated legislation. Sometimes parts of an Act are not brought into force for long periods; sometimes parts are never brought into force at all.

See 1-7 for the meaning of "delegated legislation".

1-6 Parliament has a wide power to make law. It can, for example, create new sorts or right, and new criminal offences, and take away people's property. But the power is limited in several ways. Acts of Parliament must be in accordance with:

- The law of the European Union.
- The European Convention on Human Rights, under the Human Rights Act 1998, which came into force in England and Wales on 2 October 2000.

◆ The Scotland Act 1998 and the Government of Wales Act 1998, which lay down the powers of the Scottish Parliament and the Welsh Assembly.

I-7 *Delegated legislation* Because Parliament does not have time to consider matters of fine detail, and in order to provide a degree of flexibility, Acts very often give power for "delegated" (or "subordinate") legislation to be made, usually by the government department responsible for that area of the law. This delegated legislation takes the form of rules, regulations or orders (known collectively as "statutory instruments"). It can be used to commence parts of the Act, or add detail to the Act, for example about the procedures to be followed and forms to be used. Sometimes delegated legislation can be used to amend an Act itself. The system of land registration, for example, was set up by the Land Registration Act 1925. Under this Act, delegated legislation has been made including the Land Registration Rules 1925, which deal with the detailed operation of the system, including the forms which must be used and the procedures of the Land Registry. Delegated legislation can be amended or revoked (cancelled) by later delegated legislation, just as Act can be amended or repealed by a later Act. The Land Registration Rules 1925, for example, have been amended on many occasions. About 3,000 statutory instruments are made each year, and each one is given a reference number. The Land Registration Rules 2000, for example, have the reference number S.I. (statutory instrument) "2000/429". (They make some amendments to the 1925 rules to do with electronic communications.)

For an example, see 11-25.

For sources on public law and the interpretation of legislation, see 12-25 and 12-26.

I-8 The powers given by Acts of Parliament to make statutory instruments are not always used: it is quite common to find that although a government department has the power to make rules or regulations, the power has never been used. There is a special rule by which, if an Act is replaced, the delegated legislation does not automatically have to be re-made under the new Act, but continues in force. This explains why sometimes the delegated legislation relevant to an Act has an earlier date than the Act itself.

For an example, see 9-14 for the Town and Country Planning (Use Classes) Order 1987, which predates the Town and Country Planning Act 1990.

I-9 Byelaws (also spelt "bylaws", "by-laws" and "bye-laws") are a special form of delegated legislation: local authorities are sometimes given limited power to make byelaws for their area to deal with specific questions.

> For examples, see 5-6 and 10-69.

1-10 *Decisions of the courts* Many of the decisions of the courts on questions of law are concerned with the meaning of legislation: if the meaning is in dispute, the courts have to decide. The decision is then a precedent—"case law"—and will be followed by the courts; though higher courts,in dealing with later cases which involve the same point, can disagree, and set a different precedent. Some areas of law, however, known as the common law and equity, are entirely the creation of judges over the centuries. This sort of law is not definitively written down anywhere, though writers of legal text books do their best to summarise it. Since the law has been developed over such a long period, in large numbers of cases, it is possible to be reasonably sure what the law is. Nonetheless, there is always room for the law to evolve: judges can re-interpret past explanations of what the law is, and create new exceptions—even, sometimes, discard what has been decided in the past and start again. These areas of law are gradually shrinking, as Acts are passed which replace parts of them, but they remain very important.

> See 1-6 on the limits to Parliament's power.

> See 1-20 onwards for the courts.

> See 1-17 for the meaning of "common law" and "equity".

Interpreting an Act

In *Pepper v. Hart* (1993), some staff at an independent boys' school were able to send their sons to the school on payment of a reduced fee. There was a dispute about the amount of tax which they should pay on this benefit.

The House of Lords, in dealing with the case, decided that, if an Act was unclear, it was permissible to look at what had been said in Parliament by the government minister responsible for the legislation, in order to understand what meaning Parliament intended it to have. This was a change from the existing rule, that what was said in Parliament could not be taken into account.

The House of Lords decided, in view of what had been said in Parliament, that the meaning most favourable to the staff was the right one.

1-11 In many cases, the law is clear and the court merely has to make a decision about who is right on the facts of the case. But when the courts, especially the higher courts, decide questions of law, a report of the case is published in one of the many different series of law reports, so that the court's decision can be known, and referred to as a precedent.

> See 0-22 on cases cited in this book.

1-12 *European law* The European Union has the power to make laws which apply to all the states (including the United Kingdom) which are members of the Union. In particular it can make Regulations, which apply directly in the member States, and Directives, which are in effect instructions to the members States to pass laws which have the effect specified in the Directive. Much European law is now in force, and much law has been made in the U.K. in response to Directives. Relatively little of it is concerned with land in the United Kingdom, but (for example) the Land Registry is affected by European rules on metrication of measurements; U.K. law on timeshares stems from the Timeshare Directive in 1997; and some environmental measures have a European origin.

See 8-100 for the Timeshare Act 1992.

1-13 *Customary law* In medieval times, the law relating to land was essentially local, and varied from place to place. This law—known as "customary law"—was gradually replaced by the common law. Customary law is of little significance today, but has not entirely vanished. For example, if there is a customary right to use land for recreation, the land can be registered as a town or village green, under the Commons Registration Act 1965.

See 10-65 onwards for the Commons Registration Act 1965.

1-14 *Other materials* Legislation sometimes makes provision for documents such as guidance, or codes of practice to be published by a government department or official body. While these documents are probably not law in the strict sense, they are important because they influence the way in which the law is understood and applied. In effect, they are a way in which official bodies can say more about what the law is intended to mean, but to do it in relatively informal language. Guidance, codes of practice and other documents of the same sort are pubished separately from the legislation itself, and are usually available from HMSO .

Some examples:

- *Approved Document* issued under the Building Regulations—see 10-4
- *Code of Practice under the Treasure Act 1996*—see 11-27.
- *Code of Practice on Litter and Refuse*—see 11-87.

1-15 Given the existence of codes of practice and other documents, it is often necessary to consider three "levels" of document in establishing what the law is:

Table 2: "levels"

Type of document	Made by	Effect
Act.	Passed by Parliament.	Contains the main provisions of the legislation.
Delegated legislation (e. g. Rules, Regulations, Orders).	Made by a government department, under a power given by the Act.	More detailed provisions—e. g. procedure, forms, commencement of the Act.
Code of practice, guidance, etc.	Made by a government department under a power given by the Act or the delegated legislation.	Less formal rules about how, in practice, the Act and the delegated legislation should be interpreted.

Territoriality

1-16 It should be emphasised that although the law dealt with in this book is generally the same for England and Wales, this is not invariably the case. To summarise, the main exceptions are where:

- The Welsh Assembly has made delegated legislation which is different from legislation in England.
- The law is contained in a local Act.
- The law in force depends upon whether a local authority has adopted provisions in an Act for its own area.
- Customary law applies.

See 0-28 for the position in Wales.

For examples see 4-44 and 10-55.

Common law and equity

1-17 The common law was developed by the courts, from medieval times onwards, as a body of law which applied to the whole country, replacing customary law, which was local and varied from place to place. The courts concerned with the common law became, however, very rigid in their approach, with little room for flexibility and fairness. By about 1500, different courts had started to develop a different set of rules, known as "equity" (meaning in essence "fairness") and often able to reach fairer and better decisions. Since the last quarter of the nineteenth century, the same courts have been responsible for applying both the common law and equity.

1-18 The difference remains important, though, because equitable rules have a rather different philosophy behind them: they are more flexible, and are more concerned with fairness than the common law. To take one important difference, the priority for the common law in enforcing rights over land is certainty, rather than fairness. Suppose land is made subject to some right, then sold to a person who does not know about the right. Does the right still apply? For rights which form part of the common law, the answer is Yes, even if the result is unfair. But for rights which are equitable in nature, fairness is an important consideration; and if the purchaser buys the land for a fair price, in good faith, and without knowing about the right, he will not be affected by it.

1-19 Some more examples of rules which have their origins in equity rather than the common law:

- The courts can grant injunctions (orders to do or not to do something—for example, not to trespass on someone's land). But a person bringing legal proceedings can never insist on an injunction: the courts have a discretion, and will refuse to grant one if it seems unfair.

- Though there are rules about the formalities necessary to transfer land, transactions can sometimes be enforced even though those rules are not complied with.

See 3-29 for more about the principles on which injunctions are granted.

See 7-44 for more on trusts.

See 1-38 below for more on this subject.

◆ Property can be held on trust, and the courts require trustees to manage the trust property for the benefit of the beneficiaries.

Civil and criminal law

See 3-29 for injunctions and 3-35 for possession orders.

See also 1-71 on tribunals, which can deal with certain disputes.

1-20 In one sense the difference between between civil law and criminal law is clear-cut. The civil law is concerned with redress—putting right what is wrong, by means of compensation (in legal language, "damages") or some other order, for example an injunction, or an order for possession of land. Proceedings are often brought by one private person against another, though they may be brought by or against a public body. They take place in the civil courts, the main ones being the County Court and the High Court, the latter for higher-value claims. The usual rule is that the person bringing civil proceedings has to prove his case "on the balance of probabilities". In other words, the judge decides according to who is more likely to be right.

See chapter 3 for trespass and chapter 4 for nuisance and negligence.

1-21 County courts and the High Court can deal with various types of civil dispute, including breaches of contract, disputes relating to wills and family problems, and proceedings arising from the law of torts. A tort is a type of civil wrong; and some torts—with which this book is concerned—involve land, for example trespass and nuisance. To take trespass as an example, the law carefully defines what amounts to trespass (and what doesn't), who can take legal action, and what remedies the court can award. This collection of rules makes up the tort of trespass.

1-22 The criminal law, on the other hand, is concerned with punishing people for committing criminal offences, whether major or minor—there are innumerable minor criminal offences. Bringing prosecutions is generally a matter for a public body, such as the Crown Prosecution Service, or a local authority, though private prosecutions are possible. The prosecutor must generally prove that the offence has been committed, and must do so to a high standard—"beyond reasonable doubt". (Because of this high standard, private prosecutions are relatively rare.) Proceedings take place in the criminal courts—either the Crown Court, for serious offences, or a magistrates' court for less serious offences, though some offences can be dealt with in either court. In a magistrates' court (where the proceedings are known as "summary proceedings") cases are decided by Justices of the Peace, or in some cities by a full-time, legally-qualified "stipendiary" magistrate. Magistrates' courts have more limited powers to punish those who are found guilty.

See 12-24 for sources on criminal law.

I-23 Most of the offences mentioned in this book are less serious offences, dealt with only in the magistrates' courts. For a few of these offences the magistrates can sentence a person to imprisonment; but punishment generally means a fine. The maximum fines which can be imposed by magistrates' courts have been standardised (by the Criminal Justice Act 1982 and by the Criminal Justice Act 1988). Most legislation now sets the maximum fine for an offence by referring to the appropriate level. The levels are as follows:

Table 3: levels of fines

Level	Maximum
1	£200
2	£500
3	£1,000
4	£2,500
5	£5,000

There some exceptions—offences for which the maximum is a specified amount, not one of the standard levels. £5,000 is also the "statutory maximum" fine for more serious offences which can be dealt with either in a magistrates' court or in the Crown Court.

Magistrates' courts are not exclusively criminal. For example, they deal with licensing premises for the sale of alcohol: see 10-54.

I-24 Though the difference between civil and criminal law may seem clear-cut, because of the different principles which apply and the different courts which are responsible, in practice the position is more complicated. Criminal courts have a limited power to compensate those who have suffered, by making a person convicted

See 3-29 onwards for injunctions and note also the ability of civil courts, in limited circumstances, to award "exemplary" damages: see 3-28.

See 3-40 onwards for these offences.

See 1-54 onwards for the system of land registration.

See 4-27 onwards for these procedures.

See 11-15 and 5-32 on these points.

of an offence pay compensation to the victim of the offence, though this power is really only for straightforward cases. Civil courts can punish a person who does not obey an injunction or other order made by the court. More importantly, perhaps, the civil law and the criminal tend to be used flexibly. Often criminal offences are created to reinforce or support an area of the law which is essentially civil. For example:

- Trespass is generally a civil matter, but in some circumstances the law takes a more serious view and makes trespassing a criminal offence.

- The system of land registration is concerned with the ownership of land; but criminal offences must be created for those who abuse the system.

- Noisy neighbours can be the subject of proceedings in the civil courts. But public concern has led to the creation of new procedures, by which local authority staff can take action, backed up by the criminal law.

Practical steps and self-help

1-25 It is often possible for a landowner to take practical steps to protect her position; for example, agreeing with visitors the terms on which they are to come on to her land, or putting up a notice to make sure that a public right of way is not created across her land. There is no reason why a landowner should feel hesitant about taking action of this sort.

1-26 However, "self-help", which is a term used to describe directly enforcing rights, as an alternative to legal proceedings, is another matter. Physically removing a trespasser from land, or going on to neighbouring land to stop some sort of antisocial activity, such as a smoky bonfire, would be "self-help". Such action needs to be undertaken with great care, since if the landowner finds, due to some misunderstanding or miscalculation, that he is not legally justified in what he is doing, then he is likely to have committed some wrong himself. Physically removing a person who is not in fact trespassing could amount to a serious assault on that person. The courts do not encourage landowners (or others) to try to take the law into their hands, and are sceptical about those who do. The better course is almost always to refrain from any attempt at self-help. There is, however, one exception, since it is well-established that a landowner may trim vegetation from neighbouring property which overhangs the boundary.

See 4-22 for this rule.

Describing land

1-27 Often the law (including the rules explained in the following paragraphs) is concerned with the ownership of land, or other rights over land; and for these purposes a piece of land is land in the ownership of a particular person. The word "premises" is often used to mean land, for example a house and garden, which forms a unit for the purposes of ownership. ("Premises" means the opening part of a deed, describing the land being dealt with; hence it has come to mean a piece of land in the ownership of a particular person.)

1-28 Less often, the law is concerned not with who owns or has rights over land, but with its physical characteristics. For example, under the National Parks and Access to the Countryside Act 1949, steps can be taken to give the public access to land which is "open land", including moors, heaths, downs and other land.

See 10-80 for details of how this Act works.

Classification of rights and interests in land

1-29 The law recognises a large number of different rights over land. This is natural enough, since land is the subject of so many different transactions and uses. The State, through legislation, is able to create new sorts of right over land, and does so freely—the

For examples see 2-23 onwards for the Party Wall etc Act 1996 and 7-2 onwards for the Access to Neighbouring Land Act 1992. The courts can also create new sorts of right, though this is much less common.

legislation carefully defines the rights and the ways in which they can be enforced. Members of the public do not have the same ability, so must make use of the sorts provided by the legal system. These are limited, though enough for almost all purposes.

1-30 Apart from this general limitation, the Law of Property Act 1925 imposes a classification on what might loosely be called property rights. A limited number are legal in nature, and so "absolute" meaning there are no conditions or qualifications about whether they can be enforced. The remainder cannot be legal, and so can only be equitable in nature, with the result that their enforceability is not guaranteed in the same way. The main legal rights to which this rule applies are as follows:

See 1-18 for this rule.

- Freehold ownership of land. ("Ownership" is not strictly accurate, for historical reasons, but is a perfectly adequate word for everyday use.) The right to the land must be immediate and not one which only start at some future date, and it must last indefinitely (s. 1(1) of the Law of Property Act 1925).

- Leaseholds and tenancies. To be legal in nature, a leasehold or tenancy must be for a fixed minimum period (s. 1(1)).

See 8-14 for this rule.

- Easements—rights which give a landowner some specific and limited use of nearby land, for example a right of way, enabling the landowner to cross other land to get to his own—lasting either indefinitely or for a fixed period.

See chapter 6 for easements, especially 6-6.

- Profits à prendre—rights which are in some ways similar to easements, but which allow a person to *take* something from land. Again, these must last indefinitely or for a fixed priod (s. 1(2)).

See 7-39 for the meaning of "profit à prendre".

- Mortgages (s. 1(2)).

See 7-52 onwards for mortgages.

- A landlord's right to "re-enter" the property—in other words, to end the lease or tenancy and take back the property, because of a breach by the tenant of his obligations (s. 1(2)).

See 8-33 for an explanation of this right.

1-31 Interests in land which do not fall within these categories must be equitable in nature, and their enforceability is less certain. This is true of such things as leases which are not for a definite period (an example would be a lease due to last until the next general election) or a mortgage which is not properly created because no deed was used. It is also true of a wider range of interests in land which cannot be legal in any event, for example interests under trusts, and restrictive covenants.

See 1-19 for this rule.

See 1-33 onwards for rules about formalities.

See 1-54 and 1-65 onwards for further details of these interests and how they can be protected by being entered on registers.

1-32 There are also many rights affecting land which are not within this classification into legal or equitable rights, for example the public's right to use a highway, or public rights of access to land.

See chapter 5 for highways and 10-79 onwards for public access to land.

Formalities

1-33 *Transferring land* Section 52 of the Law of Property Act 1925 provides that a deed is required for creating or transferring property rights which are legal in nature, as explained under the last heading. One of the most common transactions is the sale of freehold property, and the rule applies here, so that a deed is required. But it equally applies to such transactions as the grant of a permanent right of way (which is an easement).

1-34 The requirements for a deed are now set out in the Law of Property (Miscellaneous Provisions) Act 1989, s. 1. A deed does not have to be sealed, if it is made by an individual (i. e. a living person—an artificial legal "person" such as a company must still seal a deed). It must, however, make clear that it is intended to be a deed. It must be witnessed, either by one person if the maker of the deed signs himself, or two witnesses if someone else signs on behalf of the maker. A deed must also be "delivered", which means that the person concerned must do or say something to indicate that the deed is to take effect—usually this requirement will be satisfied by handing the deed over physically.

1-35 In interpreting deeds, the approach of the courts is to give the words used their ordinary and natural meaning, taking into account the background to the deed.

1-36 There are various exceptions to the rule that a deed is required. One important one is that a lease for up to three years can validly be created without a deed, either in writing or orally, provided it is at the best rent which may reasonably be obtained (s. 54(2) of the Law of Property Act 1925). Periodic leases, which run from week to week, month to month, or year to year, are within this rule. Other exceptions to the general need for a deed include situations where the law provides for ownership of property to be transferred automatically. This happens, for example, where a person dies and his property passes automatically to his executor or administrator (that is, the person who has the task of adminstering a deceased person's estate). Section 52 also does not affect the rule known as adverse possession.

See chapter 8 on leases and tenancies generally.

See 2-67 for the meaning of adverse possesion.

1-37 *Contracts* Although a deed is generally required in order for land actually to be transferred, a contract for the transfer of land (i. e. an agreement that one person will transfer land to another) merely has to be in writing, signed by the parties, in order to be enforceable. This is the result of s. 2 of the Law of Property (Miscellaneous Provisions) Act 1989. There are several exceptions to this rule, including:

- Short leases and tenancies.
- Contracts made in the course of a public auction.

The same leases and tenancies which do not require a deed to be to created: see 1-36.

In relation to auctions, the exception is necessary since otherwise a successful bid would not result in a legally binding contract.

1-38 Equity may assist when there has been a binding agreement to transfer land, and the agreement has not been put into effect, or where an attempt has been made to put it into effect but the proper formalities have not been complied with (for example, a deed has not been used). The court may order the person concerned to transfer the land properly.

1-39 *Buying and selling land* How do the above rules work in practice? When land is sold, buyer and seller generally start by agreeing "subject to contract", at which stage there is no legal obligation. The buyer may withdraw or make a lower offer; the seller may similarly withdraw or accept a higher offer from another

> In *Tye v. House and Jennings* (1997) Mr Tye wished to buy a golf course, which Mr House and Mrs Jennings were selling. According to Mr Tye, the parties entered into an "exclusivity agreement", which would last for a month and which prevented Mr House and Mrs Jennings from selling to another buyer within that period. When they received a better offer, and told Mr Tye that they intended to accept it, he applied for an injunction to stop them.
>
> At an initial hearing, when only Mr Tye's representatives were present, the court made an injunction. A few days later, at a second hearing, when Mr House and Mrs Jennings were present, the court decided not to continue the injunction, on the ground that monetary compensation was a sufficient remedy for Mr Tye.

Buying and selling land

person—"gazumping". One way in which the buyer and seller can reduce the risk that the other party will withdraw is to enter a "lock-out" agreement. A lock-out agreement does not legally commit either party to the sale, but it prevents one or both (depending upon the terms of the agreement) from negotiating with others for a fixed period.

Solicitors and conveyancers handling transfers of land generally use one of the two standard form conditions of sale, the Law Society's Conditions and the National Conditions. Both sets of conditions contain small print designed to deal with all foreseeable eventualities. It is the seller's responsibility to prepare the contract, and the buyer's (after making enquiries to check on the property) to prepare the transfer. 1-40

Including enquiries of the, local authority and a search of registers: see 1-54 and 1-65 onwards.

Conveyances used to list all the things which were transferred with the land, including both legal rights and physical features. Now there is no need for such a list, since s. 62(1) of the Law of Property Act 1925 provides that, unless the buyer and seller decide otherwise, a transfer of land is deemed to include: 1-41

> "..all buildings, erections, fixtures, commons, hedges, ditches, fences, ways, waters, watercourses, liberties, privileges, easements, rights and advantages whatsoever....".

See 2-47 for the meaning of "fixtures".

And by s. 62(2) a transfer of land with buildings on it includes: 1-42

> "...all outhouses, erections, fixtures, cellars, areas, courts, courtyards, cisterns, sewers, gutters, drains, ways, passages, lights, watercourses, liberties, privileges, easements, rights and advantages whatsoever...."

The effect of s. 62
Suppose the owner of The Lawns wishes to sell off part of her garden, for development. Access will be via the track on one side of the land. [See 6-33 for private rights of way.] If she also owns the wooded area on the other side of the house, and if the path has been used to gain access from the side road to the end of the garden, a right of way (an easement) will be created by s. 62, when the plot is sold, unless the effect of the section is excluded by the deed which transfers the land.

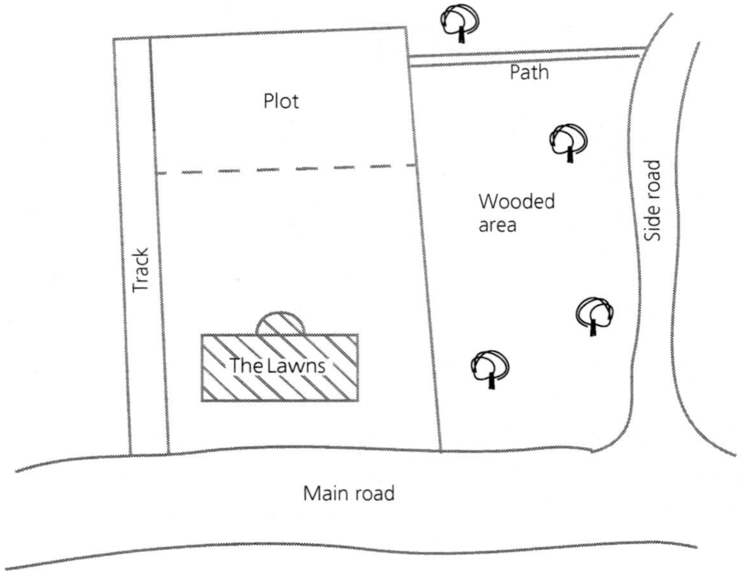

1-43 While s. 62 is useful in removing doubt about what is included when land is sold, the wording of the section can produce unexpected results, because it can create legal rights where none existed before. Perhaps the most usual situation in which this can happen is where part of a plot of land is sold off. If the land sold off has enjoyed some use of the land retained, even on an entirely informal basis, s. 62 may create a legal right. In order for this to happen, the use must be capable of forming the subject of a legal right—usually, where this is so, the right will be an easement. Suppose, then, that a landowner sells off some land which has access from the public highway, but which has also enjoyed, with his permission, access across the land which he retains. Unless the terms of the transfer make clear that s. 62 is not to apply, the section will create a permanent right of way cross the land retained. Situations of this sort thus require very careful consideration when land is transferred.

See 1-30 and chapter 6 for the meaning of "easement".

See 12-8 for sources on land law.

Who can own land?

1-44 Land in England and Wales may be owned by adults but not minors (though land may be held on trust for minors). Companies and other artifical legal persons, such as local authorities, may similarly own land. (The advantage of using a company to own land is that, unlike a real person, a company can own property indefintely, without having to pass it on to someone else.) Land can be owned jointly by more than one person, and this often happens where a husband and wife jointly own the home they live in. A trustee can own land, which must then be administered for the benefit of the beneficiary of the trust. Can land have no owner at all? It sometimes happens that a person dies without making will and without any relatives to inherit his property. In such cases the deceased person's land and other property—"bona vacantia" is the legal term—passes to the Crown, under the Administration of Estates Act 1925, s. 45.

See 7-44 for trusts.

See 1-72 for the meaning of "the Crown".

Restrictions on land transactions

1-45 Land can be the subject of many different sorts of transaction, and in general the law has not sought to restrict them. But there are two exceptions which should be briefly noted. In practice, neither is likely to arise very often. First, the courts are reluctant to enforce restrictions on a person's right to dispose of land which he owns. This is not the same as limiting the interest in land which a person has: a trust may, for example, give a person the right to live in a house for their lifetime, after which the house is to go to someone else. But if land is transferred to a person subject to a restriction preventing her from disposing of it as she wishes, that restriction may not be enforceable.

1-46 The law also forbids arrangements which seek to tie up the ownership of land far into the future, whether by means of a trust or any other method, this being known as the "rule against perpetuities". There is no need to go into further detail here, save to say that this area of the law is complex. An Act passed in 1964, the Perpetuities and Accumulations Act, improved the position somewhat.

Restrictions on the sale of land

In the case of *Caldy Manor Estates Ltd v. Farrell* (1974) Mr Farrell was the owner of Fairfield House in Caldy, in the Wirral and also an adjoinging property, known as Fairfield Cottage. He wanted to sell Fairfield Cottage but to keep Fairfield House; but a previous owner of the house had bought the cottage subject to a covenant that it should not be sold separately [see 7-13 for restrictive covenants]. The question was whether the covenant was legally valid.

The court decided that it was valid. The court said that a restriction of this sort was more likely to be regarded as valid if the person imposing it did not try to give himself the right to take back the land in the event of a breach. (Whether Caldy Manor Estates Ltd could obtain an injunction to prevent the sale, or just recover compensation if the sale took place, was not considered by the court, because the court had been asked to deal only wih preliminary legal questions.)

Possessing and occupying land

I-47 For some purposes the law is concerned not with the owner of land as such, but with whoever is in control of the land, either to protect the interests of that person, or to make them responsible in some way for the state of the land. Two key concepts here are the *possession* and the *occupation* of land. Both words mean, in effect, "control": a person who is in possession of land is in control of it, as is a person who is occupying land. It is not necessary for a person to be phyisically present on the land all the time (or, indeed, at any time) in order to be in possession or control of it, since control can be exerted in other ways. A person may exert control through other people, or (if the land can be secured in that way) by locking doors or gates or taking other measures to control what happens on the land.

See for example 8-88 onwards for the Protection from Eviction Act 1977, which safeguards occupiers of land; and 11-2 onwards for the Occupiers' Liability Acts, which make occupiers responsible for accidents on land.

I-48 The meaning of *possession* and *occupation* may vary a little, according to the context in which they are used. If there is a difference between them, it is that occupation implies a lesser degree of control over the land. It will be natural for the owner of the land to be in possession and occupation of the land, for example the owner of a house will generally be living in it, and hence in possession and control of it. But others can also be in possession or control of land—a tenant, or someone who is on the land by virtue of a licence (i. e. permission) or even a trespasser. These are all people whom the law may protect, or who may be made responsible for the state of the land. Some examples:

See 1-49 onwards for licences.

- Civil liability is imposed on the occupiers of land: they may be responsible for compensating a person who suffers injury or damage while on the land ("occupiers' liability").

See 11-2 onwards for occupiers' liability.

- A trespasser who is in possession of land is protected by the law, and can himself take legal action for trespass against someone who comes on to the land unlawfully.

See 3-9 for who can take legal action for trespass.

Licences

1-49 In legal language, a licence simply means permission. Official bodies issue licences for the use of TVs, etc. A landowner can grant permission for others to come on to his land, or use it in some other way. A licence is an alternative to many different sorts of legal right: instead of granting such a right, a landowner can simply give permission for the use in question. The use of the land is then lawful, and not a trespass. Granting a licence is a convenient way of allowing use which is intended to be temporary and personal; whereas for a permanent or long-term arrangement, which can be passed on to others, a legal right is appropriate. If a landowner wishes to create a permanent right of way across his land, for the benefit of a neighbour, he can execute a deed granting an easement. But if he merely wishes to grant temporary permission, so that, for example, the neighbour can use the land for access for a short period, then a licence will be the right course.

Official licences are granted for the use of land to sell alcohol, or for an animal boarding estblishment, and so on. See 10-54 and 10-60 for these examples.

See chapter 3 for trespassing.

1-50 A licence can be express or implied. "Express", in a legal context, means that something is done deliberately. Permission is express if the landowner actually says he is granting it. No particular form of words is required, and writing is not necessary—though it may be a good idea. "Implied", by contrast, is used where circumstances suggest that something is intended. Permission may be implied if the landowner does not actually say in so many words that he is granting permission, but it is clear from what he says, or from his conduct, that this is what he is doing, as where a shopkeeper unlocks the door of the shop and puts up the "open" sign. The implication is that customers are now invited to enter the shop.

1-51 A licence may be granted as part of a contract. Going to the cinema means, legally speaking, buying a licence to be present and see the film. (To be pedantic, there will be an implied licence, when the cinema is open, to go into the foyer; and buying a ticket will give the cinema-goer an express licence to see the film.) Equally, a licence may be unconnected with a contract, as where a landowner invites guests into her house. A licence may be given subject to conditions—for example that the person concerned can only come on to the landowner's property for certain purposes, or only on to certain parts of it. Provided such conditions are adhered to, there is no trespass.

1-52 As a general rule, a landowner can revoke (i. e. cancel) a licence whenever he wishes; though the person concerned must be given a reasonable opportunity to leave the land before he can be regarded as a trespasser. If the licence has been granted as a part of a contract, however, whether it can be revoked will depend upon the terms of the contract. The contract may say expressly that the licence may be ended by the landowner; or it may be implied that the licence can be revoked in certain circumstances.

But see also 7-46 for exceptional circumstances in which a licence may lead to a permanent right.

1-53 In short, a landowner can permit others to use his land in many different ways, and for temporary or informal arrangements this will be the best way to proceed, rather than creating one of the legal rights explained above.

See 12-8 for sources on licences.

The system of land registration

1-54 *Function of the Land Register* The point of the Land Register is to serve as an official record of the ownership of land, and some rights in land. Anyone who wishes to buy land, or has some other concern about land or rights over it, can refer to the Land Register. The Land Register is operated by the Land Registry under the Land Registration Act 1925 and delegated legislation, the Land Registration Rules 1925. Legally, the fact that land is shown on the Land Register as belonging to a person means that that person owns it (s. 5). In limited circumstances, the Land Register can be corrected (s. 82); but subject to this possibility it is authoritative, and if it does not show what it should do, any person who has been prejudiced may be able to obtain compensation.

1-55 Land registration replaces a system in which the person selling land had to show that he was the owner by tracing his "title" to the land over a certain number of years—latterly, a minimum of 15 years. All land in England and Wales is now subject to registration under the Land Registration Act 1925, both freehold land and leasehold land where the lease has more than 21 years left to run. This means that land must be put on the Register when certain transactions next take place. At first, the requirement to register was triggered by the sale of land and some other transactions; now almost all transactions trigger the requirement. The latest legislation on this point is the Land Registration Act 1997 and the Land Registration Rules 1997, S.I. 1997/3037. This does not mean that all land in England and Wales is shown on the Register: the ownership of some land may be unknown, and in some cases the requirement to register the land may not yet have been triggered.

See 1-30 for the meaning of "freehold land" and chapter 8 for leases and tenancies.

1-56 *The process of registration* Before registering the land, the Land Registry must be satisfied that the owner has a valid right to it. If so, the title is shown as "absolute", meaning that it enjoys the full protection of the system of land registration. But several less certain sorts of title can be registered, including "possessory title", meaning that the person concerned is merely in possession of the land, without any further proof of ownership; though a person in possession may become the owner, through the rule known as "adverse possession" ⚷. The Land Register is divided into three parts:

⚷ See 1-47 for the meaning of "possessing" land, and 2-67 for the meaning of "adverse possession".

- The *property register*, which identifies the land in question, by reference to a plan.

- The *proprietorship register*, which gives the name and address of the owner.

- The *charges register*, which shows some of the rights to which land may be subject.

See 1-61 for more details.

1-57 When land has been entered on to the Land Register, the Land Registry issues a "land certificate" to the owner. (If the land is mortgaged, however, the Registry issues a "Charge Certificate", instead, which goes to the bank or building society which has lent the money. The owner does not have a land certificate, since this would indicate that he was free to dispose of the land as he wished.)

1-58 *Protection of interests on the Land Register* The Land Register protects not just the owner of land, but a range of other people, with rights in the land. These rights fall into two main categories—they are either "overriding interests" or "minor interests".

1-59 "Overriding interests" are "overriding" in the sense that although they may be shown on the Land Register, they continue to apply to the land even though they are not shown, and so override whatever may be on the register. A person buying the land may find that it is subject to one of these rights, even though it is not shown on the Land Register. The rights in this category are listed in s. 70(1) of the Law of Property Act 1925 and include:

- Easements and profits à prendre, provided they are legal in nature (s. 70(1)(a)) ⚷.

⚷ See 6-1 for the meaning of "easement" and 7-39 for "profit à prendre". These rights can be shown on the Register but are still valid even if they are not.

- Rights acquired or in the course of being acquired under the Limitation Acts (s. 70(1)(f)). This is a reference to the rule known as "adverse possession", under which a person may obtain ownership of land. If a person is in adverse possession of land, a person acquiring the land takes subject to the rights of the person in possession.

- The rights of every person in actual occupation of the land, except where enquiry is made of such a person and the rights are not disclosed (s. 70(1)(g)).

- Local land charges (s. 70(1)(i)).

- Leases and tenancies for not more than 21 years (s. 70(1)(k)). These leases and tenancies do not have to be put on the Land Register, but remain valid and any person acquiring the land will be bound by such a lease.

See further 1-60 below and 1-47 for the meaning of "occupying" land.

See 1-67 for the meaning of "local land charge".

See chapter 8 for leases and tenancies.

Because of s. 70(1), a person thinking of acquiring a piece of land cannot be certain that everything she needs to know is shown on the Land Register. Other enquiries are necessary, to see whether any overriding interests exist. Particularly important is the need to contact to anyone apart from the seller who is in occupation of the land (s. 70(1)(g)). Their rights will be overriding unless the buyer contacts them but is not told about the rights. 1-60

Minor interests Interests in land which are not overriding interests are "minor interests". Minor interests must be put on the Land Register, in the charges register, since (unless s. 70(1)(g) applies) they will not otherwise be valid when the land is sold. An entry in this form is known as a "notice". Other sorts of entry are possible, including a "caution". Placing a caution on the Register is often a hostile act, done by someone whose claim to a right over the land is disputed by the owner. The effect of a caution is that dealings with the land cannot be registered until the person responsible for the caution has been notified, and thus has had the opportunity to comment (s. 55(1)). 1-61

Some examples of minor interests: 1-62

- Easements which are equitable rather than legal.

- Restrictive covenants.

See 6-10 for the difference between legal and equitable easements.

See 7-13 for the meaning of "restrictive covenant".

See 7-44 for trusts.

- Interests under trusts.

- Interests under contracts to sell land. (These are known in the legislation as "estate contracts".) The buyer can place a record of his interest on the Land Register. If he does so, his right to buy will affect any other person who acquires the land.

1-63 *Searching the Land Register* The Land Registry has its headquarters in London, and there are 19 District Land Registries which keep records and deal with enquiries. Since 1991 the Land Register has been open to inspection by the public at large, who can thus find out who is the owner of land, provided that the land been registered.

1-64 It is usually best to apply for information by post, on the appropriate form. The Land Registry keeps a series of maps, known collectively as the "Index Map", on which registered titles are shown. To find out whether land is registered, and if so what its title number is, use form 96 for a search of the Index Map. To find out what is shown on the register for that title, use form 109. The Land Registry can supply an "office copy" of the entries on the register, and a copy of the "filed plan", showing the extent of the land included. The fees are currently £4 for the office copy and £4 for the filed plan.

See 12-15 for sources on land registration.

Other registers

1-65 The register maintained by the Land Registry under the Land Registration Acts is not the only register which contains entries relevant to land: registers are also maintained under several other Acts.

1-66 *The Land Charges Act 1972* This Act is concerned only with *unregistered* land. As explained above, the system of land registration covers the whole of England and Wales and the number of unregistered properties is shrinking. The register is kept by the Land Registry, in Plymouth. The charges which can be registered fall into different classes, labelled A to F; for example, class C is concerned with mortages where the lender does not take possession of the title deeds, and other rights over land. Class D contains restrictive covenants and other sorts of right. The effect of registering a charge is to make sure that others know about it, and are affected by it if the land changes hands: however, the fact that a land charge is shown on the register does not mean that it must be legally valid, unlike the position in relation to the Land Register.

The Local Land Charges Act 1975 This Act requires local authorities to keep registers for recording a variety of "local land charges". Some examples: 1-67

- Planning obligations.
- Tree preservation orders.
- Notices under the Rights of Light Act 1959.

See 9-63 for the meaning of "planning obligations".

See 10-20 for the meaning of "tree preservation order".

See 6-45 for an explanation of how this Act works.

The fact that a local land charge is not shown on the Register does not mean that it is legally invalid. In the case of registered land, a local land charge is an overriding interest. But if a charge is not registered, and a person buys land subject to it, she may claim compensation, under s. 10 of the 1975 Act. 1-68

See 1-59 for the meaning of "overriding interest".

The Commons Registration Act 1965 Local authorities must also keep registers of common land and town and village greens. This subject is considered in chapter 10. 1-69

See 10-65 onwards for commons registration.

Courts and other public bodies

A range of public bodies is involved in the administration of the law. As explained above, the civil and criminal courts are separate at the trial level. Civil cases are dealt with in the County Courts and (for high-value claims) in the High Court. Minor criminal cases go to magistrates' courts, and serious ones to the Crown Court, where they are tried by a judge and jury. Appeals from County Courts and the High Court, and also the Crown Court are dealt with by the Court of 1-70

Appeal and appeals from the Court of Appeal go to the House of Lords (meaning not the House of Lords as a whole, but the small number of senior judges who are appointed as "law lords" to deal with these cases). The coroner's court has a number of specialised rôles, including dealing with treasure found on land.

See 11-25 for the meaning of "treasure".

1-71 Some decisions are entrusted to tribunals, rather than courts. These tend to be specialised decisions, for which a specially-designed body and procedure are more appropriate. A notable example is the Lands Tribunal. This was set up by the Lands Tribunal Act 1949, and its task is to decide a variety of issues which arise in relation to land, including the discharge and modification of restrictive covenants. The Lands Tribunal is less formal than a court—but it operates according to rules, namely the Lands Tribunal Rules 1996.

See 7-27 onwards for details of this process.

1-72 Government departments are involved in adminstering the law because they have overall responsibility for legislation: they prepare Bills, and supervise their passage through Parliament, at the end of which they become Acts; they make the delegated legislation which is usually necessary to give full effect to Acts. Often, they exercise powers under Acts. The term "the Crown" is sometimes used of central government or the monarch (on whose behalf central government is carried on). So land referred to as "Crown land" is land belonging either to a government department or to the monarch personally. The law is sometimes different in relation to Crown land.

For an example see the Limitation Act 1980, explained at 2-68.

1-73 Many public bodies have been set up under Acts of Parliament for various purposes connected with land—for example, the Environment Agency. Though they may have responsibilities extending to England and Wales (or the U. K. as a whole) they are not "the Crown"; nor are the various parts of local government.

See 2-54 for the Environment Agency.

1-74 All these public bodies, however, and central and local government, are affected by what is known as "administrative law". This is the body of law which controls the way in which public bodies exercise their powers. It has greatly increased in importance (and volume) during the twentieth century, and is now a major factor in the way in which public bodies operate. It requires that their decisions be taken in accordance with the appropriate procedures, that they take into account all the relevant factors, and that they be rational and reasonable. Bodies such as local authorities are very often given powers to take action; and whether they use those powers is then a matter for their discretion, which they must exercise properly. (Less frequently, there is not merely a power but a *duty* to take certain action.) Procedures for the exercise of powers are often laid down in legislation, and may include the giving of notices or consultation exercises, so that interested parties may comment. When comments are received, administrative law requires that they be given due weight, not ignored.

For examples see the procedures for drawing up development plans, at 9-10, or for diverting footpaths, at 5-57 onwards.

In *R v. Braintree District Council ex parte Halls* (2000) Mr Halls and his father had exercised their rights under the "right to buy" legislation, and bought their council house. The sale was subject to a covenant [see 7-14] that the land should only be used as a single dwelling. Planning permission was later granted for the erection of another house, in the garden, and the District Council was asked to agree that they would not enforce the covenant. They refused to do so unless Mr Hall paid an amount equivalent to most of the development value of the land. Their decision was challenged by means of judicial review, on the ground that it was in breach of administrative law.

The court decided that it was not reasonable for the Council to act in this way, because it was contrary to the purpose of the right to buy legislation. Other sorts of covenant—for example, preventing noise—might be reasonable, but this was not, and the Council could not enforce it.

Adminis-trative law

I-75 A person who is concerned about a decision by a public body may be able to challenge it by means of legal proceedings known as an application for judicial review. Such proceedings are dealt with by the Divisional Court, which is part of the High Court. The Divisional Court has power to set aside a decision by a public body which has not been properly taken.

See 12-25 for sources on administrative law.

Conveyancing

I-76 Conveyancing (transferring land) has been traditionally the work of solicitors, who are regulated by their professional body, the Law Society. A new type of professional, the licensed conveyancer, was created by Part II of the Administration of Justice Act 1985. Licensed conveyancers are regulated by a body known as the Council for Licensed Conveyancers, which keeps a register of all conveyancers currently licensed under the Act. Licensed conveyancers must pass examinations and must maintain insurance, to protect their clients.

I-77 The system of land registration was set up in the hope that specialised help would not be needed by members of the public wishing to transfer land. For most people, the complexity of the law and the amount of money at risk justifies the cost of employing a solicitor or a licensed conveyancer; but guides exist for those who wish to do their own conveyancing.

See 12-15 for sources on conveyancing.

Estate agents

I-78 The Estate Agents Act 1979 gives the DTI the power to make regulations laying down minimum standards of competence for estate agents (s. 22). No regulations have yet been made, however, so a person is free to set up in business as an estate agent without any sort of official permission or authorisation, unless he is bankrupt (s. 23). But the Act does regulate the activities of estate agents in a number of ways.

I-79 An estate agent must maintain a client account, into which money received from clients must be paid (s. 15). Before accepting any money from clients he must have insurance or some other arrangement, such as a guarantee, so that any loss of clients' money will be made good (s. 16). The Office of Fair Trading has power to ban a person from doing estate agency work, or estate agency work of a specified sort, on grounds which include:

- Conviction of an offence of fraud or other dishonesty, or violence, or other offences (including such things as offences under the Property Misdescriptions Act 1991).
- Discrimination (including race and sex discrimination).

- Failure to comply with certain provisions of the Act, including requirements relating to accounts.

- Engaging in practices declared to be undesirable in an Order by the DTI (including failure to disclose a personal interest) (s. 3).

In selling property, persons carrying on an estate agency business or a property development business are subject to the Property Misdescriptions Act 1991. This Act makes it an offence for anyone in the course of an estate agency business, or a property development business, to make a false or misleading statement about a "prescribed matter" relating to land (s. 1). The "prescribed matters" are set out in The Property Misdescription (Prescribed Matters) Order 1992, and fall into 33 separate categories. These include the location and physical characteristics of the land, its history, rights over it, development potential, and many other matters. 1-80

An offence under the Act can be punished in a magistrates' court in which the maximum fine is the statutory maximum, or in the Crown Court, where it is unlimited. There is a defence of "due diligence", meaning that a person is not guilty of the offence if he can show that he: 1-81

> "...took all reasonable steps and exercised all due diligence to avoid committing the offence" (s. 2).

See 1-23 for the meaning of "statutory maximum".

CHAPTER 2

Who owns what?

Introduction

2-0 This chapter deals with a number of different questions which fall under the general heading of "Who owns what?" First, there are questions about the extent of a plot of land upwards and downwards from the surface. Next, the text considers what the law has to say about boundaries: how the position can be ascertained, if there is a dispute, who owns "boundary markers" (a convenient term for walls, fences, hedges and ditches and other devices used to mark boundaries) and who should maintain them, including legislation about party walls.

See 2-10 onwards.

2-1 Then the chapter deals with the question of what is generally regarded, so far as the law is concerned, as forming part of the land. Next, the chapter discusses familar features of the landscape, such as roads, rivers, streams and lakes, and the seashore, explaining what rules there are about ownership. Finally, there is the question of adverse possession; that is, how the ownership of land may, after 12 years, change if the land is taken over by someone other than the true owner.

See 2-44 onwards.

See 2-67 onwards.

2-2 Many of the rules dealt with come from the common law; though there is some legislation, especially the Party Wall etc Act 1996. Almost all the law explained is civil law.

See 1-10 for the meaning of "common law".

Extent of plots of land

2-3 Land is generally described by referring to boundaries on the surface of the Earth, since the surface of the land is what is of most interest to landowners and others (and what gives rise to most problems).

But in reality land is three-dimensional, and the law regards land as extending both downwards and upwards from the surface

2-4 *Downwards* The owner of a plot of land is regarded as owning the subsoil, down—theoretically—to the centre of the Earth. To this principle, however, there are some exceptions, since certain minerals do not belong to the landowner.

2-5 *Upwards* Just as the owner of land generally owns the earth below the surface, so also he owns the airspace above the surface. The law provides no precise figure, applicable to all land, for the height to which a landowner is regarded as owning the airspace: it is a question of what is required for reasonable enjoyment of the land. In a city centre, where there are multi-storey buildings, more space above the ground is required than in the suburbs or the countryside.

See 2-44 for the meaning of "minerals".

See also 3-3 for aircraft flying over land.

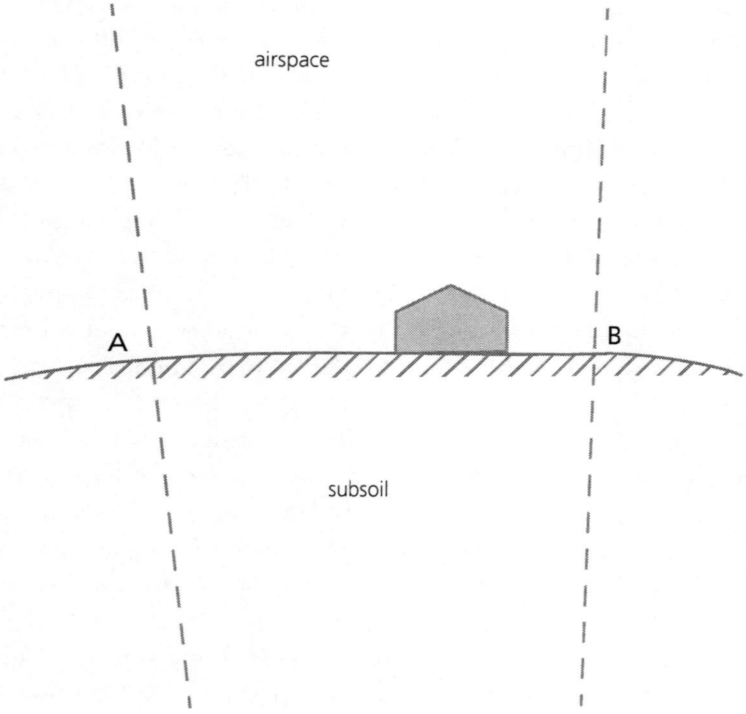

Down and up A plot of land is usually measured at the surface, from A to B, but in fact land extends down towards the centre of the Earth and also upwards, to include the airspace above the land, to a height necessary for the reasonable enjoyment of the property.

Size and shape of plots of land

2-6 There are no general restrictions on the way in which plots of land can be divided and amalgamated. Pieces of land can be very large or very small, or anywhere in between. Very small amounts of land are sometimes bought and sold: for example, one landowner may buy a thin strip of land from his neighbour, in order to make possible some development, or a small piece of land may change hands in order to give access to land from the highway. Where the land is registered, the Land Registry can be asked to make the necessary changes, whether by adding land to an existing title, or by creating a new title, as where part of a garden is sold off in order for a new house to be built.

See 5-0 for the meaning of "highway".

See 1-54 onwards for land registration.

2-7 Land can also be divided horizontally, so as to produce "slices" of land, either including the surface or consisting entirely of the subsoil (i. e. the ground below the surface) or of the airspace above the land. Pieces of land defined in this way are land for legal purposes in the same way as conventional plots (Law of Property Act 1925, s. 205(1)(ix)). An underground slice of land may be sold so that the buyer can exploit the minerals it contains, or build underground. (If he did not own any neighbouring land, he would of course need access from the surface above the land he was buying.) A section of the airspace above the surface, sometimes known to lawyers as a "flying freehold", can equally be sold. It sometimes happens, for example, that in a terrace of houses a ground floor room belongs to one house, while the room immediately above it and the roof belongs to the neighbouring house. Such arrangements can cause problems, however. One problem will be that the first-floor room relies on the ground-floor building for support; but there are legal ways of providing for this. Another is that the owner of the ground floor room is dependent upon the owner of the first floor room for protection from the elements; and there is no entirely satisfactory legal method of providing for this.

See 6-47 for easements of support.

Because of the legal difficulty of putting successive owners of the first floor room under an obligation to keep it watertight: see 7-13 onwards

2-8 For this reason, flats are rarely sold as flying freeholds, but as leaseholds. The legal arrangement between the landlord and the tenant—the lease—can then deal with such matters as maintenance of the parts of the building not included in the lease.

See chapter 7 for leases and tenancies.

2-9 The boundary of a plot of land is usually vertical, but this is not a legal requirement. It may occasionally happen, for example, that some part of a building overhangs neighbouring land; or, below the surface, the foundations of a building may extend under neighbouring land.

See also 2-29 for provisions in the Party Wall etc Act 1996 on foundations

The position of boundaries

2-10 It might be thought that, given the value of land, and the notorious unpleasantness of boundary disputes, the invariable practice would be to define boundaries precisely and fix them permanently. But being absolutely precise about boundaries poses considerable practical difficulties. In effect, the boundary must be measured from a fixed point on the land, and finding some feature which will remain unchanged indefinitely may be difficult. A building may be demolished, or extended; the line of a road or a river or stream may change. When land is entered on the Land Register, a special procedure can be followed to fix the boundaries precisely, but this is expensive and very rarely used: the Land Register almost always shows what are known as the "general boundaries" of the land, meaning that there is a lack of absolute precision about where the line of the boundary lies.

See 12-15 for sources on registered conveyancing.

2-11 In fact, there is some merit in having a degree of imprecision about boundaries, at least in relation to boundary markers. Over the years, a fence, say, might be removed and replaced by a hedge which was slightly to one side of the line of the fence. Another possibility is that one neighbour might stop maintaining the boundary marker, and the other might start to do so, as though it had changed hands. If the neighbouring landowners do not object to such slight movements of the boundary, it makes sense for the law to permit them, rather than insisting that the exact position of the boundary is fixed for all time. This is the view which the law accordingly takes. In other words, the law lets the conduct of the neighbouring landowners decide where the boundary lies, allowing it to move slightly this way and that, as the years go by. Nonetheless, if there

See 2-67 for the meaning of "adverse possession" of land; also 2-14.

As to the possibility that the boundary of land adjoining water may move, see 2-55.

is a dispute, the law must provide an answer as to where exactly the boundary lies at a particular point in time. For this purpose it provides a number of different rules, which can be summarised as follows.

2-12 *Interpretation of deeds* Although most land is now entered on the Land Register, the Register very rarely shows precise boundaries, and it may therefore be necessary to consider the deeds by which land was transferred in the past. Deeds may show boundaries in a way which is precise enough to solve the problem; but this will often not be the case. The meaning of a deed is a matter of interpretation. The land being transferred will be described in words, and usually also by reference to a map. Sometimes the plan is referred to in words such as "for the purposes of identification only", meaning that it is merely intended to show, in a general sense, where the land is. Sometimes the deed refers to the land as being "more particularly described", or "more precisely delineated" in the plan, and in this case the plan is intended to define the land being transferred. In some cases, land may be transferred by reference to Ordnance Survey maps, and this may enable a boundary to be identified. Sometimes measurements are given, to show the extent of the plot from a fixed point on the land, and hence where the boundaries lie.

See 1-34 for the meaning of "deed".

2-13 *Other evidence* In some cases it may be possible to find other evidence, such as historical records, to help prove the existence of boundaries. Practical considerations should not be forgotten. If a plot of land is surrounded by a boundary marker of the same sort, then it is highly likely, for obvious reasons, that the owner of that plot was responsible for putting up the boundary marker. Along roads, it is more likely that the owners of adjoining land have put up boundary markers to keep people from straying from the road on to their land (and perhaps, in the case of agricultural land, to keep animals in) than that the owner of the road has put up the boundary marker. If, exceptionally, the owner of the road has done so, then one would expect to find a boundary marker of the same design used along the length of the road.

2-14 *Behaviour of neighbouring landowners* The courts may give some weight to the way in which neighbours have behaved. If they have agreed, expressly or by implication, to treat the boundary as being in a particular place, or that one neighbour shall maintain the boundary marker, then the court may accept this, as evidence of where the boundary is. But this approach cannot prevail if the deeds show that the precise boundary lies elsewhere, because moving the boundary would mean transferring a strip of land from one landowner to the other, and land can generally be transferred only by means of a deed. Where this applies, ownership of land can pass from one person to another even though there is no deed.

See 1-33 onwards for this rule.

In the case of *Burns v. Morton* (2000) the deeds transferring two houses referred to the boundary between them as being a party wall or fence. Until 1979 the boundary was marked by a fence. Then Mr Morton took down the fence and built a wall about six inches on his side of the boundary. His then neighbours planted some *Leylandii* very close to the wall. (The house was transferred to Mr and Mrs Burns in 1990.) There was a dispute, which involved the question of whether Mr Morton was trespassing when he trimmed the *Leylandii* back to the line where the fence had been.

The court's decision was that in 1979 the owners of the two plots had impliedly agreed that the wall should be the new boundary. That agreement, taken together with the wording in the deeds, had transferred the strip of land between the line of the fence and the wall to Mr and and Mrs Burns, and Mr Morton had been trespassing in cutting back the *Leylandii*.

Movement of a boundary

Presumptions relating to boundaries This is an area where the courts may make use of presumptions. A presumption is a rule of law which comes into play where no evidence is presented to a court for or against a particular proposition: the court can then apply the presumption and reach a decision in line with the usual position in such cases. Presumptions deal (among many other matters) with the location of boundaries. It should be stressed that these presumptions are only relevant where there is no evidence one way or the other on which the court can reach a conclusion. 2-15

For some other examples, see 2-57 on the ownership of lakes, rivers and streams, and 2-61 on the ownership of roads.

First, walls and fences may have supports which stick out a little. If so, the presumption is that the boundary lies on the other side of the fence or wall. The reason is said to be that a landowner putting up such a boundary marker will wish to have the supports on his own land, so that he has the advantage of the tiny amount of land between them. This presumption will not apply if the landowner in question can show that for some reason the boundary marker with 2-16 the supports facing outwards. That might be the case if, for example, there was a problem with access to neighbouring land, so that the landowner had to fix the slats on to the framework of a fence from his own land.

The hedge and ditch presumption

In the case of *Alan Wibberley Building Ltd v. Insley* (1999), Mr Insley owned a cottage in Staffordshire. He bought a strip of farm land to add to his garden. Between that land and the adjoining field there was a hedge and a ditch, the hedge being on Mr Insley's side. The hedge and ditch presumption suggested that he owned the land up the far side of the ditch, and he removed the hedge and put a fence along the far edge of the ditch. The owner of the field then complained that he was trespassing. The person from whom Mr Insley had bought the land had acquired the field in 1975. For that transfer, the conveyance said that the land was "more particularly" described in an Ordnance Survey map, which was, however, "for the purposes of indentification only", and the map showed the boundary running along the centre line of the hedge.

The House of Lords considered it was most unlikely that the 1975 transfer was intended to transfer the land only to the centre line of the hedge, since this would mean that a thin strip of land (between the centre of the hedge and the far edge of the ditch) was retained by the seller, and the transfer should not be read in this way. The hedge and ditch presumption thus determined where the boundary lay, as it had done for many years, and Mr Insley was the owner of the disputed strip of land.

2-17 A special presumption applies where there is a hedge and an adjacent ditch: here the law assumes that the ditch marks the boundary, because the landowner dug the ditch at the very edge of his own land, then used the soil as a base for the hedge just inside the boundary. Again, the presumption will not apply if there is evidence that the boundary is not marked by the ditch. Along a public road, a ditch may well have been dug by the highway authority for drainage purposes.

See 5-1 for the meaning of "highway authority".

Other rules about boundary markers

2-18 For obvious reasons, a landowner will often wish to put up and maintain a boundary marker of some kind. But there is no general legal obligation on a landowner to mark the boundary of his land, or to have a fence or wall to keep animals etc out or in. It is possible for one landowner to be under a legal obligation to his neighbour to maintain a fence, but this not common.

2-19 For one landowner to be under an obligation to another *not* to put up a boundary marker presents no particular legal difficulties. This is very common, along with other sorts of negative obligations, known as restrictive covenants, relating to land. It often occurs on a new development of houses, which has been laid out with the intention that (for example) front gardens should not be fenced in, so as to maximise the feeling of spaciousness and openness. Each landowner can be made subject to the obligation, enforceable by his neighbours, not to put up a fence.

2-20 Landowners may find that they need to fence their land because of provisions in the Highways Act 1980, s. 165 and the Animals Act 1971, s. 8. The first provision says that if, on land adjoining a street, there is an unfenced source of danger the local authority may require the landowner to put up a fence.

2-21 A landowner will of course be entitled to maintain a boundary marker which he owns; but there is no general right to maintain a neighbour's boundary marker or to repair it if it is broken: the landowner's remedy is to put up his own fence, hedge or wall, on his side of the boundary. The one exception to this principle is that overhanging vegetation may be trimmed.

2-22 Planning permission may sometimes limit the height of boundary markers other than hedges. Because hedges are not subject to planning control, quick-growing plants such as *Leylandii* have been a source of public concern. The DETR has the issue under consideration. At present neighbours have no general right to complain about the effect of a high hedge, though in rare circumstances they may be able to take legal action if light to a window is seriously obstructed.

See 6-54 on fencing easements.

See 7-13 onwards for the meaning of "restrictive covenant".

See 7-21 onwards on "building schemes", to which special rules apply.

The Animals Act 1971, s. 8, is dealt with at 3-61 onwards.

See 4-22 for this rule.

See 9-35 for planning permission and boundary markers.

See 6-43 onwards for rights to light.

Party Walls

2-23 Special rules apply to the walls, often known as "party walls", which are shared by neighbouring landowners, either because the wall is built straddling the boundary, or because it is built on one side of the boundary but affects the neighbouring landowner because there are buildings on both sides of the boundary.

2-24 Before the legal reforms of the 1920s, party walls were often jointly owned, each landowner owning the whole of the party wall,this being the legal arrangement usually made when adjoining buildings were erected and sold off. But this would have caused legal difficulties under the changes being made to the law. The Law of Property Act 1925, s. 38 and Schedule 1 Part V therefore provided that ownership should be split vertically along the dividing line, the neighbouring landowners each owning half of the party wall but having a right of support from the owner of the other half, so that neither owner could weaken or remove his half of the wall.

See generally 1-3 for these reforms, and 1-44 for the joint ownership of land.

See 6-47 for easements of support.

2-25 The position was not really satisfactory, and gave rise to many disputes. Within the Inner London area, more detailed and better legislation applied (the London Building Acts (Amendment) Act 1939), and this was in effect extended to the whole of England and Wales by the Party Wall etc Act 1996. The Act, which came into force in July 1997, applies to existing and new walls. The "etc" means that it is concerned with other, related matters. "Wall" is not defined in the Act, and it is thus a matter of fact whether any particular boundary marker is a wall or not. Boundary markers built of stone, brick or concrete are likely to be "walls"; those built of other materials, or not having the thickness of a traditional stone or brick wall, may not be.

2-26 Some terms are defined in the Act, and the following are important:

- A "party wall" is a wall which forms part of a building and straddles the boundary, or which is built next to the boundary and separates buildings on different sides of the boundary. (A wall is not a "party wall" merely because its foundations run across the line of the boundary.)

◆ A "party fence wall" is a wall which straddles a boundary but which is not part of a building. (Despite the use of the word "fence", a fence in the ordinary sense of the word would not seem to be included.)

◆ A "party structure" is a party wall or a floor partition which separates buildings or parts of buildings approached solely by separate staircases or entrances (s. 20). In other words, the term includes horizontal divisions between flats and maisonettes.

◆ An "owner" of land includes a tenant, provided that his tenancy lasts for more than a year.

See chapter 8 for leases and tenancies. Periodic tenants, whose tenancies run from week to week, month to month, or year to year, are not owners for these purposes.

2-27 The Act is concerned with three main sorts of work, for which it provides procedures and lays down new rights:

◆ The construction of new walls straddling, or next to, the boundary of land.

◆ Repairs to boundary walls which are party fence walls or the external walls of buildings.

◆ Excavations which may affect neighbouring land.

2-28 *Constructing walls* A person who wishes to build a wall at a boundary (whether this will be a party wall, or a party fence wall, or a boundary wall entirely on his own land) must in some circumstances give notice to his neighbour (s. 1). This requirement applies if there are no walls or other building straddling or next to the boundary, or if there is only a boundary wall which is not a party fence wall (i. e. which does not straddle the boundary) or the external wall of a building (s.1(1)). (In other words, this procedure does *not* apply if there is already a party wall, or if the external wall of a building runs along the boundary.) A month's notice is required, and the notice must describe the proposed wall (s.1(2)). The notice must make clear whether the proposed wall is to be a party wall or a party fence wall, (i. e. straddling the boundary) or is merely to be next to the boundary, but not a party wall, because there is no building on the other side of the boundary. In the first case, the neighbour's consent is required, because the wall will be built partly on her land or will affect a building on her side of the boundary. If she gives consent—by serving a notice within 14 days—the wall will be built half on each side of the boundary, so that half belongs to each neighbour, or in whatever proportion they agree; and the costs will be shared according to the use to be made of the wall (s. 1(3)). If the wall is merely a boundary marker—a party fence wall—this will in most cases suggest that it will be used equally by both parties. But the wall may form part of a building on one or both sides of the boundary, in which case the amount of use will depend upon the actual circumstances of the case ꕥ.

ꕥ See 2-40 on how the Act provides for settlement of disputes.

2-29 If a landowner asks for consent to a party wall or a party fence wall but does not get it, or if he merely gives notice that he intends to build a wall wholly on his own land, the wall must be built entirely on his own land and there is no obligation on the neighbour to contribute to the cost of building and maintaining the wall (s. 1(4)). But the landowner has the right to put any necessary foundations, below ground level, in his neighbour's land. He must compensate his neighbour for any damage caused by the building of the wall or the installation of the foundations (s. 1(8)).

2-30 To summarise, a landowner who is served with a notice asking for consent can choose to give it, in which case the position of the wall will be a matter of agreement, and the cost of building and maintaining it will be shared by her. Or she can refuse it, in which case the wall must be built wholly on her neighbour's land, but with any necessary foundations on her land, compensation for damage being paid by her neighbour. If the notice does not ask for consent, because her neighbour has already decided to build entirely on his own land, the same consequences in relation to foundations and compensation follow.

2-31 *Repairs* Section 2 of the Act gives a number of rights to repair and do other work. It applies (firstly) where there is building of some sort which straddles a boundary. This could be a party wall or a party fence wall, or something which could be described as "building" but which is not a wall. Horizontal as well as vertical boundaries are included. Secondly, s. 2 applies where there is a boundary wall, either in the form of a party fence wall (which by definition straddles the boundary) or the external wall of a building (whether or not it straddles the boundary). The Act thus applies to a wide range of situations where there is building straddling a boundary, or next to it, but it does not apply in every case. It would not apply to a wall which was built up to the line of the boundary but which was not the external wall of a building.

See 6-50 and 7-2 onwards for other rights to maintain and repair land, and to gain access to do so.

2-32 Where s. 2 applies, a landowner is given detailed rights to carry out repairs and other work, these being set out in s. 2(2) in 14 separate categories, which include the following:

- To underpin, thicken or raise a party structure, a party fence wall, or an external wall which belongs to the building owner and is built against a party structure or a party fence wall (s. 2(2)*(a)*).

- To demolish and rebuild a party structure which is not of sufficient height or strength for some intended building of the building owner (s. 2(2)*(e)*).

- To cut into a party structure for any purpose (including the insertion of a damp-proof course)(s. 2(2)*(f)*).

- To cut into the wall of an adjoining building in order to insert flashing or other weather-proofing for a wall erected against that wall (s. 2(2)*(j)*).

- To raise a party fence wall, or to raise such a wall for use as a party wall, and to demolish a party fence wall and rebuild it as a party fence wall or as a party wall (s. 2(2)*(l)*).

- To reduce, or demolish and rebuild, a party wall or party fence wall. This must be to a height of not less than 2 metres where the wall is merely used by the adjoining owner as a boundary wall; or to "a height currently enclosed upon by the building of an adjoining owner" (s. 2(2)*(m)*). (This seems to mean that the wall must be as high as any building standing over it.)

2-33 The Act deals separately with entry on to land in order to carry out work. Conditions apply to the exercise of some of the above rights. If the work mentioned in s. 2(2)(*a*) is not made necessary by some defect in the structure or wall, the landowner carrying out the work must make good any damage caused to his neighbour and may have to extend chimneys and flues. The right to demolish a party structure under s. 2(2)(*e*) is also subject to the requirement to make good damage and to extend chimneys and flues if necessary. Under s. 2(2)(*f*) and (*j*) there is a general requirement to make good damage. Under s. 2(2)(*m*) it is a requirement that any existing parapet be reconstructed or replaced, or a new parapet constructed if need be.

See 2-39 for these rules.

2-34 Before exercising any of the rights set out in s. 2, a landowner must serve a notice (called a "party structure notice") on his neighbour, setting out details of the proposed work, and the date when the work will begin (s. 3). The notice must be served at least two months before the work is due to start and will cease to have effect if the work is not started within 12 months thereafter, or is not "prosecuted with due diligence". The adjoining landowner can give his consent in writing to the exercise of rights under s. 2, in which case the need for a notice under s. 3 does not apply. Work does not have to wait until the end of the notice period if it has to be done under statutory provisions relating to dangerous or neglected structures.

See 9-72 and10-8 and for examples.

2-35 Alternatively, the adjoining landowner may within one month serve a counter-notice under s. 4, setting out work which he wishes to be carried out, for his convenience, which can include such things as chimney copings, piers or recesses. If there is a dispute about a notice or a counter-notice, it must be dealt with under the procedures laid down by the Act.

See 2-40 for this procedure.

2-36 *Excavations* The Party Wall etc Act 1996 also requires a landowner to give notice (at least a month) to neighbours if he proposes to carry out excavations within three metres of a building or structure on neighbouring land, and the excavations will be lower than the foundations of the neighbouring structure (s. 6(1)). Notice must also be given if the excavations are to be within six metres of a building or structure on neighbouring land and they would meet a plane drawn at 45 degrees from the intersection of the plane of the external wall of the building with the plane of the bottom of its foundations (s. 6(2)).

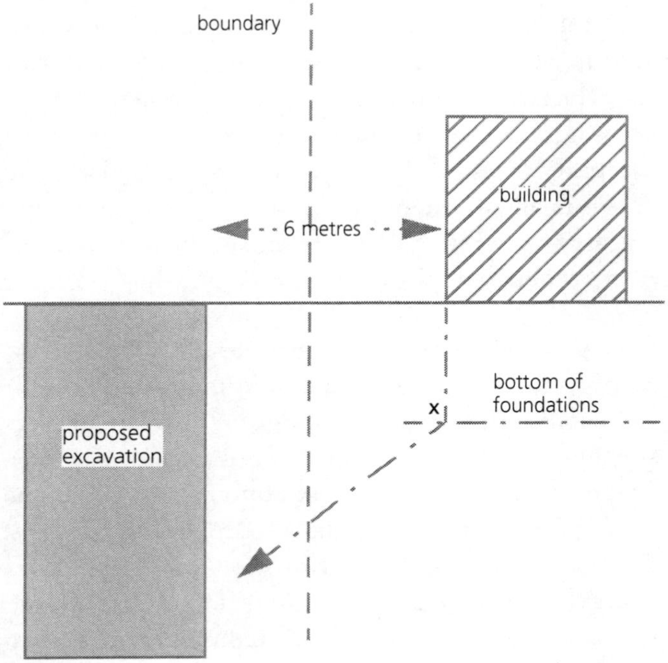

Excavations: the 6-metre rule If the 45-degree line running from point x would meet the proposed excavations, s. 6 of the Party Wall etc Act 1996 Applies. (The Act also applies to excavations within 3 metres of a building or other structure on neighbouring land.

2-37 If the neighbour does not, within 14 days, serve a notice agreeing to the work, there is deemed to be a dispute (s. 6(7)). The landowner carrying out the work may be required, at his own expense, to underpin or strengthen or otherwise safeguard his neighbour's foundations, in so far as this is necessary (s. 6(3)). After the work has been carried out, the landowner responsible must, if asked to do so, provide plans and sections showing the work which has been done (s. 6(9)).

2-38 *Compensation and other rights* Section 7(1) of the Act provides that when rights under the Act are exercised, no unnecessary inconvenience shall be caused to the owners or occupants of adjoining land. A landowner must compensate his neighbour for any loss or damage caused by work done under the Act (s. 7(2)). Work done under the Act must comply with statutory requirements,

See 1-47 for the meaning of "occupying" land.

and must be in accordance with any plans and other details settled as a result of any dispute which has occurred (s. 7(5)) ⚘.

⚘ As to statutory requirements in relation to planning and building control, see chapter 9 generally, and 10-2 onwards.

2-39 A building owner is given a right to enter his neighbour's land for the purpose of carrying out work under the Act (s. 8). Notice must be given of the intended entry—at least 14 days, unless there is an emergency, in which case the notice must be as much as is reasonably practical. The Act does not authorise any interference with existing easement of light or other easements, such as easements of support, relating to party walls (s. 9) ⚘. This will be particularly important where there is an easement of support, since a landowner who wishes to carry out work will have to make sure that his neighbour's building is properly supported, if necessary, while work is carried out.

⚘ See 6-43 for rights to light and 6-47 for easements of support.

2-40 There is a special procedure for disputes under the Act (s. 10(1)–(2)). The procedure thus covers the building of new walls, repairs and excavations. The parties must agree to the appointment of a single surveyor, or if they cannot do so they must each appoint a surveyor, and those surveyors must appoint a third. (If one party refuses to appoint a surveyor, or fails to do, the other may appoint one on his behalf: s. 10(4).) The term "surveyor" means any person (other than the parties) chosen to deal with a dispute—it is not necessary for a "surveyor" to have a qualification as a surveyor or indeed any other qualification, though in many cases it will be desirable to appoint a qualified surveyor (s. 20). The surveyor (or two of the three, if there are three) may settle any dispute, including a dispute about the right to execute work, or the timing of work, compensation, and any other matter such as the costs of resolving the dispute (s. 10(12). The decision is final, except that a party to the dispute may appeal to the County Court (s. 10(17).

2-41 It is an offence under s. 16 to refuse to allow a person to enter where he has a right to do so under s. 8, or to obstruct any person in doing what they are entitled to do under s. 8. The maximum punishment is a level 3 fine ⚘.

⚘ See 1-23 for the standard levels of fines in magistrates' courts.

2-42 The Party Wall etc Act 1996 is important in all built-up areas, particularly to terraced and semi-detached houses and other buildings which are in separate ownership with a dividing wall. The Act also applies to some walls which are not part of buildings but merely mark a boundary. Although the Act makes important changes to the law, it does not provide a comprehensive set of rules on party walls and related matters. It does not (for example) have anything to say about the need for planning permission, nor does it provide a way of fixing the location of a boundary if there is a dispute.

2-43 Whether or not the Act applies in a given situation, other areas of the law may also give a landowner the right to gain access to his neighbour's land in order to carry out repairs.

See 12-13 for sources on the Party Wall etc Act 1996.

See 7-2 onwards for the Access to Neighbouring Land Act 1992, and 6-50 for easements giving a right to repair property.

What forms part of the land?

2-44 The law has a range of rules dealing with things which form part of the land itself, things attached to it, and things found on it, such as wild animals, plants and water. Such rules are necessary in order for people to know who owns these things and how they can be the subject of buying and selling and other transactions.

2-45 *Minerals* "Minerals" is a term used by lawyers to include all potentially valuable substances found in the land, including stone, gravel, clay, oil, coal and gas, and the ores of precious and other metals. The general rule is that minerals belong to the owner of the land; but there are exceptions, since some belong to the Crown, or to an official body.

See 1-33 for the formalities involved in transactions with land.

See 1-72 for the meaning of "the Crown"

- Deposits of gold and silver have belonged to the Crown from early times. The position is governed by the Royal Mines Acts 1688 and 1693.
- Oil and gas also belong to the Crown, under the Petroleum Exploration (Production) Act 1934.
- Coal, under the Coal Industry Act 1994, generally belongs to the Coal Authority.

Licences (permissions) can be obtained, from the appropriate official body, by a landowner who wishes to extract these minerals. The

See 9-22 for the need to obtain planning permission for mining operations.

agreement of the landowner will also be required in order to come on to his land. A landowner who wishes to sell the minerals under his land can do so by selling an underground "slice" of land, or by selling a right to take the minerals. Once minerals have been extracted, they are ordinary property, not land. A seam of coal, for example, is part of the land; but once the coal has been mined, a bag of it can be bought and sold without any particular formalities, in the same way as a book or a sandwich.

See 7-39 for the nature of these rights.

2-46 *Plants and trees* Plants and trees growing on land are regarded as part of it. When land is sold, they will automatically be regarded as forming part of the land unless some other arrangement is made. Once plants (or their fruit) are picked or harvested, they cease to be land and become ordinary property.

2-47 *Fixtures* Some man-made objects may also be part of the land, or "fixtures". Buildings will (with rare exceptions) be attached to the land, and will be fixtures. Deciding whether an object is a fixture can be a difficult matter, and will be of obvious importance when land is sold: the buyer will wish to know what is included. In dealing with such problems, the courts consider (firstly) the extent to which, if at all, something is attached to the land. Things which are *not* actually attached to the land are unlikely to be fixtures, even if they are heavy and seem to have been put in position with the intention that they remain there indefinitely, as may be the case with a statue. But, exceptionally, some things which are not attached to the land may be fixtures. For example, stone steps leading to the front door of as house, might not be cemented in position, but might nonetheless be intended to be permanent, and as a matter of common sense would probably be regarded as a fixture.

2-48 Secondly, if something is attached to the land, the courts consider the purpose for which it has been attached—whether it has been attached in order to make it part of the land, or whether it has been attached for other reasons. Wooden panelling might be attached to a wall in order to make it permanent part of a house (in which case it would probably be a fixture); but a piece of modern art might be attached to a wall because that is the most convenient and safest way to display it (in which case it would probably not be a fixture).

See also 1-41 for s. 62 of the Law of Property Act 1925

2-49 When land is sold, the parties generally try to avoid disputes by agreeing specifically what objects will be treated as included in the sale. Often things will be included which are not fixtures in the legal sense but which are often sold with land. For example, a gas cooker might be included, but would probably not be regarded as a fixture since it is only attached to a house in that it is connected to the gas supply; or a carpet, which is attached only in order to keep it in position, not to make it a permanent part of the building.

> In the case of *Elitestone Ltd v. Morris* (1997), the court had to consider a wooden bungalow which was resting on (but not fixed to) some concrete pillars. It had been put up in 1945. If the bungalow formed part of the land, the occupants were protected tenants, under the Rent Act 1977; but if it was not part of the land, they were not protected. The House of Lords applied the standard test, by considering the extent to which the bungalow was attached to the land, and the purpose for which it had been attached to the land. It decided that the bungalow must have been intended to form part of the land, since it could only be removed by being destroyed. The occupants were therefore protected tenants under the Rent Act, and could not be made to leave without a court order.

When is a building part of the land?

Wild animals Wild animals such as rabbits, hares, and game birds do not belong to anyone while they remain free. It would not be practicable for the law to say that they belonged to the owner of the land on which they are present: if this were so, ownership would change constantly, as they moved to and fro across the boundaries of land. But a landowner is entitled, subject to legislation which protects certain species and also regulates sporting activity, to catch them while they are on his land, and once caught they become his property. The right to take wild animals thus belongs to the owner of the land. The rule in relation to wild fish—whether game fish or coarse fish—is essentially the same: the right to take them generally goes with the ownership of the bed of a lake, river or stream. 2-50

For the legislation which protects wild animals see 11-47 onwards.

See 2-57 onwards for the ownership of land beneath water.

The right to take wild animals or fish can be sold, so that it is separated from the land itself. Such a right is known as a "profit à prendre". A person may thus acquire the right to shoot over land, or an angling club may acquire the fishing rights in a particular lake or river. 2-51

See further 7-39 for the nature of these rights.

Water Water flowing across or underneath land does not belong to the owner of the land. Her right to take the water depends upon whether the water is in a defined channel, like water in a stream or 2-52

Even if causes subsidence which affects neighbouring properties: see 6-49.

river, or not, like rainwater falling on a roof, or water percolating underground. If the latter, the landowner is free to take the water. If the water is in a defined channel, however, a riparian owner—that is, the owner of land next to a river or stream—may only abstract as much water as is necessary for the normal use of his own land. (He may take more provided the water is returned. For example, a riparian owner who wished to divert a stream, so as to provide an ornamental water-garden, would be entitled to do so provided the water was returned to the stream.) Riparian owners can take legal action if too much water is extracted by an upstream owner and their own rights to water in the stream are affected.

Ownership of bees

The case of *Kearry v. Pattinson* (1939) concerned bees. Mr Kearry was a beekeeper. One day some of his bees swarmed, and settled in the garden of his neighbour, Mr Pattinson, with whom he was not on good terms. Mr Pattinson at first refused permission for him to collect the bees. Next day he changed his mind; but by then the bees had gone. Mr Kearry sued Mr Pattinson for the loss of the bees.

The court's decision was that Mr Kearry had no legal right to go on to Mr Pattinson's land to collect the bees. The court also decided that, while bees in a hive are the property of the beekeeper, when they swarm the rule for wild creatures applies to them, so that they cease to belong to the beekeeper.

See also 6-46 for the right to take water as an easement.

2-53 Water which is static, in ponds and lakes, belongs to the owner of the bed of the lake or pond. It is not clear how the law would treat a lake or pond which had a small inflow and outflow; perhaps in the event of a dispute the court might conclude that it was a matter of degree whether the flow was sufficient to mean that the rule for flowing water, rather than static water, should be applied.

2-54 The above common law rules, developed by the courts, are now subject to the provisions of the Water Resources Act 1991. Anybody wishing to abstract water from an underground source or from a river or stream must obtain a licence from the Environment Agency, a body with wide responsibilities in relation to environmental matters, set up under the Environment Act 1995 (s. 24 of the 1991 Act). There are some exceptions, including the abstraction of :

- Up to 5 cubic metres (or up to 20 cubic metres with the consent of the Environment Agency).

- Up to 20 cubic metres in 24 hours, this being allowed for most domestic purposes.

Subject to the above rules, one landowner can grant to another a formal right to take water from his land, and this is a right of the sort known as an easement.

See 12-8 for sources on what forms part of the land; also 12-23 on water.

The seashore and the sea-bed

Land bordering the sea can be owned in the same way as other land; and there is a presumption that the owner of land bordering the sea is entitled to the shore as far as the ordinary level of high tide—specifically, the mean between spring and neap high tides—thus including some but not all of what would be regarded as the beach. The owner of land bordering the sea is in a special position in that the extent of his land may be decreased, if the sea washes it away, or increased, if the sea deposits sand or other material so that the level of high water recedes. 2-55

In *Shetland Salmon Farmers Association v. Crown Estate Commissioners* (1990), a Scottish case, the question arose as to the ownership by the Crown of the seabed. There was a dispute between the Shetland Salmon Farmers Association, whose members were engaged in salmon-farming, by means of floating cages moored to the seabed, and the Port and Harbour of Lerwick, which was seeking to construct quays, piers and other works. To what extent did each require permission from the Crown?

The court decided that the seabed belonged to the Crown, and that permission from the Crown was therefore required for both salmon-farming and the harbour works.

Ownership of the sea bed

Below the level of high water, the shore (sometimes known as the "foreshore") and the sea bed generally belong to the Crown. This includes the beds of rivers and estuaries to the extent that they are 2-56

See 1-72 for the meaning of "the Crown".

tidal. The seabed is generally owned by the Crown for 12 nautical miles from the shore, under the Territorial Sea Act 1987. (Further out from the shore, the Crown asserts the right to fish and to extract minerals, without claiming ownership of the sea bed.) But both the foreshore and sea bed may be transferred by the Crown to others; for example so that a pier or harbour may be constructed. The Crown may in the same way grant permission for a company to drill for oil or gas on the sea bed.

See 12-23 for sources on water.

The beds of rivers, streams, lakes, etc

2-57 The beds of lakes, rivers and streams can be owned in the same way as other land. They may be owned by the owners of the adjoining land, ("riparian owners") or they may be in separate ownership. One way of giving a person the right to fish in a lake, river or stream is to transfer to them the ownership of the bed, and it may thus happen that the bed is not owned by the landowner(s) on either side. If the ownership is unknown, the law applies the presumption that, above the point at which the river is tidal, each riparian owner owns the bed to the halfway point in the lake, river or stream.

This is an alternative to the sporting rights explained at 7-39.

2-58 Sometimes canals and other waterways, and reservoirs, are constructed on land, in which case special arrangements are likely to be made concerning ownership of the land beneath the water, surrounding land, access, fishing rights and so on.

2-59 If a watercourse (the terms includes rivers, streams, ditches, drains, culverts and sewers) is not flowing properly, the Environment Agency can require any person who is in control of the watercourse, or who owns adjoining land, or who has caused the obstruction, to put matters right. Failure to comply is an offence for which the maximum punishment is a level 4 fine; and the Agency can if necessary carry out the work themselves and recover the cost of it from the person concerned (Land Drainage Act 1991, s. 25).

See 12-23 for sources on water.

Roads and paths

2-60 Most roads are public roads, and so belong, under s. 263 of the Highways Act 1980, to the "highway authority". For some roads, including motorways, the DETR is the highway authority, but generally the highway authority is the local authority—in counties, it is the County Council. Most footpaths and bridleways similarly belong to the highway authority.

See chapter 5 for more on highways generally: not all highways belong to the highway authority.

2-61 Generally, the highway authority does not own all the subsoil, but merely the surface and a sufficient depth to accommodate pipes, cables, and other apparatus. There is no fixed measurement of the depth to which the land is owned; though traditionally the amount has been described as "two spits"—in other words, twice the depth of the blade of a spade. The position is different where land has been acquired compulsorily to construct a road: in this case the body acquiring the land will generally acquire the full depth of the land, not just the top part.

Contrast the usual position of a landowner: see 2-3 onwards.

See 11-100 for compulsory purchase of land.

2-62 Where land adjoining the highway has a boundary marker such as a hedge or fence, the presumption is that all the land between the boundary markers, including verges and other small areas of land at junctions, bends, etc, belongs to the highway authority. Public ownership of verges is important since they are often used to carry pipes and cables for the utility companies.

See 11-103 onwards for services.

In *Attorney-General v. Beynon* (1965) the issue was whether a broad strip of grass verge, forming a space like a lay-by, was part of the highway. Mr Beynon owned the property on the other side the road, and used to park on the verge. The highway authority maintained that he was not entitled to do so.

The court decided that the presumption applied, and the verge was part of the highway, so that Mr Beynon was not entiled to park there

Ownership of the verge

2-63 Below the top "two spits" of the highway, the subsoil may belong to some person other than the highway authority. There is a presumption that, in the absence of evidence to the contrary, the subsoil belongs to the owners of property adjoining the road, each owning up to the mid-point in the road. This presumption is thought to apply whether or not the land has been described, in transfers, as having the road as its boundary. Ownership of the subsoil may be useful in that it allows the adjoining landowner to build cellars under the road (though building under a road requires the consent of the highway authority, under s. 179 of the Highways Act 1980).

2-64 Some roads are privately owned, whether by the owners of houses or other properties in the road, or some other person. They are likely to be subject to private rights of way, and may also be subject to public rights of way. The presumption mentioned above applies also to private roads: though in this case the adjoining owners each own not just the subsoil but the surface of the road as well.

See chapter 5 for highways generally and and 6-33 onwards for private rights of way.

See 12-18 to 12-19 for sources on highways and other roads and paths.

Ownership of a bridleway

The case of *Pardoe v. Pennington* (1997) concerned two nieghbours, whose houses were separated by a bridleway. Ms Pardoe constructed a cess-pit under the bridleway. Ms Pennington objected, and a dispute arose as to the ownership of the bridleway. Ms Pardoe's case was that, applying the presumption about the ownership of roads, half the width of the bridleway belonged to her.

The land was part of an estate known as Trethevey Manor Farm, most of which, in the 1920s, had been divided among the children of the owner. After considering the history of the estate, the court concluded that the family had deliberately refrained from including the bridleway, when land was sold off. The presumption therefore did not apply. Ms Pardoe did not own half of the bridleway, and the cess-pit had been unlawfully constructed.

Sewers, drains, pipes and cables

2-65 The utility companies which supply water, gas, electricity, telephone and cable services are now privatised, and operate under special legislation. The legislation gives them powers to install their pipes, cables and other equipment under, on and over land. Although they may be attached to the land, these remain the property of the utility companies, who are entitled, in accordance with their powers under the legislation, to maintain and repair them. A landowner may be entitled to a payment—either a lump sum or an

See 11-103 onwards.

annual amount—for the use his land. Such an arrangement is sometimes known as a "wayleave".

2-66 Apart from the utility companies, landowners may need to run pipes, cables etc over neighbouring land, for example a soakaway for a septic tank. The appropriate legal arrangement is an easement which allows the landowner to retain ownership of the pipes, and also to gain access for repair.

See 6-52 for easements of this sort.

See 12-12 for sources on pipes, cables etc.

Adverse possession

2-67 It is not uncommon for land to be appropriated by someone other than the true owner. This can happen to a plot of any size, or indeed a building, but often occurs where a landowner takes over a strip of land adjoining his own. The reason may be that there is some doubt about where precisely the boundary lies, or perhaps because the adjoining land is unused, and the owner unknown, and the landowner decides to take advantage of the situation. In certain circumstances, the law allows ownership to pass to the landowner. This is an exception to the rule that a deed is required for land to be transferred.

See 1-33 for this rule.

2-68 *The rule* The rule is the result of the basic principle, now set out in the Limitation Act 1980, that the right to take action in response to a legal wrong does not last indefinitely, but is limited. For many claims under the civil law, the period—the "limitation period"—is 6 years. The period during which the owner of land may take legal action to remove people from his land is generally 12 years (s. 15). (It is 30 years when the land is the Crown's; and 60 if it is foreshore belonging the the Crown.) After that, it will be too late, and the law will no longer assist the true owner of the land; on the contrary, it will protect the person who has appropriated the land, and he will in due course become the owner. Though it may seem harsh to impose a 12-year limit on a landowner's right to regain his land, preserving the right indefinitely would lead to uncertainty and increase the opportunity for legal disputes, since the ownership of land could then be challenged on the basis of events long ago.

See 1-72 for the meaning of "the Crown", and 2-56 for the meaning of "foreshore".

2-69 In order for land to be appropriated in this way, the person concerned must be in "adverse possession" of it, which means that he must be in sole possession of the land, not allowing others (whether the true owner, or other people) to share possession of it, and intending to be in possession of it.

See 1-47 for the meaning of "possessing" land.

Adverse possession of a strip (1)

The case of *Sturminster Holdings Ltd v. James* (1998) concerned a strip of land between a market and a road. Mr James had carried out some maintenance of the strip, but the court decided that this activity did not amount to adverse possession of the strip, and the true owner's right to the land was not brought to an end after 12 years.

2-70 It is not necessary for the person in possession to intend to *own* the land: it is enough that he intends to remain in possession of it indefinitely. Merely using the land is not enough: his actions must exclude the true owner and others from it. In many cases, the clearest way is to fence the land off and put locks on any gates (or, in the case of a building, occupying it and making it secure). When the true owner is no longer in possession, and the interloper is in adverse possession, the limitation period begins to run, and after 12 years of adverse possession the true owner can no longer take action. It is not necessary for the same person to have been in adverse possession throughout the 12 years: what matters is that the true owner has been excluded from the land for 12 years. Once that has happened, the law will protect the person currently in possession of the land.

Adverse possession of a strip (2)

In *London Borough of Hounslow v. Minchinton* (1997), a householder, Miss Minchinton, claimed a small strip of land at the bottom of her garden. There was no fence between her garden and the strip, but the boundary on the far side of the strip was marked by a hedge and fence which the Borough Council had put up. The garden as a whole, including the strip, was fenced so as to keep out dogs, and over the years owners of the house had kept the strip tidy and had a compost heap there. The court decided that these acts (which spanned more than 12 years) amounted to adverse possession, so that the land had become Miss Minchinton's.

2-71 A person in adverse possession is trespassing, and the landowner can take civil action to remove him from the land, but he cannot be accused of stealing the land merely because he is in adverse possession of it. Until the 12 years have elapsed, the true owner can take legal action to remove a person in possession of his land (i. e. to obtain an order from the court that possession of the land be restored to him). Permission by the true owner will also prevent the trespasser acquiring a right to the land by adverse possession, since a person in possession by consent cannot be in adverse possession; and permission may be implied, if the circumstances justify that conclusion. Often, however, the law takes the view that if the true owner sees that someone is in adverse possesion of his land, but takes no action, his silence does not amount to implied permission, and after 12 years the true owner will thus lose his right to regain his land. If the person in possession acknowledges that the land belongs to the true owner, he ceases to be in adverse possession.

See 11-57 for the theft of land.

If land is not registered, a person claiming to have a right to it by adverse possession may apply to the Land Registry to be registered as the owner. The Land Registry may register him with an "absolute title", or merely with a "possessory" title. But the latter can in due course be converted into an absolute title under s. 77 of the Land Registration Act 1925. If, on the other hand, the land is already registered, the true owner is deemed to hold it on trust for the person in adverse possession, and the latter can then apply to the Land Registry to be registered as the owner of the land, under s. 75 of the Act. 2-72

See 1-54 onwards for the system of land registration.

See 1-56 for the meaning of "absolute" and "possessory" title.

Application in different situations The rule described is relevant in three rather different situations: 2-73

- Where someone takes over the maintenance of a boundary marker such as a hedge.

- Where someone takes possession of an area of ground, for example by fencing off a strip of land adjoining their garden.

- Where someone takes over a building.

See 2-11 for boundary markers.

The same principles apply to all three situations. The first is perhaps the least significant: in many cases a landowner may not be greatly concerned about who owns a boundary marker. The second 2-74 is more important, and landowners need to be aware that if they are very slow to take action they may lose strips or other pieces of land which have been taken over by their neighbours. If a building is occupied by squatters who remain in adverse possession for 12 years, the landowner may find that he has lost a valuable property.

See 12-8 for sources on adverse possession.

Adverse possession of a wall

In the case of *Prudential Assurance Co Ltd v. Waterloo Real Estate* (1998) the two companies were neighbouring landowners, and ownership of a wall was of crucial importance to a property development. It appeared that the wall was originally a party wall, and that the northern face originally belonged to Waterloo. But Prudential, and the previous owners of its land, had maintained the wall since 1957: they had at one stage raised it, and had also rendered it on two occasions and carried out other work on it.

The court decided that these actions were sufficient to make Prudential the owner of the whole wall.

Assessment

2-75 It is sensible for a landowner, in the interests of good relations with neighbours and others, to have a clear idea of what forms part of his property, and what does not. Into the latter category come such things as the airspace above his property (apart from what is needed for reasonable enjoyment of the land) and also water flowing across the land. There may be grey areas, however: if, for example, there is a path running along the boundary, the ownership of which is unknown, the landowner cannot tell whether half of it is his, because of the presumption which the law applies, or whether someone else might come forward with a better right to it.

2-76 Disputes about boundaries and boundary markers are often acrimonious, and may result in legal proceedings which involve costs out of all proportion to the value of the land at stake. Common sense suggests that concessions are worth making in order to avoid such situations.

2-77 As far as party walls are concerned, the law, in the form of the 1996 Act, has intervened in order to give neighbouring landowners clearer and more extensive rights. The price is greater complexity; and a landowner thinking of building on the boundary of his land will be well advised to obtain professional advice on the implications of the 1996 Act.

Adverse possession is at first sight a difficult rule to understand. 2-78
Why should the law reward a trespasser who takes over a piece of land, by giving her, after 12 years, a right to keep it? The answer is that the law, as a matter of policy, tends to uphold the established state of affairs; and if a landowner is not sufficiently concerned to take action against a person in adverse possession, the law is content for the landowner's rights to be taken away. In other words, the law puts the burden on landowners to look after their land, and take action against anyone who tries to take possession of it. Landowners may have a range of options: it may be possible to give the trespasser permission to use the land temporarily, or to persuade the trespasser to give up possession. Direct action is inadvisable, and may be criminal if a building is involved. Legal proceedings may thus be necessary in order to prevent the land eventually being lost.

See 1-25 onwards on self-help generally, and 8-95 onwards on using or threatening violence to enter land.

Chapter 3

Trespass

Introduction

3-0 Trespassing means going on to someone else's land without their permission, or some other sort of legal justification. This is a fundamental idea, to which the law explained in other chapters is connected. For example, the fact that a road or path is a highway means that the public are entitled to use it for certain purposes, and so are not trespassing on the land. As explained below, there are many different legal reasons why going on to someone else's land may be lawful and so not a trespass. Trespass is a tort (a civil wrong), for which legal action may be taken in the civil courts; and it forms a basic protection for landowners, including those who are in possession of land.

See chapter 5 for highways

These are explained at 3-11 onwards

See 1-47 for the meaning of "occupying" land; and 1-21 for the meaning of "tort".

3-1 In some situations, the law also makes trespassing a criminal offence. In such cases there may be a prosecution in the criminal courts, as well as action in the civil courts. Some of these situations are considered below, followed by an explanation of the Animals Act 1971. This Act is not concerned only with trespassing animals, but often will be, so fits in well here.

See 1-20 for how the civil and criminal law interact.

See 3-52 onwards for the Animals Act.

3-2 Much of the law dealing with the civil wrong of trespass is common law—the product of decisions of the courts over the ages. However the criminal offences which involve trespassing have been created by Acts of Parliament.

See 1-1 onwards for sources of the law.

The nature of trespass

3-3 For the purposes of the law of trespass, "land" has the meaning explained in the last chapter. Trespassing can thus take place on

See 2-3 onwards for the extent of plots of land.

the surface of the land, or under the surface. It can also take place in the airspace above the land, but this is subject to what was said in the last chapter about ownership of the airspace. So it does not follow that every intrusion into the airspace over land is a trespass. There is also a special provision in the Civil Aviation Act 1982 (s. 76) which provides that there is no trespass when civil aircraft fly over land at a reasonable height, if the flight is in all other respects lawful. (Unless an aircraft was flying unusually low, there would probably be no trespass in any event.)

See 2-5 for ownership of the airspace.

This principle also applies to nuisance: see chapter 4.

3-4 Trespass can take many forms, of which the following activities are examples, assuming that they are not covered by some legal right:

- Walking on land.
- Leaving a car parked on land.
- Dumping waste or throwing litter on to land.
- Rebuilding a boundary wall or fence so that it is on neighbouring land.
- Operating a tower crane in such a way that it overhangs neighbouring land.
- Installing pipes or cables under land.
- Attaching something to land—for example, attaching a notice to a fence.
- Taking something from land.
- Occupying land, for example by "squatting" in an unoccupied house.

As to the criminal law on parking, see 3-49.

See also 2-23 for the provisions of the Party Wall etc Act 1996 in relation to building party walls.

See 11-103 onwards in relation to statutory undertakers.

See 2-67 onwards on adverse possession of land; and also chapter 8 on leases and tenancies.

An example of trespass

In the case of *Westripp v. Baldock* (1938) both parties lived on a housing estate. Mr Baldock was a builder, and stored building materials and equipment in his garden. Mr Westripp brought proceedings because (among other activities) Mr Baldock kept ladders, planks and other items leaning against the side wall of Mr Westripp's house.

The court decided that this was a trespass, and Mr Westripp was awarded compensation for damage which had been caused to the pointing of the wall

3-5 Trespassing is not confined to land which is protected by a fence or barrier of some kind, or which has notices warning the public not to trespass.

3-6 A trespass can be committed when a person is acting outside the terms of some legal right allowing them to go on to land. For example, a right of way may allow certain people, or the public generally, to cross land on foot. A person riding a bicyle across the land would be trespassing ✠.

✠ In relation to public and private rights of way, see chapter 5 and also 6-33 onwards.

3-7 Some of the above examples would obviously cause damage to the land; others might not. Trespass is a civil wrong, even if no damage is caused, though in the absence of any damage, compensation may be very modest. But if damage is caused to the land, compensation can be obtained for it ✠. The civil wrong of trespass is committed only where the entry is intentional or caused by carelessness. If a pedestrian is jostled, while walking along the pavement, and falls into a landowner's front garden, this is not a trespass by the pedestrian. Some trespasses may be innocent in the sense that they are free from moral blameworthiness. If, for example, a person walks across some open land in the mistaken impression that it is land to which the public has access, he still commits a trespass, because (unlike the pedestrian) he is intending to go on to the land.

✠ See 3-24 onwards for remedies for trespassing.

3-8 Trespass thus applies to a wide range of entries on to land. But one important qualification must be mentioned: trespass only applies to *direct* intrusions on to land. If there is an indirect entry on to land, as for example where a tree grows so that it overhangs neighbouring land, or where water is allowed to run on to neighbouring land, this is not a trespass but may be a different sort of legal wrong, namely a nuisance ✠.

✠ Nuisance is explained in chapter 4.

Who can take legal action for trespass?

3-9 The protection given by the law of trespass is given not to the owner of land as such, but rather to the person who has the best right to be in possession of the land. Essentially, being in possession of land means exercising control over the land. Usually the person in possession of the land will be the owner of it—most landowners are in this position. Bringing legal proceedings for trespass thus presents no problems. But it is important to note that the law has a wider effect. Suppose that a squatter moves into a holiday cottage belonging to a landowner. The landowner can bring proceedings for trespass against the squatter, because as owner of the cottage she has a better right than he does to possession of it. But while the squatter is in possession of the cottage, he can bring proceedings for trespass against someone who, for example, walks across the garden.

See 1-47 for the meaning of "possessing" land.

But this will not be the case where the house has been let, because the tenant will then have the right to possession of it: see chapter 8 generally.

In *Countryside Residential (North Thames) Ltd v. Tugwell* (2000) a firm of developers had been given a licence to go on to land for the purposes of surveying it. The question arose as to whether the firm could take action for trespass against a trespasser.

The court decided that it could not: the licence gave the firm access to the land, but did not allow it to occupy and control the land. Since it was not in control of the land, the firm could not bring proceedings for trespass.

The right to take action for trespass

Trespasses by animals

3-10 A person can commit a trespass if dogs, cats or other animals for which he is responsible go on to someone else's land; but it is necessary for the landowner to show that the person concerned intended the entry or was negligent. In practice, when animals enter on to land and cause damage, action can often be taken under the Animals Act 1971.

See 3-52 onwards for the Animals Act.

Trespasses by animals

In the case of *League Against Cruel Sports v. Scott* (1996), the League owned five pieces of land on Exmoor, which it had bought to provide sanctuaries for deer, and where it did not permit stag-hunting. The League took legal action for trespass against the master of a pack of stag hounds, after a series of incidents when the hounds had trespassed in the deer sanctuaries.

The court decided that there could be a trespass by the hounds if the master was negligent, and failed to exercise proper control over the hounds.

In the case of *Buckle v. Holmes* (1926), however, the Court of Appeal, in a case concerning a cat, took the view that it was natural for dogs and cats to stray, and that their owners were not liable if they did so. The owner of a cat was thus not liable under the law of trespass for pigeons and chickens killed by the cat.

Defences

3-11 It is for the person who takes proceedings for trespass to prove that he was in possession of the land, and to show that the person concerned came on to the land; and it is for the latter, if he can, to show that he had permission, or that his actions were legally justified in some other way, so that he has a defence to the proceedings. The matters which can form a defence can be summarised as follows.

3-12 *Licences* If the person in possession of the land (which will usually be the owner) gives a licence—permission—to come on to the land, then there is no trespass. Whenever a householder says "Please come in" to a guest, he is giving permission to enter, and the visitor does not commit a trespass in doing so. A landowner may give permission to walk across a garden or a field, or to store building materials temporarily on land. Shops and other commercial premises similarly give permission for visitors to enter, as do offices open to the public. A licence can sometimes also be implied from the circumstances ꕥ.

ꕥ See also 11-2 on occupiers' liability, where the courts are particularly concerned with implied licences because of their effect on the duty of care owed to a person who comes on to the land.

3-13 Visitors must keep within the terms of the licence they have, whether this is express or implied. It may be that they are not allowed access to parts of the premises (for example in a shop, where members are not expected to go behind counters or into storerooms). If the licence is ended, they must leave.

See 1-50 for the meaning of "express" and "implied", and 1-52 for ending a licence.

The case of *Robson v. Hallett* (1967) concerned a visit to a house by three police officers who were making enquiries about an offence. They were attacked by the occupants of the house, and the latter were charged with assaulting the police in the execution of their duty. This raised the question of whether the policemen were acting lawfully in visiting the house—if not, they would not have been acting in the execution of their duty and so no offence would have been committed.

The court decided that the occupier of a house gives an implied licence for callers to come to the door and knock. The police officers were thus acting lawfully in coming to the door.

Later cases have established that such implied licences do not allow callers to do more than call at the door. And the occupier of the house can always make clear that there is no implied licence by putting up a suitable notice, for example, "Callers by appointment only"

An implied licence to enter land

3-14 *Rights granted by the owner of the land* If the owner has granted a lease, the lessee or tenant is not a trespasser, because he has a right to be on the land, and indeed in control of it. The same is true of other rights which entitle a person to be on the land, for example private rights of way: provided a person who has the benefit of the right keeps within its terms he does not commit a trespass by going on to the land.

See chapter 8 generally.

See 6-33 for private rights of way.

3-15 *Other rights* Many Acts provide for officials to go on to land, for reasons connected with public health and safety or the regulation of agriculture, forestry and many other activities. Sometimes the right is just a right to enter the land to carry out inspections or surveys; sometimes it is a right to carry out work. But such rights are not exclusive to officialdom: sometimes they apply to private individuals. For example, a wide power, which would enable private persons to enter on to land for the purposes of preparing a planning application is contained in the planning legislation. The police have powers under the Police and Criminal Evidence Act 1984, to enter land in order to make an arrest or to search for or to seize evidence; but they may need a warrant from a magistrate or a judge in order to enter. Statutory undertakers—the utility companies and others—have powers to go on to land, and to install pipes, wires, and other equipment there.

For an example, see 9-87.

See 9-59 for this power.

See 11-103 onwards for statutory undertakers and their powers to enter land.

3-16 Various other rights allow the public to use:

- Highways ✇.
- Some sorts of land for recreational purposes ✇.

✇ See 5-7 onwards for the nature of the right.

✇ These are listed at 10-79 onwards.

3-17 Rights of access to neighbouring land are provided by two Acts, the Party Wall etc Act 1996 and the Access to Neighbouring Land Act 1992 ✇. A landowner may also be entitled to go on to a neighbour's land to abate a nuisance ⚷.

✇ See 2-23 and 7-2 for these Acts.

⚷ See 4-23 for the meaning of "abating" a nuisance.

3-18 *Other defences* In a few other circumstances the law recognises that a person going on to land has a good reason for doing so and should not be regarded as trespassing on the land. In particular, "necessity" can be relied on as a defence to trepass. By this the law means some emergency, where committing the civil wrong of trespass is justified in order to save life or property. The rule would apply where a person trespassed in order to save a child who was drowning in a stream, or to put out a fire which threatened to cause serious damage ✇.

✇ See also 7-46 on estoppel.

Preventing trespasses

3-19 A landowner can take some practical steps to prevent unlawful entries on to his land. He can put up notices making clear that entry is not allowed, though he is not under any obligation to do so ✇. Conventional security measures such as locks, gates and walls are of course in order, and it is generally accepted that walls may be topped with broken glass or spikes without exposing the landowner to the risk of liability to an intruder who injures himself (at least if the wall is high enough for the top to be out of reach of passers-by who might come into contact with it accidentally.

✇ See 3-5 on this point.

3-20 Measures which are designed to injure trespassers, and so to deter or punish them, fall into a different category. By s. 31 of the Offences Against the Person Act 1861, it is a criminal offence to set:

> "...any spring-gun, man-trap or other engine calculated to destroy human life or inflict grievous bodily harm with intent...."

There is an exception for spring-guns, man-traps, etc set at night "in a dwelling-house for the protection thereof". Although setting man-traps may not be an offence in such circumstances, the person responsible may still be liable to compensate anybody (even a burglar) who is injured.

3-21 The occupier of land is entitled to use reasonable force to prevent a trespasser coming on to his land. It will be wise to warn the trespasser first; otherwise, it may not clear that it was reasonable to use any force to stop him—he may say that if asked not to come on to the land, he would have refrained from doing so. But taking action of this sort always carries the risk that there will be a dispute about whether no more than reasonable force was used—if it was, the landowner may find that legal action is taken against him for assaulting the trespasser, assault being a civil wrong or a criminal offence or both. The better course may very often be for the landowner not to offer physical resistance, but to warn the trespasser, and afterwards take legal proceedings. The court will be able to take note of the fact that the warning was ignored, and this may make it difficult for the trespasser to argue that it is not necessary for the court to grant an injunction.

3-22 Guard dogs are subject to legal controls under the Guard Dogs Act 1975. It is an offence to use a guard dog at any "premises", unless it is under the control of a handler, or tied up so that it cannot roam freelys (s. 1). This restriction does not apply within the curtilage of a dwelling-house, nor to agricultural land, because these areas are not within the Act's definition of "premises" (s. 7). A householder can thus keep a guard dog to protect his house and its immediate surroundings, without complying with the Guard Dogs Act, and a farmer can similarly keep a guard dog to protect agricultural land. But otherwise the Act applies generally to land and buildings.

3-23 Guard dog kennels (i. e. kennels where, as a matter of busines, dogs are kept which are used as guard dogs elsewhere) must be licensed (s. 2). The Act is purely criminal in effect, and does not affect the civil law: whether a trespasser might be able to claim compensation if injured by a guard dog is a matter for the civil law

See 11-11 onwards for occupiers' liability.

If the land consists of residential premises, a trespaser who uses or threatens force commits an offence . See 8-94 for offences relating to residential premises.

See 1-26 on the dangers of self-help.

See 3-29 onwards for the principles on which injunctions are granted

See 9-18 for the meaning of "curtilage".

See also 10-56 on keeping animals.

See 11-11 and 3-52 onwards on these points.

and in particular the civil law relating to occupiers' liability and liability under the Animals Act 1971.

Remedies

3-24 The following paragraphs describe the remedies which the courts can award when a landowner brings civil proceedings for trespass.

3-25 *Compensation* Trespass is a civil wrong even if no damage is caused. The courts must thus award some compensation for a trespass, but if no damage is caused, and the trespass is otherwise trivial, the amount of compensation may be very small—perhaps no more than a pound or two.

But see also 3-27 for aggravated and exemplary damages.

3-26 If damage is caused to the land by a trespass, compensation can be awarded in respect of it. Damage may be caused, for example, by trampling flowers or crops, or breaking down a fence or hedge; or something attached to the land may be removed from it, for example fruit from fruit trees or slates from a building. There is also a class of case in which there is no damage, but neither is the trespass trivial. Suppose, for example, that while a landowner is away, her neighbour commandeers her tennis court and uses it for an afternoon. In such cases, compensation will reflect the value of the benefit obtained by the trespasser. Even if the landowner never lets out her tennis court, the court would normally award compensation to represent the sort of sum which might have been charged for an afternoon's use of the tennis court.

The question of what forms part of the land is discussed at 2-44 onwards.

3-27 Two other sorts of compensation—in legal language, "damages" —can also be awarded by the courts in appropriate cases. These apply to trespass and some other civil wrongs. "Aggravated" damages can be awarded for trespass when the trespasser's behaviour is high-handed, or offensive, and thus aggravates the injury caused: such damages are awarded as compensation for injured feelings as a result of the trespass. In the example just given, the neighbour's trespass might possibly be the result of a misunderstanding about whether permission had been given, in which cases aggravated damages would not be appropriate. But if it took place in the context of a "feud" between the neighbours, and was done to upset and annoy the landowner, the court might award aggravated damages. It is a matter for the courts to assess what figure to award as aggravated damages: the amount cannot be calculated mathematically. However, the amount would in most cases be relatively modest.

"Exemplary" damages are designed not to compensate, but to punish the person who committed the civil wrong. (And are therefore an example of a situation in which an idea relating to the criminal law has crept into the civil law ꆜ.) They are unusual, and are confined to two sorts of cases—first, where there has been oppressive action by government officials or the police, and secondly where the wrongdoer has calculated that the profit or advantage which will flow from the wrongdoing will outweigh any compensation he has to pay. Here the courts may react by awarding exemplary damages to punish the wrongdoer and make sure that he does not profit from his conduct. 3-28

ꆜ See 1-20 onwards for the way in which the civil and criminal courts work.

In the case of *A. B. v. South West Water Services Ltd* (1993) a water authority allowed 20 tonnes of aluminium suphate to contaminate the water supply at Camelford in Cornwall. About 180 people were taken ill, and sued for compensation, seeking compensation and exemplary damages. (The proceedings were brought against the privatised company which had taken over the business of the water authority.)

The court decided, among other things, that exemplary damages could not be awarded, because the water company was not by nature a governmental body.

Exemplary damages

Injunctions An injunction is an order by the court to do or (more usually) not to do something. Injunctions can be used to deal with many different sorts of civil wrong, including trespass—the order being an order not to trespass again, or, if the case was about something which had been placed on the land, such as a wall or a building, an order to remove it ꆜ. The injunction is a very powerful remedy, since the court's orders must be obeyed: failure to obey is a contempt of court, which can be punished by the court with up to two years' imprisonment. 3-29

ꆜ But see 3-31 for the court's power to award compensation instead of an injunction.

Though compensation must always be awarded for a trespass, the court has a discretion about whether to grant an injunction, so 3-30 there is no right to obtain an injunction. Nonetheless, the courts apply well-established principles in granting injunctions. The courts do not refuse to grant an injunction merely because the trespass has caused no damage. But they may do so if the trespass is very trivial, or if there is no real risk that it will be repeated. The terms of the injunction will be appropriate to the circumstances. Suppose, for example, that a neighbour has a right of way on foot over a landowner's land, but insists on driving her car over the land. In doing so she is trespassing. She points out that she is causing no damage, and offers to pay the landowner a token sum as compensation. The landowner asks her to stop, but she refuses. In these circumstances, the landowner can expect to obtain an injunction. The order will not ban the neighbour entirely from crossing the land, but merely from trespassing by driving over it.

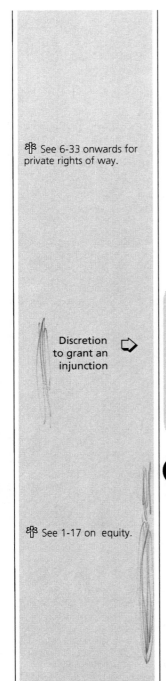

See 6-33 onwards for private rights of way.

Discretion to grant an injunction

In *Bracewell v. Appleby* (1975) a landowner built a new house in a private cul-de-sac. In order to gain access to the site he needed, but did not obtain, rights of way from the owners of the road. One of the owners took legal action, seeking an injunction.

The court refused to grant one. It pointed out that granting an injunction would mean the loss of a perfectly good house, and that the landowner had been slow to take action, and had not made a complaint until building was well under way. Compensation was awarded instead of an injunction, the measure being a fair price for the right of way assuming the owners of the land had been willing to grant one —in this case £2,000, to be split between the five owners of the road.

3-31 The court can grant an injunction in addition to awarding compensation. More important, it can award damages *instead* of an injunction, where it feels that an injunction would be oppressive or unfair. Because the injunction is an equitable remedy, the question of fairness is extremely important. Sometimes, delay by the landowner will mean that an injunction would be unfair. Suppose that a landowner builds a new house, believing that he has a right of access to the site over his neighbour's land, only to be told by her, when the building work is well advanced, that there is no such right. The unfairness is obvious: she should have objected at the outset. In such circumstances, the court would probably refuse an injunction to stop the landowner getting to the site, and award only

See 1-17 on equity.

compensation. An injunction might well, however, have been granted if there had been a prompt objection.

Another important factor is whether the person asking for an injunction has himself behaved in a way which is seriously unfair, for example by seeking to take a dishonest advantage. If so, the court may exercise its discretion to refuse an injunction. 3-32

A similar situation may occur when one neighbour has inadvertently built over the boundary by a small distance—perhaps a few centimetres—and is thus trespassing. The court may take the view that the cost and inconvenience of removing the building would be out of all proportion to the damage caused, and that there should should be compensation instead of an injunction. In such circumstances, the court's decision would be final, and it would not be open to the landowner to take any further action to remove the offending building or object from his land. 3-33

The case of *Burton v. Winters* (1993) concerned a dispute between neighbours. In 1986 Mrs Burton took legal action against her neighbours Mr and Mrs Winters because the wall of a garage, built in 1975 by some previous owners of their house, encroached by about 4 inches. The court was prepared to award compensation, but not to grant an injunction ordering the removal of the garage wall. Mrs Burton then started to build a wall, on Mr and Mrs Winters' land, in front of the garage. The court granted an injunction against her, but she persisted and was sentenced to 12 months imprisonment. Her appeal against this sentence (by now it was 1992) was allowed, and the Court of Appeal re-imposed the injunction.

Mrs Burton continued to take action, however: she made two holes in the garage wall with a sledgehammer, and was again sent to prison. She appealed, on the question of whether she had the right to remove the wall herself, despite the court's original refusal to grant her an injunction.

The court decided that she had no right to do so. Once the court had refused to grant an injunction ordering the removal of the garage wall, and awarded her compensation instead, she had no right to remove the wall herself.

Finality of an injunction

Declarations Besides granting an injunction, a court can make a declaration, which is simply a statement of legal rights. This is a discretionary remedy. Its main use is in cases where the court feels it will be enough to declare what the legal position is, without having to order one party not to trespass. That may be the case if the person concerned is a public body which can be expected to obey the law once the court has determined what the legal position is. 3-34

3-35 *Obtaining possession of land* In some cases a trespasser will put something on land, such as a building or an object of some kind; in some he will go on to the land himself from time to time. In some cases the trespasser will remain on the land. The trespasser may be, for example, a squatter in an empty house, or a protester seeking to protect an area of woodland, or a tenant whose lease has come to an end but who has stayed on unlawfully in a flat. The remedy is for the court to make an order giving the landowner back possession of his land.

See 1-47 for the meaning of "possessing" land.

3-36 The court does not have a discretion: if a landowner can show that he has a right to regain possession of the land, an order must be made. However, a landowner's right to regain possession is very much restricted by the law of landlord and tenant. The criminal law also intervenes, to prevent landowners taking the law into their own hands and physically removing trespassers who are in possession of land, so that this is lawful only in limited circumstances.

See chapter 8.

See 8-88 onwards and 8-95 onwards.

3-37 *Removing trespassers* Just as reasonable force can be used to prevent a person trespassing, so also reasonable force can be used to remove a trespasser—though this is subject to what was said in the previous paragaph. First the trespasser should be asked to leave and given the opportunity to do so. If that does not succeed, it may be reasonable to use force. There is no right to detain a trespasser for a breach of the civil law; and unlawfully detaining a person is itself a serious breach of the civil and criminal law. It is therefore highly inadvisable for a landowner to take this step.

See 1-26 for the dangers of "self-help".

3-38 *Wheelclamping* Trespassing by parking on private land presents a particular problem for landowners, because it is often not criminal. Furthermore, it may cause no damage, and so be unlikely to lead to any significant compensation if the landowner takes legal proceedings for trespass. Furthermore, unless there are repeated trespasses by the same person, it will not be worth obtaining an injunction, even if the landowner can trace the driver and establish his identity and address. Applying a wheelclamp, and charging a fee for release, allows the landowner to obtain some compensation for the intrusion, which may be significantly more than the nominal sum which a court would award as compensation,

Though see 3-49 for the offence under s. 34 of the Road Traffic Act 1984.

in the absence of damage—and a worthwhile sum. The courts have decided that subject to certain conditions, it is lawful.

Wheelclamping was the subject of the court's decision in *Arthur v. Anker* (1996). In this case, the owners of a private car park in Truro put up notices warning that cars parked without permission would be clamped, and subject to a release fee of £40. Their right to clamp cars and charge a release fee was challenged by Mr Arthur, whose car had been clamped. The Court decided that wheel-clamping was lawful, provided that three conditions were met:

- Warning notices were displayed
- The release fee was reasonable;
- It was possible for car-owners to pay the fee, and obtain the release of their cars without delay when the fee was tendered.

A later case has made clear that the clamper must show that the driver accepted the risk of being clamped. A notice positioned so that it was bound to be seen would normally show that the driver accepted the risk of clamping.

Wheel-clamping

Detaining property There is an ancient right to detain things which are doing damage on land, until compensation is paid. This was mainly relevant to animals, which are likely to cause damage when they stray, by trampling or eating crops. For animals this right has been replaced by a right under the Animals Act 1971. The right survives for things other than animals, and may sometimes be of assistance to a landowner. But it will not assist where the thing left on the land may be unsightly, and in the way, but is not actually causing damage to the land, for example a parked car. 3-39

See 3-52 onwards for the Animals Act 1971.

See 12-16 for sources on trespass as a civil wrong.

Criminal trespasses

While trespassing is essentially a civil matter, the law regards it as serious enough in some circumstances to require the intervention of the criminal law. A number of Acts make it an offence to trespass on particular sorts of property, including railways, aerodromes and property belonging to the armed forces; but this legislation is 3-40 unlikely to be of relevance to most landowners. Other situations in which trepass is a criminal offence include the following:

3-41 *Burglary* Burglary is an offence under s. 9 of the Theft Act 1968. It can take a number of different forms—either:

- Entering a building as a trespasser, with intent to commit one of a number of specified offences, including theft and causing serious injury or unlawful damage; or

- Entering a building as a trespasser and stealing or causing serious injury.

"Building" is given a special definition, so as to include inhabited vehicles and vessels. This gives the owners of caravans, mobile homes and houseboats occupants the same protection as house-owners. The offences is serious, the maximum punishment being 14 years' imprisonment in the case of a dwelling, or 10 years' in the case of some other building. There is also an even more serious offence of aggravated burglary, under s. 10 of the Theft Act 1968, which consists of committing burglary with a firearm, imitation firearm, other weapon of offence, or explosive. For this the maximum sentence is life imprisonment.

3-42 *Trespassing with a firearm* It is an offence for a person who has with him a firearm or imitation firearm to trespass in a building without reasonable excuse (s. 20(1) of the Firearms Act 1968). It is also a (less serious) offence to enter land other than a building in the same circumstances (s. 20(2)). The maximum punishment, for entering a building with a firearm other than an airgun, is 7 years' imprisonment.

3-43 *Trespassing with a weapon of offence* By s. 9 of the Criminal Law Act 1977, a person who enters any premises as a trespasser, and has with him a weapon of offence, without lawful authority or reasonable excuse, commits an offence. "Premises" is defined in s. 12 of the Act, and means a building or part of a building, and land ancillary to a building. A "weapon of offence" is something made or adapted for causing injury (such as a gun) or something intended to be used by the trespasser for causing injury. (So that a hammer, for example, would be a weapon of offence if it was clear from the circumstances that the trespasser intended to use it to cause injury.) The maximum sentence is three months' imprisonment or a level 5 fine or both.

See 1-23 for the standard levels of fines.

3-44 *Criminal Justice and Public Order Act 1994* Part V of this Act introduced some new offences which will generally involve trespassing. There are two situations in which the police have power to direct people to leave land, and in which a failure to do so is an offence. The first provision (s. 61 of the Act) is for "New Age travellers" and others who are trespassing on land with the intention of living there. If the occupier has taken reasonable steps, without success, to ask them to leave, and they:

- Are causing damage, or using threatening or abusive behaviour towards the occupier or his family or employees; or
- Have six or more vehicles (including caravans) on the land

—then the police may direct them to leave. Failing to leave (or returning within 3 months) is an offence, the maximum punishment being 3 months or a level 4 fine. The offence applies to common land, with some modifications. The police have an additional power of seizing any vehicle not removed from the land (s. 62).

See 10-65 onwards for the meaning of "common land".

3-45 The second situation relates to "raves", or, as the Act calls them in s. 63:

> "a gathering on land in the open air of 100 or more persons.... at which amplified music is played during the night ... and is such as, by reason of its loudness and duration and the time at which it is played, is likely to cause serious distress to the inhabitants of the locality".

3-46 The persons concerned need not be trespassers, though in some cases they will be, because the landowner has not consented to the use of his land. The police may direct persons to leave the land if they reasonably believe that there are two or more persons preparing for a rave, or ten or more waiting for one to begin, or attending a rave. (In other words, the police do not have to wait for 100 persons to appear, in order to direct persons to leave, provided they reasonably believe that there will be a gathering of 100 or more.) The maximum punishment for failing to leave as directed is again three months' imprisonment or a level 4 fine; and the police have power to seize sound equipment, which a court may forfeit, if there is a conviction for an offence (ss. 64–66). These sections do not apply to an event for which the local authority has granted an entertainment licence; but otherwise they can apply to any sort of musical event if the conditions as to numbers, distress to inhabitants and the absence of an entertainment licence are satisfied.

See also 10-54 onwards for how the law regulates public entertainments on land.

3-47 Section 68 of the Criminal Justice and Public Order Act 1994 introduced an offence known as "aggravated trespass". The introduction of the offence may have been prompted by the activities of hunt saboteurs, but is capable of applying more widely. The section provides that:

> "(1) A person commits the offence of aggravated trespass if he trespasses on land in the open air and, in relation to any lawful activity which persons are engaging in or are about to engage in on that or adjoining land in the open air, does there anything which is intended by him to have the effect—
>
> (a) of intimidating those persons or any of them so as to deter them or any of them from engaging in that activity,
>
> (b) of obstructing that activity, or
>
> (c) of disrupting that activity."

3-48 The offence can thus apply to a wide range of situations in which rowdy trespassers disrupt activity in the open air, whether it is a business, sporting, cultural or social occasion. The maximum punishment for the offence is again three months' imprisonment or a level 4 fine. The police have a power under s. 69 to remove persons committing the offence.

3-49 *Motorised trespassers* Landowners are given an important piece of protection against motorised trespassers by s. 34 of the Road Traffic Act 1988. The offence is committed by driving a motor vehicle, without lawful authority, on to any land which is not a "road". The word "road" has special meaning here: it means any highway or other road to which the public have access (s. 192). So some roads, which are not highways but where public use takes place and is tolerated, are roads for this purpose, and it is not an offence under s. 34 to drive on them.

See 5-0 onwards for the meaning of "highway".

3-50 Driving on to private land without lawful authority is also not an offence under s. 34, provided the driver goes no more than 15 yards from the highway and is only doing so in order to park. But to drive further, or to drive on to private land which is not a highway or a road to which the public have access, for a purpose other parking, is an offence. Often, landowners will make clear that permission is being given—for example, it is obvious that customers are being permitted to park in a supermarket car-park. The absence of gates or other barriers, or "no parking" signs, does not affect the position: the law puts the responsibility firmly on the motorist who wishes to drive on to private land to check that it is lawful to do so. The offence is not endorseable but the maximum fine is level 3.

But this may be a trespass; and if damage is caused the offence of criminal damage may be committed: see 11-57 for criminal damage.

See 12-24 for sources on trespass as a criminal offence.

3-51 *Other offences involving trespassing* A number of offences involve trespassing, and are mentioned elsewhere in the text, including:

- Poaching.
- Breach of the regulations concerned with ancient monuments.

See 11-41 onwards for poaching.

See 10-89 onwards for ancient monuments.

The Animals Act 1971

3-52 The Animals Act 1971 deals with civil liability for damage caused by animals in several different situations. Often this will happen when the animals have strayed and are trespassing (which is why the Act is dealt with here) but this is not the only situation in which liability may arise. The Act does not contain a complete set of rules on civil liability for animals, but merely deals with a number of different situations. The rest of the law of civil wrongs generally continues to apply. This means that (for example) the owner of a dog, in addition to any liability under the Animals Act 1991, may be liable if the dog trespasses, or if its barking causes a nuisance to neighbours.

See 3-10 for trespass by animals and 4-7 onwards for nuisance generally.

3-53 Some terms used in the Act should first be explained. "Damage" includes death or injury to a person as well as damage to property (s. 11). "Keeper" is also defined and includes the person who owns an animal, or who has it in his possession, and also, if the animal is owned by or is in the possession of a person under 16, the head of the household (s. 6). "Livestock" means, in the Act as a whole, cattle, horses, asses, mules, sheep, pigs, goats, poultry and deer not in the wild state (s. 11)). The main provisions of the Act deal with a number of different situations, which are summarised in the following paragraphs. These are:

But see also 3-57.

- Liability for damage caused by dangerous animals.
- Liability for dogs which kill or injure livestock.
- Liability for trespassing livestock.
- Exceptions from liability.
- Detaining trespassing livestock.
- Cattle straying on to a highway.
- Protecting livestock from dogs.

See 5-0 for the meaning of "highway".

3-54 *Liability for damage caused by dangerous animals (s. 2)* This section applies to animals which belong to a dangerous species (s. 2(1)). A "dangerous species" means one which is not commonly domesticated in the British Isles and which when fully grown is likely to cause severe damage if not restrained, or, if it causes damage, will cause severe damage (s. 6(2)). It also applies to damage caused by animals which do *not* belong to a dangerous species, if three conditions are satisfied (s. 2(2)). The conditi ons are:

- The damage is of a kind which the animal was likely to cause, or which, if caused by the animal, was likely to be severe.
- This was because of abnormal characteristics, not usually found in such animals, or only found at particular times or in particular circumstances.
- The abnormal charctaristics were known to the keeper.

In the case of *Jaundrill v. Gillett* (1996) some horses escaped from Mr Gillett's field, on to a road during the hours of darkness. The horses panicked, and galloped into a car being driven by Mr Jaundrill, who was injured. Mr Gillett had not been negligent, so the question was whether he was responsible for the injury on the basis that the horses were exhibiting characteristics not normally found "except at particular times or in particular circumstances".

The court did not consider that the horses' tendency to panic was an abnormal characteristic for the purposes of the Animals Act 1971, so the horses were not dangerous animals, for the purposes of the Act, and Mr Gillett was not liable to pay compensation to Mr Jaundrill under the Animals Act.

Liability for dangerous animals

It may be difficult to prove that all of these conditions are satisfied, so that the keeper of the animal is liable to pay compensation under s. 2(2) to a person—whether a landowner or some other person—who suffers damage. The fact that damage caused by an animal is likely to be severe may be clear enough, for example a large and powerful dog. But it is also necessary to show that the animal had some abnormal characteristics, which the keeper knew about. If this cannot be shown, then the keeper will not be liable under the Animals Act to pay compensation. (But it may still be possible to show that she is liable to pay compensation, however, on the alternative basis that she has been negligent.) 3-55

See 4-59 for negligence.

The keeper of an animal is strictly liable for damage caused by a dangerous animal, meaning that the keeper is liable to pay compensation to a person who is injured, or whose property is damaged, even where he is not at fault—for example, where the animal is safely caged, but is released by someone else and causes damage, in circumstances where the owner is not to blame. 3-56

Liability for dogs which kill or injure livestock (s. 3) This section makes the keeper of a dog liable if it kills or injures livestock. "Livestock" has the definition given above, but is extended here to cover pheasants, partridges and grouse. The Act makes the keeper liable for injury to any of these animals, regardless of whether he was at fault, unless one of the exceptions listed in s. 5 apply (see below). 3-57

See 3-53 for the meaning of "livestock".

For a criminal offence which applies where a dog worries livestock, see 11-34.

Liability for damage by trespassing livestock (s. 4) If livestock stray on to land owned or occupied by someone else, the person who owns or has possession of the livestock is liable for any damage caused by it, whether to other animals or to the land itself, or to property on the 3-58 land. Again, liability does not depend upon fault on the part of the owner of the livestock; but there are exceptions from liability, under s. 5.

3-59 *Exceptions from liability (s. 5)* Where these exceptions apply, the person concerned is not responsible for the injury or damage caused by an animal. They apply to ss. 2 to 4 as follows:

- Section 2: a person is not responsible for any damage suffered by someone who has voluntarily accepted the risk of it (for example, a person who has agreed to look after a dangerous animal at his own risk) (s. 5(2)).

- Section 2: a person is not responsible for damage caused to a trespasser, provided that the dangerous animal was not kept in order to protect persons or property, or, if it was kept with this purpose, that this was not unreasonable (s. 5(3)). (This section will not apply to a guard dog unless it has unusual characteristics, known to the keeper. If this is so, it may be diffiult for the occupier to justify keeping it for protection, unless he can show that he has something particularly valuable to protect.)

See 3-22 for the Guard Dogs Act 1975.

- Section 3: a person is not responsible for injury to livestock if the livestock has strayed on to his land, and the dog is his, or its presence is authorised by him (the latter might be the case if, for example, the dog belongs to someone visiting the land with the occupier's permission) (s. 5(4)).

- Section 4: a person is not responsible under s. 4 for damage if an animal has strayed from a highway, and its presence on the highway was lawful (s. 5(5)). (By providing this exception, the Act is leaving it up to the landowner either to fence his land, so as to keep out animals, or accept that they may stray on to it from the highway, and cause damage. Livestock would be lawfully on a highway if, for example, they were being moved from one field to another, by a farmer. In this case, there would be no liability under the Animals Act—but there might be

And see 3-61 for the opposite situation, where animals stray on to the highway.

liability on the basis that the farmer was negligent in allowing the livestock to leave the highway and trespass ✠)

✠ See 4-48 for negligence

In *Cummings v. Grainger* (1977) a trespasser entered a breaker's yard, in the East End of London, at night, and was seriousy injured by an Alsation dog. She sued the occupier of the yard, under s. 2(2) of the Animals Act 1971.

The court decided that the dog did show characteristics which were not normally found in Alsations, except in particular circumstances, namely defending what it regarded as its territory. The requirements of s. 2(2) of the Act were thus satisfied, and the landowner would have been liable to pay compensation. But in all the circumstances it was not unreasonable to keep the dog, for the protection of his property, and the trespasser knew about the dog, and had accepted the risk of injury. So the occupier of the yard had a defence under s. 5(2) and 5(3), and was not liable to pay compensation to the trespasser for the injuries she suffered.

Injury to a trespasser

◆ Sections 2–4: there is no liability where the damage was entirely the fault of the person suffering it (s. 5(1))

Detaining trespassing livestock Section 7 of the Animals Act gives the occupier of land the right to detain livestock which has strayed on to his land and is not under the control of any person. The section applies to any land. The occupier must notify the police within 48 hours that he has the livestock, and tell them (if he knows) who the owner is; otherwise the right to detain the animal ceases. It also ceases if and when compensation is tendered by the owner, to cover any damage ✠. After 14 days, the occupier may sell the livestock at auction if compensation has not been offered by the owner of the animal and the animal retrieved. If the amount received is greater than the cost of any damage caused, and the expenses of the sale itself, then the owner of the animal is entitled to any surplus. 3-60

✠ Contrast 3-39, which deals with the detention of goods causing damage to land.

Cattle straying on to a highway The general law is that a person is liable for injury and damages caused to others by his lack of care—this is the tort or civil wrong of negligence ✠. For centuries the law did not impose any general duty on a landowner to fence his land, and so landowners could not be made to pay compensation on the basis of negligence if an animal strayed on to the highway and caused damage to someone using it. This rule was changed by s. 8(1) 3-61

✠ See 4-59 for negligence.

of the Animals Act 1971, and a landowner can now be liable if animals stray on to the highway because there is no fence, or because a fence is not kept in good repair. Whether a landowner is in fact judged to have been negligent in allowing animals to stray will depend upon the circumstances. It may be that if a road is little used by cars and visibility is good, allowing animals to stray may not amount to negligence—the few motorists who use the road can slow down in good time and take avoiding action. But in most cases, it would be unwise for a landowner to let animals stray on to a highway.

On the question of obstructing a highway—which is a criminal offence—see 5-75 .

3-62 The Animals Act 1971, however, specifies that there will be no negligence, and so no liability to pay compensation for damage caused, if the land is common land; or is a town or village green; or is in an area where fencing is not customary (s. 8(2)). "Fencing", in the Act, includes "the construction of any obstacle designed to prevent animals from straying" (s. 11). Because s. 8(2) applies only to unfenced land, it does not assist a landowner where land is fenced but an animal has strayed on to the highway because of a gap in the fence.

See 10-65 onwards for the meaning of "common land", and 10-75 onwards for town and village greens.

3-63 *Worrying livestock* Section 9 of the Animals Act provides a special defence for anybody in civil proceedings for killing or causing injury to a dog. In order for the defence to apply, it must be proved by the person concerned that he was acting for the protection of livestock, and was entitled to do so. This is so if the livestock belongs to him or is on his land; and provided that s. 5(4) does not apply. (In other words, there will be no defence in respect of livestock which are trespassing and which are worried by a dog which belongs to the occupier of the land, or is there with his authority). It is also necessary to prove that the dog is worrying, or about to worry the livestock, and that there are no other ways of preventing this, other than killing or injuring the dog, or that the dog has worried livestock, and is still in the area, but is not under the control of anybody, and it is not practicable to find out who it belongs to (s. 9). A person who kills or injures a dog must also, if he is to take advantage of this defence, give notice at a police station within 48 hours.

See also 11-28 onwards for offences relating to dogs.

See 3-59 for s. 5(4)

See 12-16 for sources on the Animals Act 1971.

Assessment

The law of trespass may seem to allow a landowner to behave in a dictatorial way, constantly ordering people off his land and taking legal action against them. But this is not a very realistic picture. In the first place, the law gives many people the right go on to land belonging to others. In the second place, although a trespass is a legal wrong, the courts may well prove unsympathetic towards a landowner who has suffered only in technical sense. 3-64

See 0-5 on how the court's decision can reflect its views of the merits of the case.

Landowners are therefore wise to be tolerant of minor, temporary trespasses which do not cause any significant damage. It may be sensible for a landowner to regularise such trespasses by giving permission for the use of the land. If so, the landowner should put his permission in writing. Any terms and conditions attached should be spelt out. It will usually be wise to make clear that permission can be withdrawn by the landowner at any time; and also that any risks must be borne by the person coming on to the land. 3-65

See 11-2 for occupiers' liability.

The position is different where the activities of a trespasser will in due course lead to the loss of land, or rights over it. This may occur where land is fenced off and occupied by a trespasser, or a boundary moved, or where repeated comings and goings over land may lead to the creation of public or private rights of way. Here the landowner may be able to take some practical steps to safeguard his position; and can always try to reach agreement with the trespasser. But if these steps are not successful, and legal proceedings become unavoidable, the courts are likely to be more sympathetic. The criminal law may also be able to assist in some cases, since some sorts of trespass are considered serious enough to be criminal offences, not just civil wrong. 3-66

See 2-67, 5-22 and 6-15 for these areas of the law.

In relation to animals, the law of trespass and the Animals Act 1971 have to strike a balance between imposing too much responsibility on the owners and too little. Damage or annoyance caused by straying pets will not usually be a matter for complaint in legal terms: landowners are expected to put up with intrusions of this sort. The exception is where dogs kill or injure livestock—here 3-67 the law generally makes the owner or keeper of the dog liable to pay compensation, regardless of whether he was at fault.

Chapter 4

Nuisance

Introduction

4-0 Some disputes between neighbours are caused by trespassing; for example by building over the line of the boundary, or taking short cuts across a neighbour's front garden. But many others are caused by behaviour which is not a trespass, because it does not involve a direct entry on to land, but which causes disturbance to a landowner, whether by noise or in some other way. This sort of behaviour is dealt with by the law of nuisance.

See chapter 3 generally, and 3-3 on what amounts to a trespass.

4-1 Although most legal terms are relatively precise, "nuisance" is not. It is a broad term, which covers many different sorts of anti-social behaviour, and is generally regarded as falling into three different categories, according to the sort of legal proceedings which can be brought to deal with it:

- A "private" nuisance is one which interferes with a landowner's right to enjoy his land in some way. It is a civil wrong, for which a landowner can take action in the civil courts.

See 1-20 for civil and criminal law, and 4-5 onwards for private nuisance.

- A "public" nuisance is one which affects a section of the public at large (whether or not they are occupiers of land), either by interfering with their health and comfort or by creating a danger to the public. A public nuisance is a crime, and can thus result in a prosecution against the person(s) responsible. It may also be a civil wrong; but this is subject to the rule that a person may only take action in the civil courts if he has suffered to a greater extent than the public generally.

See 4-25 onwards for public nuisance.

- "Statutory nuisances" are particular sorts of nuisance which are listed in legislation. They are partly nuisances in the sense used above, and partly also a matter of public health. The legislation gives local authorities special powers to deal with these nuisances, including bringing prosecutions; and it also allows private persons to bring proceedings ꙮ.

ꙮ See 4-27 onwards for statutory nuisance.

4-2 Some activities may fall into more than one of the above categories, in which case a landowner who is affected has more than one possible course of action. If, for example, a neighbour is keeping dogs in overcrowded and unhealthy conditions, and the dogs are causing noise and smells, the landowner might be able to bring civil proceedings for nuisance, or ask the local authority to take action, on the ground that there is a statutory nuisance. If the local authority are not prepared to take action, the landowner could herself bring criminal proceedings for statutory nuisance.

Public nuisance ⇨

In the case of *R. v. Shorrock* (1993), an "acid house party" was held in a field owned by Mr Shorrock, a farmer. This caused a great deal of noise and disturbance to local residents, and Mr Shorrock was prosecuted for causing a public nuisance.
Mr Shorrock said that he had given permission to a man named Kevin Read to use the field, charging £2,000, and he had no idea of how large the event was going to be—Kevin Read had said he wanted to hold a disco, to raise some money to buy a wheelchair. This raised the legal question of what the prosecution needed to prove, in relation to Mr Shorrock's state of mind, in order for him to be guilty of the offence. The judge directed the jury that a person was guilty of causing a public nuisance if he knew or ought to have known that this would be the result.
The court decided, on appeal, that this was a correct direction on the law, and that Mr Shorrock was rightly convicted of causing a public nuisance.

4-3 In addition to nuisance, this chapter also explains a number of Acts, which are not concerned with the law of nuisance as such, but which are relevant because they have a very similar effect, controlling anti-social activities by neighbours and others. These include: the Noise Act 1996, the Protection from Harassment Act 1997, the Control of Pollution Act 1974 (in relation to noise) and the Crime and Disorder Act 1998, which introduced a new legal procedure, the anti-social behaviour order.

4-4 The law explained in this chapter is thus a mixture of civil and criminal law. Much of the law of private and public nuisance is common law; whereas statutory nuisance, as the name suggests, is to be found in legislation. Byelaws may also be important, since local authorities have power to make byelaws to deal with nuisances.

See 1-10 onwards for the common law and 1-1 onwards for legislation

Private nuisance

4-5 Under the heading of private nuisances, the law is concerned with three rather different sorts of activities. First, there are some which interfere with the enjoyment of land, without damaging the land or injuring those present on it. Second, some amount to indirect intrusions on to the land, without causing damage. (Direct entries on to land are regarded by the law as trespasses, whereas indirect ones are nuisances.) Third, some cause damage.

See 3-3 for what activities may amount to trespassing.

4-6 The courts have decided that only a person with an interest in land can take legal proceedings for nuisance. In other words, a person who is only an occupier, without being the owner or the tenant of the land (for example a squatter) cannot complain about a nuisance.

An important case on the law of nuisance was *Hunter v. Canary Wharf Ltd* (1997). The case was brought by a number of people living in the Docklands area of London, who were concerned about interference to television reception caused by the Canary Wharf Tower, which was nearly 250 metres high.

The case came to the House of Lords, who decided (firstly) that since the interference with television signals was the result merely of the presence of the building, this was not a nuisance.

Secondly, the House of Lords decided that only a person with an interest in the land could bring proceedings for nuisance; so not all those who occupied houses in the Docklands area could do so. (The law on this point had become uncertain as a result of a case in 1993.)

Principles of nuisance

4-7 *Interferences with the use of land* There are many different ways in which activities on land can interfere with the use of neighbouring land, the main ones being:

- Noise.

- Smells.
- Smoke.
- Fumes.
- Dust.
- Vibration.

4-8 It is not necessary for any injury or damage to the property to be caused to the landowner or her land, provided that the activity prevents the landowner from using and enjoying her land. It may do so by annoying the landowner in the ordinary sense of the word, and so making the landowner angry, upset or indignant, or by preventing the landowner from doing certain things. For example, smoke and fumes may prevent the landowner from sitting in her garden; while loud noises late at night may prevent her from sleeping. The list given above is not exhaustive, though these are the common sorts of nuisance. It is not a nuisance, however, to spoil the view from a house or other property by letting trees or shrubs grow, or by putting up a fence or building.

See 4-14 for the situation where there is damage or injury,

In rare cases there may be a right to light: see 6-43 onwards. And see 2-22 generally on problems with *Leylandii*.

Light as a nuisance

A case in New Zealand, *Bank of New Zealand v. Greenwood* (1984), concerned sunlight which was being reflected from a building, on to neighbouring properties. The light was reflected off a glass surface which had the unusual effect of concentrating it and causing a dazzling glare, too bright to look at.

The court decided that the light was capable of amounting to a nuisance, so that the occupier of a building affected by it could take action against the occupier of the building from which the light was being reflected.

4-9 The key question considered by the courts, in deciding whether an activity is a nuisance, is whether it is reasonable in all the circumstances. The law has to balance the interests of neighbouring landowners, and to give one landowner complete freedom from any interference would mean imposing severe restrictions on his neighbours. What is reasonable will depend on a

See 0-13 for the meaning of "reasonable".

number of factors. A certain amount of interference with the use of land may be reasonable in relation to an activity such as building work which lasts only for a limited time and serves a useful purpose. This does not mean that building work can never amount to a nuisance; but if steps are taken to reduce noise, vibration, dust etc as far as reasonably possible, and to limit the times of day when the noise etc was produced, a court would probably conclude that there was no nuisance.

Also important is the location of the land. Noise and fumes that might be regarded as acceptable on an industrial estate might well amount to a nuisance in a quiet residential area. The question sometime arises of whether the grant of planning permission, and the development which then takes place, can change the nature of a neighbourhood, so that some activity ceases to be—or becomes—a nuisance, for example where a new industrial estate is built. The grant of planning permission does not mean that an activity automatically becomes lawful. In the case of large-scale developments, development can change the character of the area, and so have an effect on what activities would amount to a nuisance, but this is much less likely to be so for small-scale developments. 4-10

In *Wheeler v. J. J. Saunders Ltd* (1995) Dr Wheeler and his wife bought a house and some outbuildings which were part of a farm run by J. J. Saunders Ltd. The outbuildings were converted into cottages. J. J. Saunders Ltd erected two buildings for rearing pigs, each capable of holding 400 pigs. One of the buildings was only 11 metres from one of the holiday cottages.

It was clear that for pigs to be reared so close to the cottage would normally be a nuisance—European guidelines generally set a minimum distance of 100 metres between such buildings and houses. But J. J. Saunders Ltd argued that planning permission had been granted for the buildings, and this made them lawful, so that there could be no nuisance.

The court decided that planning permission might in some cases change the character of an area, in such a way that a particular activity ceased to be a nuisance, but that was not so here. The smell from the pigs was thus a nuisance.

Planning permission and nuisance

Motive may be an important factor in deciding whether an activity is a nuisance. In the course of a "feud" between neighbours, one party may cause noise, etc for no reason other than to irritate the other. The court is likely to regard such behavour as a nuisance, 4-11 even if the same amount of disturbance, produced without any intention to irritate, would not be:

4-12 The fact that a landowner is an unusually sensitive person, or is carrying on some business which is very easily affected by disturbance, is not regarded by the courts as relevant: the standard remains what is reasonable for the neighbourhood.

4-13 *Indirect intrusions* Branches overhanging a boundary are regarded by the law as a nuisance, as are roots crossing the boundary underground, even if they cause no damage. Other indirect entries on to land may also come within this category, for example where water is allowed to leak on to land. The principles which apply to nuisances of this sort are different from those mentioned above, in relation to interferences with the enjoyment of land. No question of reasonableness arises: these indirect entries on to land are nuisances, and the landowner is entitled to take action to deal with them.

This is different from the situation in which water drains naturally on to neighbouring land: see 6-4.

See 4-22 in relation to trimming branches and roots.

4-14 *Nuisances which cause damage* If one landowner causes his neighbour's land to subside, or damages it by means of vibration, or by allowing water to flow on to it, the activity is again a nuisance. And, as in the second category, no question of reasonabless arises. The difference between this type of nuisance and those in the first and second categories may be slight. Smoke which merely annoys a landowner and others on his land, but causes no damage, falls into the first category; so that whether it amounts to a nuisance will depend upon whether it is reasonable. In contrast, airborne smuts which cause damage—for example, by dirtying clothes on a washing line—would fall into the present category: the smuts would amount to a nuisance and no question of reasonableness would arise. If the evidence is not clear about whether damage has been caused, it will be for the judge to decide which category the nuisance falls into, and so whether reasonableness is involved.

4-15 One important point which should be mentioned here is that where it is not foreseeable that damage will be caused, the person responsible for the nuisance will not be liable to pay compensation. Damage will not be foreseeable if it occurred as a result of a freak accident, or if science had not identified the risk that a particular activity could lead to damage.

In the case of *Cambridge Water Co v. Eastern Counties Leather plc* (1994) the latter company had for some years allowed a chemical known as PCE, to leak into the ground below their works. The PCE contaminated an aquifer from which the Cambridge Water Co drew its water. It was not foreseeable, however, that the PCE would accumulate in the aquifer; nor that the water company's supply would be damaged.

The House of Lords held that in the circumstances the Eastern Counties Leather Co was not responsible for the nuisance.

Foresee-ability and nuisance

4-16 *Defences* The law recognises a range of defences, which will enable a person accused of causing a nuisance to avoid responsibility. It is a defence that the owner of the land affected agreed to the nuisance—for example, by saying that he would not object to noisy building work. It is not a defence as such that the landowner knew about the nuisance when he bought the land: he is stil entitled to complain and to take legal action.

4-17 A right to commit a nuisance may be acquired over a period of time by the process known as prescription. The right to commit a nuisance will arise 20 years after the time when the landowner was aware of it and could have started legal proceedings against the person responsible.

See 6-15 onwards for the meaning of "prescription" in relation to easements.

4-18 Sometimes an Act of Parliament gives the legal right to carry out certain work. This is true particularly of "statutory undertakers" such as the utility companies, which supply water, gas, electricity and telecommunications services such as telephones and cable television. The principle is that where work is authorised by an Act, it cannot be a nuisance. A special rule applies, however, which is that any person seeking to rely on authorisation by statute must prove that he caused only the minimum interference or damage to others. This is an important principle. If, for example, a utility company sets up a pump or generator in a road, in the course of doing work to install or repair pipes or cables, the company must be in a position to prove that any noise or other disturbance caused to those living nearby was the minimum which could reasonably be achieved—otherwise the company may be liable for causing a nuisance. The extent to which the statutory undertaker is entitled

See 11-103 onwards for the meaning of "statutory undertaker".

to cause a nuisance may also depend upon the terms of the Act which authorises the work.

4-19 A legal right to commit a nuisance may exist in different forms, including an easement.

See 6-1 onwards for the meaning of "easement".

A right to cause a nuisance?

In the case of *Gardner v. Davis* (1999) the owner of two houses had the right to use a septic tank, which was located in the garden of a third house. The septic tank overflowed, allowing sewage to escape into the garden, but use of the septic tank continued.

The question for the court was whether this was lawful, or whether it was a nuisance, about which the owner of the garden could take legal action.

The court decided that it was a nuisance. The right to use the septic tank was a right to use it without causing escapes of sewage; and the escapes were therefore not lawful.

4-20 *Remedies* Where damage has been caused by a nuisance, the law allows the landowner to obtain compensation from the person responsible. If the nuisance is one which does not cause damage, but interferes with the right to enjoy land, the measure of damage is how much the value of the land is reduced by the nuisance, while it lasts. There is no mathematical basis for working out how much compensation should be awarded for this sort of nuisance; the courts must do their best to fix an appropriate amount to compensate the landowner for the period during which his land was less enjoyable, as a result of the nuisance. As explained above the wrong is done, legally speaking, to the owner of the land; and this means that the compensation is not increased according to the number of people on the land who are affected by the nuisance—for example, the members of a family, or employees in the case of business premises.

4-21 A landowner may be able to obtain an injunction, that is, an order from the court requiring the person responsible to stop causing a nuisance. The general principles on which injunctions are granted were explained in relation to the law of trespass. If the nuisance is trivial and unlikely to be repeated, an injunction may be refused. But the courts do not allow a person to continue committing a nuisance just because they are willing to pay compensation. So a landowner can generally expect to find that the court will grant an injunction if this is necessary to stop the nuisance.

See 3-29 onwards for these principles.

4-22 "Self-help" is often an unwise course for a landowner to pursue, in seeking to put an end to some legal wrong. But it is well-established that a landowner may deal with overhanging branches, and with roots growing under his land, by cutting them back at the point where they cross the boundary, whether or not they are causing damage to his property. He has the right to do so, and will not be responsible for any damage to the tree or other vegetation trimmed. Vegetation cut off does not become the property of the person who cut it off, and so should not be taken by him.

See 1-26 onwards for self-help generally.

Even where the tree is protected by a tree preservation order: see 10-23.

4-23 Beyond the special case of overhanging vegetation and roots, a landowner may in certain circumstances go on to a neighbour's land to "abate" (i. e. to stop) a nuisance. Such action may easily lead to confrontation and violence, so landowners are generally wise to refrain from exercising this right. Since the courts are rarely called on to consider cases in which a landowner has exercised such rights, the legal principles involved are in any case not entirely clear. It may be that the right is confined to cases of real urgency. A landowner may need to give notice, if he can, so that his neighbour has the chance to put matters right himself.

See 12-16 for sources on private nuisance.

4-24 A landowner should certainly cause only the minimum damage necessary to abate the nuisance. If he goes beyond what the law allows him to do, he may himself be liable for trespassing or some other civil wrong, or for breaches of the criminal law.

For example criminal damage or using force to enter property: see 11-59 and 8-95.

In *Co-operative Wholesale Society Ltd v. British Railways Board* (1995) a wall on BRB's land had started to bulge and lean over CWS's land. There was a dispute about whether the wall was dangerous. CWS went on to BRB's land, and demolished and rebuilt the wall. They then claimed the cost of doing so from BRB, but BRB refused to pay.

The court underlined the principle that the right to abate a nuisance should be confined to cases in which urgent action was necessary. It ordered BRB to meet the cost of demolishing the wall, which was £1,400, but not the cost of rebuilding it, since this was no business of CWS's.

Abating a nuisance

Public nuisance

4-25 The activities listed above as examples of private nuisance could be public nuisances if they affected a section of the public at large. If, for example, a landowner held a party which was so loud and disorderly that it affected not just his immediate neighbours, but the public for some distance around, this might be a public nuisance. A wide range of activities which caused a danger to the public might also constitute a public nuisance; and this is particularly true where the public's use of the highway is threatened by dangerous activities on land bordering the highway. Over the centuries, landowners have been punished for such activities as keeping explosives on their land, adjacent to the highway, or for having unfenced excavations near a highway.

Obstruction of a highway is also a public nuisance, and this is dealt with at 5-75.

4-26 If an accident results from a danger of this sort, and a person using the highway is injured, she may be able obtain compensation from the landowner, under the principles explained above. The cases which have come before the courts, in which the law has been laid down, have often been concerned with things which overhang the highway—trees or structures of some kind—and which collapse, causing injury to a user of the highway. The law is that a landowner may be responsible, if he knew or ought to have known of the risk of an accident. Whether this is so will depend upon the circumstances: it may be obvious that a tree (for example) is rotten or damaged, and liable to collapse on the highway, or there may be no visible sign of the dangers.

See 4-1 for these principles.

A structure overhanging the highway could be a trespass against the owner of the highway: see 3-1 generally.

See 12-16 and 12-24 for sources on public nuisance.

Statutory nuisance

4-27 The main provisions on statutory nuisance are contained in Part III of the Environmental Protection Act 1990, which has been amended by other legislation, including the Clean Air Act 1993, the Noise and Statutory Nuisance Act 1993 and the Environment Act 1995. Provisions on enforcement are also set out in the 1990 Act.

Types of statutory nuisance The list of nuisances, which is set out in s. 79(1) 1990 Act, is as follows:

"*(a)* any premises in such a state as to be prejudicial to health or a nuisance;

(b) smoke emitted from premises so as to be prejudicial to health or a nuisance;

(c) fumes or gases emitted from premises so as to be prejudicial to health or a nuisance;

(d) any dust, steam, smell or other effluvia arising on industrial, trade or business premises and being prejudicial to health or a nuisance;

(e) any accumulation or deposit which is prejudicial to health or a nuisance;

(f) any animal kept in such a place or manner as to be prejudicial to health or a nuisance;

(g) noise emitted from premises so as to be prejudicial to health or a nuisance;

(ga) noise that is prejudicial to health or a nuisance and is emitted from or caused by a vehicle, machinery or equipment in a street or in Scotland a road;

(h) any other matter declared by any enactment to be a nuisance."

4-28 By s. 79(7), "prejudicial to health" means "injurious, or likely to cause injury, to health"; and "premises" includes land and any vessel. Some limitations are applied, however, by the remaining provisions of s. 79. For example, paragraph *(b)* does not apply to smoke from the chimneys of private dwellings within smoke control areas. Paragraph *(c)* applies only to premises other than private dwellings; and paragraph *(ga)* does not apply to noise made by traffic, or by public demonstrations. But the section is wide enough to cover such things as bonfires which have been lit inconsiderately, and noisy dogs. The question is whether in each case the activity is either prejudicial to health or is a nuisance; and "nuisance" simply means a private or public nuisance.

See 1-27 for the meaning of "premises".

But see also 11-62 on air pollution.

4-29 Although the Environmental Protection Act 1990 says that it applies only to premises, and "vessels" (ships and boats), s. 268(1) of the Public Health Act 1936, following its amendment by the 1990 Act, applies these provisions also to "tents, vans, sheds and similar structures used for human habitation". So a tent or caravan which was a source of smoke or noise to the extent that it was a threat to health, or a nuisance, could be the subject of action. The 1936 Acts adds some statutory nuisances which apply to "tents, vans, sheds", etc: these are a nuisance if they are so overcrowded as to be prejudicial to the health of people living in them, or if their use, because of a lack of sanitation or otherwise, gives rise to a nuisance or conditions prejudicial to health (s. 258(2)) ♣. The 1936 Act also creates some other statutory nuisances, including "any pond, pool, ditch, gutter or watercourse which is so foul or in such a state as to be prejudicial to health or a nuisance" (s. 259(1)*(a)*).

♣ See 10-51 for local authorities' power to regulate "moveable dwellings". For other legislation relating to overcrowding and other public health issues, see 11-90 onwards.

Statutory nuisance

In the case of *R v. Bristol City Council, ex parte Everett* (1999) the question for the court was whether some steep stairs could be a statutory nuisance, within s. 79(1)(a), because they were "prejudicial to health", or "injurious, or likely to cause injury, to health".

The court observed that the words seemed wide enough to cover situations where there was a danger of accident; but it was clear from the history of the legislation that it was concerned with harm caused by disease. The steep stairs could therefore not be a statutory nuisance.

4-30 *Enforcement* Sections 80–82 of the Environmental Protection Act 1990 allows both local authorities and private individuals to take action against statutory nuisances. Where a local authority is satisfied that a statutory nuisance exists, or is likely to occur or recur, it must serve an "abatement notice" ♣. The notice may, as appropriate, require the nuisance to be abated (i. e. ended), or forbid or restrict its occurrence or recurrence. The notice may also require work to be carried out for any of those purposes (s. 80(1)). The notice must be served on the person responsible for the nuisance, or failing that on the owner or occupier of the premises in question (s. 80(2)). Where the nuisance comes from an unattended vehicle or unattended machinery in the street, the notice can be served by fixing it to the vehicle or machinery (s. 80A).

♣ This is an example of a situation where a local authority has a *duty* to act, not just a power. See generally 1-74.

4-31 Failure to comply with an abatement order without reasonable excuse is an offence, though the person served with the order has a right of appeal, within 21 days, to a magistrates' court. Appeals are governed by Schedule 3 to the Act and the Statutory Nuisance (Appeals) Regulations 1995. If an abatement notice is not complied with, the local authority may abate the nuisance themselves, and do any work specified in the notice, recovering the cost from the person responsible for the nuisance (s. 81(3) and (4)). Where the nuisance consists of a noise, the local authority can use this power to seize equipment being used to make the noise (Noise and Statutory Nuisance Act 1996, s. 10(7)). Equipment which has been seized in this way can be forfeited by the court, using its general powers. Taking action in this way does not prevent the local authority from bringing proceedings for the offence of failing to comply with the order. The maximum punishment is level 5 on the standard scale, and also a daily fine of one-tenth of that amount for every day on which the nuisance continues (s. 80(5)).

See 1-23 for the standard scale of fines in magistrates' courts.

In the case of *R v. Wakefield Magistrates' Court, ex parte Wakefield Metropolitan Borough Council* (2000) the local authority served a notice on a pig-farmer, requiring him to stop smells coming from the farm, and prohibiting any recurrence of the smells, but not specifying the work which had to be carried out to prevent a recurrence. The magistrates' court found that the notice was invalid, because no work was specified. The local authority applied for judicial review of the decision [see 1-74 for judicial review].

The higher court held that, depending on the facts, a local authority could either serve a notice requiring a statutory nuisance to cease, or one requiring work to be carried out. The magistrates' court had taken the wrong approach because it had not established the facts, and so could not judge what was appropriate.

Abatement notices

A private individual affected by a statutory nuisance can take action himself. First it is necessary to give notice in writing, to the person responsible for the nuisance, that he intends to bring proceedings (s. 82(6)). The notice is generally three days' notice for noise nuisances, and 21 days for others. Proceedings in the magistrates' court may then be started. If the court is satisfied that the nuisance exists, or is likely to recur, it may make an order covering essentially the same matter as a local authority's abatement notice (s. 82(2)). The maximum punishment for contravening an order is the same as for proceedings brought by the local authority (s. 82(8)). In some circumstances, however, it is a defence to prove that "the best practicable means were used to prevent, or to counteract the effects of, the nuisance" (s. 82(9)). Although a private person who 4-32

See 12-16 and 12-24 for sources on statutory nuisance.

brings proceedings for a statutory nuisance cannot expect to obtain compensation, the proceedings may achieve the purpose of stopping the activity in question.

Defence of 'best practicable means"

In the case of *Manley v. New Forest District Council* (1999) the owners of a dog-breeding establishment in a residential area were served with an abatement notice, which stated that noise from dogs was a statutory nuisance. The owners argued that they had used the best practicable means to minimise the nuisance. But the court decided that the best practicable means would have involved moving the business to a non-residential area.

The owners appealed, and the higher court decided that this was the wrong approach: it was not necessary to move the business elsewhere in order to show that they had used the best practicable means to minimise the nuisance, since this would make a nonsense of the defence.

Byelaws

4-33 Local authorities may make byelaws, under s. 235 of the Local Government Act 1972, for various purposes, including for the "prevention and suppression of nuisances". Byelaws cannot be made if other legislation already deals with the matter in question. The procedure laid down requires that the byelaws are available for public inspection (s. 236)); and byelaws cannot come into force unless confirmed by the DETR. Byelaws may provide that breach of their requirements is punishable by a fine. The maximum is generally level 2 on the standard scale, though may in some case be higher; and there may be an additional fine of £5 for each day the offence continues after conviction (s. 237). So landowners should be aware that besides the nuisances specified in the Acts referred to above, it is possible that byelaws are in force in the area in question, making other activities a nuisance.

See 12-25 for sources on byelaws.

Noise

4-34 A number of Acts have addressed the problem of noise, in different ways, either creating criminal offences, or giving powers to local authorities to take action, or both.

4-35 *Control of Pollution Act 1974* Part III of this Act deals with two sorts of noise—noise from construction sites and noise in streets. In relation to construction sites, the local authority can take action on a wide range of construction (or demolition) work, by serving a notice which imposes requirements on the way the work is carried out (s. 60). A notice may be served before the work starts or while it is in progress—no doubt the service of a notice may be triggered by complaints from the public about noise. It may specify:

- The plant or machinery which is or is not to be used.
- The hours during which the work may be carried out.
- Permitted noise levels.

4-36 The DETR has power, under s. 71 of the 1974 Act, to issue Codes of Practice giving guidance on how noise can be minimised. A code has been issued on noise from construction sites, entitled the *Code of Practice on Noise Control on Construction and Open Sites* (1984). Local authorities, in using their power under s. 60, must take into account the Code of Practice. Contravening a notice without reasonable excuse is an offence, the maximum fine being level 5 on the standard scale, with a further £5 for each day the offence continues after conviction. Alternatively, a person about to carry out work may seek consent from the local authority before starting, in which case conditions may be imposed as to the noise which can be made, contravention being an offence.

See 1-14 for codes of practice generally.

4-37 Section 62 of the Act is concerned with the problem of loudspeakers in streets. (A "street" for this purpose is "a highway and any other road, footway, square or court which is for the time being open to the public".) The Act forbids the use of loudspeakers in a street between 9 in the evening and 8 in the morning, for any

See 5-4 onwards for the meaning of "highway"

purpose(s. 62(1)(a)), and at any other time for the purpose of advertising any entertainment, trade or business (s. 62(1)(b)) There are exceptions for a number of purposes, including the emergency services, car stereo systems (provided they do not give reasonable cause for annoyance to people in the area) and vehicles selling perishable food, between midday and 7 in the evening (s. 62(2) and (3)).

4-38 In addition to these exceptions, local authorities can give consent to the use of loudspeakers in streets, under the Noise and Statutory Nuisance Act 1993, s. 8 and Schedule 2; but they cannot give consent in connection with elections, or for advertising any entertainment, trade or business. Where there is no consent, and the Control of Pollution Act 1974 does not allow the use of a loudspeaker, it is an offence to use one, and the maximum fine is a level 5 fine, and £50 for each day on which the offence continues after conviction (s. 74 of the Control of Pollution Act 1974).

4-39 A noise abatement zone may be set up by a local authority under the Control of Pollution Act 1974. The local authority must first measure and record the level of noise coming from premises in the zone. The reading must be served on the owner and occupier of the premises, and must also be made available on a public register (ss. 63–4). The noise level must then not be exceeded, except with the consent of the local authority, a contravention being an offence for which the maximum fine is level 5 on the standard scale, with £50 for each day on which the offence continues after conviction (s. 74). A local authority can also take action to reduce noise levels, under s. 66, provided that a reduction is practicable at reasonable cost and would benefit the public.

4-40 *London Local Authorities Act 1991* This Act deals with burglar alarms (which it calls "audible intruder alarms"). Its provisions apply only in those London Boroughs which adopt them. The Act is mentioned here because a very similar scheme is set out in the Noise and Statutory Nuisance Act 1993, s. 3 and Schedule 3; but these parts of the 1993 Act have *not yet been commenced* ✠. When they are commenced, local authorities throughout England and Wales will be able to adopt them.

✠ See 1-5 for commencement of Acts of Parliament.

Meanwhile, the requirements of the 1991 Act can be summarised as follows. Any person installing a burglar alarm (or becoming the owner or occupier of property where an alarm is fitted) must: 4-41

- Make sure it is fitted with a device which cuts off the noise after 20 minutes.

- Notify the police of nominated keyholders for the property.

- Notify the local authority of the installation and tell them which police station has been notified of the keyholders (s. 23(1)).

The Act does not compel the keyholders to assist, when an alarm goes off; but if an alarm is still operating an hour after it has gone off, and unsuccessful efforts have been made to gain access with the assistance of the keyholders, and the alarm is causing a nuisance to people living or working nearby, the local authority can apply to a Justice of the Peace for a warrant allowing them to enter the property—by force if need be—and de-activate the alarm. When they do so, however, they must be accompanied by a police officer (s. 24(7)). 4-42

Failure by a landowner to comply with the Act is an offence. Depending on the nature of the failure, the maximum punishment may be a level 5 fine (s. 24(6)). 4-43

Noise Act 1996 This Act, which came into force in July 1997, was introduced in order to deal with noise from dwelling-houses during the night, it being felt that the provisions of Part III of the Environmental Protection Act 1990 needed reinforcing. Most of the Act applies only if the local authority for the area in question has resolved that it should (or if the DETR has made an order that it should apply) (s. 1). Enforcement is a matter for the local authority. 4-44

See 4-27 for Part III of the 1990 Act.

If the Act is in force in a particular area, the local authority must make sure that an "officer of the authority" (i. e. a member of their staff) takes "reasonable steps" to investigate any complaint from someone in a dwelling, between 11 p. m. and 6 a. m., that there is excessive noise coming from another dwelling (s. 2). The noise may be music or any other noise. "Dwelling" here includes gardens, 4-45 yards and outbuildings: the noise need not come from within the dwelling itself (s. 11(2)). Noise, as measured from within the dwellling of the person who complained, must not exceed the "permitted level", that is the level laid down by the DETR in Directions (s. 5(1)). The Department issued the necessary Directions in July 1997. They are set out in the DETR Circular 8/97 on the Noise Act 1996. Where the underlying level of noise does not exceed 25dB (decibels) the permitted level is 35dB; and where the underlying level exceeds 25dB the permitted level is 10dB more than the underlying level. The DETR can also approve devices for use in measuring noise levels (s. 6).

4-46 If the initial investigation reveals that the noise would or might exceed the permitted level, the local authority's officer may serve a warning notice. It is for him to decide whether the noise would or might exceed the permitted level (s. 2). The warning notice must be served on the person who appears to be responsible for the noise, or if it is not reasonably practicable to identify such a person, the notice must be left at the dwelling in question. It must state the time at which it is served, and must specify a period, beginning at least 10 minutes after that time, and lasting until the following 7 a. m., and it must give warning that any person causing noise above the permitted level during that period may commit an offence (s. 3).

4-47 Once a warning notice has been served, it is an offence for any person to cause noise above the permitted level, as measured from within the dwelling of the person who complained (s. 4). The maximum penalty is a fine not exceeding level 3 on the standard scale. But the local authority's officer may take action at once if the noise does not stop after a warning notice, by serving a fixed penalty notice. The penalty fixed by the Act is £100; and, if it is paid, the person concerned cannot be prosecuted. Only one fixed penalty notice may be served on a person during one night; but if the noise continues after a warning notice and after a fixed penalty notice, the person responsible may be prosecuted for the offence (s. 7).

4-48 Local authorities have an extra power, in s. 10, which is to enter a dwelling and seize and remove any equipment used to cause noise. This may be amplifying equipment, for music, or any other sort of equipment which makes a noise—for example, noisy power tools being used for DIY work. The power may be used if a warning notice has been given, and afterwards the noise exceeds the permitted level. The Schedule to the Act allows equipment which has been seized to be forfeited.

See 12-24 for sources on these Acts.

Protection from Harassment Act 1997

4-49 This Act (which came into force in June 1997) applies to the public at large, not just to landowners; but it could be relevant where neighbours are on bad terms and one is harassing the other. The Act provides that:

> "1.-(1) A person must not pursue a course of conduct—
>
> (a) which amounts to harassment of another, and
>
> (b) which he knows or ought to know amounts to harassment of the other.
>
> (2) For the purposes of this section, the person whose course of conduct is in question ought to know that it amounts to harassment if a reasonable person in possession of the same information would think that the course of conduct amounted to harassment of the other."

4-50 Isolated incidents cannot amount to harassment for the purposes of the Act, since there has to be a "course of conduct"; but otherwise any sort of annoyance or pestering will be harassment if a reasonable person would think that it amounted to harassment, whether prompted by hatred or ill-will or by misplaced affection, or by devoting obsessive attention to someone else (sometimes referred to as "stalking").

4-51 The Act does not attempt to provide a list of all the actions which might amount to harassment, since that depends only on human ingenuity, but it says that harassment can include alarming someone or causing them distress (s. 7). The effect of the Act is to provide a degree of basic protection for the privacy of landowners and others. A landowner who was subjected to a "feud" by a difficult neighbour, or who was a public figure, and was subjected to unwelcome attentions at her private address by press photographers, might be able to rely on the Act.

Harassment

In *Director of Public Prosecutions v. Williams* (1998) Mr Williams was prosecuted for harassing a lady who was a householder. He had on one occasion put his hand through the bathroom window, while a guest was showering; and on another occasion he climbed on to a roof to look through a bedroom window. He was convicted, and appealed, arguing (among other things) that his behaviour was not "stalking", which was what the Protection from Harassment Act 1997 was concerned with.

The court decided that the conviction was right: if the behaviour caused alarm and distress it was harassment, even if it did not constitute stalking.

4-52 The Act goes on to provide that harassment is both a crime and a tort (a civil wrong). As a crime, harassment is subject to a maximum of six months' imprisonment on summary conviction, or a level 5 fine. As a civil wrong, harassment can result in compensation for the victim, or an injunction, to prevent further acts of harassment. Furthermore, if an injunction has been granted by the court, and the person concerned does something which appears to be in breach of the injunction, the court can issue an arrest warrant, so that the person is taken into custody.

See 1-22 onwards for summary proceedings and 1-23 for the standard scale of fines.

See 3-29 on injunctions.

See 12-16 and 12-24 for sources on the Protection from Harassment Act 1997.

Anti-Social Behaviour Orders

4-53 The Crime and Disorder Act 1998, s. 1, introduced a new way of dealing with anti-social behaviour—the anti-social behaviour order ("ASBO"). This is a new concept, designed to deal with serious bad behaviour in the community. The Home Office have issued guidance which explains how this part of the Act (which came into force on 1 April 1999) is meant to work.

4-54 An application for an order can be made, to a magistrates' court (acting in its role as a civil court) against a person who is acting in a way "likely to cause harassment, alarm or distress to one or more persons not of the same household as himself", if it is necessary to protect persons in the area from the behaviour (s. 1(1)). The application must be made by the police or by the local authority. In practice, the procedure is intended to apply to unruly, intimidating or bullying behaviour, perhaps backed up by vandalism and perhaps fuelled by drink or drugs. In some cases the behaviour may be directed at a minority group or at people who are vulnerable such as the elderly. The Act is not intended to catch behaviour which is just a one-off incident: it must appear that repetition is likely. The anti-social behaviour which is relied on to justify an ASBO may consist of criminal offences, but non-criminal behaviour may also be relied on. The point of the ASBO is that is is a civil order, and it is easier for the police or local authority to satisfy the court that an order should be made.

See 1-22 for proving criminal offences.

4-55 Consultations between the police and the local authority, and perhaps other bodies, must take place before an application is made. An order can be made against anyone over 10; though it is expected that orders against those as young as 10 will be rare. An ASBO will prohibit the person concerned from doing specified things and must last for at least two years (s. 1(4)). Breach of an ASBO—by doing what is prohibited by the order—is an offence which carries a maximum of 5 years' imprisonment.

See 12-24 for sources on anti-social behaviour orders.

Weeds Act 1959

4-56 This Act relates to certain "injurious" weeds listed in the Weeds Act 1959, these being:

- Spear thistle.
- Creeping or field thistle.
- Curled dock.
- Broad-leaved dock.
- Ragwort.

4-57 The Act gives the MAFF the power, if satisfied that any of these weeds are growing on any land, to serve notice on the occupier requiring him to take action to prevent the weeds from spreading (s. 1). Failure to comply with a notice is an offence punishable with a fine of up to level 3 on the standard scale (s. 2). If the landowner does not comply, the MAFF can enter the land and carry out the necessary work, and recover the cost from the landowner (s. 3). These powers can be delegated to local authorities, so that they can take action; and this in practice is what is done (s. 5).

See 12-2 for sources on the Weeds Act 1959.

Other civil wrongs

4-58 Although the torts of trespass and nuisance above are likely to cover the large majority of the interferences with land, and the comfort and health of the owner or occupiers, these are not the only civil wrongs which can apply to landowners. One which should be mentioned briefly is negligence. The law lays down that people owe a duty of care to those who are closely affected by their actions; and if a person fails to take sufficient care, and causes injury or damage to someone else, he may be liable to pay compensation.

4-59 This principle applies to people in many different situations, including landowners in relation to their neighbours. A landowner who is careless, and causes damage or injury to a neighbour, may be liable under the tort of negligence. Often, negligence covers the same ground as nuisance. If, for example, the owner of a factory allows industrial waste to escape on to nearby land, causing damage, the landowners affected may be entitled to compensation either on the basis of nuisance or negligence. If they start legal proceedings, they can rely on both, in the alternative. (But they can only be compensated once for the loss which they have suffered.)

In relation to people who come on to land, the duty of care is the special duty laid down by the Occupiers' Liability Acts: see 11-2 onwards.

See 12-16 for sources on civil wrongs.

Assessment

The law of trespass is one of the main protections which the law gives to landowners; the law of nuisance is another. It is different in that it is not as clear cut: whether there is legally a nuisance depends to a large extent on what is reasonable. Landowners must be prepared to accept a certain degree of disturbance from their neighbours, knowing that their own activities may well cause some disturbance in return. What is reasonable will depend upon the circumstances, including the nature of the area. Probably as good a test as any is for the landowner to ask himself, before embarking on some noisy or smoky operation, "Are other people in the area regularly making this sort of disturbance?" and perhaps also "How would I feel if my neighbour were to do this?" What can confidently be said is that the courts take a dim view of "feuds". A landowner who tries to deal with noise of some other form of nuisance by retaliating in kind is likely to find the courts very unsympathetic and may also find that the disturbance he causes is a nuisance, because it was done purely to annoy, even if his neighbour's was not. 4-60

The statutory procedures for dealing with nuisance cover all the main forms of nuisance, including noise, smoke and smells. They may offer a better way of proceeding if a landowner finds that legal action is necessary: there may be no compensation, but the proceedings may succeed in stopping the nuisance, which may be the main thing from the point of view of the suffering landowner. 4-61

Noise can be a particular problem, and there are extra legal procedures to deal with it. The assistance of the local authority may be necessary. Local authorities have a discretion about whether to act, and although they must act properly and responsibly, this does not mean that they must take action in every possible case, not least because they may not have the resources to do so. 4-62

See 1-74 for administrative law generally.

Overhanging branches (and also roots which grow under the boundary) are also dealt with by the law of nuisance; and a landowner is entitled to trim them at the boundary. But it is probably wise to let the neighbour know about the problem in case she wishes to do the trimming herself. 4-63

4-64 For cases of really serious disruptive behaviour, the law provides other remedies, in the form of procedures under the Protection from Harassment Act 1997 and anti-social behaviour orders. These are likely to be rare; but they are there if needed.

Chapter 5

Highways

Introduction

This chapter is concerned with public rights of way, or in other words (the two terms mean the same thing) highways. The law is here defining and protecting the right of the public to travel from place to place along roads, paths and other "ways". Many highways are very ancient, though new ones are being created all the time. In limited circumstances, the public's right to use a highway can be ended ("stopping up" a highway is the legal term for this process). Otherwise, the rule is "once a highway, always a highway", and the public's right to use the highway continues indefinitely. 5-0

Because highways are a matter of public concern, their upkeep is generally—but not always—a matter of public responsibility; and the law protects highways by means of a range of criminal offences, such as obstructing or damaging a highway, and also by giving local and central government a number of powers over highways. In this context, the term "highway authority" is used by the legislation. For motorways and trunk roads, the highway authority is the DETR. Otherwise the highway is a local government body—usually the County Council or Metropolitan District Council, though some responsibility for highways can be delegated to the bodies responsible for smaller areas. The term "highway authority" is generally used in this chapter. 5-1

See 5-72 onwards for these powers.

Some of the law relating to highways is common law; but much comes from legislation, particularly the Highways Act 1980. Some is civil and some criminal. For footpaths and bridleways, the Wildlife and Countryside Act 1981 is also important. The Countryside and Rights of Way Bill presently going through 5-2

See 1-10 for the meaning of "common law" and 1-1 onwards for "legislation".

Parliament will make some important changes to the law on public rights of way.

5-3 Landowners may be concerned about highways for two rather different reasons:

- They gain access to their property by means of a highway, in the form of a public road, and in many cases live next to the road, and so are concerned about what happens on the road and how the law controls the use of the road.

- Their land may be subject to a public right of way—for example, a footpath—and this restricts the use of the land.

Both aspects of the law are covered in this chapter.

Classes of highway

5-4 Highways are regarded as falling into three main classes, according to the traffic which has a right to use them:

- *Carriageways*, for pedestrians, equestrians and motorists in cars and other vehicles.

- *Bridleways*, for pedestrians, equestrians and also (in most cases) cyclists.

- *Footpaths*, for pedestrians.

For particular classes of unsurfaced highway, see 5-45 onwards.

5-5 Ordinary public roads are carriageways, and thus freely open to vehicles of all kinds, and also equestrians and pedestrians. Bridleways and footpaths often run across country, and their appearance will be familiar. The law is concerned with the nature of the right, not physical characteristics of the land; so it is perfectly possible for a footpath (say) to exist along a private road, or across the paved forecourt of commercial premises.

5-6 The right for cyclists to use bridleways was added by s. 30 of the Countryside Act 1968. Cyclists using bridleways must give way to pedestrians and equestrians. Local authorities may make byelaws excluding cyclists from bridleways.

See 1-9 for the meaning of "byelaws".

The public's right to use a highway

5-7 The public's right to use a highway is determined in the first instance by the class of highway. Motor vehicles, for example, may not be driven on footpaths. Furthermore, the right is essentially a right to "pass and repass", or in other words to go to and fro. But the law does not concern itself with the reason for the journey, which may thus be purely recreational. Walking or jogging for enjoyment or exercise are within the public's right to use a highway.

The case of *Director of Public Prosecutions v. Jones* (1999) was concerned with a demonstration at Stonehenge. Dr Jones was one of the demonstrators, who were on the verge by the side of the A344. The demonstration was peaceful and was not obstructing the highway. She and others were prosecuted for holding a "trespassory assembly", contrary to s. 14B(2) of the Public Order Act 1986. Whether there was a trespassory assembly depended upon whether the demonstrators were exceeding the public's right to use a highway.

The House of Lords decided that the use of the highway for a peaceful demonstration which did not interfere with the use of the highway was within the public's right to use the highway, and so not a trespass. Dr Jones and others were therefore acting lawfully, in demonstrating, and should not have been convicted of holding a trespassory assembly.

Use of the highway

5-8 Incidental activities are deemed to be within the public's right to use a highway; so that a walker, for example, may stop to rest and admire the view. The right to use a highway extends to activities which are not strictly incidental, but which are reasonable and usual, provided they do not interfere with the use of the highway. Picnicking by the side of road, in a way which did not interfere with the use of the road, would probably be regarded as within the public's right to use the road; but picnicking on a narrow footpath, and obstructing it, would probably not.

5-9 Provided that these rules are observed, the use of the land is lawful. Otherwise, the use is unlawful, and will be a trespass against the owner of the land, whether this is the highway authority or a private person.

See chapter 3 on trespassing. Straying from the highway on to adjoining land is also a trespass.

5-10 There is no general legal right to park in a carriageway, either for the owners of houses or property in the road, or for the public at large, even where there are no specific restrictions on parking. Local authorities are general tolerant, unless they have introduced parking restrictions using their powers to regulate traffic. Parking may be an offence, particularly if it causes an obstruction or danger.

See 5-74. For the offence of driving or parking away from public roads, see 3-49.

5-11 It is a general rule of the common law that the owner of land running along a highway can gain access to the highway at any point along his boundary. An access point is sometimes known as a "crossover"—the landowner will often have to cross over a pavement or verge in order to reach his own land. The right has, however, been restricted by the rule that planning permission is required for a crossover.

See 9-19; see also 6-39 for access to private roads.

Other rights

5-12 The right to use land as a highway does not belong to any particular person, but to the public at large. It is a quite different sort of right from a private right of way, which is a form of legal property and which does belong to a particular person. Land may be subject to both sorts of right: for example, a private road may be subject to private rights of way, which allow landowners living in the road to gain access to their houses, and at the same time subject to a footpath, allowing the public at large to walk along the road—but not to drive along it.

See 6-33 onwards for private rights of way.

5-13 The public's right to use a highway is also different from the right of public access to land. A number of different legal arrangements can provide for public access to land. The difference is essentially that a public right of way is confined to a specific route, and the

ee 10-79 onwards for public access generally.

activities permitted are limited; whereas a public right of access means access to the land as a whole, for recreation or fresh air and exercise. Land can be subject to both sorts of right: a common may be subject to public rights of way and also a public right of access.

See 10-65 onwards for the meaning of "common".

Creating highways

5-14 It might be thought that creating a highway would involve a single legal procedure, which would do three things:

- Give rise to a public right of way.
- Transfer ownership of the highway to the some public body.
- Make maintenance a public responsibility from then on—or, in legal language, make it "maintainable at the public expense". (This process is sometimes known as "adoption"—hence the phrase "unadopted road", meaning one which is *not* maintainable at the public expense.)

See 2-61 onwards. Generally, ownership of a highway means owning only the top layer of the land—the "top two spits".

5-15 In fact, although these are the main steps, the position is considerably more complicated than this. There is a whole range of different legal procedures for creating highways. They do not always involve the second and third steps (which go together): where this happens, the result is that the public have the benefit of a highway, but do not have to bear the cost of maintaining it. They may involve an extra step, namely the "making up" of the highway, or bringing it up to a proper standard. Some knowledge of the history of the law is also necessary in order to understand the position, since some highways are very old.

5-16 Much of the present law is contained in the Highways Act 1980, and this Act contains a number of procedures for creating highways and (sometimes) making them maintainable at the public expense. The process of "dedication and acceptance" is also important. In

See 5-22 onwards for the meaning of "dedication and acceptance".

effect, the law is that a highway can be created by public use over a period of time. This is an ancient concept of the common law (though it has been modified by the Highways Act 1980). These procedures are explained below, followed by a brief account of the earlier law.

5-17 A separate line of Acts, starting with the National Parks and Access to the Countryside Act 1949, has laid down additional rules which are also important. These relate to footpaths and other highways which run across country, and are at risk of being damaged or obliterated. The main effect of the legislation—particularly the Wildlife and Countryside Act 1981—is that local authorities have to prepare a "definitive map and statement" recording the existence and route of these highways. "Definitive" means that, subject to various qualifications, if a footpath or other highway is shown, then legally it exists. This legislation does not actually create highways; but it guarantees their existence once they have been created.

See 5-43 onwards for the Wildlife and Countryside Act 1981.

Procedures under the Highways Act 1980

5-18 The Highways Act 1980 contains a number of different procedures by which land may become a highway. Some of these provisions may be mentioned by way of example. Some are for any of the classes of highway mentioned above; some are only for footpaths and bridleways. The Highways Act makes clear which highways are maintainable at the public expense: some are listed in s. 36, and other sections of the Act also provide that particular sorts of highway are to be maintainable at the public expense. When a highway is maintainable at the public expense, public ownership follows, under s. 263 of the Act. At the same time, a duty to maintain the highway is placed on the highway authority by s. 41.

See further 5-66 on repair and maintenance of highways.

5-19 *Highways of all classes* As one would expect, highways constructed by the highway authority are maintainable at the public expense (s. 36(2)(a)). Section 37 contains a procedure by which a highway created by dedication and acceptance can become maintainable at the public expense, if the highway authority agree. Under s. 38(3) of the Act, the highway authority may make an agreement with a landowner to undertake the maintenance of a way which will become a highway of one of the three classes mentioned above. On the date specified in the agreement, the way will then become a highway maintainable at the public expense. There are also complicated provisions, in Part XI of the Highways Act 1980, by which both new and existing private streets may become highways maintainable at the public expense. Generally, the expense of making up the road falls on the frontagers. (It is also possible, under Part XI, for a private road to become a highway without becoming maintainable at the public expense.)

See 12-19 for sources on private roads.

5-20 In practice, when new roads are built by a developer, they are built to the standard required by the highway authority. They can then be adopted by agreement under s. 38 of the Highways Act 1980 (which is more usual), or under Part XI; alternatively, they can remain as private roads. There will then be no public right of way; and those who need to use the road for access will have to rely on private rights of way.

See 6-33 onwards for private rights of way.

5-21 *Footpaths and bridleways* Sections 25 and 26 of the Highways Act 1999 are confined to footpaths and bridleways. Under s. 25, a local authority can make a "public path creation agreement" with a landowner, which has the effect of creating a footpath or a bridleway. Under s. 26, the local authority can make an order—a "public path creation order"—which results in the creation of a footpath or bridleway without the agreement of the landowner. But under s. 26 an order must be confirmed by the DETR before it takes effect, and the local authority may have to pay compensation to any person whose land loses value, or who is disturbed in the enjoyment of land (s. 28). Compensation is not confined to the person over whose land the new highway runs: if the owner of nearby land finds that it has lost value or that he is disturbed, he can claim compensation.

Dedication and acceptance

5-22 *Generally* In addition to the procedures mentioned above, highways of any class can be created by the process known as "dedication and acceptance". The rule is that if the owner dedicates a way to the public as a highway (or, more importantly, is deemed to have done so) and if the public then accept the dedication, by using the way, a highway is created. Any land can become a highway in this manner. The use which has taken place determines what sort of highway is created. For example, if the public have crossed a field on foot, a footpath may be created; and if the public have drive through a private road, a carriageway may be created. The rule is a very ancient common law rule, though it is now reinforced by s. 31 of the Highways Act 1980. Highways have for centuries been created by the process of dedication and acceptance, and can be created in this way today. The width of the way subject to the right will depend upon the circumstances—a narrow strip for a footpath, rather more for a bridleway and more still for a carriageway.

See 5-4 for the different classes of highway

See 5-25 for s. 31

5-23 The fact that a highway is created by means of dedication and acceptance does *not* mean that it automatically becomes maintainable at the public expense. Ownership does not automatically pass to the highway authority under s. 263 of the Highways Act 1980, and the highway authority does not have a duty to maintain the highway under s. 41.

5-24 A landowner might make a positive decision to dedicate land as a highway. The law does not lay down what acts amount to dedication; but a landowner might make clear by means of signs, or perhaps notices in the local press, that he intended to do so. If so, the period of public use required to establish acceptance is likely to be quite short—perhaps some months. This is likely to be a rare event, however: if a landowner wishes to create a highway, the procedures in the Highways Act 1980 will be more attractive. A landowner wanting to create a highway for the benefit of the public will almost certainly want its maintenance to be a public responsibility.

5-25 A much more likely situation is that the landowner has not made any conscious decision to dedicate his land as a highway, but use by the public has taken place. The absence of a deliberate decision by the landowner is not the end of the matter, because the law presumes that, after use of a certain nature for a particular period, the owner must have intended to dedicate the land. Section 31(1) of the Highways Act 1980 now provides that where a way:

> ".....has been actually enjoyed by the public as of right and without interruption for a full period of 20 years, the way is deemed to have been dedicated as a highway unless there is sufficient evidence that there was no intention during that period to dedicate it."

5-26 The use by the public must be open, "as of right" (that is, as though there was a right to use the land as a highway) and without interruption. Use must continue for 20 years; and the period of 20 years must be measured backwards from the date when the public's right is challenged. (This rule was formerly set out in the Rights of Way Act 1932, so some highways may have been created in this way between 1932 and 1980.) The fact that the Highways Act 1980 lays down a 20-year period does not mean that the common law—which does not specify a particular period—no longer applies. But the Highways Act is clearer, and anybody seeking to show that a highway has been created will tend to rely on the fact that there has been 20 years' use by the public.

See 6-19 for the meaning of "as of right" in relation to easements created by prescription.

5-27 *Evidence of use by the public* In establishing whether sufficient public use has actually taken place, the Highways Act provides that a court or other tribunal must give appropriate weight to "any map, plan or history of the locality or other relevant document which is tendered in evidence" (s. 32). Maps and other documents may be relevant either directly, by showing that there was a public right of way, or indirectly, by showing that there was something such as a shop which the public are likely to have visited. It may also be possible for a person wishing to establish that a right of way has been created to rely on the word of someone who has known the land over a period of many years, and seen the public use it. But if there is no such first-hand evidence, it may still be possible to draw inferences about likely use from the nature of the land, or to rely on a presumption which the law makes about use. Where a way serves as a through-route between two existing highways, there is a presumption that the public has used the way to pass between the two highways, and the way may thus become a highway too. The presumption is rebuttable—in other words, it does not apply if there is evidence to the contrary. In the absence of other evidence, this may be the only way in which the necessary use can be established.

5-28 Public use cannot create a highway, however, if the use amounts to a criminal offence. (The fact that it is a trespass, and so a civil wrong, does not matter for this purpose.)

Criminal acts can't create a highway

In the case of *Robinson* v. *Adair* (1995) there was a dispute about a metalled road leading to Praa Sands, in Cornwall. The road had been blocked by Mr Adair. Mr Robinson alleged that it was a highway, having been used by cars, and that Mr Adair had committed an offence by obstructing it. On appeal, the court decided that use which was prohibited by statute could not lead to the creation of a highway. Here the use was prohibited because the road was part of a common, and driving on it was an offence under s. 34(1) of the Road Traffic Act 1988, so no public right of way for vehicles could have arisen.
[See also 6-22 for the case of *Hanning v. Top Deck Travel* (1994) for a similar rule aplying to the creation of *private* rights of way.]

5-29 The dedication of land as a highway may be subject to conditions. A footpath, for example, may be dedicated as a highway on condition that there is a gate or a stile across the path. This means that when the land becomes a highway, the existence of the gate or stile does not amount to an unlawful obstruction of the highway.

See 5-75 for the meaning of "obstructing" a highway.

5-30 Whether land has become a highway through the process of dedication and acceptance may be unclear or in dispute, because it often depends upon events spanning a relatively long period of which there may well be no records. (The procedures under the Highways Act 1980 are much less likely to be in dispute, since they are likely to be the subject of official records which can be referred to.) A person who wishes to claim that land has become a highway, and that the public can exercise a right of way across it, may be challenged by the owner of the land. The landowner will ask the person concerned to stop crossing his land, and if the use continues may bring proceedings for trespass, asking the court to grant an injunction to stop the unlawful use. It is for the person claiming that a public right of way exists to prove that this is so. A definite answer can only be given by a court, or, in relation to footpaths and

See chapter 3 generally, and 3-29 onwards for injunctions.

other vulnerable ways by the procedures applicable to the "definitive map and statement" ⌘.

⌘ See 5-43 onwards for definite maps and statements.

Preventing dedication and acceptance

5-31 Because of the way the law has developed, a landowner who sees that the public are using his land to pass to and fro but takes no action may in due course find that a public right of way has arisen. However there are various steps which can be taken to stop this happening.

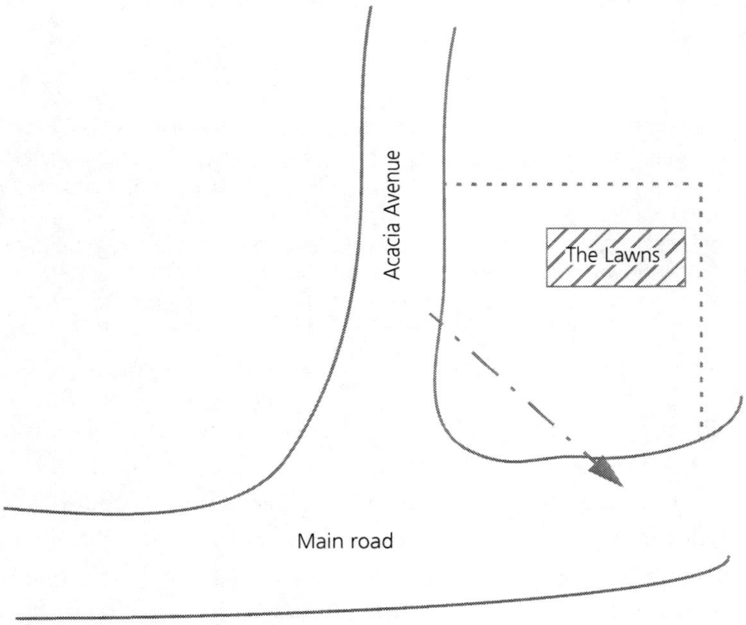

Dedication and acceptance If the garden of The Lawns is unfenced, and the public walk across it, to cut the corner between Acacia Avenue and the Main Road, the path will eventually become a highway unless the owner of The Lawns takes some action to prevent dedication and acceptance.

5-32 *Notices* A landowner can put up a notice making clear that he does not intend to dedicate his land as a highway. The Highways Act 1980, in s. 31(3), provides that a notice which is "inconsistent with the dedication of the way as a highway" is sufficient to negative any intention to dedicate the way as a highway, "unless the contrary intention is proved". The latter phrase means that if the landowner actually does wish to dedicate his land as a highway, the existence of a notice will not prevent this happening (an unlikely event).

5-33 No special form of words is laid down by the Act: the landowner merely has to make clear that he has no intention to dedicate the land as a highway. In built-up areas, where development leaves an area of land open to the public—for example, a strip of land next to a pavement, or a path between two buildings—it is common to put up a notice which says that the land is not dedicated to the public, and the notice will prevent a public right of way from arising. A notice saying "no public right of way", "private property—keep out", or words to the same effect, would be sufficient. But a notice which merely said "private" might well not be sufficient, since the fact that land is private property is not inconsistent with the dedication of the land as a highway.

But note 5-86 on misleading notices.

Preventing dedication as a highway

In the case of *Jacques v. Secretary of State for the Environment (1994)* the landowner's estate had three footpaths running over it. The public had used the footpaths "as of right and without interruption" for 20 years; but the landowner had made clear to users, by putting up notices and by fences and gates, that he had no intention to dedicate the land as a highway. The court decided that, despite the nature of the use which had taken place, the actions of the landowner prevented the land from being dedicated as a highway, in view of the final words of s. 31(1) of the Highways Act 1980.

5-34 Provision is made in s. 31(5) of the Highways Act for situations in which a notice is put up but is later torn down or defaced: the owner of the road can then give notice to the local authority that the way is not dedicated. The giving of such notice is, similarly, sufficient evidence of an intention not to dedicate the land, and so prevents the creation of a highway by dedication and acceptance.

5-35 *Interruption* If the use by the public is interrupted, before the 20-year period under the Highways Act 1980 has expired, the land cannot become a highway. This is why private roads often have gates which are closed once a year: the interruption makes sure that any use by the public cannot lead to the creation of a highway.

5-36 *Giving permission* A landowner can prevent the creation of a highway by giving permission for the use of his land. But in doing so he should be careful not to express himself in such a way as to make it seem that he is dedicating the land to the public. As in the case of other licences, the landowner should give permission in writing, expressing himself with care and making clear that the permission may be withdrawn at any time.

See 1-49 on licences generally.

5-37 *Lodging information with the local authority* A further alternative exists, under s. 31(5) of the Highways Act, and that is for the landowner to deposit with the highway authority a large-scale map (at least 6 inches to the mile) and a statement setting out what if any public rights of way the landowner admits exist over the land. This procedure may be intended for use mainly by the owners of farms and other large areas of land, but it could equally be used by the owner of any land. Once the map and statement have been deposited, their effect can be continued by the making of statutory declarations, at intervals of not more than six years, affirming that no further ways have been dedicated. (A statutory declaration is a formal statement, made before a solicitor or other qualified person: making a false declaration is an offence.) These documents, deposited with the highway authority, constitute sufficient evidence to negative an intention of dedicating. Strictly speaking, therefore, they make other options, such as notices and gates unnecessary; but there is an obvious advantage in retaining one or both of the latter.

Some history

5-38 The above paragraphs summarise some of the ways in which highways can be created under the present law. Some highways are relatively modern, having been created under the Highways Act 1980, or its predecessor, the Highways Act 1959. But many are older—indeed, some are very ancient—and a brief explanation of the law is necessary in order to understand the position in relation to older highways. The law differs according to whether the highway is a road or not.

See 1-10 for the meaning of "common law".

See 5-14 for the meaning of "adoption".

Though such roads may occasionally become maintainable at the public expense: see 5-19 on Part XI of the Highways Act 1980.

5-39 *Roads* It was a rule of the common law over the centuries that the inhabitants of a parish were responsible for the maintenance of the highways of all classes in that parish. But in relation to new roads which became highways, through the process of dedication and acceptance, the position was altered by the s. 23 of the Highway Act 1835: after 1836, new roads only became a public responsibility if the appropriate procedures were followed for them to be adopted by the parish. It has thus been possible since 1836 for roads to become highways without any public obligation to maintain them. Where, however, there was a duty to maintain existing roads, this was preserved by the 1835 Act, and by the Highways Acts of 1959 and 1980.

5-40 In short, all carriageways created before 1836 are maintainable at the public expense. After that date, carriageways are maintainable at the public expense only if made so under some statutory procedure. This leaves some carriageways, especially those created by dedication and acceptance, which are not maintainable at the public expense. The land is subject to a public right of way, but the highway is not maintainable by anyone—the public has no duty to maintain it, nor does the landowner.

5-41 *Footpaths and other ways* have a slightly different legal history. The common law duty to maintain them applied in the same way as to roads; but s. 23 of the Highway Act 1835 did not apply to them, so public responsibility for new footpaths and bridleways was never interrupted by that Act. It continued until the National Parks and Access to the Countryside Act 1949. Sections 47 and 49 of that Act confirmed that all existing footpaths and bridleways were maintainable at the public expense, but laid down that, from the end of 1949 onwards, public responsibility would apply only to footpaths and bridleways created by a procedure introduced by the Act, known as "public path agreements". These have now been replaced by public path creation orders and public path creation agreements, under ss. 26 and 27 of the Highways Act 1980.

See 5-21 onwards for the meaning of public path creation orders and agreements

5-42 So all highways, other than carriageways, created before 1949 are maintainable at the public expense; and since then they are maintainable at the public expense only if created under a public path creation order or agreement, or adopted under the procedures mentioned above. A footpath (for example) created today by

See 5-18 onwards for these procedures.

dedication and acceptance will not be maintainable at the public expense unless a further step is taken to make it so.

See 12-18 for sources on highways.

Recording of footpaths, etc

The National Parks and Access to the Countryside Act 1949 introduced a special procedure for footpaths, bridleways and other highways running across country, which are at risk from being damaged or lost. The main requirement is that local authorities must record the existence of these highways on a "definitive map and statement". The record is then evidence that the highway exists (but not that it is maintainable at the public expense). 5-43

The definitive map and statement The 1949 Act required that local authorities prepare a definitive map and statement for their area, showing the location of all "public paths"; and that there must be revisions at fixed intervals, to keep the map and statement up to date. The law was simplified by the Countryside Act 1968, and is now set out in the Wildlife and Countryside Act 1981, Part III (ss. 53–66) and also the regulations made under it. The 1981 Act lays down that the definitive map and statement must be kept continuously up to date, rather than revised at intervals (s. 53); and where no map and statement had yet been prepared (the process was in some areas a very slow one) this had to be done. 5-44

One important change was made to the classification of public rights of way. Besides providing for footpath creation orders and agreements, the 1949 Act introduced the concept of a "road used as a public path", often referred to as a RUPP, which meant: 5-45

> "a highway, other than a [footpath or bridleway] used by the public mainly for the purposes for which footpaths or bridleways are so used".

This was intended to apply to carriageways—highways with a right of way for vehicles—which were not surfaced and which were not in regular use as roads, but which were mainly used by pedestrians and equestrians.

5-46 This classification was not satisfactory, since it left unclear what exactly the public right of way was. So highway authorities were required (first by the Countryside Act 1968, and now by s. 54 of the Wildlife and Countryside Act 1981) to reclassify RUPPs, so that they became, according to the nature of the public right of way shown to exist, footpaths, bridleways, or as "byways open to all traffic". The latter are sometimes known are "BOATs"; and the term "green lane" is also used for these unsurfaced, cross-country roads subject to a right of way for vehicles. After reclassification, all three sorts of highway become maintainable at the public expense (s. 54(4) of the Wildlife and Countryside Act 1981).

RUPPS and BOATs

In *Masters v. Secretary of State for the Environment, Transport and the Regions* (2000) the Somerset County Council made an order under s. 53(2)(b) of the 1981 Act, changing a RUPP into a BOAT. Mr and Mrs Masters were the owners of a farm through which the BOAT passed. They appealed to the DETR and when the appeal was unsuccessful they challenged the decision by applying for judicial review [see 1-74 for judicial review]. They argued that it was wrong to show the existence of a BOAT on the definitive map when there was no evidence of it being currently in use by vehicles.

The court decided that the right test was not the nature of the current use of the highway, but past use, which had established which class of highway it was. Because of the rule "once a highway, always a highway", the highway remained a highway of that class. The highway was a BOAT.

5-47 However, the 1981 Act, in s. 54(7), relieves highway authorities of the duty to provide a metalled surface for BOATs, which would otherwise arise under the Highways Act 1980. Because they are carriageways they can lawfully be used by motorists and motorcyclists who are "off-road" enthusiasts; though motor vehicles must be taxed and tested and otherwise comply with the law, just as for any other public road.

See 5-66 for the duty to maintain a highway.

5-48 Local authorities must keep copies of the definitive map and statement available for public inspection (s. 57(3) of the Wildlife and Countryside Act 1981). The statement accompanying the map gives the date of the map and may contain other details about the rights of way shown. The Wildlife and Countryside (Definitive Maps and Statements) Regulations 1993 lay down requirements for definitive maps: these must be a scale of at least 1/25,000, and Schedule 1 provides for how the different sorts of highway are to be shown on the map.

Table 4: markings on the definitive map

Highway	Marking
Footpath	Continuous purple line, or continuous line with short bars at intervals.
Bridleway	Continuous green line, or continuous line with cross bars at intervals, or a broken line with cross bars in the intervals.
RUPP	Broken green line, or a broken line and small arrowheads.
BOAT	Continuous brown line, or continuous line with arrowheads alternately above and below the line.

Modifying the definitive map and statement The local authority must keep the definitive map and statement up to date, and this means modifying them to reflect the following events: 5-49

- A highway being stopped up, diverted, widened or extended; or ceasing to be a highway of the type shown; or a new public path (i. e. a footpath or a bridleway) being created (s. 53(3)*(a)*(i), (ii) and (iii)).

- The end of any period which raises the presumption of dedication to the public (in particular, the period of 20 years mentioned in s. 31 of the Highways Act) (s. 53(3)*(b))*.

- The discovery of evidence which shows that a highway exists which is not shown in the map and statement; or that a highway of one type ought to be shown as another type (e. g. a footpath as a bridleway); or that there is no highway over land shown on the map (s. 53(3)*(c)*(i), (ii) and (iii)).

See 5-25 for this rule.

5-50 The local authority can act on its own initiative; and any member of the public can make an application to the local authority for an order modifying the map and statement; but they may apply only under s. 53*(b)* and *(c)*, not *(a)*. The Wildlife and Countryside (Definitive Maps and Statements) Regulations 1993 lay down the form of such applications. The owner of the land in question must be given notice of the application, unless the landowner is the person making the application. Regulation 7(3) and Schedule 6 of the 1993 Regulations provide that notice must also be served on certain special interest groups, including the British Horse Society and the Ramblers Association. By Schedule 14 to the 1981 Act, the application must include a map showing the way to which it relates.

Modifying the definitive map

In *Trevelyan v. Secretary of State for the Environment, Transport and the Regions* (2000) the Ramblers' Association brought legal proceedings to challenge the deletion of a bridleway from the definitive map. The Association argued that this was wrong because it would result in anomalies: some footpaths would become dead-ends, and another bridleway would have no connection with the public road. The court decided that despite these anomalies it was not wrong to delete the bridleway.

5-51 The local authority must consider the application; and there is a right of appeal to the DETR if the local authority refuse to make an order modifying the map and plan. If the local authority decides to make a modification order under s. 53(3)*(b)* or *(c)* they must follow the procedure laid down in the 1981 Act (s. 53(6) and Schedule 15) and the 1993 Regulations (reg. 7(1) and Schedule 4). They must publish a notice in at least one local newspaper, serve a copy notice on any landowners affected by the order, and display it at the ends of the highway in question and at Council offices in the area and anywhere else which the local authority considers appropriate.

5-52 If no objections or representations are made, the local authority can confirm the order or, if they wish to amend it in any way before making it, they must submit it to the DETR for confirmation. If, on the other hand, the making of the order is opposed, the order must be submitted to the DETR for confirmation; and the DETR must either hold a local enquiry or give any person who has made representations or objections the opportunity of being heard by a person appointed by the DETR. The DETR can then, after taking into account representations and objections, and the report of the local enquiry or the person appointed to hear representations or objections, confirm the order. The confirmation can be made with or without modifications; but before it can be confirmed with modifications it may be necessary (depending on the nature of the modifications) to give those concerned a further opportunity to make representations or objections. Any person aggrieved can challenge the Department's decision in the High Court on limited grounds (Schedule 15).

"Stopping up" and diverting highways

Once a highway has been created over some land, whether by dedication and acceptance or by one of procedures in the Highways Act, the process cannot be reversed by the owner of the land by himself, the rule being "once a highway, always a highway". The fact that the highway is no longer in use by the public, or that its existence has become burdensome for the landowner, for example because of damage caused by users, does not in itself cause the public right of way to cease. 5-53

Parliament, however, does have power to provide in legislation for the "stopping up" of a highway—in other words, for ending the public's right to use the land as a highway—and also for the diversion of highways, i. e. changing their course. Several Acts give power to local and central government to stop up or to divert a highway. 5-54

Highways generally Under s. 116 of the Highways Act 1980, any class of highway can be stopped up if it is "unnecessary", or if it "can be diverted so as to make it nearer or more commodious to the public". The test of whether a highway is necessary is whether it is needed for the purpose of passing and repassing, other matters such as parking, and the convenience of owners of property in the road, being irrelevant. The fact that the owner of the land in question 5-55 would like the highway to be stopped up—for example a farmer with a footpath running across a field—is not in itself a ground on which the procedure can be used. If a highway is used by the public, a stopping-up order will generally not be appropriate unless a suitable alternative exists. Private persons cannot apply as such; but the application can be made by the local authority on behalf of another person, under s. 117. A visit may be made to inspect the highway, if the magistrates think fit. In the case of a carriageway, the order may close the highway to all traffic, or may leave a footpath or bridleway in existence. Notice must be served on the owners of property adjoining the road, and on statutory undertakers with pipes, cables or other apparatus under or over the highway. The stopping up of a highway means that the public right of way ceases, and ownership of the land passes from the highway authority back to the person who owned the land before it became a highway.

See 11-103 onwards for the meaning of "statutory undertaker".

See 2-64 as to the position if it is impossible to trace the owner.

Stopping up a highway

In the case of *Ramblers Association v. Kent County Council* (1990) the County Council obtained an order from a magistrates' court, under s. 116 of the Highways Act 1980, for the stopping up of some highways which ran across military land. The Ramblers' Association challenged the order, in a higher court, on various grounds. The higher court considered that the notices given by the County Council were misleading, because they wrongly said that alternative routes were going to be provided. In addition, there was some evidence that the highways were being used by the public. Where that was so, it would be difficult for a magistrates' court to conclude that a way was "unnecessary" unless an alternative was provided. The court decided that the magistrates' order was of no effect, so that the highways remained in existence.

5-56 Other Acts have provisions which allow a local authority to stop up or divert a highway; for example, there is a power in s. 258 of the Town and Country Planning Act 1990 which allows them to do so in order to assist development.

5-57 *Footpaths and bridleways* Sections 118 and 119 of the Highways Act 1980 allow for the stopping up and diversion respectively of footpaths and bridleways. These sections are unlike s. 116 in that it is not necessary to apply to a magistrates' court. Instead, local authorities may make orders, known as "public path extinguishment orders" and "public path diversion orders". The procedures are set out in Schedule 6 to the Highways Act 1980 and in some regulations, the Public Path Orders Regulations 1993.

5-58 First, the local authority must give notice of the order, which must be in the form laid down, including a map (s. 118(3) and 119(7)). The notice must be published in a local newspaper and served on the landowners affected and others. "Others" includes every parish and community council affected, and any person who has required the local authority to give him notice of public path creation and diversion orders. The notice must also be displayed at the ends of the path and at the local authority's offices (Schedule to the Highways Act). If representations or objections are made, the DETR must either hold a local enquiry or allow the person concerned the opportunity to be heard by a person appointed by the DETR (Schedule 6). A report then goes to the DETR, which can decline to confirm the order or confirm it with or without modifications.

5-59 The test of whether a footpath or bridleway can be *extinguished* is whether it is "expedient" for the path to be stopped up, on the ground that it is not needed for public use (s. 118(1)). Before the order can be confirmed, the local authority or the DETR must be satisfied that it is:

> "expedient to do so, having regard to the extent (if any) to which it appears ... that the path or way would, apart from the order, be likely to be used by the public, and having regard to the effect which the extinguishment of the right of way would have as respects land served by the path or way..." (s. 118(2)).

At this stage (that is, after there has been an opportunity for public comment) the question is slightly different, namely whether the path ought to be stopped up, given the degree of use. The question of compensation can also be taken into account. The local authority may have to pay compensation because s. 121(2) says that s. 28 applies to the extinguishment and diversion of footpaths and bridleways, as well as their creation.

See 5-21 for s. 28 and compensation generally.

5-60 A landowner over whose land the footpath or bridleway runs may claim compensation if the value of her property is affected, or if she is disturbed in the enjoyment of it by an extinguishment or diversion order. A claim might be made where, for example, a footpath is diverted so that it runs nearer to her house, and so causes some disturbance. Compensation may also be paid to a landowner who does *not* own the land over which the footpath or bridleway runs—but only if she would have been able to bring legal proceedings in the absence of statutory authority for making the order. Such a case might arise if, for example, a footpath was diverted so that it ran along the boundary of land, and caused enough disturbance for action to be taken for nuisance. Claims must be made within 6 months, in accordance with the Public Paths Orders Regulations 1993. If the person claiming and the local authority cannot agree the amount payable, the dispute can be settled by the Lands Tribunal.

See chapter 4 for nuisance.

See 1-71 for the Lands Tribunal.

5-61 Where the order is for the *diversion* of a footpath of bridleway, the local authority act at the request of a landowner. The test is whether, in the interests of the landowner or of the public it is "expedient" for the line of the path to be altered (s. 119(1)). The end of the path must not be moved, unless the path ends on another highway, in which case it may be moved along the highway, provided the new route is as convenient to the public (s. 119(2)). Before the order can be confirmed, the local authority or (if there is an objection) the DETR must be satisfied that the diversion is expedient as required by s. 119(1), that the new route will not be substantially less convenient to the public, and also that it is expedient to confirm the order, having regard to the effect of the diversion on:

- Public enjoyment of the path.
- Other land served by the path.
- Any land which will be subject to the new right of way (s. 119(6)).

5-62 But, as in the case of an extinguishment order, compensation may be taken into account. Before the necessary steps are taken the landowner may be asked to enter into an agreement that he will contribute towards the payment of compensation (if the local authority has to pay compensation) or towards the costs of making the order and diverting the path (s. 119(5)). The question of costs is dealt with by the Local Authorities (Recovery of Costs for Public Path Orders) Regulations 1993.

Information about highways

5-63 Highway authorities are required, by s. 36(6) and (7) of the Highways Act 1980, to keep a list of the streets which are maintainable at the public expense. "Street" means the same in the Highways Act 1980 as it does in the New Roads and Street Works Act 1991, that is, "any highway, road, lane, footway, alley or passage", "any square or court", and "any land laid out as a way whether it is for the time being formed as a way or not" (s. 48 of the New Roads and Street Works Act 1991).

See 11-106 for the New Roads and Street Works Act generally.

5-64 Footpaths and bridleways which are maintainable at the public expense are thus included, as well as carriageways, because they are highways. The list must be kept up to date, and open to public inspection. Footpaths, bridleways and BOATs, whether or not maintainable at the public expense, will also appear on the definitive map and statement.

See 5-44 for the definitive map and statement.

5-65 Highway authorities may also keep, for their own and others' information, unofficial lists of private roads (perhaps differentiating between those which are and are not highways); but there is no legal obligation to keep such lists.

And see 5-70 onwards in relation to signposts—which are also a source of information about highways.

Maintenance and other work

5-66 In some circumstances, the law provides for a road or path to be "made up", meaning that work must be undertaken to bring it up to a proper standard. This is true particularly of the adoption of a private street under Part XI of the Highways Act 1980, when the expense will usually fall on the owners of property fronting the road. Once the road has been made up to a standard satisfactory to the highway authority, the expense of maintaining the road falls on the highway authority. In some circumstances, new paths and bridleways may have to be made up, under s. 27 of the Highways Act.

See 5-19 for Part XI of the Highways Act 1980.

5-67 In relation to maintenance generally, s. 41 of the Highways Act is not specific about what work the highway authority must do in the course of maintaining a highway. In the case of metalled roads, the surface will need attention from time to time, and the highway authority must also be concerned about other matters such as drainage of surface water and structural damage. The surfaces of footpaths, bridleways and other unmetalled highways may need relatively little maintenance, but the highway authority is nonetheless under an obligation to do whatever is required. Quite apart from the obligation which rests on the highway authority under s. 41, where there is no obligation on any person to maintain a footpath or bridleway, a district, parish or community council has power to undertake maintenance if they wish—but they are not under any obligation to do so.

Failure to repair a highway

In *Westley v. Hertfordshire County Council* (1998) the East Herts Footpath Society took action against the County Council under s. 56 of the Highways Act 1980. Their complaint was that the Council had failed to deal with some vegetation within fencing which was encroaching on and obstructing a bridleway.

The court's decision was that the real problem was an obstruction, not a lack of repair, and s. 56 was not appropriate. However, the Council might have been in breach of its duty under s. 130 of the Highways Act, for failing to remove an obstruction.

5-68 Where the highway authority are under a duty to maintain a highway, and the highway appears to be out of repair, any person may apply to a magistrates' court for an order requiring them to repair the highway (s. 56(4) of the Highways Act 1980). If an order is made, but the work is not done, the person concerned can be authorised by the court to do the work himself and recover the cost from the highway authority (s. 56(6)).

5-69 The Highways Act 1980 also contains provisions on specific sorts of work on highways. By s. 146, the owner of land subject to a footpath or bridleway must keep stiles and gates in safe condition, and "to the standard of repair required to prevent unreasonable interference with the rights of the persons using the footpath or bridleway" (s. 146(1)). The local authority must contribute at least 25% to the cost of any expenses reasonably incurred in complying with this requirement (s. 146(4)). In the event of a failure to do so, the local authority can carry out the work and recover the cost from the landowner (s. 146(3)).

Highway authorities have powers under s. 27 of the Countryside Act 1968 in relation to signposts for footpaths, bridleways and BOATs. They can, after consultation with the landowner, put up and maintain signposts along these highways (s. 27(1)); and they must use their power to put up sufficient signs to assist a person not familiar with the locality to follow the route of the highway (s. 27(4)). Others may put up signposts with the consent of the highway authority (s. 27(5)). There is a specific duty on the highway authority to put up a sign at the point where the footpath, bridleway or BOAT leaves a metalled road, showing, "so far as the highway authority consider convenient and appropriate", where the highway leads, and the distance. 5-70

Under s. 62 of the Wildlife and Countryside Act 1981, local authorities may appoint one or more persons to act as wardens in relation to footpaths, bridleways and BOATs, for the purpose of advising and assisting the public. Wardens can provide information about the use of these public rights of way and act as a reference point for information about problems such as obstruction or a lack of repair. 5-71

Protecting highways

Highway authorities have a general duty under s. 130 of the Highways Act 1980, which extends to all the highways (whether or not they are maintainable at the public expense) in its area. By s. 130(1): 5-72

> "It is the duty of the highway authority to assert and protect the rights of the public to the use and enjoyment of any highway for which they are the highway authority, including any roadside waste which forms part of it."

"Roadside waste" includes grass verges and other small pieces of land next to the highway which form part of it. The section goes on to require highway authorities to prevent obstruction and

See 2-61 on the question of what land forms part of a highway.

encroachment on highways. They can do this by prosecuting people who commit offences relating to highways, and also by using the powers they have been given.

See 5-74 and 5-87 onwards for these offences and powers.

5-73 The law is not concerned solely with highways: some of the legislation mentioned in the following paragraphs also applies to "streets". This term covers roads, lanes, footpaths etc, whether or not they are highways and (if so) whether or not they are maintainable at the public expense. The following paragraphs consider some offences and some of the powers which highway authorities have. These are overlapping categories, since sometimes there is an offence and a power in relation to the same problem.

See 5-63 for the meaning of "street" in the Highways Act 1980.

Offences

5-74 Some of these offences are created by the Highways Act 1980, and some by other Acts. The aim of the law is to safeguard the highway itself, and prevent it from being obstructed or damaged, and to protect members of the public when using the highway.

For other offences which may be relevant to highways, see 11-85 on litter, and 11-57 on criminal damage.

5-75 *The Highways Act 1980* Perhaps the most important offence is the offence of obstruction, under s. 137. A person is guilty of an offence if he "without lawful authority or excuse, in any way wilfully obstructs the free passage along a highway". A person using the highway may often get in the way of others; and whether an offence is committed depends upon what is a reasonable use of the highway. Obstructions which are minor, or last only for a short space of time, do not necessarily amount to an offence.

5-76 It is also an offence under s. 22 of the Road Traffic Act 1988 to leave a vehicle or trailer is such a position as to involve injury or danger to other road users.

5-77 Other specific offences include:

- Damaging a highway (which includes digging a ditch or excavation, removing soil or turf, depositing anything on the highway so as to damage it, or lighting a fire within 50 feet from

In the case of *Torbay Borough Council v. Cross* (1995) a shop display covered about 5% of a wide pedestrianised street, and so did not block the whole of the highway. The question was whether this was an offence.
The court decided that it was. The obstruction was not so small that it could be disregarded, and it was unreasonable.

Obstructing the highway

the centre of a carriageway so as to damage the highway) (s. 131).

◆ Making unauthorised marks on a highway, or any tree or structure in the highway (s. 132). The highway authority has power to remove any unauthorised marks.

◆ Erecting a building, or planting a hedge in a carriageway (s. 138).

◆ Planting a tree or shrub within 15 feet of the centre of a made-up carriageway and failing to remove it when given notice to do so by the highway authority (s. 141). (A "made up carriageway" is one which has been metalled or otherwise surfaced so that it is suitable for vehicles (s. 329(1)). This offence could cover planting on land adjoining highway, if the carriageway was narrow. But an offence (the maximum punishment being a level 1 fine on the standard scale) is committed only if occupier of the land fails to remove the tree or shrub when required to do so.

See 1-23 for the standard levels of fines.

◆ Without lawful authority, depositing things on a made-up carriageway, including rubbish and booths and stalls for trading (s. 148).

See also 5-87 for local authorities' power to regulate street trading. Trading under a licence from the local authority is lawful, and so not an offence under s. 148.

◆ Depositing anything on a highway so as to injure or endanger a user; lighting a fire on a carriageway, or discharging a firearm or firework within 50 feet of the centre of a carriageway, so as to injure, interrupt or endanger a user; playing football or any other game on a highway to the annoyance of a user; allowing

See 1-27 for the meaning of "premises".

dirt or filth to flow on to a highway from adjoining premises (s. 161).

- Lighting a fire on land so as to injure, interrupt or endanger a user of a carriageway (s. 161A).

- Putting up scaffolding, or any other structure which obstructs the highway, without a licence from the highway authority (s. 169). Highway authorities are entitled to charge for granting a licence, under the Local Authorities (Transport) Charges Regulations 1998 (which cover a range of other activities as well).

- Mixing mortar, or any other substance which is likely to stick to the surface or solidify in drains (s. 170).

5-78 The Highways Act 1980 also contains provisions which deal with skips on highways. Under s. 137, the permission of the highway authority is required if a skip is to be deposited in a highway. The authority can grant permission either unconditionally or subject to conditions relating to the siting, size, marking of the skip and other matters. It is an offence to deposit a skip in a highway without permission. Skips must always be lit during the hours of darkness, must be marked with the name of the owner, and his telephone number or address, and must be removed as soon as is practicable after being filled; and any conditions imposed by the highway authority must be complied with. Failure to comply with these requirements is an offence. In each case, the maximum fine is level 3 on the standard scale. Regulations made by the DETR, The Builders' Skips (Markings) Regulations 1984, deal with the marking of skips.

5-79 The highway authority, or a police officer, may remove or reposition a skip, or may direct the owner of the skip to do so, under s. 140 of the Highways Act 1980. For the purposes of ss. 139 and 140, a person hiring a skip is not regarded as the "owner" unless he hires it for a month or more. So if a householder hires a skip for (say) a week, it is the firm supplying the skip which is the owner, and whose name must appear on the skip.

The highway authority can charge for allowing a skip to be placed on a highway: see 5-77.

5-80 *Other legislation* Apart from the Highways Act 1980, there are offences relating to highways in older legislation, which is still in force. The Highway Act 1835 contains several offences which are still in force. Under s. 72, it is an offence to ride a horse on a footpath by the side of a road, or to lead or drive horses, cattle, sheep etc along such a footpath, or to tether horses and certain other animals on a highway. The maximum fine is level 3 on the standard scale. Under s. 78, there is a range of minor offences, including riding or driving "furiously", for which the maximum fine is level 1. The Town Police Clauses Act 1847 contains, in s. 28, a long list of activities which may cause annoyance or danger to residents, or users of a street, and which are made offences. These include throwing stones or other missiles, wilfully ringing doorbells or knocking on doors, flying kites, making slides in the ice or snow, fixing or placing flower-pots, boxes or other heavy objects in upper windows without making sure that they are guarded from being "blown down", throwing things into the street from a building (apart from snow, thrown so as not to fall on persons using the street). The maximum fine is level 3 on the standard scale, or an offender may be sentenced to a maximum of 14 days in prison. There is a similar list in s. 54 of the Metropolitan Police Act 1839, which applies within the metropolitan police district.

5-81 *Offences relating to footpaths and bridleways* The Highways Act 1980 was amended by the Rights of Way Act 1990, so as to provide extra protection for footpaths and bridleways. It is an offence, under s. 131A, for any person, without lawful authority, to disturb the surface of a footpath, bridleway or other highway which is a carriageway (but not a made-up carriageway) "so as to render it inconvenient for the exercise of the public right of way". A "made up carriageway" is one "which has been metalled or in any other way provided with a surface suitable for the passage of vehicles" (s. 329). The offence (which can be committed by the owner of the land or any other person) carries a fine not exceeding level 3 on the standard scale. Only the highway authority or other local authority can prosecute for the offence; and they are under a special duty to ensure that "where it is desirable in the public interest such proceedings are brought"—in other words, they cannot simply ignore s. 131A.

See 5-77 for the meaning of "made-up carriageway".

5-82 The Highways Act, as amended by the Rights of Way Act, also lays down rules for the ploughing or other disturbance of a footpath or bridleway on agricultural land. By s. 134, if the occupier of a field or enclosure which consists of agricultural land, "in accordance with the rules of good husbandry" wishes to plough or otherwise disturb the surface, and if it is not reasonably convenient to avoid disturbing the surface of the path or bridleway, the public right of way is deemed to be subject to the right to plough or otherwise disturb the surface (s. 134(1)). Disturbing the surface thus becomes lawful and is not an offence under s. 131A. But the surface of the footpath or bridleway must be made good afterwards, to the "minimum width", which is:

- For a footpath, 1 metre.
- For a bridleway, 2 metres.
- For any other highway, 3 metres.

The surface must be made good within the "relevant period", which is 14 days where the occupier is sowing a particular crop, or 24 hours in all other cases (s. 134(7)); though the period may be extended by up to 28 days (s. 134(8)). The occupier of the land must also make clear the line of the path on the ground, so that it is clear to members of the public wishing to use it. Otherwise, they might accidentally stray from the path and be liable for trespassing.

5-83 "Agriculture"—which is relevant to the meaning of "agricultural land"—has a wide definition in the Highways Act, and includes horticulture, fruit growing, market gardening, etc, and woodlands where ancillary (s. 329(1)). The right to disturb footpaths and bridleways does not apply to "field-edge paths", i. e. paths which follow the edges or headlands of a field or enclosure (s. 329(1)). Failure to make good the footpath of bridleway is an offence which carries a fine of up to level 3 on the standard scale.

5-84 Section 134 does not apply to an "excavation or engineering operation" on agricultural land, for which there are separate rules in s. 135. The landowner must apply to the highway authority for an order allowing him to disturb the surface of a footpath or bridleway for a period not exceeding 3 months (s. 135(1)). The path must be diverted temporarily, or steps must be taken to ensure that it remains open (s. 135(2)). If the landowner does not make good the path within the period allowed, he commits an offence under s. 131A; and it is also an offence under s. 135 to fail to comply with conditions laid down by the highway authority.

By s. 59 of the Wildlife and Countryside Act 1981, it is an offence to keep a bull on land crossed by a public right of way. The prohibition does not apply to bulls under 10 months old, and those which are not of a "recognised dairy breed", the breeds being listed in the section. The maximum fine for the offence is level 3 on the standard scale. 5-85

Landowners tempted to put up notices designed to deter people from using a public path may be prosecuted under s. 57 of the National Parks and Access to the Countryside Act 1949. The offence consists of putting up a notice which contains a false or misleading statement. The maximum fine is level 1 on the standard scale. When a fine is imposed, the court may also order the landowner to remove the notice, in which case there is an additional fine of £2 for failing to remove the notice. 5-86

See 12-2 for sources on these offences.

Powers of local authorities

Local authorities have a wide range of powers which they can use in relation to highways (and, often, in relation to other roads). Some are powers given by the Highways Act 1980, some by other Acts. The following are examples: 5-87

- Carrying out work of various sorts on highways; for example widening a highway, or installing street lighting (ss. 72 and 97 of the Highways Act 1980).

- Stopping up and diverting highways. A highway authority can also stop up a private access to a highway, if it is dangerous (s. 124).

See 5-53 onwards for the meaning of "stopping up" and diverting highways.

✠ See 10-26 for dangerous and overhanging trees.

◆ Dealing with dangerous and overhanging trees (s. 154) ✠.

◆ Serving notice on a person who has deposited something on the highway, requiring them to remove it (s. 149).

✠ See 1-74 on administrative law.

◆ Removing obstructions caused by snow, or the falling down of banks, or other causes (s. 150). (This is a *duty*, not just a power ✠.)

The duty to remove an obstruction

In the case of *Worcesterhire County Council v. Newman* (1974) there was a complaint that some footpaths were blocked by overgrown hedges and barbed wire. One question which arose was whether the County Council was under a duty to remove the obstruction, as a result of a requirement in the Highways Act 1959 which was similar to s. 150 in the 1980 Act.

The court decided that there was no duty here: the duty applied only to snow, collapsed banks and obstructions of a similar nature, which meant sudden, natural occurrences, which needed an immediate response. An overgrown hedge did not fall into this category.

◆ Constructing a "crossover", to give access across a verge or footway (s. 184).

◆ Regulating street trading under Part III of Schedule 4 to the Local Government (Miscellaneous Provisions) Act 1982.

◆ Taking "traffic calming" measures, under ss. 90A –91. These include road humps. There are regulations, the Highways (Road Humps) (Local Inquiries) Regulations 1986 and the Highways (Road Humps) Regulations 1999, on this topic.

◆ Making "traffic regulation orders", under the Road Traffic Regulation Act 1984, for example to make roads one-way, or limit the classes of traffic which can use them. There is a special power under s. 29 of the Act to make orders prohibiting traffic on roads to be used as playgrounds. These orders can be used in urban areas, to turn a quiet residential road into a playground, where there are no convenient playgrounds nearby. Local authorities can then make byelaws for the use of the road as a playground (s. 31).

See 12-2 and 12-18 for sources on local authority powers in relation to highways.

Assessment

5-88 Landowners may be concerned about a road or other highway which passes their property and which they use for access. In this respect the law protects the interests of landowners well: there are ample remedies against obstruction of the highway, and damage to it and other forms of abuse of it. If problems arise, they should be raised with the local authority, so that they can consider bringing a prosecution or using their powers. As is very often the case, whether the local authority take action is a matter for their discretion; though in one respect—obstructions such a snow or collapsed banks—they have a duty to take action.

Including dangers caused to users by landowners: see 4-25 onwards.

5-89 A highway is in effect a neighbour; and just as the law of nuisance requires landowners to put up with a certain amount of disturbance from other neighbours, so also the needs of highways users have to be balanced against the wishes of landowners whose property adjoins the road to enjoy as much peace and quiet as possible. Such things as street trading, and the positioning of skips in the highway, may be lawful; and landowners may therefore have to put up with them even though they cause a degree of annoyance and inconvenience.

But see 4-34 onwards for controls over noise.

5-90 Landowners may find that their land is subject to a public right of way—particularly a footpath or bridleway. They may perhaps be forgiven for thinking that there is a certain unfairness in the situation: many of these highways were created long ago, because they were needed by the inhabitants of the area, and use would have been limited. Yet now they are available for unlimited recreational use by members of the public, including those who arrive by car from some distance away. Nonetheless, these highways enjoy as

See 10-68 for a similar process relating to common land.

much or more legal protection than public roads, and landowners must accept that the existence of a highway is a burden to which their land is subject. In some circumstances it may be possible to stop up or divert a footpath or bridleway, though the scope for this is limited.

5-91 One step which landowners can take is to prevent the unintended creation of highways by the process of dedication and acceptance. If a landowner is clear that she wishes to create a public right of way for some reason, the wise course will be to use one of the statutory procedures, under which the highway authority assume responsibility for maintenance. Otherwise, the steps explained above should be taken, to avoid the creation of a public right of way.

Chapter 6

Easements

Introduction

The owner of a piece of land may find that she needs to make some limited use of a nearby piece of land in order to enjoy her own land. For example, she may need to cross neighbouring land in order to get to her land. Mere permission from the neighbour (legally speaking, a "licence" to cross the neighbour's land) may be all that is necessary if the need is temporary. But if there is a need for a permanent right of way, something more than permission is required—namely, an arrangement which is not just a personal matter between the two landowners but which can continue despite a change of ownership of either or both pieces of land, and which can last indefinitely. For this purpose, the law provides a special means of achieving the desired result, namely an easement. 6-0

See 1-49 onwards for licences.

An easement is a piece of abstract legal property—in effect, just a right. It cannot exist on its own, but must always be attached (in legal language "annexed" or "appurtenant") to a piece of land, which has the benefit of it. Suppose that one landowner has an easement giving him a right of way over a neighbour's land. The easement is regarded as attached to the first landowner's land. It cannot exist separately from the land; while it exists, it will change hands when the land itself changes hands—there is no question of it being sold separately. The first land has the benefit of the right of way; the neighbour's land is said to be subject to, or burdened with, the right of way. Lawyers also call land with the benefit of an easement the "dominant" land, and land subject to an easement the "servient" land. 6-1

An easement The track and the field are in the same ownership as The Farm. There is no *public* right of way over the track, but the house and garden known as Rose Cottage have a private right of way over the track (an easement) in order to gain access to a garage. Rose Cottage is the dominant land, and has the benefit of the easement. The track is the servient land, and is subject to the easement.

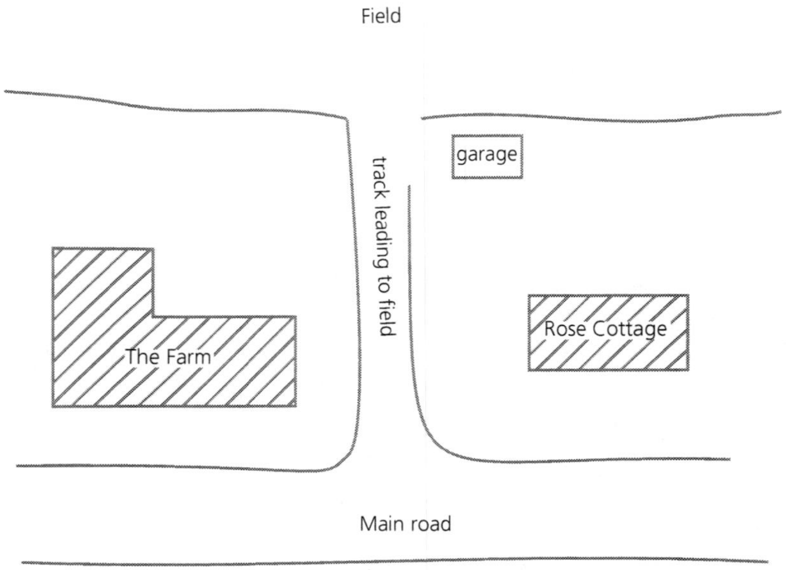

6-2 It is common for land to have the benefit of, or to be subject to the burden of, one or more easements. These rights are important to a landowner. They may enhance his land by allowing him to make some use of nearby land. They may limit the possible use of his land, and so restrict its value; though this will depend upon the circumstances. A right of way (for example) over land which is already in use as a road is unlikely to lessen the value of the land, so long as the road remains in existence. But if there is a desire to redevelop the whole site, and remove the road, the existence of the right of way may pose real problems.

See 1-10 for the meaning of "common law".

See 1-54 onwards for land registration generally; also 6-27 onwards for registration of easements.

6-3 Much of the law on easements is common law—law laid down by the courts in deciding cases. But some legislation is also relevant, including the Prescription Act 1832 and the legislation which deals with land registration. All of the law explained in this chapter is civil law: this is not an area in which the criminal law has intervened directly.

Requirements for an easement

6-4 The law requires that certain conditions be fulfilled if a right is to be recognised as an easement. These are essentially that:

- There are two pieces of land, nearby (not necessarily adjoining) in separate ownership, one with the benefit of the easement and the other subject to it.
- The right granted must relate to the use of the land which has the benefit of it. If, for example, Alice runs a tea shop, the right to put a sign on neighbouring land saying "Alice's Tea Shop →" could be an easement, since the sign relates to the use of Alice's land. But the right to put *any* advertisement or notice on neighbouring land could not be an easement.
- The right must be of the sort which the law recognises as an easement.

In the case of *Palmer v. Bowman, The Times* 10 November 1999, there was a dispute about the natural drainage of rain water from one piece of land on to another, lower, piece. The owners of the first piece claimed that there was an easement, in the form of a right for rain water to run down on to the other land.
The court decided that this was not a right which could exist as an easement, and in any event there was no need for such a right—the owners of the lower land could not complain about rain water flowing on to the land from higher ground. [But see also 4-13 for the position where water leaks on to neighbouring land from (say) a pipe.]

A right which cannot be an easement

6-5 The last point merely begs the question; but the law will not recognise as an easement an arrangement which is too vague, or which interferes too much with the land subject to it. The use made of the land must be limited, so that the land remains valuable to the owner. This is so (for example) in relation to a right of way across a field: the use being made of the field by someone exercising the right of way is limited, and the field remains valuable to the owner. So the right can exist as an easement. The same is true of the example

See particularly 6-39 on storing things on land as an easement.

given above relating to a sign. With one exception, an easement cannot require the owner who is subject to it to spend money ꙮ

ꙮ See 6-54 on fencing easements.

Scope of easements

6-6 Many different sorts of use of land can be the subject of easements. The only limitation is that the rules explained above must be complied with. No complete list of possible easements can ever be given, though the easements mentioned in this chapter include all the most common sorts ꙮ The use of land which is allowed by the easement may be occasional or regular, and may be essential to the land which has the benefit of the easement, or merely convenient. The easement may have been created in order for the land to be developed (which is often the case with rights of way) or it may have been created since then, to improve the usefulness of the land in some way.

ꙮ See 6-33 onwards

6-7 Easements generally take two rather different forms. Most allow the owner of the land which has the benefit of the easement to go on to the land subject to the easement, for a particular purpose, or to put things on it. The easement makes the use of the neighbouring land lawful, and so not a trespass. Some, however, allow the owner of the land which has the benefit of the easement to insist that no change be made to it in a particular respect. This is true of rights to light: the dominant owner can insist that nothing be built on the servient land in such a way as to obstruct his right to light ꙮ Similarly, a right of support enables the dominant owner to insist that the servient owner does not demolish buildings, or carry out excavations, in such a way as to endanger his land or the buildings on it ꙮ

ꙮ See 6-43 onwards for rights to light.

ꙮ See 6-47 onwards for easements of support.

6-8 Not all easements fit neatly into these categories, however. The right to have fences maintained by a neighbour is recognised by the law as an easement (though an unusual one). A right to take water from land can also be an easement, though taking other things from land (such as game and minerals) is a different sort of right ꙮ

ꙮ See 6-54 for fencing, 6-46 for water, and 7-39 onwards for sporting and other rights.

Easements and other arrangements

6-9

To put them in context, easements can be contrasted with other sorts of arrangement for the use of land.

- A licence—that is, permission to use land. Permission can be given for any type of use of land, including use which could form the subject of an easement. It may be possible to pass on the benefit of the licence (if the person giving it has agreed that it can be passed on). But the licence will not generally continue when the land subject to it is transferred to a new owner. A licence is thus not a reliable long-term arrangement.

- A restrictive covenant. A restrictive covenant is an undertaking in a deed, given by the owner of one piece of land to the owner of another. Provided it is negative in its effect (an undertaking *not* to do something) it will generally be binding on later owners of the two pieces of land.

See 7-13 onwards for the meaning of "restrictive covenant".

- The right to obtain access to neighbouring land, for maintenance or repair, under the Access to Neighbouring Land Act 1992 or the Party Wall etc Act 1996.

See 7-2 onwards and 2-23 onwards for these two Acts.

- The right to enter land, and to install and maintain pipes, cables, etc, which the privatised utility companies enjoy under special legislation. (Such rights are sometimes known as "wayleaves".) Electricity companies operate under the Electricity Act 1989, gas companies under the Gas Act 1986, water companies under the Water Industry Act 1991, and cable TV and telephone companies under the Telecommunications Act 1984.

See 11-103 for statutory undertakers and their powers.

- Rights which apply to the public at large, including the public's right to use a highway, and to have access to some sorts of land, including commons, for recreation.

See 5-7 for the public's right to use a highway and 10-79 onwards for public rights of access to land.

See 8-9 for the rights of lessees and tenants.

- A lease or tenancy, which gives the lessee or tenant *exclusive* use of the land in question.

Creating easements: deliberately

See 1-17 onwards for the meaning of legal and equitable rights.

See 1-33 for this rule; and 1-35 for the interpretation of deeds.

Though it may be protected by entering it on the Land Register: see 1-61 onwards for the registration of minor interests.

6-10 Easements can be either legal or equitable in nature. The main difference is that a legal easement is enforceable against anyone who buys the land subject to the easement, but an equitable easement is enforceable against the person who buys the land only if she knew about the easement at the time of the sale. A landowner who wishes to obtain an easement over neighbouring land will want it to be legal in nature, so that he can be sure it will always be enforceable. Since the law puts a legal easement in the same class as land itself, under s. 1 of the Law of Property Act 1925, a deed is necessary to create the easement. In order for the easement to be legal it must also last indefinitely, or be for a fixed period. (A lease of a flat or maisonette can thus have easements over neighbouring land which last as long as the lease itself.)

6-11 If these requirements are not complied with (that is, if the easement is not created by means of a deed, or does not last either indefinitely or for a fixed period) then it will be equitable and not necessarily enforceable against successive owners of the land which is subject to the easement.

6-12 The deed creating an easement will not necessarily use the word "easement", but will make clear that the right conferred is an easement, rather than an arrangement which is personal to the landowners concerned, by saying that it will be attached to the land having the benefit of it. Alternatively, the deed may say that the right is to continue for the benefit of later owners of that land. In this way the deed makes it clear that the right granted is not just a personal arrangement between the parties to the deed, but is intended to create a permanent or long-term right, which will apply to later owners of the two pieces of land.

6-13 The deed will define carefully the extent of the use conferred. A map or plan is generally used to show what land has the benefit of the easement and what land is subject to it. This will not necessarily be all of the land included in the title: a landowner who owns a house and driveway might grant a right of way over the driveway , for the benefit of his neighbour's land; in which case only the drive is subject to the easement. There may be conditions, for example that the right can be enjoyed only so long as a payment is made. A right of way may thus be subject to the payment of a contribution towards the cost of upkeep of the road or path. There may be circumstances in which the right will come to an end; for example, the deed may say that the easement will cease if the land which has the benefit of it is split into separate plots. In the event of a dispute the precise meaning of the deed may have to be considered by the court.

See 7-16 on enforcing a right to payment in such circumstances.

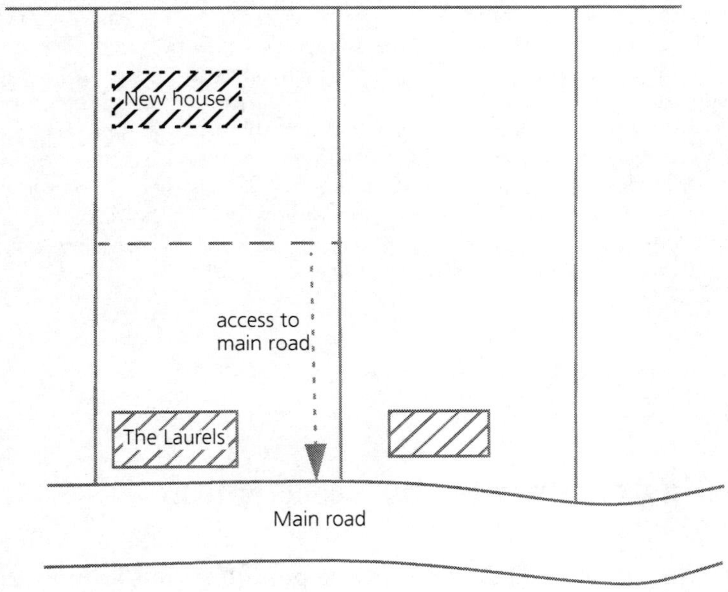

An implied easement
If the owner of "The Laurels" sells off the back part of the garden, so that a new house can be built, the buyer of the land will wish to have a right of way, in the form of an easement, to gain access to the highway. Even if no right of way is expressly granted, there will be an implied right of way—because without a right of way, the land sold off is useless to the buyer.

6-14

An easement can also be created by a transfer of land, even though nothing is said in the deed which makes the transfer, if the person selling the land owns other land. An implied easement may be created if it is necessary for an easement to exist in order for the land sold to be of any use. This might occur if the land sold had no access except over land being retained by the person selling—for example, in the case of "backland" development. An easement may also be implied if it is clear from the circumstances that the parties intended there to be one. The same result may follow if some use has been made, by the occupier of the land sold, of the land retained, for example, a right of way across it. While the land is all in the same ownership an easement can't exist. But when the land is sold, the rule is that an easement may arise if this is necessary for the reasonable enjoyment of the land sold, and if the use was "continuous and apparent". Finally, s. 62 of the Law of Property Act 1925 can create an easement where part of a piece of land is sold off.

See 6-4: there must be two pieces of land in separate ownership.

See 1-41 for the effect of s. 62.

An implied easement

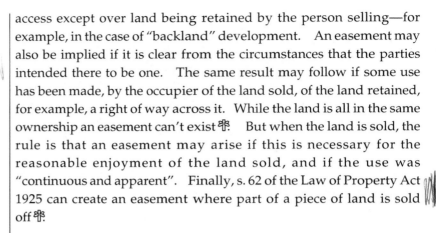

Millman v. Ellis (1996) concerned a large house and surrounding land. The house and some of the land was sold. There was a right of way over a drive leading to the highway. At the end of the drive was an area shaped like a lay-by, which was not expressed to be subject to the right of way granted when the house was sold, but which had been used by drivers in coming and going. The new owner of the house claimed the right to use the lay-by, on the ground that there was an implied right of way over it, though nothing was said in the deed transferring the land.

The court decided that there was indeed such a right. The lay-by had been used by vehicles for some years, and was surfaced in the same way as the drive, so the use had been "continuous and apparent"; it was also reasonably necessary, since using it made the turning safer for vehicles.

Creating easements: by prescription

6-15 Easements can be created by use over a period of time, without any agreement from the owner of the land subject to the use, the legal name for this process being "prescription". This is a good example of the creativity of the law. It may seem odd that the law creates rights when the owners of the land did not intend to do so, and that the law "rewards" trespassing by eventually giving the trespasser a right, so that he can continue doing lawfully what he has been doing unlawfully. The explanation may be partly that these rules are very ancient, and date back to a time when many people were uneducated and unable to arrange their own affairs, so that the courts felt a need to intervene by creating such rights. It may be partly that it makes sense for the law to recognise the existing state of affairs. If, for example, a landowner has been acting as though he had a right of way across neighbouring land, and this has continued for long enough, it is sensible for the law to say that he actually has that right.

6-16 The rules for creating easements by prescription resemble those applicable to highways, and the creation of *public* rights of way by dedication and acceptance. But the two processes are different, and should not be confused. An easement created by prescription is legally just as valid as one created by deed, and is attached to the land having the benefit of it in the same way. However, the process is more likely to give rise to disputes, since there may be disagreements about whether the necessary use has actually taken place to create the right—and, if it has, the exact scope of the right created.

See 5-22 onwards for the meaning of "dedication and acceptance".

See 6-25 on this question.

6-17 *Different sorts of prescription* There are no less than three differents types of prescription, though the three sets of rules have much in common. The first, known as common law prescription, depends upon the proposition that use of land has been taking place since 1189. It does not apply if it can be shown that the use cannot go back that far. For example, if a right of way is said to have arisen over a track, it may be possible to show that the track dates from some time after 1189, and that this sort of prescription cannot apply. Such arguments will very often succeed, because of changes to the landscape over the centuries, and so it will be rare for an easement to be created by this sort of prescription. Nothing further is said here about this sort of prescription.

6-18 The two other sorts of prescription are:

- Prescription under the Prescription Act 1832.

- The legal fiction that there has been a "lost modern grant".

The second sort depends upon a fiction, devised by the courts, that an easement has been granted by deed in modern times, and use has

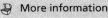

been taking place in accordance with the deed, but that the deed has been lost. The fiction is just that: the argument cannot be defeated by showing that there was in fact no deed. Since the two sets of rules are similar, they can be considered together.

6-19 *The use required* Both sorts of prescription require that there has been use "as of right"; in other words, that the persons using the land have acted as though they had the right to do so. If it is said (for example) that a right of way has arisen by prescription, the landowner who claims to have the benefit of the right must show that he and others visiting his land have passed to and fro, across neighbouring land, as though they had the right to do so. They must not do so secretly, so that the owner of the neighbouring land has no chance to object. They must not do so by force or the threat of force, or by permission of the neighbouring landowner, since this would mean they were not acting "as of right".

Use "as of right"

In the case of *Mills v. Silver* (1991) the owners of a hill farm had, between 1922 and 1981, used a track running across another hill farm, for access. The owners of the latter farm never gave express permission for the use of their land, but knew about it and tolerated it. There was little use after 1981, until the first farm changed hands.

The new owners then put down about 700 tonnes of stone, so as to make the track usable in all weathers. This led to a dispute about whether a right of way had arisen by prescription and whether there was a right to put down the stone

The court decided that a prescriptive right of way had arisen, but that there was no right to put down the stone. It was open to the owners of the farm with the benefit of the right of way to maintain the track, but not to improve it. [See 6-38 on repairs to paths and roads.]

See 1-50 for implied licences.

6-20 Permission may be specifically given, by the owner of land, or it may be implied. It will be implied if a landowner has not said in so many words that permission is granted, but his words and behaviour give the impression that permission is granted. Difficulties may arise if use takes place, and the owner of the land affected knows about it, but takes no action to stop it. Does this mean that he is impliedly consenting, so that the use is not "as of right", and no easement can be created? Or is the correct view that there is no implied permission, and the use is "as of right", so that an easement will arise after the necessary period of use? The courts seem to prefer the latter approach.

6-21 Finally, the use being made of neighbouring land cannot give rise to an easement if it was not just a trespass but also a criminal offence. This rule is a matter of policy by the courts: it is seen as acceptable that a person may benefit from committing civil wrongs, but not from committing criminal offences.

6-22 For the creation of a prescriptive easement, there must generally be a minimum of 20 years' use. The use may be begun by one owner of the land, and continued by later owners. However several qualifications must be made to this statement. The 20-year period is laid down by the Prescription Act 1832, s. 2, for prescription under the Act. For the purposes of the prescription by lost modern grant, a 20-year period of use is not a strict requirement. The courts will tend to require the same period, but may in some cases accept a shorter one. Furthermore, the Prescription Act says that the 20 years must run right up to the time when legal proceedings are started to prove the right. If there is a "gap", before proceedings are started, an easement cannot be established under the Act. This particular rule does not apply to prescription by means of a "lost modern grant."

In *Hanning v. Top Deck Travel Group Ltd* (1993) there was a claim that a right of way had arisen, by prescription, over a track which led across Horsell Common to a farm. The track had been used by buses, which were taken to the farm for maintenance and repair. Whether a right had arisen was disputed by the trustees of Horsell Common.

The court decided that no right of way could arise by prescription, because it was an offence under s. 193 of the Law of Property Act 1925 to drive a motor vehicle on a common without lawful authority, and an easement could not arise by prescription if the use of the land had been an offence. [See 10-70 for the public's right of access to common land under s. 193.]

Prescription and criminal offences

6-23 The 20 years' use "as of right" must in any event be uninterrupted. If the owner of the land in question grants permission, this will interrupt the use, because it will not then be "as of right". The use will also be interrupted if the user is asked to stop, and does so; or if he is forced to stop by legal action. But in order to count under the Prescription Act, the interruption must last for at least a year. What is a sufficient interruption for the purposes of a claim by virtue of a claim of lost modern grant will be matter of fact.

6-24 Although the period is generally 20 years, the Prescription Act 1832 adds a further complication: an easement can generally arise after 40 years' use even though oral permission was given before the 40 years started. But if permission in writing is given before the 40 years, or if any permission is given during the 40 years, no easement can arise.

The exception is rights to light: see 6-43.

6-25 When an easement arises by prescription, the nature of the right acquired is usually determined by the use which has taken place. If, for example, one landowner establishes a right of way by walking over his neighbour's land, then the right of way is for pedestrians only: driving a car over the land would not be within the right acquired, and so would be a trespass. The neighbour could take legal action to stop such use.

See 3-29 onwards on injunctions.

Preventing prescriptive easements

6-26 A landowner who sees that some use is being made of his property by a neighbour, and wishes to make sure that no easement can arise (whether or not he is content for the use to continue) has a number of ways of doing this. He can:

- Give permission in writing for the use to continue. If there has not already been 20 years of use "as of right", no amount of further use can give rise to an easement, because it will not be use "as of right".

It will be wise for the landowner to make clear that permission may be withdrawn at any time: see 1-49 onwards for licences.

- Interrupt the use. For the purposes of the Prescription Act 1832 the interruption must be for at least a year and the person claiming the right must "submit" or "acquiesce" to it (s. 4).

- Stop the use altogether—if necessary, by taking legal action to obtain an injunction.

Easements and the Land Register

6-27 The rule is that easements which are legal in nature do not have to be shown on the Land Register in order to be valid, because they are overriding interests in land. Their legal nature means that an easement is effective even against a person who is unaware of it when he buys land subject to it. However a legal easement can be shown on the Land Register and this is often done as a matter of convenience (Land Registration Act 1925, s. 70(3)). The Land Register shows the easement both in relation to the land which has the benefit of it and the land which is subject to it. The Register does not necessarily give all the information about the easement: it may refer to the deed which created the easement for full details.

See 1-59 for the meaning of "overriding interest".

6-28 Before entering an easement on the Land Register, the Land Registry is required by the Land Registration Rules 1925 to give notice to the landowner whose land would be subject to the easement. The landowner then has the opportunity to comment, which is particularly important if is claimed that an easement has been acquired by prescription but there is a dispute about it.

6-29 An equitable easement cannot be shown on the Register in the same way as a legal easement. But it can be entered on the Register as a minor interest, and the purpose of the entry is to alert any purchaser of the land to the existence of the right. He cannot then escape the effect of the easement on the ground that he bought the land in good faith, paid value for it, and had no notice of it.

See 1-61 onwards for the meaning of "minor interest", and protection of minor interests on the Land Register.

See 12-12 for sources on easements generally.

Interfering with easements

6-30 Interfering with an easement is a civil wrong; namely a nuisance. It fits into this category, because an easement is technically land, and because nuisance is the tort which allows landowners to take action where there has been an interference with their right to enjoy their land. In the case of a right of way, obstructing the road or path so as to make it more difficult—or impossible—to pass to and fro would be a nuisance. The culprit might be the owner of the land subject to

See 3-29 onwards for injunctions.

the easement, but legal action can equally be taken against anyone else interfering with the right. If necessary, the court could grant an injunction to prevent further interference.

Interfering with an easement

In the case of *Groves v. Minor* (1997) there was a dispute about a right of way over a lane in which both Mr Groves and Mr Minor lived. Mr Groves had put up a storm porch, on a raised shelf, along the side of his house. Mr Minor said that the storm porch interfered with his right of way along the lane.

The court found that the shelf was not subject to the right of way, that the lane was wide enough for vehicles to pass, and the construction of the storm porch did not interfere with the right of way.

Ending easements

See 6-4 for this rule.

6-31 An easement will come to an end if the land with the benefit of it, and the land subject to it, come into the same ownership, because an easement cannot exist in such circumstances. An easement can also be ended—or varied—in the same way that it can be created, that is by means of a deed made by the current owners of the two pieces of land. Finally, an easement can be abandoned by the landowner whose land has the benefit of it. The courts, however, are not easily persuaded that an easement has been abandoned. Lack of use over a long period is not in itself enough to show that the easement has been abandoned. But if the owner of the land with the benefit of the easement takes some step which shows that he never intends to use it again, then the court may be prepared to conclude that the easement has been abandoned and has ceased to exist. For example, if a landowner has a right of way over a path leading from his property across neighbouring land, and builds across the line of the path, this would seem to indicate that he has no intention to use the right of way in the future and so has abandoned the right of way.

The case of *Benn v. Hardinge* (1992) concerned a track over which a right of way had been created, in 1818, for the benefit of a farm near Hailsham, East Sussex. The track gave access to a field, but had never been used for this purpose since there was alternative access. When the farmer tried to start using the track, to gain access to the field, the owners objected.

The court decided that the lack of use for some 175 years did not mean that the right of way had been abandoned. The right still existed, and the farmer was entitled to use it for access.

Abandoning an easement

6-32 It is odd that the law does not regard long disuse as bringing an easement to an end, given that use for a relatively short period can have the effect of creating one.

See 6-15 onwards for prescription.

Some common easements

6-33 *Rights of way* Private rights of way may be needed in many situations where land does not have access from the highway, or where an additional access in the form of a road or path is needed over neighbouring land. Such rights may be found, for example, in a private road, where a pair of houses shares a driveway, or where a terrace of houses has an alley or path giving access to back gardens. Rights of way may be vital in order for development to take place. Sometimes the right is needed over a small strip of land—hence the term "ransom strip", since the owner can demand his own price for granting the necessary right of way, unless the developer has legal powers enabling it to acquire land or rights over land compulsorily.

See 5-7 onwards for the public's right to use a highway.

See 11-100 for compulsory purchase of land.

6-34 An easement in the form of a right of way can be granted in general terms, so that it allows any type or amount of traffic, regardless of the use of the land which has the benefit of the right. More usually, the deed granting the right will be subject to conditions. The conditions may define the amount of use permitted, and this may be limited to certain sorts of traffic (for example, noncommercial traffic only). Or the deed may limit the width of the path or road, and so in effect prevent certain sorts of traffic from using it.

See 6-13 for the use of maps and plans in defining easements.

6-35 The deed may also—or instead—limit the right of way by reference to the use being made of the land which has the benefit of the right of way. For example, the right of way may be expressed so that it applies only where the land with the benefit of it is in residential use, or (more narrowly) only when it is used as a single dwelling. If the use of the land changes, then the right of way ceases, and further use of the road or path is a trespass, for which legal action can be taken. Rights of way granted in modern times are very likely to be subject to carefully-devised limitations of this sort. The deed is likely to define, usually by means of a plan, the land subject to the right.

See 3-29 onwards for injunctions.

6-36 A right of way (like other easements) may be restricted in that it is expressed not to be "severable". This means that the right exists only so long as the land with the benefit of it remains as one plot. The land cannot be split into separate plots, each of which has the benefit of the right of way. Equally, a landowner cannot increase the land which has the benefit of the right of way by buying adjoining land.

Misuse of a right of way

In *Jobson v. Record* (1997) Mr Jobson sold a farm house and some land to Mr Record, and granted a right of way over a private road. Mr Record bought some woodland. He used the road to gain access to the woodland, and he also brought felled timber to the farm for storage. There was a dispute about whether he was entitled to use the road in this way.

The court decided that he was not entitled to use the road for access to the woodland, nor to bring timber to and from the farm: the right of way was for the benefit of the farm, not the woodland.

6-37 Where a right of way has arisen by prescription, the extent of the right created will depend upon the extent of the use which has taken place. But the courts have shown some flexibility on this point, in relation to rights of way, and use which goes beyond the original use may still be within the right of way acquired by prescription.

See generally 6-25 on this point.

6-38 When a right of way is granted, the landowners may make arrangements for the repair of the road or path. Typically, the owner of the land which has the benefit of the easement will be obliged to contribute to the cost of repairs. If no arrangements are made, the owner of the land subject to the right is not under an obligation to keep the road or path in good repair. The owner of the land with the benefit of the easement will have an implied right to make repairs in order to keep the road or path in good repair. But there is no right to improve the surface.

See the case of *Mills v. Silver*, at 6-19.

Giles v. County Building Constructors (Hertford) Ltd (1971) concerned a plot of land containing two house which had the benefit of a right of way acquired by prescription. The site was developed so as to contain a block of 6 flats, a bungalow and 7 garages. The use of the right of way was challenged.
The court decided that the increased use was within the scope of the right of way.

A prescriptive right of way

6-39 Where a landowner has a private right of way, his own land may run alongside the road or path which gives him access. His right will usually be to gain access to his land at a specific point, not at any point along his boundary. If the right of way was granted in a deed, the deed will usually make clear the point(s) at which the landowner can gain access to a road or path; and if the right of way was acquired by prescription, it will be a right to gain access at the point(s) where access has in fact been gained.

The position is different for highways: see 5-11.

See 12-12 for sources on rights of way.

6-40 *Parking* Surprisingly, perhaps, it was until recently not entirely clear whether an easement can give the right to park a car on neighbouring land. Although parking is a familiar source of problems today, it was not a problem experienced in past centuries, since horse-drawn carriages and wagons could not simply be left where they stood indefinitely. So the law has not been called on until relatively recently to answer this question. In some cases in the past, however, the question arose as to whether there could be an easement permitting the storage of things such as building materials on land. The problem was that storing things on land may effectively monopolise the area of land in question, and prevent the owner having any worthwhile use of it. For these reasons there was for many years some doubt about parking as an easement. Then the courts decided that a right to park could exist as an easement if granted expressly, in a deed.

6-41 This left some doubt about whether a right to park could be acquired by prescription. But the courts have recently decided that the an easement to park can be acquired by prescription.

6-42 Some questions may remain however. In dealing with the right to park as easement, the law is concerned with two rather different situations—first, the right to park in a defined car-sized parking space, and secondly the right to park somewhere within a defined area which is bigger than a car. The courts may in future have to clarify whether a right to park can exist in either situation. If so, the first situation seems to be a departure from the rule that an easement must still leave the land subject to it capable of some use: while a car is parked in a car-sized parking space, there is little else which the landowner can do with the land. Another question with which the courts may have to deal is whether landowners can now claim that they have acquired the right on the public highway, if they have been doing so "as of right" for 20 years.

6-43 *Rights to light* A right to light can exist as an easement. The benefit it gives, to one piece of land, is that the supply of natural light to a window must not be obstructed by building on neighbouring land. The right to light can only exist in relation to buildings, not open land. Besides windows, it also applies to skylights, glass roofs, glazed doors and other openings designed to let in light. The law does not recognise the existence of a right to a view, nor to a right to direct sunshine as such—the fact that a window is in shadow some or all of the time does not mean that the amount of light reaching the window is inadequate. And a right to light does not mean that the flow of light cannot be reduced, but merely that it cannot be reduced below what is reasonably required for the use of the building. Rights to light can be very relevant in inner citites, where buildings are large and built close together, but are likely to be much less important in the suburbs and other areas where the height and spacing of buildings mean that a reasonable amount of light is available at all times.

6-44 Rights to light can be expressly granted, though this is in practice rare; more often they are acquired by prescription. Notices saying "ancient lights" are sometimes seen on old buildings, meaning that a right to light is being asserted for a particular window(s). The rules explained above apply, save that the

See 6-15 onwards for prescription.

Prescription Act 1832 treats rights to light differently from other easements. It is not necessary for there to have been enjoyment "as of right", though this is necessary for other easements. Written permission will mean that no right to light can be acquired, since the Act says so, but an oral agreement will not be an obstacle. As for other sorts of easement, no right can be acquired by prescription if it has been interrupted.

See 6-19 for this rule.

6-45 The owner of land which might become subject to a right to light could erect some sort of temporary screen, to obstruct the flow of light, and so prevent a right to light from being acquired by prescription. But this would be highly impractical in the case of a tall building, as well as being unsightly, to say nothing of the planning problems which it would cause. To solve these problems, a special procedure was introduced by the Rights of Light Act 1959. The owner of the land in question can, instead of putting up a screen, file a notice with the local authority, as a local land charge. The notice must describe the size and position on the land of an imaginery obstruction of light. It must be accompanied by a certificate from the Lands Tribunal confirming that notice has been given to all persons affected. Once registered, a notice under the Rights of Light Act generally expires after a year, this being long enough to amount to an interruption. A fresh notice must then be registered, no later than 19 years from that date, so as to make sure that 20 years use are not completed, and a permanent right to light acquired.

See 1-67 for the meaning of "local land charge".

See 12-12 for sources on rights to light.

6-46 *Water* The right to take water from a neighbour's land can exist as an easement. This is an exception to the rule that the purpose of an easement is to allow some use of neighbouring land, not to allow things to be taken from the land. A right to take water would generally allow the landowner whose land had the benefit of the right to put pipes and other equipment on or under the land, to extract the water and channel it to the land having the benefit of the easement. It might limit the amount of water which could be taken or the purposes for which it could be taken, or impose other conditions.

See also 6-52 in relation to pipes.

See 12-12 for sources on water.

6-47 *Support* An easement of support is a right not to have the support for a building removed. The support may come from a building on adjoining land—the buildings may in effect be leaning together—or from the land itself. In either case, it may be difficult to tell whether a building is being supported by the adjoining land, until the neighbouring building or land is removed. The right to support can be granted expressly, or acquired by prescription, as explained above. Although the owner of land which is subject to an easement of support must not remove the support by demolishing the building, or excavating soil; he has no positive obligation to keep buildings in good repair so that they continue to provide support.

See also 2-23 onwards for the effect of the Party Wall etc Act 1996.

6-48 Quite apart from the possibility of an easement of support, a landowner has what the law calls a natural right of support from adjoining land, which means that the neighbouring owner cannot carry out excavations or underground works in such a way as to cause the ground to subside.

6-49 Where subsidence is caused by the extraction of water percolating below neighbouring land, the law gives no right to compensation.

See 12-12 for sources on easements of support.

Abstraction and loss of support

In *Langbrook Properties Ltd v. Surrey County Council* (1970) the County Council pumped water out of excavations on their land. This had the effect of removing water which was percolating below land owned by Langbrook Properties, causing some buildings to settle on their foundations. Langbrook claimed compensation for the damage.

The court decided that the County Council had committed no legal wrong, and that Langbrook Properties therefore had no right to compensation for the damage.

6-50 *Repair* An easement can give a landowner the right to go on to neighbouring land in order to gain access to her own land for repair. If, for example, a landowner built a wall right up to the boundary of her land, she might not able to repair it without going on to his neighbour's land. Any landowner building right up to the boundary should perhaps make sure she obtains an easement from her neighbour, allowing her to repair and maintain what she has built, but in practice it has been relatively rare for landowners to obtain such rights. It is now possible to obtain access under the Acces to Neighbouring Land Act 1992.

See 7-2 onwards for this Act.

6-51 *Recreational use of land* A right to use a garden for recreation may exist as an easement for the benefit of a number of nearby houses. There seems no reason why similar rights should not be granted, for example to walk dogs on land, or perhaps to play ball games on open land.

6-52 *Pipes and cables* An easement may allow pipes and cables to be laid under neighbouring land, in order for the land to have a supply of water, or a private drainage system. Such an easement is an oddity, since it contradicts the principle that an easement must not interfere too much with the use of land: the small amount of space within a pipe, drain etc is being devoted entirely to the land which has the benefit of the easement, and cannot be used at all by the owner of the land which is subject to the easement. Nevertheless, the law recognises that this sort of right can exist as an easement.

6-53 Like other sorts of easement, a "pipe easement" can arise by prescription; but if the owner of the land subject to the right is unaware of the existence of pipes under his land (as may well be the case), the use will not be "as of right", because it will not be open, and no easement will arise.

6-54 *Fencing* The right to have a neighbouring landowner fence his land can exist as an easement, and can be created by deed or by prescription. However, it is not at all common, since it depends on the idea that the neighbour is fencing his land not for his own benefit but for the benefit of the landowner. As an easement, an obligation to fence breaks the general rule that it must not force the owner of the land subject to the easement to spend money. But the courts have nonetheless recognised that this can be an easement.

Assessment

6-55 By no means all land is subject to easements, but these rights are common. Their importance is obvious, and a landowner will be wise to make sure he understands what rights he has over neighbouring land, and what rights his neighbours have over his. Where easements have been granted expressly, the deed should make clear what exactly the right is—what can be done, and what land is

See also 10-79 onwards for the various forms of public rights of access to land.

See 6-5 for this principle.

See 12-12 for sources on easements relating to pipes and cables.

affected. The existence of the easement should appear on the Land Register, but this is not essential to its validity.

6-56 It is difficult to see any advantage in allowing use to continue which will lead to the creation of a prescriptive easement. A landowner can prevent this happening in one of the ways explained above. The use itself can be allowed to continue, by permission, or by granting an express easement, if the landowner wishes to do this.

6-57 Where it is clear that an easement has arisen by prescription, but its scope is unclear, it may be possible for the landowner with the benefit of the easement to clarify the position by applying for it to be entered on the Land Register. Alternatively, if both landowners agree, the existing easement can be cancelled, and a new one granted in its place, thus removing any uncertainty.

6-58 Legal advice will be important when an easement is granted, to make sure that its scope—the use of land which it allows—and any terms and conditions are set out clearly. Landowners will need to consider whether granting an easement may impede some future use of the land. When land as a whole is transferred, the subject will also be important, because the process of transfer may give rise to easements.

See 6-14 onwards for how this may happen.

Chapter 7

Other rights over land

Introduction

7-0 This chapter is concerned with a selection of rights over land not dealt with in other chapters. The first sort—rights of access under the Access to Neighbouring Land Act 1992—applies automatically to almost all land in England and Wales. The others are common, and will affect many landowners.

7-1 The law explained in this chapter is almost all civil law. Some of it comes from legislation; some from case-law.

See 1-1 and 1-10 onwards for the meaning of "legislation" and "case law".

Access to Neighbouring Land Act 1992

7-2 A landowner may need to go on to his neighbour's land for the purposes of carrying out work on his own land—for example, putting up a fence or wall on the boundary, pointing a wall, or erecting scaffolding so that work can be carried out on the roof. It has always been possible for neighbours to create rights of access in the form of easements, though this is not particularly common. In the absence of an easement, no difficulty arises provided that a licence (permission) can be obtained from the neighbouring landowner. But in the absence of a licence, there was no general right to gain access to neighbouring land in order to carry out work. The Access to Neighbouring Land Act 1992, now provides a legal procedure by which, if a landowner cannot obtain a licence from his neighbour, he can go to the court for an order allowing him to enter.

See 6-50 on easements giving access to land for repair.

See 1-49 on licences.

Also relevant is the Party Wall Act 1996: see 2-23 onwards.

7-3 In practice, an application to the court will rarely be necessary: a landowner asked to give permission for entry will realise that if he does not agree he may face legal proceedings. There may, however, be differences of opinion about the terms and conditions on which entry should be allowed, and if these cannot be settled by the neighbouring landowners there may have to be an application to the court.

The Access to Neighbouring Land Act 1992 The owner of The Ferns has built a large greenhouse along the edge of his property, and may need access from the garden of Lily Cottage to maintain the wall running along the boundary. The owner of Rosewood may need access from the garden of Lily Cottage to bring in heavy equipment to fell and remove some large trees. The Act can deal with both situations—the fact that Rosewood and Lily Cottage are separated by a narrow strip of land does not prevent the Act from working.

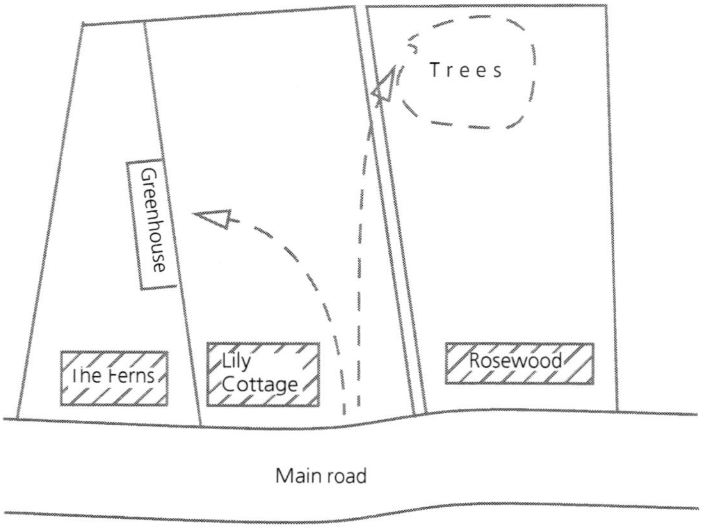

⚷ See 5-0 for the meaning of "highway".

7-4 The Act applies to all land except highways, because highways are excluded from the definition of "land" in the Act (s. 8(3)).⚷. The Act does not apply only to pieces of land which share a boundary: if a landowner's land is bordered by a thin strip it may be necessary for her to enter the land on the far side of strip in order to gain access to her own land. Access can be obtained only to carry out repair and maintenance: the Act has nothing to do with obtaining new rights of way for access generally. Landowners cannot agree between themselves that the Act will not apply (s. 4(4)).

7-5 A person who wants to carry out work on land, and needs access to neighbouring land in order to do so, but does not have permission from his neighbour, may apply to the court (generally the County

Court) for an "access order" (s. 1(1)). Generally, the court must make an order if the work is:

- "Reasonably necessary for the preservation" of the land. And:

- It cannot be carried out, or would be substantially more difficult, without access to the neighbouring land (s. 1(2)).

An access order must not be made, however, if entry on to the neighbouring land would cause disturbance or hardship—despite the terms or conditions in the access order—to an unreasonable degree (s. 1(3)).

> The case of *Dean v. Walker* (1996) concerned a party wall. There was a dispute about whether the court could make an order under the Access to Neighbouring Land Act 1992 in relation to the wall, so that one of the neighbouring landowners could go on to the other's land to repair the wall.
> The court decided that it could make an order, since the definition of "land" for the purposes of the Access to Neighbouring Land Act was wide enough to include a party wall.

Access under the 1992 Act

7-6 Some sorts of work (assuming that they need doing) are called "basic preservation work" by the Act, and are deemed to be "reasonably necessary for the preservation" of the land, namely:

> "(a) the maintenance, renewal or repair of any part of a building or other structure comprised in or situated on the dominant land";
>
> (b) the clearance, renewal or repair of any drain, sewer, pipe or cable so comprised or situate;
>
> (c) the treatment, cutting back, felling, removal or replacement of any hedge, tree, shrub or other growing thing which is so comprised and which is, or is in danger of becoming, damaged, diseased, dangerous, insecurely rooted or dead;
>
> (d) the filling in, or clearance of any ditch so comprised (s. 1(4))"

7-7 In other words, a landowner who wishes to obtain an access order need only show that "basic preservation work" needs doing, not that it is necessary for the preservation of the land, since this is assumed.

In many cases, the work which a landowner wishes to carry out will be "basic preservation work". If he wishes to do other work, it may still be possible to obtain an access order, but he will have to show that the work is necessary for the preservation of the land. Furthermore, the Act also provides that, if the court considers it fair and reasonable, work can be regarded as covered by the Act even though it involves a certain amount of demolition or improvement—things which would not be covered by themselves (s. 1(5)). An access order may also be made so that land can be inspected, to see whether work is necessary (s. 1(7)).

7-8 An access order must specify the work which can be carried out by entering on to the neighbouring land, the part of the neighbouring land which can be used for access, and the date(s) on which access is permitted (s. 2(1)). It may also set terms and conditions designed to minimise loss and damage, and also inconvenience and loss of privacy to the occupier of the neighbouring land (s. 2(2)). These terms and conditions can deal with:

- The manner in which the specified works are to be carried out.
- The timing of the works (including the hours when the work may be carried out).
- The persons who may come on to the neighbouring land.
- Precautions to be taken by the person applying for the access order (s. 2(3)).

So, when an access order is made, the court has the ability to impose conditions which will protect the landowner whose land will be subject to the order.

7-9 The court can impose terms and conditions requiring the landowner applying for the order to pay compensation for any loss and damage caused (s. 2(4)). Where the access order is required for non-residential land, the court can order a payment to be made for the privilege of access; but no payment is possible were the land is residential (s. 2(5)). The payment may reflect the degree of inconvenience suffered by the occupant of the neighbouring land and the financial advantage gained by the carrying out of the work.

A person carrying out work under an access order (and builders, surveyors and others acting for him) has a legal right to enter the land subject to the access order (s. 3(1)). Unless the access order provides otherwise, he can temporarily bring materials and tools on to the land, and leave waste there (s. 3(2)); but he must remove the waste promptly, make good the land and pay for any damage (s. 3(3)). 7-10

Access orders are not necessarily confined to one-off entries: they can set the terms of access for the future. If, for example, access to neighbouring land is needed every year to clear gutters, the court can make an order accordingly. What if the land subject to the order changes hands? The Act deals with this by providing for access orders to be registered, either under the Land Charges Act 1972, if the land is not registered land, or under the Land Registration Act 1925 if it is registered. The rights and obligations of the access order then apply to new owners of the land subject to the order (ss. 4 and 5). 7-11

See 1-66 for the Land Charges Act 1972 and 1-54 onwards for registration under the Land Registration Act 1925.

The court can alter or discharge (that is, bring to an end) an access order; and breach of an order gives a right to compensation to any person affected by the breach (s. 6). A landowner who refuses to let a neighbour exercise a right of entry under the Act may be required to pay compensation; though perhaps more significant is the fact that an access order requires a landowner to permit access, and a failure to comply may be punished as a contempt of court (s. 3(1)). A landowner who has a right of entry under an access order but does not abide by its terms—for example, because he does not complete the work within the time allowed, or fails to make good damage—may similarly be required to pay compensation. 7-12

See 3-29 for the meaning of "contempt of court".

See 12-8 for sources on the Access to Neighbouring Land Act 1992.

Restrictive covenants

When land is sold, or subject to some other sort of transaction, there may be a desire to restrict its future use. If, for example, a landowner 7-13 sells off part of her garden for development, she may wish to impose restrictions on the future use of the land sold—perhaps that only one house be built on the land, or that no commercial activity take place there, or that no caravans can be stationed on the land. She will want the restriction to apply not to just to the first owner of the land being sold, but to later owners as well; and when she sells the land she has retained, the buyer will want the restriction to be enforceable by him. The way in which such restrictions are usually imposed is by means of a restrictive covenant.

The need for restrictive covenants
If the owner of High Beeches sells off part of her garden so that a new house can be built, she will be affected by what the owners of the new house do, and will probably want to impose restrictive covenants to control the use of the land. These may deal with such things as further building, business use of the land, noisy pets, caravans, and so on. The restrictive covenants will continue in force even though the two houses change hands.

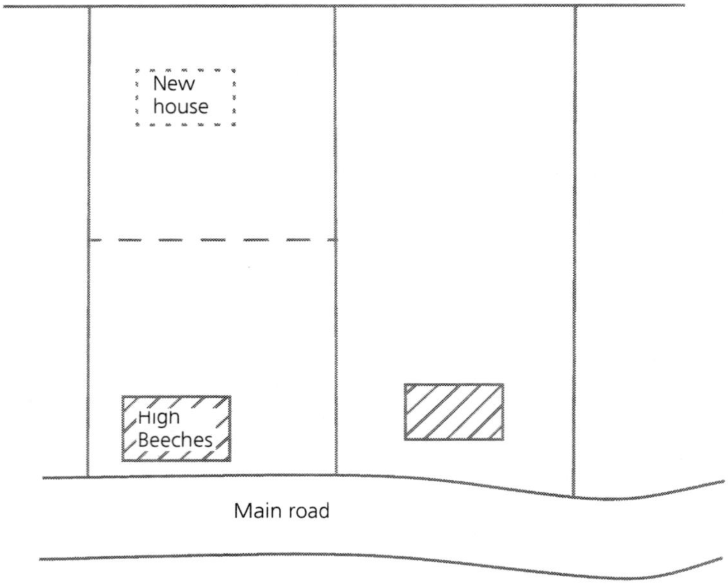

7-14 "Covenant" is a general term for an undertaking in a deed; usually an undertaking to do or not to do something. When a person gives an undertaking in a deed, the undertaking is enforceable against him by the other party (or parties) to the deed. If a person selling land wants to limit its use in the future, as in the example just mentioned, she may be able to obtain a covenant from the buyer not to use the land in certain ways, and she can enforce the covenant against the buyer. However, the law goes further and subject to certain conditions allows later owners of both pieces of land to be affected by the covenant. Legally, the rules which govern the transfer of the covenant to later owners are complex (and have

See 1-34 for deeds.

long been regarded as in need of reform) but the essentials are as follows.

Conditions for enforcing restrictive covenants First, the covenant must be negative in its effect—an undertaking *not* to do something. Hence the term "restrictive covenant": it is only covenants which are negative in their effect, and restrict the use of the land, which can be passed on. 7-15

There is an exception to this rule, however: the law does not allow a person who is receiving some benefit under a deed to take that benefit but refuse to carry out some obligation which goes with it. This might be the case if, for example, a landowner was granted a right of way over a private drive and undertook, in return, to contribute to the cost of upkeep. 7-16

The case of *Rhone v. Stevens* (1994) concerned a house which had been divided into two separate dwellings. The roof of one part covered a bedroom in the other smaller part, which was known as "The Cottage". When The Cottage had been sold off, in 1960, the owner of the rest of the house had covenanted to keep the roof in good repair. By 1984, the roof was leaking, and the current owner of The Cottage tried to enforce the covenant against the current owner of the rest of the house.

The case reached the House of Lords, which confirmed the principle that a *positive* covenant could not be enforced against a later owner of land. The current owner of the house was thus not liable to maintain the roof over the cottage.

Enforcing a covenant

Secondly, the parties who made the deed must have been the owners of the respective pieces of land, and must have intended the covenant to be enforceable between later owners. (It is perfectly possible for the parties to the deed, if they wish, to insert a covenant which is intended apply only to themselves, not to later owners of the two pieces of land.) Thirdly, the covenant must have something to do with the land which has the benefit of it. A covenant not to use the land as a public house or off-licence would meet this test, but a covenant by a landowner never to drink alcohol would not: the court would regard this as a purely personal matter. 7-17

Finally, the owner of the land subject to the covenant must have had notice of it before acquiring the land. This is because of the influence of equity, which is concerned with fairness. 7-18

See 1-17 for equitable principles.

See 1-61 for the registration of minor interests.

See 1-66 for registration under the Land Charges Act 1972.

See 6-1 onwards for easements.

See 6-7 for easements of this sort.

See 10-38 onwards for keeping caravans on land.

See 9-10 for the meaning of "amenity".

Nowadays, the existence of a restrictive covenant can be shown on the Land Register, under s. 50(1) of the Land Registration Act 1925, and this is deemed to be notice of the covenant to buyers (s. 50(2)). So there is no reason for a restrictive covenant to be unforceable for lack of notice. For land not yet registered, restrictive covenants can also be shown on the register kept under the Land Charges Act 1972, with the same effect.

7-19 Legally, restrictive covenants are in some ways like easements; and the same language can be used of the two pieces of land involved, one being the dominant land, which has the benefit of the restrictive covenant, and the other the servient land, which is subject to it. And it is true that some types of easement can be negative in their effect, restricting what can happen on the land subject to the easement. But the law of easements does not allow restrictions to be placed on the use of neighbouring land generally: to do this, landowners must use restrictive covenants.

7-20 Restrictive covenants amount to a form of DIY planning control. They were widely used before the planning system introduced a general way of regulating the use of land in the interests of the public as a whole; and covenants going back many years are common. But the planning system has not eliminated the need to control the use of land by private agreements, and restrictive covenants are still often imposed today. This applies both to large-scale developments, such as housing or industrial estates, and to one-off situations, where one landowner wishes to restrict the use of neighbouring property.

7-21 *Building schemes* Mention must be made of a special situation in which the above rules are altered slightly in order to make them effective. Suppose that an estate of houses (or other property) is built, and the developer imposes restrictive covenants on each house as it is sold. On a modern housing estate such covenants might prevent residents from fencing their front gardens, or hanging washing in them, or keeping caravans. The intention will be that each resident can enforce the restrictive covenants against all the others, and that if all residents abide by the convenants this will help to preserve the look and amenity of the estate.

7-22 But the rules explained above would not allow all the residents to enforce the covenants. This is because the land which obtains the benefit of the covenants, as each house is sold, consists of the unsold houses belonging to the developer. As more and more houses are sold, fewer and fewer would obtain the benefit of the covenants. Hence the special rule for what are generally known as "building schemes", which is that the restrictive covenants will apply to all the plots of land, and be enforeceable by all the owners, provided that the land as a whole was laid out in plots by a person who then sold off the plots with restrictive covenants which were intended to benefit all the land sold. If this is so, the courts will enforce the covenants. The covenants need not be identical, since the estate may contain plots which differ—for example, a housing estate might contain a mix of houses, to which slightly different covenants applied.

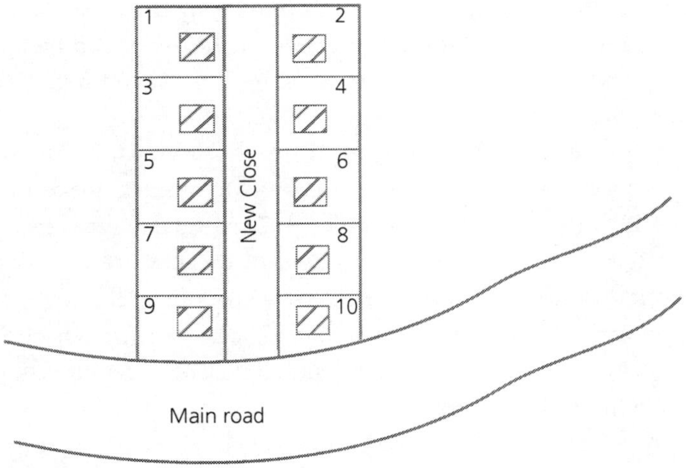

A building scheme A developer acquires some land and lays out New Close. He wants to make sure that all the houses are subject to restrictive covenants, in favour of all the others, in the interests of amenity. The law allows him to do this. Otherwise there would be difficulties. When he sold the first house (No. 1), he could make sure that all the remaining houses had the benefit of the covenants. But when he sold the second house (No. 2), he could not make the owner of No. 1 agree to have the benefit of the covenant. The problem would get worse as more and more houses were sold.

7-23 *Remedies for breach of a restrictive covenant* A landowner who is entitled to the benefit of a restrictive covenant, and finds that the owner of the land subject to the covenant is not complying with it, may take action in the civil courts. His concern will usually be to obtain an injunction, to stop the activity which represents a breach of the covenant. The grant of an injunction is not automatic: the court has a discretion about whether to grant one, and will consider questions of fairness in deciding whether an injunction is

See 3-29 onwards for injunctions.

appropriate. One factor which may mean that an injunction is refused is delay, because it may cause unfairness if a landowner delays in applying to the court for an injunction.

Whether to grant an injunction

In the case of *Jaggard v. Sawyer (1995)* Mr and Mrs Jaggard were the owners of a house in a private cul-de-sac. Mr and Mrs Sawyer also lived in the cul-de-sac. All the houses were subject to a restrictive covenant which prevented further building. The Sawyers bought some land behind their house and started to build a new house on the site. Access was to be by means of a drive through their garden—which was a breach of the restrictive covenant. Mr and Mrs Jaggard objected to the development but were slow in bringing proceedings: they did not take action until building work at the Sawyers' new house was at an advanced stage.

The court decided that it would be unfair to grant an injunction, in view of the delay; instead, damages would be awarded for Mr and Mrs Sawyer.

7-24 In deciding whether to grant an injunction to stop a breach of a restrictive covenant, the court may also take into account the behaviour of the person applying. If he has behaved badly towards the person against whom he is asking for an injunction, this may make the court reluctant to grant one.

7-25 Compensation can sometimes be awarded instead of an injunction. The courts also have power to make a declaration, under s. 84(2) of the Law of Property Act 1925, about whether freehold land is affected by a restriction, or what the nature and extent of a restriction is, and who is entitled to enforce it. This may be an appropriate remedy if there is a dispute about whether land is subject to a restrictive covenant, but, if the court declares that it is, the covenant will be complied with.

See 7-27 onwards for more on s. 84.

7-26 A restrictive covenant can be discharged (i. e. cancelled) or modified by the current owners of the two pieces of land involved. Another possibility is for a landowner to agree that a particular use of neighbouring land may take place, and that the restrictive covenant will not be enforced so as to prevent it. In either case, this will usually be a matter for negotiation: the covenant will have a value to the owner of the land which is benefited by it, and he will probably expect payment.

7-27 *Applications to the Lands Tribunal* The jurisdiction of the Lands Tribunal includes discharging and modifying restrictive covenants in certain circumstances. (The Tribunal can also deal with some

See 1-71 for the rôle of the Lands Tribunal.

other sorts of legal restriction which affect the use of land; but it cannot deal with restrictions in leases unless the lease was for a period of at least 40 years, of which at least 25 years have expired ꆧ.) The reason why the Tribunal has this jurisdiction, and can sometimes undo or alter agreements made between landowners, is that it is considered to be in the public interest to override the agreement. This is true particularly of restrictive covenants which become obsolete with the passage of time. A restrictive covenant may continue in force for decades, or even centuries. Land subject to restrictions on (say) commercial use at a time when it was in a quiet village may become part of a busy urban area. In addition, transactions over the years, by which plots of land are split up or joined, sold and leased may make it difficult to discover which if any landowners are entitled to enforce a restrictive covenant.

ꆧ Leases for more than 3 years must be made by deed, and covenants in the deed may impose restrictions on the use of the land. See 8-17 onwards for covenants in leases.

The Lands Tribunal can discharge or modify restrictive covenants and other similar restrictions on the use of land, in circumstances laid down by s. 84(1) of the Law of Property Act 1925, with amendments made by the Law of Property Act 1969. The Lands Tribunal can act if it is satisfied: 7-28

> "*(a)* that by reason of changes in the character of the property or the neighbourhood or other circumstances which the Lands Tribunal may deem material, the restriction ought to be deemed obsolete; or
>
> *(aa)* that (in a case falling within subsection (1A) below) the continued existence thereof would impede some reasonable user of the land for public or private purposes or, as the case may be, would unless modified so impede such user; or
>
> *(b)* [that the owners of the land have agreed to the discharge or modification of the restriction]; or
>
> *(c)* that the proposed discharge or modification will not injure the persons entitled to the benefit of the restriction".

Subsection (1A) provides that subs. (1)(aa) applies where the Lands Tribunal is satisfied that the restriction: 7-29

> "*(a)* does not secure to persons entitled to the benefit of it any practical benefits of substantial value or advantage to them; or
>
> *(b)* is contrary to the public interest;
>
> and that money will be an adequate compensation for the loss or disdavantage (if any) which any such person will suffer from the discharge or modification."

7-30 Subsection (1B) of the Act is also important:

"In determining whether a case is one falling within subsection (1A) above, and in determining whether (in any such case or otherwise) a restriction ought to be discharged or modified, the Lands Tribunal shall take into account the development plan and any declared or ascertainable pattern for the grant or refusal of planning permissions in the relevant areas, as well as the period at which and the context in which the restriction was created or imposed and any other material circumstances."

7-31 These provisions allow the Lands Tribunal to act in four different circumstances, which can be summarised as follows:

Table 5: Discharge and modification of restrictive covenants

	Circumstances in which Lands Tribunal can act	
	Effect of 1925 Act	Effect of 1969 Act amendments
1.	Restriction obsolete (s. 84(1)(*a*))	Planning relevant (s. 84(1B))
2.	Restriction would impede reasonable use of land (s. 84(1)(*aa*))	Planning relevant (s. 84(1B)) Restriction gives no practical benefits; *or* restriction against public interest; *and* in either case money is adequate compensation (s. 84(1A))
3.	Agreement to discharge or modification of restriction (s. 84(1)(*c*))	Planning relevant (s. 84(1B))
4.	Discharge or modification will not cause injury (s. 84(1)(*d*))	Planning relevant (s. 84(1B))

7-32 The first ground is that the restriction is obselete, but it is *not* necessary to show that the covenant is ancient in order for this argument to succeed—the covenant could be relatively recent, but still arguably obsolete in the light of changes to the area in question.

7-33 The second ground covers two rather different situations. It could be argued that the covenant did not provide any real benefit to the person entitled to enforce it if, for example, it was a covenant against commercial use of land in an area where the surrounding land was already in commercial use. It is much less common for the public interest to justify the discharge or modification of a covenant.

The case of *Re Lloyd's and Lloyd's Application* (1993) concerned a large house which was to be converted into a home for some psychiatric patients. This, however, would have been in breach of a restrictive covenant against using the house for any trade or business. An application was made to the Lands Tribunal to modify the covenant so as to permit this use.

The Lands Tribunal decided to modify it. The Tribunal considered that the covenant was contrary to the public interest, because the current policy was for patients to receive care in the community. Furthermore the covenant did not confer any practical benefit on the landowners entitled to enforce it because a residential home for the elderly had already been built close by. A final factor was that plannig permission had been granted for the development.

Modifying a restrictive covenant

7-34 The third ground is where the persons entitled to enforce the covenant have agreed to the discharge or modification of the covenant. The agreement can be express or implied. If the agreement is express, but has not been carried into effect by the making of a deed, an application to the Tribunal can be made. An application can also be made where it can be implied, from what is said or done by the person who has the benefit of the covenant, that he agrees to the discharge or modification of the covenant. Suppose that a restrictive covenant forbids the use of some land for commercial purposes. The owner of land which has the benefit of the covenant makes clear that he would not allow use of the land for industrial use, but has no real objection to use of the land for offices. The land is accordingly used for offices, without objection. Finally, the Lands Tribunal can act where the discharge or modification of the restrictive covenant will not injure the person entitled to enforce it.

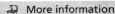

7-35 Planning permission is a particularly important matter, in relation to all four of the grounds upon which a restrictive covenant may be modified or discharged It may be that a restrictive covenant forbids a certain sort of development, but that the local authority have given permission for development. The owner of the land which is subject to the covenant may wish to make an application to the Lands Tribunal for the covenant to be modified or discharged, so as to allow the development to take place. The existence of planning permission is an important factor, but is not decisive.

7-36 During the proceedings, the Tribunal must try to find out which landowners are entitled to the benefit of the restriction—there may be a number—and make sure they can participate in the proceedings if they wish. If a restrictive covenant is discharged, it ceases to exist. If it is modified, the Tribunal will in effect rewrite the restriction, so as to permit some activity. A restriction might, for example, forbid any commercial activity on land; and the Tribunal might rewrite the restriction so as to permit certain types of commercial activity.

7-37 Where the Lands Tribunal exercises its jurisdiction to discharge or modify a restrictive covenant, it can direct the applicant (i. e. the person applying for the covenant to be discharged or modified) to pay compensation to the person entitled to enforce the covenant. The Act makes it clear that this may be *either* compensation for any loss or disadvantage he may suffer as a result, *or* a sum to reflect any effect which the restriction had on the sale price of the land benefiting from it.

See 12-14 for sources on restrictive covenants.

Other powers to alter covenants

7-38 Restrictions on the use of land can be made ineffective in several other situations. Under s. 237 of the Town and Country Planning Act 1990, a local authority which has aquired land in order to carry out development can act on planning permission, despite the fact it is in breach of a restrictive covenant. In other words, the restriction can be ignored: if this were not so, restrictive covenants could be used to impede development by the local authority, who would have to apply to the Lands Tribunal to discharge or modify the restriction. County Courts also have power, under s. 610 of the Housing Act 1985, to discharge a covenant which restricts a building to use as a single dwelling, thus allowing for conversion into flats or maisonettes. The County Court can act if it can be shown that the building cannot easily be let as one dwelling, but could be let if converted.

See 12-2 and 12-20 for sources on these powers.

Sporting, grazing and mineral rights

7-39 The law provides a special sort of right—an easement—to enable a landowner to *use* nearby land in a particular way. A different sort of right provides a way of allowing things to be *taken* from land. This goes by the ancient name of a profit à prendre (pronounced *prender*) or "profit" for short. The things which can form the subject of a profit, and can be taken from the land, fall into three broad categories:

See chapter 6 for easements.

- Game or fish.
- Grass or other vegetation.
- Minerals.

See 2-45 for the meaning of "minerals".

The case of *Tehidy Minerals v. Norman* (1971) concerned a claim by some farmers that they had acquired a right to graze cattle over some down-land by prescription—in other words, a profit. The owner of the down-land did not agree, and a dispute arose when the owner put up a fence and the farmers took it down. The court decided that the farmers had not grazed their cattle on the down for 30 years before the legal proceedings were started, and so no right had arisen under the Prescription Act 1832. But some of the farmers had acquired a profit under the "lost modern grant" rule [see 6-18 onwards for this rule].

Profits and prescription

7-40 A profit relating to fish or to game is conferring fishing or sporting rights. The person who has the benefit of the right may come on to land and take fish or game, as the case may be. Profits can be, and often are, drawn up so as to relate to specific fish or game—for example a right to take trout or to shoot pheasants. Grazing rights may be the subject of a profit: the person with the benefit of the land may then send sheep or cattle on to the land to graze there. Limits may be set on the amount of cattle or other animals which may graze on the land.

7-41 Profits are like easements in that a profit is strictly speaking a piece of legal property, but is best thought of as being a right. A profit is within the meaning of "land" and so can only be created or transferred by means of a deed. They can be shown on the Land Register but their validity is not affected if they are not shown there, because they are "overriding" interests in land. In one important respect, however, profits are different from easements: they can be, but do not have to be, attached to a piece of land, as easements do. So fishing or sporting rights, for example, may belong to an individual or to a club even though they have no land in the area. Profits are also different from easements in that they can be granted either to one person on his own, or to a number of people, who enjoy the right in common with each other. Hence the expression "right of common", which is often applied to grazing rights but can be applied to other sorts of profit, for example the right to take fish, and "common land". Rights of common must be registered under the Commons Registration Act 1965 in order to remain valid.

An alternative way in which a person can enjoy the right to fish is to own the bed of the river, stream or lake in question. See 2-57 onwards.

See 1-33 onwards for this rule.

See 1-59 for the meaning of "overriding interests" and their entry on the Land Register.

See also 10-65 onwards for common land.

Selling grazing rights

In *Bettison v. Langton* (1999) the court had to consider some grazing rights, which were limited to 10 head of cattle and 30 sheep and which were attached to a farm. The question was whether they could be sold separately, or whether the law required that they remain permanently attached to the farm.

The court's decision was that provided grazing rights were limited to a fixed number of animals, they could be sold separately.

7-42 Profits can arise by prescription (use over a period of time); but the period which must elapse, under the Prescription Act 1832, s. 3, before the right arises, is normally 30 years (and 60 where there is permission other than written permission). Takings things from land without permission may involve committing an offence. The law does not allow an easement to arise by prescription where the

See 6-22 for prescription under the 1832 Act in relation to easements—where the periods are 20 and 40 years.

use of land which has taken place amounts to an offence, but it may be that profits are different in this respect, and can be created even though the activity which gives rise to them is criminal in nature.

See 12-8 for sources on profits.

Some equitable rights

7-43 Chapter 1 explained the development of equity, as a set of rules and principles which have had a wide influence in the legal system. The effects have been described in relevant parts of the text. Two further examples may be mentioned here.

See 1-17 onwards for equity generally.

See for example 3-29 onwards for injunctions and 7-13 for restrictive covenants.

7-44 *Trusts* A trust is an arrangement in which one person (the trustee) holds property not for his own benefit but for another person (the beneficiary). It is not necessary to use the word "trust" to create a trust. Trusts may be created deliberately, so that one person can hold property for another. And they are sometimes imposed by legislation in order to regulate dealings in property, including land. The courts too, using the rules of equity, have developed rules by which a trust is held to exist, even though no deliberate steps have been taken to create one, in order to achieve fairness. A trust of this sort is sometimes known as a constructive trust.

The case of *Yaxley v. Gotts* (1999) concerned a converted house in Cromer, Norfolk. Mr Gotts and his son bought the property, having entered into an agreement with Mr Yaxley, a friend of theirs who was a builder, that he would do work on the flats in the upper floors, and let and manage them. In return, he would have the ground floor of the house, to convert into two flats. Mr Yaxley spent a good deal of time working on the property, and managing it. But Mr Gotts and his son would not transfer the ground floor to him. There was no written agreement which Mr Yaxley could enforce [see 1-37]. The question was whether Mr Yaxley had any rights.

The court decided that a constructive trust arose; and the right result was for Mr Yaxley to have a 99-year lease of the ground floor of the house.

Constructive trust

7-45 To take a particular example, a trust may be imposed, in the interests of fairness, where a family home is in the ownership of only one of the couple, but the other has contributed towards the cost of buying the home, whether by means of a lump sum or helping to make mortgage payments. It would be unjust, if the relationship broke up, for the owner to have all of the proceeds of sale. So if the court detects an agreement between the couple, either express or implied, to share the proceeds when the home is sold, the court will find that there is a trust, the owner being a trustee in respect of the non-owner's share. (How large that share will be will depend upon the circumstances: it may be more or less than half.)

See 7-48 for how the law regulates the right to *occupy* a family home.

7-46 *Estoppel* This strange word conceals an equitable rule which can prevent unfairness by giving a person an interest in property. Suppose that a landowner agrees that she will sell a small area of land at the end of her garden to her neighbour, so that he can build a garage for his own use. Relying on this statement, but before the land is transferred, the neighbour proceeds to build the garage; but the landowner changes her mind and tries to insist that the garage is hers. The court may decide that because her actions are so unfair she is "estopped" (prevented) from saying that the land is hers—and she may be ordered by the court to transfer the land to her neighbour, to remedy the unfairness caused by her behaviour.

Proprietary estoppel

In the case of *Gillett v. Holt* (2000) Mr Holt was an unmarried farmer. Mr Gillett was much younger; and Mr Holt met him while he was still a boy, and persuaded him to leave school and work in his farming business, rather than going on to take O and A levels. Mr Gillett did so. He (and, later, his wife) worked for many years on the farm, helping to build up the business. Mr Holt repeatedly assured him that he would inherit the business on Mr Holt's death. Mr Gillett relied on these assurances, and took no steps to start his own business elsewhere or to make other arrangements to provide for the future. In 1992, however, their relationship became less friendly. Mr Holt rewrote his will, treating Mr Gillett much less favourably; later he dismissed Mr Gillettt and cut him out of his will altogether. Mr Gillett claimed that he had the right to a share in the farming business, and brought legal proceedings.

The court decided that proprietary estoppel applied, and ordered Mr Holt to transfer to Mr Gillett a farm known as The Beeches and also £100,000 in lieu of his entitlement to share in other parts of the business.

7-47 The limits of the rule are hard to define. In some cases the courts have applied strict conditions; in others they have adopted a more flexible approach. But in essence a landowner should be aware that if she lets another person use her land, allowing him to think that he will obtain some right; and if that person acts accordingly, and spends money or in some other way acts to his cost, the landowner may then be prevented by the court from changing her mind, and may be required by the court to transfer land or rights over land, or allow the other person to go on using the land.

See 12-2 and 12-8 for sources on equity.

Rights under the Family Law Act 1996

7-48 Part IV of the Family Law Act 1996, which came into force in the autumn of 1997, set out rights which apply where a man and woman are living together as a couple in a "dwelling-house". A "dwelling house" can be a flat or maisonette, as well as a house, and for *some* purposes it includes other forms of dwelling such as a caravan, mobile home or houseboat (s. 62). The Act is concerned essentially with the right to live in the couple's home. In many cases the couple will be be the joint owners or tenants of the dwelling house, and in this situation there is no need for the Act, because both have sufficient rights. The Act comes into play when only one is the owner or tenant of the home: it gives rights to the person who is not the owner. It is likely to be needed when the couple cannot agree; particularly when the relationship is breaking up. The Act is mainly concerned with family law, but Part IV is relevant to a book on land law because of the rights it gives.

See 10-38 onwards for the law on caravan sites and mobile home parks.

See 1-44 for joint ownership of land, and chapter 8 for leases and tenancies.

7-49 Section 30 of the Family Law Act applies to married couples. Where one of them is the owner or tenant of the family home, the other has what the Act calls "matrimonial home rights", meaning a right to occupy the home. The right is a right against the owner or tenant; and it can be entered on the Land Register, so that it will affect a third party who buys the property. In other words, the matrimonial home rights do not cease to exist when the property is sold (s. 31).

See 1-61 for entry of rights of this sort on the Land Register.

7-50 Matrimonial home rights generally last only while the marriage lasts. But the courts can make a range of orders to enforce matrimonial home rights, to make sure that a person with the benefit of such rights can live in the home, and regulating the terms on which he or she does so; and the court can make an order that the rights continue after the end of the marriage (s. 33). In making an order the court must take into account the needs of the couple and any children they have. When a marriage has ended, and one of the couple has a right to live in the couple's home, but the other does not, the latter can make an application for an order allowing him or her to do so. But in this case the order can only last for 6 months, though it can be extended for a further 6 months (s. 35).

7-51 Some protection is also given to "cohabitants", by which the Act means a man and a woman living as though they were married. (The Act does not include same-sex couples in the definition.) The same underlying idea applies: if one person is the owner or tenant of the home, and the other is not, the court can make an order enforcing the latter's right to live there, or regulating the way in which they both live there (s. 36).

See 12-2 for sources on the Family Law Act 1996.

Mortgages

7-52 A debtor may run away, but land stays where it is; and land is therefore an ideal security for a debt—the lender is given the right to enforce the loan by exploiting the value of the land, if the debtor does not pay, and can thus be sure, or almost sure, that he will get his money back. A transaction of this sort is generally known as a mortgage, though the word is also used loosely to refer to the amount of money borrowed. In legal documents, the "mortgagor" is the person who borrows the money, while the "mortgagee" is the person who lends the money and gets security over the land. The word "equity" is sometimes used to refer to the value of the owner's interest in land—in other words the sale value less any amounts borrowed on the security of the land. "Negative equity" describes the situation in which the amount borrowed exceeds the value of the land.

See 0-10 for rights of this sort.

See 8-41 for the Unfair Terms in Consumer Contracts Regulations, which may also apply to mortgages.

7-53 The traditional way for the lender to get security for the loan was for ownership to be transferred to him, on the understanding that it would be transferred back when the debt was repaid. If the loan was not repaid, he could sell the land to get his money back. Since the law reforms of the 1920s, the lender does not have ownership of the land, but a different sort of interest. This can be either a long lease (usually 3,000 years) or what is known as a "charge"; that is, an interest in the land which gives the lender the same rights as if he had a long lease (Law of Property Act 1925, ss. 85 and 87.) The latter is in practice common. A legal mortgage (equitable mortgages are considered below) must be made by deed (s. 53 of the Act). The deed will in practice impose detailed conditions on the lender, for example:

See 1-1 for these reforms.

- That the lender may vary the interest rate.
- That the borrower may repay by instalments.
- That the borrower must keep the land insured.
- That the borrower must not let the land without consent (this is because a tenant would make it more difficult for the lender to enforce the security and recover his money)

See chapter 8 for leases and tenancies.

7-54 The deed will generally allow the borrower to remain in possession of the land, so long as the repayments on the mortgage continue to made promptly. The borrower thus remains the legal owner of the land, and can expect to retain the use of it. But the lender is legally in a very strong position, provided that he does not lend too much. Indeed, it is the near certainty of being able to get his money back which enables the lender to charge a rate of interest which is lower than the rates for unsecured loans.

See 1-47 for the meaning of "possessing" land.

7-55 If land is unregistered, the lender has a right to hold the title deeds to the land (ss. 85–87 of the Act). This makes it very difficult for the borrower to dispose of the land to some unsuspecting third party, and so deprive the lender of his security. In the case of registered land, the Land Registration Act 1925 says that a mortgage must be by way of charge (s. 25). The borrower must surrender his land certificate. This is kept by the Land Registry; meanwhile the lender receives a separate document, known as a "charge certificate", which is evidence of his interest in the land.

See 1-57 for land and charge certificates.

7-56 *Types of mortgage* The division between legal and equitable rights applies here too, with consequences for the enforceability of the mortgage. A mortgage will be equitable in nature if the interest in land being mortgaged is equitable; for example, a lease which is equitable because it is not for a fixed period. If there has been an agreement to create a mortgage, and the money has been handed over but the mortgage deed has not been executed, there will be an equitable mortgage—but (since 1989) the agreement must be in writing, signed by the borrower and lender, to comply with the basic rule for contracts relating to land. Before 1989, it was possible to create an equitable mortgage merely by depositing the title deeds (or the land certificate) with the lender; but since then it has been necessary for there to be an agreement in writing if there is to be an equitable mortgage. If there is no written agreement, the lender will not obtain any security.

See 1-17 onwards for legal and equitable interests.

See 1-37 for this rule.

7-57 *Priority of mortgages* If only one lender has lent money against the security of a given piece of land, he will wish to make sure that all the formalities are complied with, so that he has a legal mortgage, and also that he does not lend more than he can expect to get back if he has to enforce the loan against the land. By taking these steps he maximises his chances of getting his money back. But it is possible for the same piece of land to serve as security for more than one loan. In this case, another question arises, namely the order in which the lenders are paid, if it is necessary to enforce the mortgages against the land. The first lender is in the best position. Later lenders will no doubt try not to lend unless they can be sure that the land is valuable enough to pay off the loan even after other loans have been satisfied. But they will be more at risk, if the value of the land has fallen. The question of priority—the order in which lenders get paid, if the land has to be sold—is thus a very important one. The law has developed complicated rules for determining this question; but the main principles are that legal mortgages come first, and then equitable mortgages.

7-58 *Enforcement* If the borrower fails to repay, the lender can enforce the mortgage in a number of different ways. He can:

- Start legal proceedings against the borrower for the money. This can be done for a mortgage as it can for any other debt;

though of course it will only be worthwhile if the borrower has sufficient money to repay the loan without selling the land.

- Take possession of the property, unless this possibility is excluded by the mortgage deed. This allows the lender to let the property, and receive the income; but strict rules govern what happens to the income received, and a court order will be necessary in many cases in order for the lender to obtain possession—he cannot simply evict the borrower by force. The lender may also wish to take possession of the property as a preliminary to selling.

See 8-88 onwards for the Protection from Eviction Act 1977.

- Sell the land. The lender must obtain the best price he reasonably can. Under s. 105 of the Law of Property Act 1925, the proceeds of sale must go first to pay the expenses of the sale, then to pay off the mortgage, then to the next lender according to the rules of priority mentioned above, or if there is no other lender, to the borrower.

- Foreclose. The effect of this legal action is to end the borrower's rights in the land, and to make the lender the owner of it. In practice, this Draconian remedy is subject to safeguards which make it less useful to the lender.

See 7-59 for these safeguards.

- Appoint a receiver; that is, a person to take charge of the property and manage it with the aim of producing money for the lender. (This is a right which is often given to lenders if the property is commercial.)

Given the strong position of the lender, the legal system has developed rules which offer the borrower extra protection. The borrower is regarded as having a right to redeem (pay off the debt) and so regain full rights over the land. This right must not be unduly interfered with, and it is regarded as continuing, subject to certain limitations, after the date when the debt was due to be repaid. 7-59

The courts have a discretion, where a lender is seeking possession of a dwelling, or foreclosing in respect of a dwelling, to delay making the appropriate order for a reasonable time, if they think that the 7-60

Suspending an order for possession

In the case of *Cheltenham & Gloucester Building Society v. Norgan* (1996) Mr and Mrs Norgan borrowed money on their house for business purposes. The business ran into difficulties and substantial arrears built up. The Cheltenham applied to the County Court for an order giving them possession. An order was made but suspended under s. 8 of the Administration of Justice Act 1973 on condition that arrears were paid off. When this was not done there was a series of further applications by the building society and a further suspended order. Eventually the judge decided that he could not grant further suspensions because there was no prospect of the the arrears being paid off within a reasonable period, which he regarded as 2–4 years.

There was an appeal, and the Court of Appeal decided that the judge was wrong: the correct starting point was the remaining period of the mortgage: subject to other factors, if the arrears could be paid off during that period the order for possession should remain suspended.

borrower will be able to pay any sum due within that time. These powers were granted to the courts by the Administration of Justice Act 1970, ss. 36 and 39, and the Administration of Justice Act 1973, s. 8. The borrower may thus have an extra chance to pay the money he owes and avoid losing his property.

7-61 While it is very common in the United Kingdom for lenders to give themselves the power to vary the rate of interest charged, Parliament has in some cases set a limit on their ability to charge very high rates to private individuals, under of the Consumer Credit Act 1974. The Act applies only where the amount lent is less than £15,000. First mortgages are unlikely to be so small; but later, additional mortgages may come into this category.

7-62 Sections 137 to 140 of the Consumer Credit Act 1974 allow the court to reopen a credit agreement (including a mortgage by a private person) if it finds that the agreement is "extortionate". By s. 138, an agreement is "extortionate" if if requires the person or a relative of his to make payments which are "grossly exorbitant", or which "otherwise grossly contravene principles of fair dealing". The court may take into account, in deciding whether an agreement is extortionate, interest rates prevailing at the time the agreement was made, and a number of other factors such as the age, experience and health of the borrower, and whether he was under financial pressure. The agreement can be altered by the court, for example by

The Unfair Terms in Consumer Contracts Regulations 1999 may apply to mortgages, as they do to leases: see 8-41.

substituting a lower rate of interest, or by deleting some unfair term. While the court's powers are wide, they are not for use merely because the borrower has committed himself to an interest rate which is higher than the norm—the agreement must be "grossly exorbitant", or the agreement "grossly unfair", before the court can intervene.

See 12-2 for sources on mortgages.

Assessment

7-63 It is surprising that for centuries there has not seemed to be a need for a general right allowing landowners to gain access to their land, via neighbouring property, for the purposes of repair and maintenance: it is after all very common for landowners to build right to the boundaries of their land, so that they must go on to neighbouring land to get access to the wall on the boundary. Perhaps common sense has generally prevailed, and permission has been given when requested. In any event, the Access to Neighbouring Land Act 1992 now provides a way for landowners to apply to court for an access order, if they need to.

7-64 The intention is, however, that landowners should reach agreement between themselves, knowing that the court will make an order if they cannot do so, and that the process of applying to the court will be expensive to one or both landowners. It is therefore sensible for a landowner faced with a request for access to grant permission voluntarily. But this does not mean that there should not be discussion about terms and conditions: the aim should be to agree a reasonable basis on which access will be granted. This cannot include payment, however, unless the land to which access is sought is commercial rather than residential.

7-65 Restrictive covenants can be a valuable way of controlling the use of neighbouring land. But enforcement—particularly of old covenants—can be an uncertain business. There may be doubts about which land is entitled to the benefit of the covenant, and which is subject to it. If the covenant has been ignored in the past, the court may be reluctant to enforce it by granting an injunction; and an application can always be made to the Lands Tribunal to discharge or modify a restrictive covenant. It is partly becuse of the unreliability of restrictive covenants that careful attention is given to the granting of rights of way, where one piece of land is dependent upon a right of way over another: limiting the terms of the right of way may be a better way of controlling the use of the land which has the benefit of it.

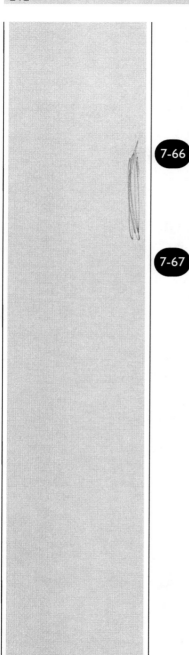

7-66 Landowners should be aware that allowing others to use their land, in the expectation of acquiring some right over it, may mean that the expectation has to be honoured, in the interests of fairness. It is undoubtedly better, before getting into this situation, to take professional advice and draw up a proper agreement, defining the rights which will be granted.

7-67 Borrowing money on mortgage gives the lender powerful rights over land. These rights are to some extent balanced by rights which the law gives to the borrower; but at the end of the day the point of a mortgage is to give the lender a guarantee of being able to get his money back by enforcing his rights over the land, and while borrowers in difficulties can be given "second chances" by the courts, before being deprived of their property, the rights of lenders must in the end be allowed to prevail.

Chapter 8

Leases and tenancies

Introduction

The subject of this chapter is leases and tenancies. The words "lease" and "tenancy" mean, in a legal sense, the same thing. In practice, "lease" is sometimes used to describe long-term arrangements, and "tenancy" short-term arrangements, but this chapter uses the words interchangeably. "Landlord and tenant" are equivalent to "lessor and lessee". 8-0

See 1-30 for the meaning of "freehold" and "leasehold".

This is a complicated subject, and the chapter deals with it only in outline. It looks at the general law, then at some particular sorts of lease, and the protection given to tenants. Finally it deals with the way in which the criminal law gives some added protection, both to people who are in occupation of residential property and to landowners who want to regain possession of residential property in order to live there. 8-1

A landowner may be a landlord, and so concerned to know what rights he and his tenant have. Equally it is right to describe a tenant as a "landowner" for the purposes of most of this book—the owner of leasehold rather than freehold land—since a lease can also be a piece of legal property. If so, the landowner will be interested in the relationship from the other point of view. 8-2

Much of the law explained in this chapter comes from legislation; Parliament has intervened with a great deal of legislation which adjusts the rights of landlords and tenants, mainly to protect tenants. There are also many decisions of the courts on how the legislation works, and on points not covered by legislation. The law explained is civil law—backed up at appropriate points by criminal law. 8-3

Use of leases and tenancies

8-4 The effect of a lease or tenancy is to give the tenant the entire use of a piece of land, to the exclusion of the owner of the land and others. Lease and tenancies are flexible legal arrangements, since the terms can be adapted to suit short or long term use of land, and different sorts of use (residential, commercial and so on).

8-5 Furthermore, complicated arrangements can be constructed by sub-letting and by assigning leases. Unless the terms of the lease forbid it, a tenant can sub-let; in other words, he can grant a lease (which must of course be shorter than his own lease) to a sub-tenant. Or he can assign his lease, meaning that he passes his interest in the land to another person, and drops out of the picture. Such complications are common for large commercial properties, but are not considered further in this chapter.

Assigning and sub-letting A, the owner, lets property to B. B can then sub-let to C, or he can assign his lease to D, so that D is then A's tenant. D in turn can sub-let to E. See 8-18 for the effect of assignment or sub-letting on covenants in leases.

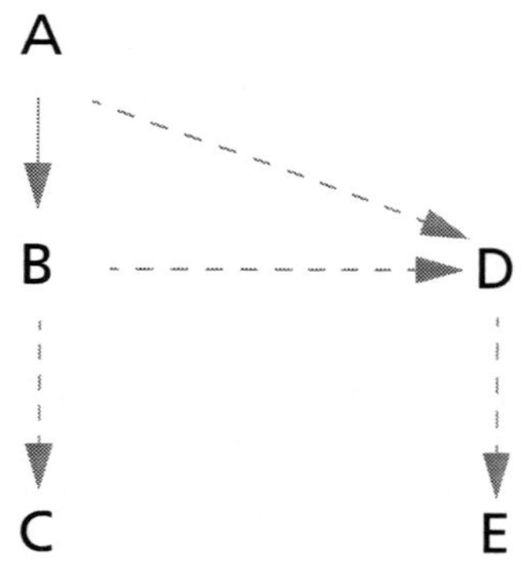

8-6 Building leases were common during the 19th century and the early part of the 20th. A builder would acquire land for development, would put up houses for customers, and would then grant a lease, usually of 99 years. The builder would receive a modest "ground rent" and would be entitled to get the land back after 99 years, a landlord's right to have the land back at the end of the lease being known as the "reversion".

8-7 Any sort of land can be leased, including houses and commercial property, as an alternative to being sold freehold. Flats are almost always sold leasehold, rather than freehold. It is not legally impossible for a flat to be sold freehold, but unless the flat is a ground floor flat the result will be a "flying freehold"—freehold land which consists of a volume of space above the surface of the earth. The contents of the space will not stay in place by themselves. They will need support and also a roof. To make the arrangement work in practice, it will be necessary to impose continuing obligations which will apply between the landlord and the tenant. In essence the owner of the surface of the land must be under an obligation to maintain the structure as a whole, and the tenant to contribute to the cost. This poses problems in the case of a flying freehold, since the general rule is that *negative* obligations can be binding on successive owners of land, but not positive obligations like a requirement to pay money or do work.

See 2-6 on plots of land.

See 7-13 onwards for restrictive (i. e. negative) covenants.

8-8 A lease is a way of making sure that a flat is subject to positive obligations, since positive obligations in leases can be enforced by successive landlord against successive tenants, and vice versa. The same ability to construct long-lasting obligations between landlords and tenants is also useful in other contexts, for example in the case of commercial developments.

See 12-11 for sources on leases generally.

Contrast with other legal arrangements

8-9 The key characteristic of leases and tenancies is that the owner of the land gives exclusive possession to it to someone else. "Exclusive possession" means that, subject to one exception, the owner of the land gives up entirely the right to come on to the land and bring others on to it. (The exception is that a lease may provide for the landlord to enter for specified purposes, for example to inspect the property.) A lease is thus different from an easement: an easement can give the right to make use of land; but the use must be limited, and must not interfere too much with the right of the owner to go on making reasonable use it.

See 1-47 for the meaning of "possessing" land.

See chapter 6 for easements.

8-10 If the owner of a house takes in a lodger, the nature of the arrangement is likely to be that the lodger will not have exclusive possession of his room, because the owner of the house will make clear that she reserves the right to go into the room. The arrangement will therefore not be a lease, but merely a licence—in other words permission by the owner to use the room.

See 1-49 for licences.

8-11 Whether an arrangement creates a tenancy, with all the rights and obligations which go with it, or merely a licence, can be a difficult question. The courts apply one important rule, however, which is that the way in which the arrangement is described does not matter very much. What counts is the whether the owner of land has given exclusive possession of the land to someone else. If so, the courts are likely to conclude that there is a tenancy. This is an understandable response to the desire of some landowners to avoid the legal consequences of creating a tenancy by describing the arrangement as a licence.

See also 8-100 for timeshares, which are usually licences rather than leases.

Leases and licences

In the case of *Bruton v. London & Quadrant Housing* (1999) the question was whether a tenancy of a flat had been created. If so, the tenant, Mr Bruton, had rights under the Landlord and Tenant Act 1985 to have the flat repaired. His agreement with London & Quadrant (a charitable housing association) was described as a licence; and London & Quadrant had only a licence from the local authority, who would require the property in due course for development.

The House of Lords decided that the agreement had all the characteristics of a tenancy, and the fact that it was described as a licence made no difference. Nor did the fact that London & Quadrant was itself a licensee: there was still a landlord and tenant relationship between the association and Mr Bruton. Mr Bruton thus had rights under the Landlord and Tenant Act 1985.

8-12 The payment of rent, in money or money's worth, is not an essential ingredient of a lease. An incoming tenant may be asked to a pay a "premium"—a lump sum. For a long lease, the tenant will often have to pay a substantial premium, and perhaps a relatively small annual rent.

See also 8-54 and 8-67 for rules on premiums.

Creation and registration

8-13 Like other sorts of property, leases can be equitable or legal in nature. To be legal, a lease must be created by deed. However there is an exception to this rule for leases which start immediately, are for not more than three years, and which are at the best rent reasonably available, without any premium being paid. These leases can be created by writing which is not in the form of a deed, and they can even be created orally. The exception applies even if the tenant is able to extend the period of the lease, provided the initial period is for not more than three years (Law of Property Act 1925, s. 52(2) and s. 54(2)).

See 1-17 onwards for the difference between legal and equitable interests in land.

8-14 In addition, to be legal in nature, a lease must be for a definite period. This requirement will be fulfilled if it is for (say) one year, or 99 years; equally it will be fulfilled if the lease is "periodic", and runs from week to week, month to month, or year to year, since each period has a fixed maximum duration. The fact that the lease or tenancy may be brought to an end before the expiry of the period does not prevent the lease from being legal. Rent usually has to be paid under a lease, either in money or money's worth; but this is not an essential ingredient of a lease.

8-15 If, on the other hand, a lease has an uncertain maximum duration —for example, because it will end when the tenant dies—it cannot be legal in nature. Nor can a lease for which a deed is required, but which has not been created by deed. Such leases can only be recognised by the rules of equity, and the principles explained in chapter 1 apply to them.

See 1-17 onwards for these principles.

8-16 A lease for more than 21 years must be entered on the Land Register in order to be valid, whether or not the land is already registered (Land Registration Act 1925, ss. 123(1) and 19(1)). A lease for 21 years or less does not have to be entered on the register: the purpose of this rule is to prevent the system of land registration being clogged up by short leases. Instead, the Land Registration Act 1925 provides that leases for up to 21 years, provided that they are legal in nature, are overriding interests. This means that if the land is sold, it remains subject to the lease whether or not the purchaser knows about it. Purchasers of land must therefore take care to check

See 1-59 for the meaning of "overriding interest".

whether there is a sitting tenant (i. e. a tenant occupying the property).

Covenants in leases

See 1-34 onwards for deeds.

See also 1-50 for the meaning of "express" and "implied".

8-17 A "covenant" is an undertaking in a deed. Covenants in a lease set out the rights and obligations of the landlord and tenant. (The term "covenant" is sometimes used even where there is in fact no deed, because the lease is for less than three years and is created without one.) Covenants may be "express", meaning that they have been specifically agreed by the landlord and tenant, or "implied", meaning that the law inserts a covenant, imposing an obligation on the landlord or the tenant. Where a covenant is intended to be of fundamental importance, so it is clear that breach of it means that the other party is entitled to end the lease, it is known as a "condition".

8-18 The rules about how covenants affect the landlord and tenant when there is an assignment (transfer) of the lease, or where the tenant sub-lets, are important, but outside the scope of this book. The law has been changed in fundamental ways, for leases made after the start of 1996, by the Landlord and Tenant (Covenants) Act 1995.

8-19 *Express covenants* Depending upon the purpose of a lease, and the length of time involved, covenants may be very lengthy, setting out the obligations on the tenant and the landlord in great detail, and dealing with rent review, the use of the land, repair, and many other matters. In other circumstances, especially where the lease is for only a short period, the express covenants may be very brief. The following express covenants are common:

- A covenant by the tenant to pay rent. This may be expressed as a specific sum, or the lease may set out a formula for calculating the rent. If the lease is to be for a lengthy period, it is common for there to be a review of the rent after a certain number of years, so that it reflects current market conditions.

- A covenant by the tenant that he will not sub-let the property or assign the lease, or let someone else take possession of the property.

Covenants of the latter sort are very important to the landlord, who will wish to be sure that the person using the property is someone she trusts. Without such a covenant, tenant would be free to transfer the lease to anyone he wished, no matter how unwelcome to the landlord. Restrictions on disposing of the lease are also very important to tenants, especially in the case of long leases, since they may affect the value of the lease. A covenant in the lease may prevent the tenant from sub-letting or assigning the lease altogether (though the landlord may still agree to sub-letting or assignment if she wishes). Alternatively, a lease sometimes provides that the tenant may only sub-let or assign with the landlord's consent. In this case, in almost all leases, the law is that the landlord's consent must not be unreasonably withheld (s. 19(1) of the Landlord and Tenant Act 1927). The landlord can then refuse consent only if there are reasonable grounds for doing so. Additional rules have been added by the Landlord and Tenant Act 1988, s. 1: if the landlord is asked by the tenant for consent (the request must be in writing) the landlord must respond within a reasonable time and if she refuses consent she must explain why she is doing so. 8-20

In the case of *Welsh v. Greenwich London Borough Council* (2000) there was a covenant by the landlord of a flat (the Council) to "maintain the dwelling in good condition and repair". The tenant complained that there was a breach of the covenant because the flat was affected by damp and mould. The landlord argued that the dampness was caused by bad design of the flat, and was not covered by the covenant.

The court's decision was that the obligation to maintain the flat was separate from the question of repairs; and since the flat was not in good repair the landlord was under an obligation to do the necessary work.

The court added that the meaning of a covenant in a lease was to some extent a matter of impression, and depended upon the circumstances.

A covenant to repair

Express covenants may cover a wide range of subjects, including such things as: 8-21

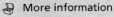

- Restricting the use which the tenant may make of the property.

- Requiring the tenant to insure the property.

- Requiring the tenant to repair the property when necessary, or redecorate it from time to time.

- Giving the landlord the right to enter the property and inspect it at certain times for particular purposes.

8-22 *Implied covenants* The law implies covenants in certain circumstances. The implied covenant does not appear in the written document (if there is one) containing the terms of the lease, but is nonetheless effective, and imposes obligations on the landlord or tenant. Generally, implied covenants apply only if there are no express covenants dealing with the point.

8-23 In any lease there is an implied covenant by the landlord that he will allow the tenant "quiet enjoyment" of the property. This means that the landlord will not disturb the tenant in any way in his enjoyment of the property. The implied covenant is not mainly concerned with noise as such, since noise which interfered with the use of the property could be dealt with under the law of nuisance. It is concerned with other sorts of disturbance caused by the landlord, for example harrassing the tenant by cutting off electricity or other services, or obstructing his use of the property in some other way.

See 4-7 onwards for nuisance.

See also 8-89 for the offence of harassment, under the Protection from Eviction Act 1977.

8-24 A landlord is not under any general obligation to repair because of an implied covenant. But there is an implied covenant where the lease is for less than seven years and is a lease of a "dwelling house", which includes flats and maisonettes (Landlord and Tenant Act 1985, s. 11). The implied covenant obliges the landlord to keep in good repair:

- The structure and exterior of the dwelling-house, including drains, gutters and external pipes.

- The supply of water, gas and electricity, and sanitation (including basins, sinks, baths and lavatories).

- The central heating and water heating system (s. 11(1)).

In the case of *Southwark London Borough Council v. Mills* some tenants in a block of flats brought legal proceedings against the landlord, Southwark Council. They complained that the walls of the flats were so thin that they were disturbed by the everyday noises made by other tenants, and that this was a breach by the landlord of the covenant for quiet enjoyment..

After a succession of appeals, the House of Lords decided that there was no breach of the covenant. Although the covenant could apply to noise, it did not cover noise due to the state of the property at the start of the lease, or from use which the landlord and tenants must have expected. The tenants were therefore not entitled to compensation. [The House of Lords also decided that the noise did not amount to a nuisance for which the tenants could be compensated: see chapter 4 for nuisance.]

Quiet enjoyment

If the property forms part of a building, then the landlord's obligation extends to other parts of the building in which the landlord has an interest. If, for example, a flat in a block receives hot water or heating from a central boiler, not located in the flat itself, then the landlord has an obligation to keep the boiler in good repair. However this rule only applies to leases made after 15 January 1989 . 8-25

This implied covenant applies regardless of what the landlord and tenant may agree. Any attempt to agree to disregard or alter it will be of no effect (s. 12(1) of the 1985 Act). However if the landlord and tenant agree, and it appears reasonable, the County Court may make an order which allows them to ignore or alter the implied covenant (s. 12(2)). 8-26

Some implied covenants apply to the tenant. There is an implied covenant that the tenant will pay any tax due on the property, such as Council tax. In negotiating a lease, especially a short one, the tenant may thus wish to exclude this obligation, if he can, so that it falls on the landlord. Most leases will have an implied covenant by which the tenant must repair the property; but the nature of the covenant will depend upon the length of the lease. For tenancies which run from week to week or month to month, the tenant is 8-27 responsible for any damage which he actually causes, but is not generally responsible for damage which occurs through neglect. (Though the law is not entirely clear, it is sometimes said that a tenant must act in a "tenant-like manner", suggesting that there may be an implied obligation to take at least obvious steps to prevent damage.) For yearly tenancies, it is generally considered that the tenant also has the obligation of keeping the property "wind and water-tight", and so may have to carry out limited repairs if necessary for this purpose. Where there is a lease for a number of years, there is an implied covenant that the tenant will maintain the property and keep it in the condition it was in at the start of the lease.

8-28 Since the nature of the implied covenant may be uncertain, it will make sense for the landlord and tenant to reach agreement about what repairs each will be responsible for. There will then be no need to rely on the implied covenant.

8-29 Tenants and landlords may commit legal wrongs other than breaches of covenants, express or implied. A tenant, for example, may be guilty of stealing from the property, or damaging it.

See 11-57 for stealing and 11-59 for criminal damage to land.

Remedies for breach of covenants

8-30 Covenants in a lease will impose obligations on both the landlord and the tenant. One can take legal action for breach of covenant by the other. What action is possible will depend upon the nature of the breach and whether the law intervenes to regulate what happens. The law does this for breaches both by tenants and by landlords; though it tends to intervene more to protect tenants, because they may be in a more vulnerable position.

8-31 *Landlords* Where a tenant is in breach of a covenant, the landlord can take legal action to obtain compensation for any loss suffered. Typically the tenant may have failed to pay rent due, and the landlord can then sue the tenant for the arrears. Another course open to the landlord is "distress": the landlord may in certain circumstances be entitled to enter the property and "distrain" (seize) property found there, with a view to selling it. The law on this point

See 8-39 on this point.

is complicated, however (a bailiff must be used) and like other "self-help" remedies the right needs to be exercised with great care.

See 1-25 for self-help.

8-32 If a landlord wants to carry out repairs, he may be entitled to do so under the terms of the lease; or, in circumstances where his obligation to repair is imposed by an Act, the Act will also give a right to enter the property to carry out those repairs.

8-33 The most powerful remedy which may be open to a landlord is to forfeit the lease—that is, to end the lease by taking back possession of the property. This sometimes known as "re-entering" the property. The landlord can take this course if it is clear that there has been a breach of a condition in the lease, or if the lease provides that the landlord can forfeit the lease for breach of a covenant. Forfeiting the lease may have a harsh effect on the tenant, whether the property is the tenant's home or business address or is put to some other use, and the law lays down rules which lessen the harshness by giving the tenant relief in certain circumstances, allowing the tenant to remain. The way the law works depends upon the nature of the breach of covenant for which the landlord is seeking to forfeit the lease.

See 8-17 for the meaning of "condition" and "covenant".

8-34 If the breach consists of a failure to pay the rent, the overdue rent must first of all be formally demanded (though the lease may well provide that this step does not need to be taken). The landlord may then take action, and will usually need to do so by taking legal proceedings to regain possession of the property. The basis of the court's order is that, once the tenancy has ended, the tenant is a trespasser, and he can therefore be ordered to give possession of the property back to the landlord. The tenant can avoid forfeiture by paying the overdue rent before the case is heard by the court. But even if the landlord shows that the rent is overdue, the County Court may suspend an order for possession for four weeks or more, thus giving the tenant the opportunity to pay off the arrears and so remain in the property. And even when the landlord has regained possession, the tenant may still, within six months, apply to the court for relief, and if the court grants it the lease comes back to life (County Courts Act 1984, s. 138). (The terms imposed by the court are likely to include payment of all arrears of rent, and the landlord's costs.)

See 8-88 for the Protection from Eviction Act 1977.

See chapter 3 for trespass.

8-35 For breach of any covenant other than one to pay rent, a landlord who wishes to forfeit the lease must first serve a notice on the tenant under s. 146(1) of the Law of Property Act 1925. The notice must:

- Specify the breach which the landlord is complaining of.
- Require the tenant to remedy the breach, if it can be remedied (this will be so if the lease imposes an obligation to do something which the tenant has not done, but may not be possible if the tenant has done something which the lease forbids).
- Require the tenant to pay compensation.

8-36 If the tenant fails to remedy the breach (assuming it can be remedied) or fails to pay compensation, the landlord can take action, which will usually mean bringing legal proceedings. Once the landlord has started to take action, the tenant can apply to the court to ask for relief (s. 146(2)). The court has a wide power to grant relief, taking into account all the relevant circumstances, including the conduct of the parties. Suppose, for example, the tenant has broken a covenant which forbids noisy parties, and the landlord has the right under the lease to forfeit for breach of the covenant. The breach cannot be remedied; but if the tenant offers reasonable compensation the landlord cannot bring proceedings to forfeit the lease. If the tenant does not offer compensation the landlord can bring proceedings; and the court may grant or refuse relief. It might, for example, allow the tenant to remain, on condition that he pays compensation, and the costs incurred by the landlord in bringing the proceedings, and on condition that there are no more noisy parties.

8-37 An additional rule applies to some leases where the landlord wishes to forfeit the lease because of a failure to repair the property. This applies to leases of more than seven years (but not agricultural leases) where there is at least three years left to run, under the Leasehold Properties (Repairs) Act 1938. A landlord who wishes to forfeit the lease for breach of a covenant to repair must, as explained above, serve a notice under s. 146 of the Law of Property Act 1925. The 1938 Act provides that the same sort of notice must be served before the landlord can bring proceedings for compensation, for a failure to repair, even if he does not wish to forfeit the lease (s. 1(2)). In either case the landlord's notice must draw attention to the tenant's right to serve a counter-notice (s. 1(4)). If the tenant serves a counter-notice, the landlord can take no action without the permission of the court (s. 1(3)). Permission can only be given on specific grounds set out in the 1938 Act, including the need for repairs to prevent "substantial diminution" in the value of the property (s. 1(5)). The court can impose terms and conditions in giving leave (s. 1(6)). The purpose of this Act is to give tenants extra protection against oppressive action by landlords in cases where the property is in poor repair and the landlord might use this fact to pressurise a tenant.

A different situation, where extra rules apply, is where the landlord wishes to forfeit the lease (or obtain compensation) for breach of a covenant to carry out "internal decorative repairs", and so serves a notice on the tenant under s. 146 of the Law of Property Act 1925. The tenant can apply to the court for relief under s. 147 of the Act, and the court can grant relief if it is satisfied that the notice is unreasonable. The tenant may be relieved from doing any redecorating, or merely from doing some. But in some cases s. 147 does not apply, and the tenant cannot obtain relief, including: 8-38

- Where there is an express covenant to put the property in good decorative order, and the tenant has never done so.

- Where the repairs relate to the property's sanitary condition or structure.

- Where there is a covenant to hand over a house or other building, at the end of the lease, in a certain state of repair (s. 147(2)).

When a landlord wishes to forfeit a lease, he may be able to do so by physically going on to the property and taking possession, this course being known to the law as "peaceable re-entry". But this course will usually not be open to him in relation to residential 8-39 property, because of the protection which the law gives to those living there.

See 8-93 for restrictions on the right to regain possession of residential property.

8-40 *Tenants* When a tenant finds that his landlord is in breach of a covenant in the lease he may take legal action against the landlord to obtain damages (compensation), or an injunction—for example to stop the landlord disturbing him, in breach of the covenant for quiet enjoyment. A tenant may also be able to obtain an order from the court requiring the landlord to carry out an obligation in the lease, for example making repairs. (The courts generally do not make such orders against tenants, because the landlord will usually be in a position to enter the property and carry out the repair and then take legal action against the tenant to make him pay for it, if repair is in fact the tenant's responsibility.)

See 8-23 for these covenants.

8-41 Where a tenant is a private individual, and the landlord is acting in the course of business, the Unfair Terms in Consumer Contracts Regulations 1999 may apply to a lease. These Regulations provide that a term in a contract which is "unfair" is not valid. Whether a term is unfair has to be assessed in all the circumstances. But the Regulations deal specifically with standard-form agreements (which includes leases):

> "A contractual term which has not been individually negotiated shall be regarded as unfair if, contrary to the requirement of good faith, it causes an imbalance in the parties' rights and obligations to the detriment of the consumer."

So covenants in a standard-form lease may be unfair, and of no effect, if they put the landlord in too strong a position.

See 8-82 for a different piece of legislation, the Unfair Contract Terms Act 1977.

8-42 *Generally* The remedies described above are in addition to those provided by the general law for legal wrongs, both civil and criminal. A landlord will generally reserve the right to enter the property in certain circumstances; but a landlord who enters without such a right, or some other legal right, will be trespassing, and the tenant can take action in accordance with the civil law. The criminal law also applies, and some particularly relevant offences are explained below.

See chapter 3 for trespass generally.

See 8-88 and 8-94 onwards for these offences.

8-43 Where a building contains two or more flats, there is a special procedure under Part II of the Landlord and Tenant Act 1987. This applies if the landlord does not carry out his obligations to repair, maintain or insure the property. A tenant can serve notice on the landlord to remedy the breach; and if the landlord does not do so the tenant may apply to the court for the appointment of a manager to take over the care of the property.

Ending leases and tenancies

Generally Apart from forfeiture, explained above, a lease or tenancy may come to an end in a number of different ways. A lease granted for a fixed period will expire at the end of that period, or before then, if the terms of the lease provide for this to happen. A periodic tenancy will come to an end if the landlord or the tenant gives notice that he wishes to end the lease. Subject to anything in the terms of the lease, or an agreement between the landlord and tenant, the period of notice required will generally be six months for a yearly lease, and a month for a monthly lease. 8-44

A lease may also be ended if the tenant surrenders it, with the agreement of the landlord. If the tenant buys the landlord's interest in the land—the reversion—then the lease is said to have "merged" with the reversion, and the tenant becomes the freehold owner of the land. It was common for this to happen in the case of a building lease. A house would be built on the land, and at some point during the lease the owner of the house would buy the landlord's interest in the land and so become the freehold owner of the land. 8-45

A tenancy may come to an end in a friendly way, the tenant being happy to leave the property. But there may be a dispute. The landlord may (for example) claim that there has been a breach of covenant, entitling him to forfeit the tenancy, and the tenant may deny it. When this happens, the landlord will have to take two steps. First, he must end the tenancy. Then, assuming the tenant refuses to leave, he must obtain possession, generally by means of an order for possession, not by taking direct action himself.

Just as the law intervenes in many cases to restrict a landlord's right to end a lease by forfeiture, so also there are wider rules which apply to leases of particular sorts, particularly residential leases. The main purpose of these rules is to protect the tenant by: 8-46

For weekly tenancies, the minimum period will be 4 weeks, under the Protection from Eviction Act 1977: see 8-47.

See 8-6 for the meaning of "reversion" and also for building leases.

◆ Controlling the rent which can be charged for the property.

◆ Limiting the circumstances in which the landlord can end the lease.

These rules are considered below.

See 8-48 onwards.

8-47 *Notices to quit* Some special rules apply to many periodic tenancies of residential property. By s. 5 of the Protection from Eviction Act 1977, a notice to quit, whether given by the landlord or the tenant or other occupier, must generally be in writing, must contain the prescribed information, and must be given at least 4 weeks before the date on which it takes effect. "Prescribed" means prescribed in regulations, and the relevant regulations are the Notices to Quit (Prescribed Information) Regulations 1988. The information which must be given, set out in the Schedule to the Regulations, is as follows:

See 8-14 for the meaning of "periodic" tenancy.

It does not apply to those which are "excluded" under the 1977 Act, as to which see 8-93.

> "1. If the tenant or licensee does not leave the dwelling, the landlord or licensor must get an order for possession from the court before the tenant or licensee can lawfully be evicted. The landlord or licensor cannot apply for such an order before the notice to quit or notice to determine has run out.
>
> 2. A tenant or licensee who does not know if he has any right to remain in possession after a notice to quit or a notice to determine runs out can obtain advice from a solicitor. Help with all or part of the cost of legal advice and assistance may be available under the Legal Aid Scheme. He should also be able to obtain information from a Citizens' Advice Bureau, a Housing Aid Centre or a rent officer."

Protection for residential tenants

8-48 The Rent Act 1977 set up a system of protection for residential tenants with short leases. This system dealt with security of tenure—the tenant's right to remain in the property unless certain conditions are fulfilled—and control of rent. Since 15 January 1989, with a few exceptions, it has not been possible to create new tenancies under the

1977 Act; instead, a new (and in some ways weaker) system of protection under the Housing Act 1988 applies. The following paragraphs look at these Acts, which are both concerned with short-term tenancies.

See 8-72 onwards for protection for longer-term residential tenants.

The Rent Act 1977

When the Act applies In order for the Rent Act 1977 to apply, the following conditions must be satisfied: 8-49

- There must be a separate dwelling, whether this is a house, flat, or maisonette (s. 1). In other words, the Act applies only to residential property. There can be some sharing of rooms; but the property which is let must generally have its own living area, and cooking and bathroom facilities, though the bathroom may be shared. (Bed-sitting rooms cannot be subject to protection under the Act.)
- The value of the property must be within certain limits, thus excluding properties with a high rental value from the protection (s. 4).
- The tenancy must not be excluded under ss. 5–16 (see below).
- The tenancy must have been created before 15 January 1989.

The cases in which a tenancy is excluded under ss. 5–16 include the following: 8-50

- Where the rent is very low (s. 5) (The point of this provision is to exclude long leases, where the tenant is likely to have paid a premium for the lease, often with a small annual payment.)

See 8-12 for the meaning of "premium".

- Where the tenancy includes meals (s. 7).

- Where the tenant is a student (s. 8).

- Holidays lettings (s. 9).

- Where the dwelling forms part of a building (but not a block of flats) in which the landlord also lives (s. 12).

- Where the landlord is a public body (ss. 13–16). This includes central and local government and also some other bodies.

See 8-30 and 8-44 onwards.

8-51 *Security of tenure* The way in which the Rent Act 1977 works is that if the landlord wishes to regain possession of the property, he must first end the tenancy in accordance with the rules explained above. He may need to give notice, or rely on a breach by the tenant, or if the tenancy is for a fixed period it will come to an end in that way. But when the tenancy has been ended, the Act creates a further tenancy, known as a statutory tenancy, on the same terms, provided the property is being used by the tenant as his or her residence (ss. 2 and 3). The statutory tenancy can only be ended in accordance with the Act.

8-52 The Act lists two main sets of circumstances in which the court may make an order for possession, so that the landlord gets the property back (s. 98 and Parts I and II of Schedule 15). First, the court may make an order if it reasonable to do so, and if one of the following conditions, mostly listed in Part I of Schedule 15, is satisfied (the list is not exhaustive):

- Suitable alternative accommodation is available for the tenant to go to (s. 98(1)(a)).

- The tenant has failed to pay rent, or has broken any other obligation of the tenancy (Case 1 in Part I of Schedule 15).

- The tenant or others living in the property have caused a nuisance to neighbours, or have used the property in a way which is illegal or immoral (Case 2).

- The lease was linked to the employment of the tenant by the landlord, the employment has ended and the landlord has a reasonable need for the property, for a new employee (Case 8).

- The landlord has a reasonable need for the property for his own use or the use of a close relative (Case 9).

Where the above grounds apply, the court has a discretion about whether to end the tenancy and give the property back to the landlord. But for the grounds listed in Part II of Schedule 15, there is no discretion and the court must make an order giving the landlord possession. In each case the landlord must generally give the tenant notice, before the start of the tenancy, that he may require possession of the property on the ground in question: 8-53

- The landlord lived in the property before the tenancy, and now needs it for himself or a member of his family (Case 11).

- The landlord needs the property to live in during his retirement (Case 12).

- The property has previously been lived in by an agricultural worker and the property is needed again for that purpose (Cases 16–18).

- The landlord gave notice to the tenant, before the start of the tenancy that the tenancy was a "protected shorthold tenancy" (Case 19). (This ground was introduced by the Housing Act 1980.)

Rent control The Rent Act 1977 allows either the landlord or the tenant to apply to a rent officer to set a "fair rent" (s. 67). The rent officer must take into account certain factors, including the age, character, location and state of repair of the property, and whether it is furnished. But he must not take into account any shortage of rented accommodation (s. 70). Because of this requirement, fair rents are likely to be lower than market rents, and the system favours 8-54

See 1-23 for the standard scale of fines.

tenants. The Rent Act also controls rents in another way, namely by preventing landlords from charging a premium for granting a tenancy to which the Act applies. Charging a premium is an offence, for which the maximum punishment is a level 3 fine (s. 119). The landlord cannot get round this rule by requiring the tenant to pay an excessive amount to purchase furniture and fittings (s. 123). However a landlord can ask for a deposit of up to one-sixth of the annual rent (s. 128).

8-55 *Passing on a protected or statutory tenancy* The original tenant who enjoys the protection of the Rent Act 1977 can in some circumstances pass on his or her rights (s. 2 and Schedule I). If the tenant dies, the tenancy can be passed on to his or spouse or partner if living with him at the time. If there is no such person, the tenancy can be passed on to a member of the family living with the tenant for at least two years.

Passing on a Rent Act tenancy

The case of *Fitzpatrick v. Sterling Housing Association* (1999) concerned a homosexual couple. On the death of Mr Fitzpatrick's partner, he claimed that he was entitled to succeed to the tenancy in the same way that a wife or husband could.

The House of the Lords decided that Mr Fitzpatrick was not a "spouse"; but that the courts could decide who was a member of the tenant's family, for the purpose of the Rent Act 1977, and that Mr Fitzpatrick could become the new tenant on this basis.

(The House of Lords pointed out that when the Human Rights Act 1998 was in force it might mean the court would have to interpret "spouse" differently.)

The Housing Act 1988

8-56 The Housing Act 1988, in an attempt to reduce the shortage of accommodation available for letting, cut back the protection for tenants, so as to make the market more attractive to landowners who wished to let residential property. The 1988 Act has been amended by the Housing Act 1996. The legislation applies to tenancies created after 15 January 1989. It lays down a new set of rules which deal with security of tenure and control of rent for short-term residential tenancies. The Act is thus quite similar in its aims to the Rent Act 1977, though there are important differences.

8-57 Tenancies to which the Act applies are called "assured tenancies", and there is a special class of assured tenancy known as the "assured shorthold tenancy", under which the landlord can be sure of regaining possession of her property. This sort of tenancy developed from the "protected shorthold tenancy" under the Rent Act 1977.

See 8-53 for the meaning of "protected shorthold tenancy".

8-58 *When the 1988 Act applies* The 1988 Act applies when:

- The property is let as a separate dwelling.
- The tenant is an individual (i. e. not a company) and occupies the property as his only or main home.
- The tenancy is not "excluded" (s. 1).

8-59 The cases in which a tenancy is excluded, and so cannot be an assured tenancy, are listed in Schedule 1 to the 1988 Act, and include the following:

- Where the rent does not fall within certain limits. For a tenancy created before 1 April 1990, the rent must be at least two-thirds of the rateable value of the property, and the rateable value must not exceed £1,500 in Greater London or £750 elsewhere. For a tenancy created on or after that date, the rent must be more than £250 (£1,000 in Greater London) and less than £25,000 a year.
- Business tenancies to which Part II of the Landlord and Tenant Act 1954 applies.
- Where the tenant is a student, and the landlord is a "specified educational institution" (meaning specified in regulations made by the DETR).
- Holiday lettings.

See 8-84 for these provisions.

- Where the landlord is a public body—which includes central and local government and some other public bodies such as housing action trusts.

8-60 *Assured shorthold tenancies* There is a class of assured tenancies known as assured shorthold tenancies. Between the start of the 1988 Act and February 1997 (when some amendments made by the Housing Act 1996 came into force) an assured shorthold tenancy would be created if the landlord served notice on the tenant, before the start of the tenancy, making clear that the tenancy would be an assured shorthold tenancy. The tenancy also had to last for at least six months. Since February 1997, a different rule has applied: assured tenancies will automatically be assured shorthold tenancies, unless certain exceptions apply, including:

- Where the landlord and tenant have agreed that the tenancy is *not* a shorthold tenancy.

- Some agricultural tenancies.

8-61 *Security of tenure* For assured tenancies apart from shorthold ones, the effect of the 1988 Act is that a fixed term tenancy is replaced by a statutory periodic tenancy when it expires. To end a periodic tenancy, the landlord must give notice; and for these and for fixed-term tenancies he may be able to forfeit the tenancy, in the way explained above. (If there are no grounds for ending a fixed-term tenancy, the landlord will have to wait for it to expire and be replaced by a statutory periodic tenancy, then give notice.) At this point, the landlord must take legal proceedings, since the 1988 Act provides that the statutory periodic tenancy can only be brought to an end by means of a court order, and that the order can only be made on certain grounds.

See 8-33 onwards for forfeiture.

8-62 On some of the grounds in the Act, the court *must* end the tenancy and give the landlord possession of the property, and these include the following, which are listed in Part I of Schedule 2 to the 1988 Act. For these grounds to apply, the landlord must have served notice before the beginning of the tenancy, as under the Rent Act 1977:

- Where the landlord occupied the property as his only or principal home before the tenancy and now requires it for himself or his wife's only or principal home (Ground 1).

- Where the property has in the past 12 months been let for holiday use, and where the tenancy is for a fixed term of up to 8 months (Ground 3). This enables a landlord to let holiday property over the winter and still be sure of regaining possession.

- Where the property has been let to students in the last 12 months, and where the tenancy is for a fixed term of not more than 12 months (Ground 4). This serves a similar purpose, allowing a landlord to grant a fixed-term tenancy between student lettings.

- Where the landlord needs to regain possession in order to carry out substantial work on the property, which cannot be done while the tenant remains (Ground 6).

- Where there are substantial arrears of rent. For a weekly tenancy, the rent must be at least 8 weeks' overdue both when the landlord starts proceedings and when the case is heard by the court (Ground 8).

In *Artesian Residential Developments Ltd v. Beck* (2000), Mr Beck had an assured tenancy of a house in Bridgnorth for a fixed period of 10 years. The terms of the lease were that it could be ended if the rent was more than 14 days in arrears. The landlord took legal proceedings to end the lease on this basis, but Mr Beck argued that the court could still grant relief against forfeiture, by suspending the order giving the landlord possession, using the power in s. 138 of the County Courts Act 1984.

The court decided that the power in s. 138 did not apply: under the Housing Act 1988, arrears of rent was a ground on which the court must order possession (Ground 8).

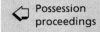

Possession proceedings

8-63 Other grounds are listed in Part II of Schedule 2 to the 1988 Act. Where these apply the court has a discretion about whether to end the tenancy and give the landlord possession of his property. (The court also has a wide discretion allowing it to adjourn or suspend proceedings—it can thus, for example, adjourn proceedings on the condition that the tenant pays off arrears of rent.) These grounds include the following:

- Suitable alternative accommodation is available for the tenant (Ground 9).

- Rent is overdue, or there has been persistent delay in paying rent (Grounds 10 and 11).

- The tenant has broken some other obligation under the tenancy (Ground 12).

- The tenant or others living in the property have caused a nuisance to neighbours or have used the property in a way which is illegal or immoral or has been convicted of a serious offence in or near the property (Ground 14).

- The tenant has damaged the furniture (Ground 15).

- The tenancy was linked to the employment of the tenant by the landlord, the employment has ended, and the landlord has a reasonable need for the property for a new employee (Ground 16).

- The landlord was persuaded to grant the tenancy by a false statement from the tenant (Ground 17).

8-64 In the case of an assured shorthold tenancy, the landlord can be sure of regaining possession of his property provided the tenancy has come to an end and he has given the tenant at least two months' notice that he requires possession (s. 21). The grounds mentioned above also apply, so that the landlord can use these if he wishes.

8-65 *Rent control* The Housing Act 1988 does not intervene in relation to rent if the tenancy agreed between the landlord and the tenant is for a fixed term, or if it is a periodic tenancy with a rent review clause (i. e. built-in arrangements to alter the rent after a certain period or in other circumstances). If the tenancy is a periodic tenancy *without* a rent review clause, whether it is a tenancy agreed between landlord and tenant or the statutory periodic tenancy which arises at the end of a fixed term tenancy, then the Act is relevant to rent.

8-66 If the landlord wishes to increase the rent, he can serve a notice on the tenant, proposing a new rent (s. 13). The tenant can accept the new rent, or can negotiate with the landlord and reach agreement with him about the new level of the rent; or the tenant can apply to a Rent Assessment Committee to decide the rent (s. 14). This must be the amount at which the property "might reasonably be expected to be let in the open market by a willing landlord under an assured tenancy". The Committee must disregard any improvements carried out by the tenant and also any reduction in value caused by the tenant's failure to carry out his obligations under the tenancy.

8-67 The Housing Act 1988 is thus very different from the Rent Act 1977 in relation to the fixing of rent, and is much more favourable to the landlord. The 1988 Act is also different in that it is does not prevent the payment of a premium for the grant of a tenancy.

8-68 Rent control applies to assured shorthold tenants: they can apply to a Rent Assessment Committee for their rent to be fixed (s. 22). They also have the right to require the landlord to supply a written statement of the terms of the tenancy (s. 20A of the 1988 Act, inserted by the Housing Act 1996).

8-69 *Passing on an assured tenancy* Section 17 of the Housing Act 1988 allows a periodic tenancy to be passed on to the tenant's partner (married or not) when the tenant dies, provided the latter was using the property as his or her only or principal residence.

See 8-55 in relation to same-sex partners under the Rent Act 1977.

8-70 *Other points* The Housing Act 1988 also intervenes in several other ways. It implies a term into periodic assured tenancies so that the tenant cannot assign or sub-let the property without the landlord's consent (s. 19). (Section 19(1) of the Landlord and Tenant Act 1927 does not apply, so the landlord's refusal of consent does not have to be reasonable.) This is perhaps only fair, in view of the way in which the Act allows a tenancy to be passed on. But if, in the case

See 8-20 for s. 19(1) of the 1927 Act.

of a non-statutory periodic tenancy, there is an express term which either allows assignment and sub-letting, or prevents the tenant from doing so, the implied term does not apply.

See 8-5 for the meaning of "assign" and "sub-let".

8-71 Another term implied into all assured tenancies is that the landlord can have access to the property to carry out repairs (s. 16). The 1988 Act also provides that the landlord cannot exercise his right to distrain for rent without obtaining permission from the County Court (s. 19).

See 8-31 for the meaning of "distrain".

Long residential leases

8-72 Parliament has also, in a series of different Acts, given some protection to residential tenants who have long leases, including in some cases the right of enfranchisement, meaning the right in some circumstances to "buy out" the landlord and become the owner of the property. This legislation is not concerned with rent control, since tenants with long leases will generally pay a substantial premium, to buy the lease, and usually no more than a modest annual rent.

The law explained above on covenants in leases, forfeiture, and other matters applies to long leases as well as short ones: see 8-17 onwards.

8-73 *Security of tenure* Where a residential lease is for a fixed period of at least 21 years, the tenant may have the right to continue the tenancy at the end of the period. The legislation which produces this result is the Local Government and Housing Act 1989 (which now applies to long leases granted before as well as after the date of the Act). It amends the Landlord and Tenant Act 1954, which used to provide that a Rent Act tenancy could be created at the end of the fixed period; now an assured tenancy, under the Housing Act 1988, can be created. The landlord can serve a notice, with a view to ending the lease, and the tenant can then serve a counter-notice, saying that he wishes to remain in the property. (Alternatively, he will be entitled to remain if he would be an assured tenant, apart from the fact that the rent is low.) If the landlord wishes to pursue the matter he must take legal proceedings, and the grounds on which he can obtain possession are:

- Ground 6 in Part I of Schedule 2 to the 1998 Act.

- Most of the grounds in Part II of Schedule 2.

- Several additional grounds, including the fact that the landlord wishes to demolish and redevelop the property.

See 8-62 onwards for Parts I and II of Schedule 2.

8-74 *Extending leases and buying the freehold* The Leasehold Reform Act 1967 gives residential tenants with a long lease of a house (the Act does not apply to flats or maisonettes) the right to acquire the freehold or to obtain an extended lease. The existing lease must be for at least 21 years, and the rent generally less than two-thirds of the rateable value; or, for leases granted on or after 1 April 1990—when domestic rating was abolished—the rent must not be more than £1,000 in Greater London or £250 elsewhere (ss. 3 and 4). The tenant must have been occupying the house, as her only or main residence, for three years (s. 1).

In the case of *Bello v. Oakins* (2000) Mr Oakins had a 99-year lease and gave notice that he wished to purchase the freehold of the house, from Mr Bello, who had bought it at auction in 1988. The Leasehold Valuation Tribunal fixed the price at £10,800. Mr Bello appealed to the Lands Tribunal, arguing that the value should have been £19,750, which was what he paid when he bought the house in 1988. The Lands Tribunal rejected this argument, and decided that the price to be paid was to be calculated in accordance with the Leasehold Reform Act 1967, at the date when the tenant gave notice that he wished to purchase the freehold.

Buying the freehold

8-75 In order to exercise these rights the tenant must serve a notice on the landlord, saying whether she wishes to purchase the freehold or extend the lease (s. 5). The landlord may be entitled to gain possession of the house if he wishes to carry out rebuilding work or to demolish it, or if it is needed for a member of the his family (ss. 17 and 18). If the tenant wishes to have an extended lease, this will be for a period of 50 years, starting at the end of the existing lease (s. 14). The Act lays down the way in which the price is to be calculated (s. 9). In the event of a dispute a tribunal, the Leasehold Valuation Tribunal, deals with it.

See 1-71 for tribunals.

8-76 The scope of the 1967 Act was extended by the Housing Act 1996, so that some tenants of houses with leases of more than 35 years can buy the freehold even though they do not pass the low rent test. Meanwhile, and more importantly, the Leasehold Reform, Housing and Urban Development Act 1993, gave rights to tenants of flats with long leases. As explained above, the 1967 Act does not apply to flats. The 1993 Act applies where there are two or more flats (or maisonettes) in one building. Tenants can take action if they have a long lease (at least 21 years) at a low rent (generally no more than two-thirds of the letting value of the property, or less than £1,000 per year in Greater London or £750 elsewhere)(ss. 5–8). A tenant who meets these conditions has a right under s. 37 to acquire a fresh 90-year lease, starting when the existing lease ends. The price to be paid for the lease is calculated in accordance with the 1993 Act.

8-77 Furthermore, if two-thirds or more of the tenants meet these conditions, they can usually acquire the freehold of the building from the landlord. (There are some exclusions, including where there are not more than four flats, and the landlord lives in one of them (s. 4).) The procedure is for the tenants to serve the appropriate notice on the landlord. If the parties cannot agree on the price to be paid (which must be calculated in accordance with Schedule 6 to the 1993 Act) the dispute is dealt with by the Leasehold Valuation Tribunal (s. 21).

See 8-43 for Part II.

8-78 Some of the rights given to tenants by the Landlord and Tenant Act 1987, Parts II and III, have already been mentioned. Part I of the Act also assists tenants since it gives them a right of "first refusal": in other words, if the landlord wishes to sell the freehold, it must first be offered to the tenants (ss. 1 and 5). The Act applies where there are two or more flats in a building; the landlord must not be a public-sector body, nor someone who is resident (but this does not apply to a purpose-built block of flats)(ss. 1 and 58). More than half of the tenants must be residential tenants who do not have tenancies protected under the Rent Act 1977 or the Housing Act 1988. If the landlord serves notice on the tenants, offering the freehold to them, the tenants can serve a notice accepting the offer, or they can serve a counter-notice proposing their own terms (ss. 6 and 7). If the tenants do not respond, the landlord is then entitled to sell the freehold to whom he wishes, during the next 12 months; if the tenants agree to buy, they must put forward a nominee (which is likely to be a company) to be the new owner of the freehold.

See 12-11 for sources on enfranchisement.

Other provisions on residential tenancies

The Landlord and Tenant Act 1985 contains several provisions which are designed to help residential tenants generally. Tenants can insist on knowing the landlord's name and address. The procedure is for the tenant to make a written request of the person to whom he pays rent, and that person must then disclose the name and address of the landlord. Failure to do so is an offence for which the maximum punishment is a level 4 fine (s. 1). If the landlord turns out to be a company, the tenant can make a further request, for the names of directors of the company and the company secretary. The maximum punishment is the same (s. 2). Because of these provisions, a landlord cannot hide behind an agent or go-between. 8-79

A new landlord must tell the tenant when ownership of the property is transferred to him; and he must in some circumstances tell the tenant about the tenant's rights under the Landlord and Tenant Act 1987 (ss. 3 and 3A). 8-80

Any residential tenant who pays rent weekly can insist on having a rent book. Rent books must contain the name and address of the landlord, and details required by the Rent Books (Forms of Notice) Regulations 1982. Failure to comply with these requirements is an offence for which the maximum punishment is a level 4 fine (s. 4). 8-81

In *Unchained Growth III plc v. Granby Village (Manchester) Management Co. Ltd* (2000) some tenants in a block of flats objected to the level of service charges. When the management company took legal action, the tenants argued that the covenant to pay service charges was not valid because it was not reasonable as required by the Unfair Contract Terms Act 1977.

The court decided that this Act did not apply. The covenant was an integral part of the lease, and therefore outside the scope of the Act, which did not apply to interests in land.

Service charges

8-82 Service charges for residential tenants are also controlled by the Landlord and Tenant Act 1985. A "service charge" is a charge which covers services, repairs, maintenance, insurance or management, and which varies according to the circumstances (s. 18). Only reasonable costs can be taken into account by the landlord in fixing the charges, and any work to which the charges relate must be of a reasonable standard (s. 19). The tenant can ask the landlord for a summary of the costs, and can inspect accounts, receipts and other documents which the landlord has (ss. 21 and 22). A landlord who fails to comply with sections 21 or 22 commits an offence, the maximum punishment being a level 4 fine (s. 25). However, these provisions generally do not apply to tenants of local authorities and some other public bodies (s. 26).

8-83 Finally, the Accommodation Agencies Act 1953 makes it an offence to:

- Ask for or accept a payment to register a person who is looking for residential accommodation to rent.
- Ask for or accept a payment for supplying details of residential accommodation which is to let.
- Issue advertisements describing property as being to let without the authority of the owner.

The maximum punishment is a level 3 fine, or three months' imprisonment, or both.

Protection for business tenants

8-84 Part II of the Landlord and Tenant Act 1954 gives some protection to business tenants. The Act applies where property (or part of it—for example, where shop premises include a flat occupied by the shopkeeper) is used for business purposes (s. 23). "Business" has a wide definition, and includes the activities of clubs and other organisations . However, the Act does not apply to business lettings for a fixed period of not more then six months, nor to certain sorts of business, including agriculture and the licensed trade (s. 43).

8-85 A business tenant enjoys a degree of security of tenure. Once the tenancy has come to an end, because it was for a fixed term which has expired, or because it was a periodic tenancy, and the landlord has given notice to terminate it, the tenant simply remains in place, on the same terms, and the landlord can only regain possession by following the procedures laid down in the Act (s. 24).

See 8-14 for the meaning of "periodic" tenancy.

8-86 To do this the landlord must serve a notice, saying that he wishes to have possession of the property, and if the tenant wishes to remain he must, within two months, serve a counter-notice, and then within a further two months must apply to the court (usually the County Court) for the grant of a new tenancy (s. 25). The grounds on which the landlord can obtain possession, and stop the tenant getting a new tenancy, are set out in the Act; and the landlord must indicate in his notice which he will rely on, if the tenant applies for a new tenancy. They include:

- Failure to repair by the tenant.
- Persistent delay in paying rent.
- Breach of other covenants by the tenant.
- The landlord's wish to demolish and rebuild the property.
- The landlord's wish to occupy the property himself (s. 30(1)).

8-87 If the tenant is seeking a new tenancy, the terms of it can be agreed between tenant and landlord, and there will then be no need for the Court to make a decision. But if there is no agreement, and the Court has to decide, it can grant a tenancy of up to 14 years, and settle the terms (s. 33). On the other hand, the landlord may be successful in showing that he should regain possession of the property. The tenant may then be able to claim compensation from the landlord, for disturbance (i. e. the inconvenience of moving) and for any improvements made to the property with the landlord's consent (s. 37(1) of the 1954 Act, and the Landlord and Tenant Act 1927).

See 12-11 for sources on business tenancies.

Termination of a business tenancy

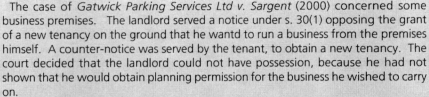

The case of *Gatwick Parking Services Ltd v. Sargent* (2000) concerned some business premises. The landlord served a notice under s. 30(1) opposing the grant of a new tenancy on the ground that he wantd to run a business from the premises himself. A counter-notice was served by the tenant, to obtain a new tenancy. The court decided that the landlord could not have possession, because he had not shown that he would obtain planning permission for the business he wished to carry on.

The landlord appealed, and the Court of Appeal decided that he should not have been denied possession. All the landlord had to show was that there was a reasonable chance he would get planning permission. (In any event, by the time of the appeal the landlord had obtained planning permission.)

The Protection from Eviction Act 1977

8-88 The Protection from Eviction Act 1977, as amended by the Housing Act 1988, protects tenants and other residential occupiers of land by imposing restrictions on landlords and others who may want to regain possession of land (including lenders under a mortgage). It creates offences, and also imposes requirements as to notice.

See 7-52 for the meaning of "mortgage".

8-89 *Unlawful eviction and harassment* The Act defines, in s. 1(1), the concept of a "residential occupier". A "residential occupier" is a person who is occupying premises as a residence, whether under a lease or tenancy, or merely a licence, or who has the benefit of a right to remain in occupation or a restriction on the landlord's ability to regain possession. (Though it should be noted that a licence may in some circumstances be terminated, so that the licensee becomes a trespasser, and ceases to enjoy the protection of the Act.)

See 1-27 for the meaning of "premises".

See 1-49 onwards for licences.

8-90 Section 1 of the Act creates three separate offences, namely:

- Unlawfully depriving the occupier of his occupation of the premises (in other words, evicting him) (s. 1(2))

◆ Interfering with the peace and comfort of the residential occupier, or his household, with intent to make him give up his occupation of the premises, or to refrain from exercising any right or remedy in respect of the premises (s. 1(3))

◆ In the case of a landlord, or his agent, doing any act likely to interfere with the peace or comfort of the residential occupier or his household, or persistently withdrawing or withholding services, in either case knowing or having reasonable cause to believe that the conduct is likely to make the occupier give up the premises or refrain from exercising any right in connection with them (s. 1(3A)).

> In the case of *R. v. Phekoo* (1981) Mr Phekoo went to a house which he owned. He found two men there, threatened them, and asked them to leave. He was prosecuted under s. 1(3) of the Protection from Harassment Act 1977.
> Mr Phekoo accepted, at the trial, that the two men were "residential occupiers", but his case was that he did not know it when he went to the house, and thought he was dealing with squatters. He was therefore not guilty.
> On appeal, the court agreed: the offence was a serious one, and in order for a person to be convicted, the prosecution must show that he knew or believed that he was dealing with a residential occupier.

⇦ Harassment

The third offence is confined to landlords—but it has a wider scope in that it does not require the prosecution to prove a specific intent, merely knowing or having reasonable cause to believe that the act will have the result mentioned. It is a defence for a person to prove that he had reasonable grounds for what he did (s. 1(3B)). The maximum punishment in a magistrates' courts is a fine of the statutory maximum; and in the Crown Court an unlimited fine or two years' imprisonment. 8-91

Where an offence under s. 1 of the Protection from Eviction Act 1977 has been committed, the victim may also be able to make a civil claim, and obtain compensation, under s. 27 of the Housing Act 1988. 8-92

Forfeiture of leases and eviction Section 2 of the 1977 Act applies where there is a lease of a dwelling, and the lease gives the landlord the right to forfeit the lease (i. e. take back possession): in these circumstances, it is unlawful for the landlord to enforce the right 8-93

See 8-33 for forfeiture generally, and 3-35 for proceedings for possession.

See earlier in this chapter for the various forms of protection.

See 12-11 and 12-24 for sources on the Protection from Harassment Act 1977

except by legal proceedings for possession—and is therefore an offence under s. 1(1) of the Act. In other words, the landlord cannot simply remove the tenant physically. Section 3 deals with a slightly different situation, namely where a tenancy has come to an end. It imposes the same restriction: the landlord cannot take back possession by means of physical action, but must obtain possession by obtaining an order from the court. However, this provision is more complicated. It does apply to licences, as well as tenancies; but it does not apply to tenants who already have protection against the ending of their tenancies. Some arrangements are specifically excluded, including where:

- The landlord shares accommodation with the tenant.
- The occupier has the right to occupy only for a holiday.
- The right is granted otherwise than for money or money's worth (s. 3A).

Offences under the Criminal Law Act 1977

8-94 This Act creates two offences which are of general importance and concern the occupation of land. (They are dealt with here for the sake of convenience, because they will be most relevant where property is let; but they could be relevant to a landowner who is occupying his land himself, or indeed to a trespasser.) It is an offence to use or threaten violence in order to secure entry to premises; and it is an offence in limited circumstances for a trespasser to fail to leave premises if required to do so.

8-95 *Using or threatening violence to enter* By s. 6(1) of the Act, it is generally an offence for any person, without lawful authority, to use or threaten violence for the purpose of securing entry to any premises, if there is someone on the premises who is opposed to the entry, and the person making the threat knows that this is so. The threatened violence can be against a person or against property (s.

6(4)(a)). "Premises" in this context, means any building or part of a building which is in separate occupation, and land ancillary to a building. The premises need not be residential, but must include a building if the Act is to apply. The maximum punishment is a level 5 fine, or six months' imprisonment.

The Act narrows the concept of "lawful authority". It is not enough to have an interest in the premises, or a right to possession or occupation. What is a required is a specific right to enter. The main example will be the right granted by the court as a result of proceedings for possession; people with a statutory right to enter land will also be able to make a threat (for example, a threat to break down a door, if it isn't opened) in order to gain entry to premises. 8-96

In addition, however, the Act provides (in ss. 6(1A), 12 and 12A) that the offence in s. 6(1) does not apply to a person who is a "displaced residential occupier" or to a "protected intending occupier of the premises". A "displaced residential occupier" is any person who was occupying the premises as a residence, before being excluded by someone who entered the premises—unless he was occupying as a trespasser (s. 12(3)). Subject to that, a displaced residential occupier may use force to regain entry to premises from which he has been excluded. Three different sorts of person are "protected intending occupiers", namely: 8-97

- A person with a freehold interest, or a leasehold interest with at least two years to run, who requires the premises for his own use, is excluded from them by a trespasser, and who holds a written statement setting out his interest in the property, signed by him and witnessed by a justice of the peace (s. 6(2)).

- A person with a tenancy, or a licence to occupy the premises, granted by a person with a freehold interest or a leasehold interest with at least two years to run, the other conditions mentioned above being satisfied (s. 6(4)).

- A person who has a tenancy or a licence granted by one of a number of specified bodies, including the Housing Corporation and registered housing associations, the other conditions mentioned above being satisfied, except that the person has a certificate from the body in question, rather than a statement (s. 6(6)).

8-98 *Adverse occupation of residential premises* It is an offence for a person who has entered residential premises as a trespasser, and who remains there as a trespasser, to fail to leave after being required to do so by a displaced residential occupier, or a protected intending occupier. The maximum punishment is again a level 5 fine or six months' imprisonment (s. 7).

8-99 "Premises" has the same meaning as for the s. 6(1) offence, but the offence can only be committed if there is a displaced residential occupier or a protected intending occupier. It is a defence for the person trespasssing to prove that he thought the person requiring him to leave was not a displaced residential occupier or a protected intending occupier of the premises, or that he was not on any part of the premises used wholly or mainly for residential purposes (s. 7(2) and (3)). It is also a defence for the trespasser to prove that no statement or certificate was produced to him by a protected intending occupier (s.12A(9)(a)). In other words, a protected intending occupier must show the trespasser his statement or certificate, before the trespasser can be prosecuted for remaining on the premises.

See 12-24 for sources on the Criminal Law Act 1977.

Timeshares

8-100 The idea behind timeshares is well known: it means buying the right to occupy property—almost always a holiday home—for a certain period each year. Legally, a timeshare can take the form of a lease or a licence; but generally the buyer receives a licence, with detailed terms and conditions relating to the use of the property. The licence can usually be assigned (i. e. transferred) so that the timeshare can be exchanged or sold.

8-101 The law protects buyers under the Timeshare Act 1992, and some regulations made under it, particularly the Timeshare Regulations 1997. The Act applies to living accommodation, in the United

Kingdom or elsewhere, intended to be used wholly or mainly for leisure purposes. ("Accommodation" includes caravans and mobile homes.) The Act does not apply, however, to a timeshare agreement which is made abroad. When a timeshare is sold in the course of business, and the buyer is not a business, the buyer has the right to cancel the agreement (and any linked finance agreement) within 14 days, and must be given a notice explaining this right.

See 12-2 for sources on the Timeshare Act 1992.

Assessment

Leases and tenancies are undoubtedly a useful and flexible way of arranging for someone to have the exclusive use of land. Many landowners, whether their property is residential or commercial, will sooner or later be involved in letting. The fact that the law intervenes in so many different ways to protect the rights of landlords and tenants is one sense helpful; but the sheer complexity of the law is a drawback, since those involved have to take into account not merely what they have agreed between themselves but the ways in which the law might intervene to modify that agreement. 8-102

Landowners should (in the first place) be careful about granting any lease, particularly of residential property, remembering that for short leases no special formalities are required, the key question being whether thee is a right of exclusive occupation, and that regaining possession, if there is a dispute, will almost certainly involve legal proceedings. Legal advice will therefore be important, even for what is intended to be a short-term, informal arrangement. In this context, the advantage of the shorthold assured tenancy is that the landlord can be sure of regaining possession of the property, though while the tenancy lasts the tenant is strongly protected by the law from harassment and interference. 8-103

Granting a long lease, for residential or commercial purposes, certainly calls for even more careful consideration of the legal position, with professional assistance, including the rights which the law will give to the landlord and the tenant; and the lease itself will 8-104 need careful drafting, to deal with repair, rent reviews and other points.

8-105 Landowners who are tenants with long residential leases have a range of rights enabling them to extend their leases or acquire the freehold of the land, or sometimes, in the case of a block of flats, to exercise some control over the management of the block. Exercising these rights, against the wishes of an unhelpful landlord, has sometimes proved difficult. Forthcoming legislation, however, should improve the position of these tenants.

Chapter 9

Planning

Introduction

9-0 The planning system is a relatively recent phenomenon: the first legislation on planning dates from the early years of the twentieth century. It is partly concerned with the pattern of land use—making sure that the right development goes in the right place, with the infrastructure (roads, etc) to support it; and partly with more specific objectives, such as preserving old buildings of merit, safeguarding the countryside, and protecting the environment. In pursuing these objectives, planning law blends into other areas of the law, including the law which is concerned with protecting the environment.

See for example 9-73 on conservation areas.

9-1 Planning law is likely to be relevant to landowners at two different levels. At one level, there may be questions about whether minor and uncontroversial work on land requires planning permission. Such questions don't generally need a detailed knowledge of planning law. But rather different are situations where planning permission is required, and a grant or refusal of permission can cause significant gains or losses to a landowner. Here a knowledge of the planning system as a whole may be important. The system is rather self-contained: it consists of rules and procedures which do not apply to other sorts of issues.

9-2 At the heart of the system of planning control is the concept of "development", for which planning permission is generally required. Planning law defines development, and in some cases provides that planning permission is not in fact required, though it otherwise would be, or that it is granted automatically, so that no application has to be made. But in many cases the grant or refusal of planning permission calls for a decision—both central

See 9-13 onwards for the meaning of "development".

government (mainly the DETR) and local government have rôles to play in taking these decisions, and in the planning system generally.

9-3 Sometimes planning law does not apply because there are other forms of regulation for the activity in question; sometimes different sorts of regulation overlap, so that a particular activity is regulated both by planning law and by another area of the law. Planning law as a whole embraces rules on two related subjects:

See for example 10-34 on forestry; and contrast 10-38 on caravans.

- Outdoor advertisements.
- Trees.

But these are really separate subjects, and they are dealt with in chapter 10.

See 10-11 and 10-19 onwards for these subjects.

Sources of planning law

9-4 The planning system is the creation of statute. At the moment the main Act is the Town and Country Planning Act 1990 (which will be referred to from now on as the "1990 Act"). Three other Acts concerned with planning were also passed in 1990: the Planning (Listed Buildings and Conservation Areas) Act, the Planning (Hazardous Substances) Act, and the Planning (Consequential Provisions) Act. A further Act, the Planning and Compensation Act 1991, made some alterations to the system, and in particular strengthened the procedures for enforcing planning law (i. e. making sure that the rules are observed). Delegated legislation is important, since it contains many of the more detailed rules which are significant in practice. Planning law has its own procedures; but the courts also have a rôle, and there are decisions by the courts on planning law just as there are on other areas of the law.

See 9-84 onwards for enforcement.

See 1-7 for the meaning of "delegated legislation".

9-5 An important feature of planning law is that central government, the DETR, publishes information and guidance on planning. Since 1988 this material has consisted of:

- Departmental Circulars, which give guidance to local authorities on changes in the law and planning procedures.

- Guidance Notes of different types.

The main series of Guidance Notes is the Planning Policy Guidance Notes, the Notes being numbered PPG1, PPG2, and so on. There are also separate series of Mineral Policy Guidance notes ("MPG1", etc) and Regional Policy Guidance notes ("RPG1", etc). These Notes deal with matters of policy. PPG1 (1997), for example, contains a general review of the government's planning strategy. These materials are not law in the way that Acts and delegated legislation are law, but they are indirectly relevant to legal issues, because local authorities and others concerned with the workings of the planning system must give them due weight in taking planning decisions. 9-6

See 1-74 for administrative law and how this affects decisions by public bodies and officials.

Table 6: some Planning Policy Guidance Notes

No.	Subject
PPG1	*General Policy and Principles*
PPG2	*Green Belts*
PPG3	*Housing*
PPG7	*The Countryside: Environmental Quality and Economic and Social Development*
PPG12	*Development Plans*
PPG15	*Planning and the Historic Environment*
PPG18	*Enforcing Planning Control*
PPG19	*Outdoor Advertising Control*
PPG24	*Planning and Noise*

Most of the law explained in this chapter is civil law; but there are also criminal offences for breaches of planning law which are designed to ensure that the planning system is effective in practice. 9-7

Administration of the planning system

9-8 Central government, in the form of the DETR, is responsible for the system as a whole, and makes delegated legislation. The DETR issues Circulars and Guidance Notes, and handles some planning decisions, including appeals. The system is flexible: in some circumstances the DETR can give give directions to local government about what should be done, or can take over planning decisions from local authorities ☞.

☞ See particularly 9-58 for "calling in" planning applications.

9-9 Most day-to-day planning decisions are taken by local authorities, sometimes by officials rather than the local authority itself. It is also for local government to draw up development plans. Here the aim is to plan for an area as a whole, dealing with infrastructure, the preservation of the countryside, and the amount and location of new development such as industrial estates and housing. A development plan does not automatically determine in advance which individual applications for planning permission will be granted, but is highly relevant to those applications ☞.

☞ See 9-48 onwards for the significance of development plans for planning applications.

9-10 Since 1947, the system of development plans has been changed on several occasions. But in most areas, development plans now take the form of "structure plans" at County level, and "local plans" at District level, the latter being much more detailed (Part II of the 1990 Act, as amended by the Planning and Compensation Act 1991). Local plans must generally be consistent with the structure plan for the area. (More specialised local plans may also deal with minerals and waste disposal.) In metropolitan areas, the development plan may be a "unitary" plan, with only one level. Local authorities must undertake consultation in drawing up development plans. A development plan must include a statement of the local authority's planning policies, and the latter must include policies relating to the conservation of the natural beauty and amenity of the land, the improvement of the physical environment and the management of traffic (s. 36(3)). ("Amenity" is a vague but useful word used in planning law and elsewhere to describe the pleasantness or attractiveness of land.) The point of drawing up policies of this sort is that the local authority should then be in a position to decide individual applications in a consistent and coherent way. If there was no policy behind its decisions, they might well be inconsistent and unfair. The Town and Country Planning (Development Plan) (England) Regulations 1999 contained detailed rules for the preparation of development plans.

If there are objections to a local plan—for example, by local pressure groups concerned that there is too much or too little new housing, or by commercial interests pressing for new roads—the local authority must hold a public inquiry at which objectors can make representations, unless the objectors have said that they do not wish to do so. The inquiry will be chaired by an Inspector appointed by the DETR, who will consider written and oral representations, and make a report to the local authority, which may contain recommendations for modifying the plan. The local authority must then (under the 1999 Regulations) prepare a statement explaining, where necessary, whether they accept what the Inspector has said. They may modify the development plan in the light of the Inspector's report; and, if so, further comments and representations can be made by interested parties, and the local authority have a discretion about whether to hold a further public inquiry. 9-11

When this process has been concluded, the final step is for the local authority to resolve to adopt the plan, which then comes into force. However there is a final safeguard, since the DETR may require that a local plan be submitted for its approval, under s. 44(1) of the 1990 Act, before coming into force, so the DETR can influence the contents of the local plan. 9-12

Development: basic definitions

The concept of "development" of land is central to the planning system. The word covers two sorts of activity: 9-13

- "Operations" of various sorts on land. (This is sometimes known as "operational development".)

- Material changes of use of land.

See 9-46 for where both are involved.

See 9-84 onwards for enforcement.

See 9-31 onwards for the GPDO and 9-30 onwards for the Use Classes Order.

The difference between the two sorts is important, because although both require planning permission, different rules sometimes apply. Depending on the circumstances, one or both sorts may be involved in any given project.

9-14 By s. 57 of the 1990 Act, planning permission is required for development, and enforcement action may be taken against those who do not abide by the law. The general proposition that planning permission is required is modified in two main ways: in some cases, the legislation provides that permission is not required, though it otherwise would or might be, and in some cases permission is granted automatically, so there is no need to make an application for planning permission. These rules are set out in the 1990 Act, and also in delegated legislation made under the Act, the Town and Country Planning (General Permitted Development) Order 1995 (often known as the "General Permitted Development Order", or simply the "GPDO") and also the Town and Country Planning (Use Classes) Order 1987 (or simply the "Use Classes Order").

9-15 The main definition of "development" is in s. 55(1) and (1A) of the 1990 Act, which deals with operations and changes of use and contains some further provisions about what does and does not constitute development. The most important parts of the definition in s. 55(1) and (1A) are as follows:

> "(1) Subject to the following provisions of this section, in this Act .... "development" means the carrying out of building, engineering, mining or other operations in, on, over or under land, or the making of any material change in the use of any buildings or other land.
>
> (1A) For the purposes of this Act, "building operations" includes":
>
> (a) demolition of buildings;
>
> (b) rebuilding;
>
> (c) structural alterations or other additions to buildings;
>
> (d) other operations normally undertaken by a person carrying on business as a builder."

9-16 There is a partial definition of "building", in s. 336(1) of the Act, which is important because of its effect on the meaning of "building operations", and this needs to be taken into account as well:

""Building" includes any structure or erection, and any part of a building, as so defined, but does not include plant or machinery comprised in a building".

The definition does not define everything which is a "building", just some of the things which are included in the definition.

9-17 Section 55(2) provides that some sorts of operation and uses of land do not constitute development at all, and so do not require permission, even though they might otherwise amount to (say) building operations:

"The following operations or uses of land shall not be taken for the purposes of this Act to involve development of the land:

(a) the carrying out for the maintenance, improvement or other alteration of any building of works which:

(i) affect only the interior of the building, or

(ii) do not materially affect the external appearance of the building.....

(d) the use of any buildings or other land within the curtilage of a dwellinghouse for any purpose incidental to the enjoyment of the dwellinghouse as such.

See 9-18 for the meaning of "curtilage".

(e) the use of any land for the purposes of agriculture or forestry (including afforestation) and the use for any of those purposes of any building occupied together with land so used;

(f) in the case of buildings or other land which are used for a purpose of any class specified in an order made by [the DETR] under this section, the use of the buildings or other land or, subject to the provisions of the order, of any part of the buildings or the other land, for any purpose of the same class.

(g) the demolition of any description of buildings specified in a direction given by [the DETR] to local planning authorities generally or to a particular local planning authority".

See also 9-23 for demolition.

9-18 Section 55(2)(d) refers to the "curtilage" of a house. This is an important concept, which is relevant elsewhere. What is meant is the land around a house, which goes with it. Typically this might mean modest areas at the front and back of the house, such as a garden or a yard, and often a garage. A house in the country might have attached to it other pieces of land, for example a paddock or an orchard, but these would probably not be regarded as within the curtilage of the house.

See for example 3-22 and 10-31.

"Curtilage" of a dwelling

In *Skerritts of Nottingham Ltd v. Secretary of State for the Environment, Transport and the Regions* (2000) the question was whether a stable block, about 200 metres from the Grimsdyke Hotel, Old Redding, was within the curtilage of the hotel. This was important for reasons to do with the listing of the hotel [see 9-66 onwards for listing].

The court's view was that "curtilage" was not a precise term; much depended on the facts of each case. Often, where houses were built close together, the curtilage of each would be small. But the area involved was not necessarily small in a case such as this, where the building was originally a large country house, the home of W. S. Gilbert. The court also made clear that land can only be within the curtilage of one house at a time—it cannot be shared between houses.

9-19 "Engineering operations" is also partly defined in s. 336(1), which says that they include forming or laying out an access to a highway.

See 5-0 for the meaning of "highway"; note also 9-35.

9-20 Section 55(3) of the 1990 Act provides that, for the avoidance of doubt, certain activities *do* involve a material change of use and so require planning permission. Finally, some other sorts of activity are not subject to planning permission, because they do not involve development. In particular, the planting and felling of trees does not require planning permission, because of the separate rules on tree preservation orders; and advertisements which comply with the rules do not require planning permission.

See 9-28 and 11-71 for these provisions.

See 10-19 onwards for tree preservation order and also 10-34 onwards for controls over forestry. For advertisements, see 10-11.

Building and other operations

9-21 *Building operations* As noted above, the term "building operations" is partly defined in s. 55(1A) of the 1990 Act. In addition, the courts have on a number of occasions had to consider whether a structure or erection was within the definition of "building". Much will depend upon the facts of each case. However, some general principles have been developed by the courts—the important factors will be:

- The size of the structure.

- Whether it is intended to be permanent.
- Whether it is attached to the land.

Skerritts of Nottingham v. Secretary of State for the Environment, Transport and the Regions (No. 2) (2000) concerned the owners of an hotel, who each year put up a marquee on a lawn next to the hotel. The marquee stood on the lawn between February and October, and had a supply of electricity—erecting it took several days. The local authority served an enforcement notice [see 9-84]. The owners of the hotel appealed, and the Planning Inspector upheld the enforcement notice. The owners then appealed to the court.

The court decided that the Planning Inspector was right to conclude that the marquee was a building, bearing in mind its size, degree of permanence and attachment to the land. Putting up the marquee was therefore a building operation, and since the landowners had not applied for planning permission the local authority were entitled to serve an enforcement notice.

What is a "building"?

Engineering and other operations Generally speaking, the term "engineering operations" should probably be regarded as bearing its ordinary meaning. It would include operations which would normally be thought of as engineering, rather than building; and it might include such things as landscaping or earth-moving on a significant scale. The meaning of "mining operations" is clarified in s. 55(4), in a way which gives the term a wide meaning. The Act does not define "other operations", and the courts have rarely had to consider the meaning of the phrase; but this category would include operations which did not fit easily into any of the other categories. 9-22

Demolition of buildings ""Demolition of buildings" is mentioned in s. 55(1A) as being a "building operation", and is therefore development; but this rule would have a very far-reaching effect, bearing in mind the definition of "building", and s. 55(2)(g) allows the DETR to give a "direction" specifying types of demolition which will *not* be development. A Direction was issued in 1995, namely the Town and Country Planning (Demolition—Description of Buildings) Direction 1995, and this lists certain sorts of buildings which can be demolished without planning permission, including: 9-23

Note also 10-9 on the requirements of building control in relation to demolition.

◆ Buildings which are listed buildings, buildings in conservation areas, and ancient monuments—all of which are subject to controls under other legislation.

◆ Buildings under 50 cubic metres (measured externally).

◆ Buildings other than dwelling-houses (and buildings which adjoin dwelling-houses).

◆ Gates, fences, walls and other means of enclosing land (except in a conservation area).

See 9-66; for listed buildings, 9-73 for conservation areas and 10-87 for ancient monuments.

Outside these categories, demolition of a building *does* amount to development, and so requires planning permission. One important category is dwellings and buildings attached to them.

But see 9-39 for provisions in the GPDO which automatically grant permission for demolition in certain circumstances.

Material changes of use

9-24 While planning permission is required for various sorts of development involving "operations" on the land, it is also required, under s. 55(1) of the 1990 Act, where there is a "material change in the use of any buildings or other land".

9-25 Whether there has been a material change of use in any given case is a matter of fact and degree. Difficult questions can arise when a landowner changes the use of part of the property, rather than the whole. The courts have developed some principles which help to clarify decisions in this area. First, it is necessary to establish what is the "planning unit"—the area of land which should be regarded as a single unit. This will often be the whole area of land owned by the person concerned, especially in the case of a house and garden, but there will be some cases in which the land will be regarded as consisting of two or more planning units, or as part of a larger planning unit. Much depends on the facts of each case. Secondly, within a planning unit, it is the main use of the land which matters, and other, ancillary uses are not counted.

9-26 Suppose that a landowner owns a small farm, and sells produce from the farm at a shop on the farm. For the purposes of planning control, the land would probably be regarded as one unit, in use as a farm. The use of a small part of it as a farm shop would not affect the position. But it might well be different if the landowner wished to set up a general-purpose shop, which sold not only his own produce but a full range of groceries, since the shop would not then be ancillary to the main use of the land as a farm. And planning permission would certainly be required to turn the whole site into a supermarket, because that would involve a change in the main use of the land.

9-27 Apart from these general principles, the legislation itself contains some important rules about changes of use. In practice, these will in many cases determine whether planning permission is required. First, as explained above, s. 55(2)(d) of the 1990 Act covers uses which are within the curtilage of a dwellinghouse, and incidental to the use of the land as a dwellinghouse: for changes of this sort, no development is involved, and so planning permission is not needed. Changing a garage into a hobby room, for model trains, would thus not require planning permission (assuming that no operation development was involved). On the same basis, the use of a room in a house might be changed, so that it was available for bed and breakfast accommodation; or a room might be set aside for business use. Many other changes are permissible, provided always that they are within the curtilage of the house and for an incidental purpose.

See 9-17 for s. 55(2)(d).

9-28 Section 55(3)(a) of the 1990 Act makes clear, for the avoidance of doubt, that changing the use of a building from one dwelling to more than one—in other words, subdividing a dwelling—is a material change of use. Planning permission is thus required for the change of use.

9-29 Householders sometimes seek to enlarge their gardens by buying part of an adjoining field. This requires planning permission, because it involves a material change of use, that is, a change from agricultural to residential use. The planning legislation does not automatically grant permission for such a change.

9-30 In addition, many changes of use are permitted because of the Use Classes Order (in full, the Town and Country Planning (Use

See also 9-36 for other changes of use which are allowed, under the GPDO.

Classes) Order 1987, made under s. 55(2)(f) of the 1990 Act). Classes of use are listed in the Schedule to the Order, and changes of use within each class are deemed not to be material, so that they do not amount to development, and planning permission is not required. So, for example:

- Class A1 (Shops) includes most sorts of retail premises, as well as post offices and funeral parlours. Changes within this class do not involve a material change of use, so do not amount to development. But the sale of hot food is in a separate class (A3), so change of use from a grocery shop to a take-away restaurant does constitute development, and planning permission will be required.

- Class C3 (Dwellinghouses) includes use by a single person, or by people living together as a single family, and use by up to six people living as a single household. So if a large flat ceases to be used by a family and is let to more than six people living as flatmates, the change will not be permissible by virtue of the Use Classes Order. Whether planning permission is required will depend on whether, in the particular circumstances, there is a material change of use.

Development Permitted by the GPDO

9-31 In addition to the cases mentioned in the 1990 Act, where planning permission is not required because there is deemed to be no "development", planning applications are unnecessary where permission is granted by virtue of a "development order", made by the DETR under s. 60(1) of the Act. One way of getting planning permission is to apply to the local authority: this is another.

9-32 Development orders may relate to specific areas or projects, for example the large-scale redevelopment of a run-down area of a city, where it is appropriate to grant permission for the whole scheme by means of a single decision. They may also be of general application.

The GPDO (the Town and Country Planning (General Permitted Development) Order 1995) is the latter kind of order, and contains a long list of sorts of development for which planning permission is automatically granted. Some are operations and some are changes of use; all are minor sorts of development for which it is generally thought to be unnecessary to require an application for planning permission to be made. The list is set out in Schedule 2 to the GPDO, which is divided into 33 Parts. Each Part contains one or more class of development, marked A, B, C, etc. Besides indicating what development is permitted, the GPDO makes clear for each class, where appropriate, what development is *not* permitted.

9-33 The GPDO does not apply in the same way to all land. Under article 4, the DETR and local authorities can direct that the GPDO shall not apply to specified classes of development. The result of a direction is that planning permission is not automatic and an application has to be made. Use is often made of this provision in conservation areas. In addition, the GPDO itself makes clear that it does not apply fully to certain sorts of land. These are:

- Land in certain counties, including the West Country, much of Wales, and Yorkshire, which the GPDO refers to as "article 1(4) land".
- Land in a National Park, an area of outstanding natural beauty, a conservation area, and certain other areas ("article 1(5) land").
- Land in a National Park or in neighbouring areas, or in the Norfolk Broads ("article 1(6) land").

See 9-83 and 10-80 for National Parks, 9-73 for conservation areas, and 9-83 for areas of outstanding natural beauty.

Some of the Parts in Schedule 2 have a wide application, while some are very specific. The following are the most important for the purposes of this book:

9-34 *Part 1: development within the curtilage of a dwellinghouse.* Under this heading the following classes are included.

See 9-18 for the meaning of "curtilage".

- Class A: enlargement, improvement and alteration of dwellinghouses. The restrictions and conditions which apply include the following. For article 1(5) land (i. e. in conservation areas and some other areas) or a terraced house, there is a limit of 50 cubic metres or 10%; elsewhere the limit is 70 cubic metres or 15%, subject to an overall limit of 115 cubic metres. The height of the building must not be increased, and there must be no extension of a building in the direction of any adjoining highway, or nearer than 20 metres to it. Development under this heading cannot include the erection of a satellite antenna, an alteration to a roof, or cladding a building with stone or other material.

See 5-0 for the meaning of "highway".

But see Classes B and C for roofs and Class H for satellite antennas.

◆ Class B: additions or alterations to the roofs of dwelling-houses. The roof must not be made higher, and there must be no alterations to the plane of a roof fronting a highway. The same restrictions on cubic content apply, to article 1(5) land and other land, as in Class A.

◆ Class C: any other alterations to the roof of a dwellinghouse. There must be no material alteration to the shape of the dwellinghouse.

◆ Class D: the construction of a porch outside any external door of a dwellinghouse. The ground area (measured externally) must not exceed 3 square metres; the porch must not be more than 3 metres high; and it must not be within 2 metres of any boundary between the house and a highway.

◆ Class E: buildings and other enclosures, and swimming and other pools, required for a purpose incidental to the enjoyment of the dwellinghouse as such. This covers outbuildings: it does not permit the enlargment of the house itself. Restrictions include the following—the building must not be nearer to any adjoining highway than the house, or nearer than 20 metres to a highway; the building must not exceed 10 cubic metres if within 5 metres of the house; the height of the building must not exceed 4 metres, if it has a ridged roof, or 3 metres in any other case; the total area of buildings and enclosures within the curtilage must not exceed 50% of the area of the curtilage (excluding the house); for article 1(5) land, or land within the curtilage of a listed building, there must not be building exceeding 10 cubic metres.

See 9-66 for the meaning of "listed building".

- Class F: hardstanding, within the curtilage of a dwellinghouse for any purpose incidental to the use of the dwellinghouse as such. (The hardstanding could be for a car, or for some other purpose such as for a caravan or a boat.)

See 10-38 onwards for caravans generally.

- Class G: the erection within the curtilage of a dwellinghouse of a container for oil for domestic purposes. The capacity must not exceed 3,500 litres; the container must not be more than 3 metres above ground level; and if the curtilage is bounded by a highway (as will in the majority of cases be so), the container must not be nearer to the highway than the existing building, or (if that is nearer to the highway) 20 metres.

- Class H: the installation, alteration or replacement of a satellite antenna on a dwelling house, or within the curtilage of a dwellinghouse. Only one antenna is allowed by the GPDO. The maximum size is 45 centimetres if on a chimney, or 90 centimetres on a dwellinghouse within article 1(4) land; or 70 centimetres in any other case. If installed on roof or chimney, the antenna must be no higher than the roof or the chimney. In article 1(5) land, an antenna cannot be installed on a chimney, on a building which exceeds15 metres in height, or on a wall or roof slope which fronts a highway. So far as practicable, the effect on the external appearance of the building must be minimised, and the antenna must be removed when it is not needed.

Part 2: minor operations Part 2 is concerned with "minor 9-35
operations", and consists of the following classes:

- Class A: the erection, construction, maintenance, improvement or alteration of a gate, fence, wall or other means of enclosure. In some cases, the work will be so minor—for example, replacing a small part of a fence—that it will not involve any development; but in so far as it does involve development, permission is granted. But permission is not granted by the GPDO where the height of the gate, fence, etc would exceed one metre if adjacent to a highway used by vehicles, or 2 metres in any other case; nor is permission granted in the case of a gate, fence etc surrounding (or within the curtilage of) a listed building.

◆ Class B: the formation of an access to a highway other than a trunk road or classified road, where the access is required for the purposes of any development permitted by the GPDO (apart from Class A of Part 2). This (though it applies only to minor roads) means that if a landowner puts up a garage, making use of permission under the GPDO, any necessary access to a highway does not require planning permission either.

◆ Class C: painting the exterior of a building. This speaks for itself. The GPDO does not automatically treat conservation areas differently; but the local authority can use their power under article 4, if they wish, to restrict the automatic grant of planning permission for painting.

See 9-33 for the article 4 power.

9-36 *Part 3: changes of use.* Part 3 lists some specific changes of use for which permission is granted, including the following:

See also 9-30 for situations in which development is not involved because the new use comes within the same class in the Use Classes Order.

◆ Class A: *from* use for the sale of food and drink, or motor vehicles, *to* a general retail shop.

◆ Class B(a): *from* use for general industrial purposes, or use for storage and distribution, *to* business use.

◆ Class F(a): *from* use as a retail shop *to* use as a shop and a single flat.

9-37 *Part 4: temporary buildings and uses* Certain sorts of temporary development are allowed by the GPDO, including the following:

◆ Class A: buildings, plant, etc, required for building and other operations. This does not apply where planning permission for the building or other operations is needed but has not been granted; but where the necessary permission has been granted for those operations, permission for such things as temporary site offices follows automatically. The temporary development must cease when the main operations have been carried out, and the land must be re-instated.

◆ Class B: the use of any land for any purpose, for not more than 28 days a year. This permits a wide range of temporary uses, and it includes "moveable structures" (such as tents, stands, etc) which may be required for those uses. But there are a number of exclusions. Under this heading the GPDO does not permit temporary buildings or uses on land within the curtilage of a building, or use of land as a caravan site, or land within a site of special scientific interest for motor sports, clay pigeon shooting or war games. Temporary buildings and uses are also limited to 14 days in any calendar month in relation to markets, and motor sports.

In the case of *Ramsay v. Secretary of State for the Environment and Suffolk District Council* (2000) some land had been used for motorsport. Events did not take place on more than 28 days a year, and the organisers relied on the temporary permission granted by the GPDO.
The court decided that the exemption for temporary use did not apply here. The land was laid out with tyres, fences and markers, and remained in this state throughout the year. In the circumstances, the land was in permanent use for motor sports, even though events took place only on certain days.

Temporary use of land

Part 5: caravan sites This part is concerned with caravan sites. Permission is granted automatically in most (not all) of the cases where there is an exemption from the need to obtain a licence for a caravan site, under the Caravan Sites and Control of Development Act 1960. Permission is also granted automatically for any development which is required by the terms of a site licence, for example the provision of washing facilities, or landscaping. 9-38

See 10-40 for these exemptions.

Part 31: demolition of buildings Because of the Town and Country Planning (Demolition—Description of Buildings) Direction 1995, demolition of some buildings is deemed not to involve 9-39

See 9-23 for the effect of the Direction.

development, so does not require planning permission. But other sorts of demolition does require planning permission. Part 31 grants permission for two sorts of demolition:

- Class A is concerned with buildings generally. Permission is granted, except where the building has been rendered unsafe or uninhabitable, whether by action or neglect, and repair (temporary or otherwise) is possible. The purpose of this restriction is to prevent landowners from letting buildings—particularly listed buildings—deteriorate, so that they can then be demolished. Where demolition is permitted, the permission is conditional on following a procedure laid down in the GPDO. If demolition is urgently necessary, the developer must give the local authority, as soon as possible, a written justification of why the demolition was necessary. Otherwise, the developer must apply to the local authority for a "determination as to whether the prior approval of the authority will be required", in relation to the method of demolition and restoration of the site. The developer must also put up a notice on the site, so that the public are aware of the proposal. The local authority may then decide that no approval is required; or that it is required, and may only be carried out in accordance with details (as to the method, and restoration of the site) which they have approved. As noted above, a Direction under the 1990 Act means that in many cases planning permission will not be required at all. But it will generally be required for houses. The GPDO allows the local authority to exercise control over the method of demolition. Or, if they wish to prevent the GPDO from granting permission in a particular class of cases, they can use their power under article 4.

See 9-66 onwards for the meaning of "listed building".

See 9-33 for this power.

- Class B consists of the demolition of any "gate, fence, wall, or other means of enclosure".

9-40 To summarise the requirements in relation to demolition, the demolition of a building is a "building operation", by s. 55(1A)(a); but some demolition is within the Direction given by the DETR, and so does not require planning permission, and some (particularly the demolition of houses) is within the GPDO, so has automatic planning permission, subject to conditions.

GPDO generally Other Parts in Schedule 2 to the GPDO cover 9-41 agricultural buildings and operations (Part 6), and forestry buildings and operations (Part 7). Permission is granted by Part 9 for the repair of private roads, while Part 10 grants permission for works to sewers, pipes, cables and other apparatus. Local authorities have permission to carry out certain development under Part 12, street lamps, bus shelters and other items of "street furniture". Some Parts are very specialised: Part 30, for example, deals with toll road facilities, while Part 33 permits the installation of closed-circuit TV cameras in certain circumstances.

Is a planning application required?

The following flow-chart summaries the above headings: 9-42

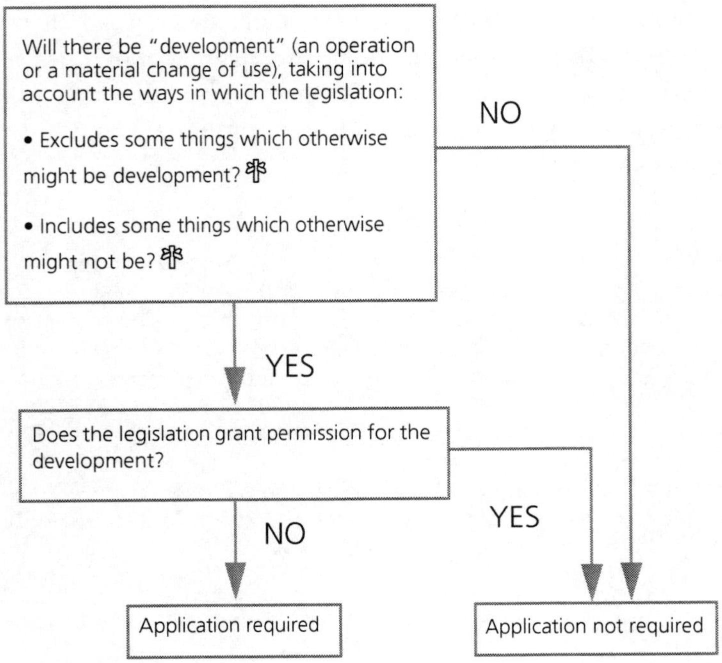

Such as maintenance, ancillary development within the curtilage of dwelling, and changes within a class in the use Classes Order: see 9-17 and 9-30.

Such as subdividing a dwelling: see 9-28.

Nature of planning permission

9-43 Planning permission goes with the land: it does not belong to the person who obtained it. In most cases it is the owner of the land who makes an application for planning permission, but there is no reason why a person other than the owner—for example, someone who is thinking of making an offer to buy the land—should not apply. The owner and anyone else with an interest in the land must be informed, but their consent to the application is not necessary. Planning permission is reversible, in that the local authority can revoke or modify it; but if they do they may be required, under s. 107 of the 1990 Act, to compensate the owner of the land for any loss suffered, and revocation is in practice rare.

See 9-52 for the notification requirements.

9-44 Under s. 70(1) of the 1990 Act, planning permission can be, and usually is, granted subject to conditions. In the case of building or other operations, a condition must be imposed that the development be started within five years, or some other specified period (s. 91). (If the permission granted is outline permission, the application for full permission must be made within 3 years (s. 92).) Other conditions may relate to such matters as the re-instatement of the site after the completion of the development, or the planting of trees: s. 197 puts a duty on local authorities to ensure that in granting planning permission they include conditions, if appropriate, to deal with the preservation and planting of trees.

See 9-50 for the meaning of "outline planning permission".

See also 10-19 onwards for tree preservation orders.

The start date of development

In the case of *Leisure Great Britain plc v. Isle of Wight County Council* (2000) planning permission had been granted for the construction of some holiday chalets and a club. The conditions included the requirement that fencing be erected, and that the building work start within a certain period. The development company began work within the period, but were in breach of planning control because they had not put up the necessary fencing. The period then expired. This raised the question of whether the work had been validly started within the period—if not, the planning permission was of no effect.

The court decided that, although there were some exceptions, work which was a breach of planning control did not count as a start to the development. The permission had therefore expired.

9-45 Conditions must be reasonable, and must be imposed for planning reasons: they cannot be imposed because of some policy which the local authority wish to pursue but which is not concerned with planning. Where permission has been granted subject to conditions, the person who applied may appeal against the conditions just as he may appeal against a refusal of planning permission.

See 9-56 for the appeal procedure.

9-46 Where permission is granted for a change of use, this does not include permission for any building or other operations unless they are specifically included in the grant. Where permission is granted for the erection of a building, however, s. 75 of the Act provides that the permission may specify the use of the building (in which case any other use may require further planning permission, because there will be a material change of use) or if nothing is said about the use of the new building, the permission is deemed to cover the use for which the building is designed. Planning permission for the building of a new house thus does not need to specify that the building is to be used as a house.

Grant and refusal: relevant factors

9-47 In granting or refusing an application, the local authority must take into account the general principles set out by the DETR in its series of Guidance Notes. The local authority must also have regard to the development plan for the area, and to the arguments for and against the proposed development, as put forward by the applicant, and by anyone objecting to it.

See 9-5 for Guidance Notes

See 9-9 onwards for development plans.

9-48 How important is the development plan, compared to the merits of the case? No simple answer can be given, but the Planning and Compensation Act 1991 added a new s. 54A to the 1990 Act, in order to make matters clearer:

> "Where, in making any determination under the planning Acts, regard is to be had to the development plan, the determination shall be made in accordance with the plan, unless material considerations indicate otherwise."

In other words, the local authority must follow what is said in the development plan, unless there is some reason why they should not do so. There is also a general requirement, for the local authority to "have regard to the development plan, so far as material, in determining an application for planning permission", under s. 70(2) of the 1990 Act.

9-49 The development plan must therefore be considered, and it can be expected that the local authority's decision will generally be in accordance with the plan; but there is freedom to depart from the plan if there is a sufficient case for doing so. Much will depend upon what the plan has to say: if there is a clear statement in the development plan for or against a certain sort of development, a planning application will usually be decided in accordance with the development plan. But if the development plan is less clear-cut, and calls for a balancing of different considerations, planning permission may be easier to obtain.

Significance of a development plan

In *Faradene Ltd v. Secretary of State for the Environment, Transport and the Regions* (1999) Faradene Ltd was refused permission for some commercial development on a seafront, and appealed. The planning inspector dismissed the appeal on the ground that it could prejudice the preparation of the development plan for the area. Faradene Ltd appealed again.

The court decided that the planning inspector was wrong to focus on the new development plan, rather than the existing policy, and the development would not in any event prejudice the preparation of the plan.

Grant and refusal: procedure

9-50 *Applications to the local authority* When an application is made, details of the proposed development must be given, in accordance with the Town and Country Planning (Applications) Regulations 1988, on the proper form and accompanied by a plan and drawings. If the application is for the erection of a building, it can be an "outline" application, meaning that full details are not given of the siting of the building, or its external appearance or means of access, or the landscaping of the site, these being reserved to the detailed application which must follow later (s. 92). If outline permission is granted (and the local authority may decline to deal with the matter as an outline application) it will be subject to the approval of these "reserved matters".

9-51 Fees are payable in accordance with the Town and Country Planning (Fees for Applications and Deemed Applications) Regulations 1989. The Town and Country Planning (General Development Procedure) Order 1995 deals with the procedure for making applications. The person making the application must send in a certificate to confirm that persons with an interest in the land have been notified of the making of the application. It may be that the applicant is the owner of the land, and that no-one else has an interest in it; but there may be tenants to be notified. There is nothing to prevent one person from making an application for permission in respect of land which he does not own: the owner's agreement to the making of the application is not necessary, but the owner must be notified that an application is being made.

9-52 An application must also be publicised, and for this purpose applications are divided into three classes:

See also 9-65 and 9-72 for action which the local authority must take in relation to listed buildings and conservation areas.

- Some applications, including those which are not in accordance with the development plan, or which affect rights of way to which Part III of the Wildlife and Countryside Act 1981 applies, must be advertised in a local newspaper and there must be a notice on the site for at least 21 days:

See 5-44 for Part III of the 1981 Act.

- Some, including those where 10 or more houses will be built, or the site consists of more than 1 hectare, must be advertised in a local paper, and there must be either a notice on the site or notification to neighbours.

- Other applications require a notice on the site or notification to neighbours.

9-53 Local authorities must, under s. 69 of the 1990 Act, keep a register of planning applications which is open to public inspection at all reasonable hours. The 1995 Order requires that this contain copies

See 9-44 in relation to planning conditions.

See 5-1 for highway authorities.

of drawings and other details; and also, where permission has been granted, information about conditions imposed by the local authority. Members of the public can thus check whether development being carried out has permission, and whether conditions are being observed.

9-54 The 1995 Order also requires a local authority to consult certain government departments or public bodies, if they have an interest in the proposed development. For example, for development likely to result in a material increase in the use of a public road, there must be consultation with the local authority responsible for roads (which means that a District or Borough Council will often have to consult the County Council). And for development likely to affect an inland waterway or canal, there must be consultation with the British Waterways Board.

9-55 In limited circumstances, a local authority may refuse to deal with an application altogether: s. 70A of the 1990 Act allows the local authority to do this if the application is not significantly different from one which has already been dealt with. Otherwise the application must be granted (with or without conditions) or refused.

9-56 *Planning appeals* There is a right of appeal to the DETR against the refusal of planning permission, or against conditions imposed in granting permission (s. 78 of the 1990 Act). An appeal can also be made if the local authority fails to deal with the application in eight weeks. Only the person who made the planning application can appeal. The DETR must arrange a hearing (usually in the form of a public local enquiry) if either the applicant or the local authority wish to have one (ss. 320–323 of the 1990 Act). Persons other than the applicant and the local authority may send in comments, opposing or supporting the appeal; and they may speak at a hearing if permission is given. An Inspector is appointed by the DETR to conduct the hearing, and in almost all cases takes the decision on behalf of the DETR. (In a few cases, the Inspector merely makes a recommendation, which the DETR can accept or reject.) The DETR can require a party to an appeal to pay the costs of the other side. Three pieces of delegated legislation lay down the procedure for these appeals, and deal with documentation and other matters: the Town and Country Planning (Inquiries Procedure) (England) Rules 2000, the Town and Country Planning Appeals (Determination by

Inspectors) (Inquiries Procedure) (England) Rules 2000, and the Town and Country Planning (Hearings Procedure) (England) Rules 2000.

9-57 Alternatively, if the applicant and the local authority agree, the appeal can be dealt with by means of written representations. Regulations—the Town and Country Planning (Appeals) (Written Representation Procedure) (England) Rules 2000—lay down the procedure. The appeal is then dealt with on the papers, without a public hearing.

9-58 *Other procedures* If a planning application is thought to be very important, because it is controversial or would set a very significant precedent, the application can be "called in" by the DETR, which means that the decision is taken by the DETR, not by the local authority (s. 77). This procedure is in practice confined to decisions of major public importance. There is a limited further right of appeal to the courts, under s. 288 of the Act, from a decision by the DETR on appeal or in relation to a planning application which has been called in.

9-59 The 1990 Act provides a wide power of entry on to land for the purposes of preparing development plans, applying for planning permission and appealing. Any person (not just the local authority's officials) may enter land, if authorised in writing by the DETR or a local authority, for the purpose of surveying it (s. 324).

The power of entry also applies to the control of advertising and to tree preservation orders: see 10-11 and 10-19 onwards for these subjects.

Other planning procedures

9-60 The planning system is not concerned only with granting and refusing planning permission: other procedures form part of the system. The following paragraphs briefly describe some of these procedures.

9-61 *Certificates of established and proposed use* A landowner may wish to obtain confirmation that the existing use of the land, or operations which have been carried out on the land, are lawful—for example, before selling the land, so that the purchaser could see there was no objection from the local authority to use or development which has taken place. This can be done by applying to the local authority for a "certificate of lawfulness of existing use or development", under s. 191 of the 1990 Act. The person applying must give the local authority the necessary information, and it is his responsibility to show that the use or development appears to be lawful (not the local authority's to show that it is unlawful). "Lawful" in s. 191 means either that there was no breach of planning control or that there was, but it is now too late to do anything about it, because of the rules which impose time limits on enforcement action by the local authority. If the local authority are satisfied that this is so, they must issue a certificate, and the effect of the certificate is that lawfulness is "conclusively presumed", so that it cannot afterwards be challenged by anyone.

See 9-84 for the meaning of "breach of planning control" and 9-90 for the time limits.

9-62 An application may also be made for a "certificate of lawfulness of proposed use or development", under s. 192, so that the landowner can be sure about the future use of the land. The local authority must grant the certificate if they are satisfied that the proposal would be lawful. This procedure is not a substitute for an application for planning permission: it applies where a person wishes to check that what he wishes to do will not require planning permission (or that the necessary permission has been granted by the GPDO or some other development order). Again, once a certificate has been granted, lawfulness is "conclusively presumed", provided that the person concerned keeps within the terms of the certificate.

Certificates of lawful use

The case of *Panton v. Secretary of State for the Environment, Transport and the Regions* (2000) concerned a mill, which had been put to various uses over the years, including use for sculpting and making models, and use for a catering business, but these had not been carried on for some time. The question was whether a certificate under s. 191 could be granted to cover these uses.

The court decided that it could. Even though these uses were dormant, the right to use the mill in these ways still existed, and the right would not be lost unless it was abandoned, or by a material change of use of the land.

9-63 *Planning obligations* The 1990 Act (as amended by the Planning and Compensation Act 1991) contains provisions under which a "planning obligation" may be imposed on a developer (ss. 106, 106A and 106B). A planning obligation may:

- Restrict the use of the land.
- Require the developer to carry out work on the land.
- Require the land to be used in a specified way.
- Require money to be paid to the local authority.

The developer of a supermarket might thus be placed under an obligation to pay for improvements to a road junction leading to the site. A planning obligation is a local land charge, and so should appear on the register of local land charges.

See 1-67 for the register of local land charges.

9-64 *Purchase notices* If a refusal of planning permission means that land has no practical use, the owner may serve notice on the local authority, requiring them to buy the land. The local authority may decline to do so, in which case the dispute is decided by the DETR (ss. 137–148 of the 1990 Act). The land is valued in essentially the same way as if it was being compulsorily acquired by the local authority.

See 11-100 for compulsory purchase.

9-65 *Abandoning the use of land* Most land has an established use, and planning permission is not necessary in order for the landowner to go on using the land in this way. An established use of land will cease, however, if there is a long period when no actual use takes place, as where a house is left unoccupied for many years. The law does not lay down a fixed period; whether a particular use of land has been abandoned will depend upon the circumstances.

See 12-9 for sources on planning law.

Listing of buildings

9-66 The process of listing is designed to give extra protection for buildings of special architectural or historic interest. When a building is listed, permission is required for demolition of the

Abandoning the use of land

The case of *Hughes v. Secretary of State for the Environment, Transport and the Regions* (1999) concerned a bungalow. The owner moved out in 1963, and the bungalow then stood empty. In 1986 the slates were stolen from the roof. The bungalow was sold in 1990, and was by then in very poor condition. The new owner's application for planning permission to build a replacement house on the site was refused: the local authority's policy was to grant such applications only if the residential use had not been abandoned, and they considered that the use had been abandoned here, due the lapse of time.

The court considered four factors laid down in an earlier case as being relevant to the question of abandoning the use of land:

- The physical state of the building
- The period for which the building had not been used
- Whether any other use had taken place
- Evidence about the intentions of the owner.

The court decided that the residential use had not been abandoned: both the previous owner and the new owner intended to resume residential use of the land.

building, or work which affects its character. This consent is known as "listed building consent", and is additional to any planning permission which may be required. The legislation which deals with listing is the Planning (Listed Buildings and Conservation Areas) Act 1990, and also some regulations made under this Act, the Planning (Listed Buildings and Buildings in Conservation Areas) Regulations 1990.

9-67 The DCMS is the department responsible for maintaining the list, under s. 1 of the Act. The DCMS must work with and consult English Heritage (full name, the Historic Buildings and Monuments Commission for England) and other relevant bodies. English Heritage has a special rôle in protecting and preserving historic buildings and ancient monuments, under the National Heritage Act 1983.

9-68 The term "building" has the same wide meaning in this Act as in the main 1990 Act (s. 91(2)). The DCMS can thus list "any structure or erection or part of a building". A part of a building includes:

See 9-16 for the meaning of "building" in the 1990 Act.

- Any object or structure fixed to the building.

◆ Any object or structure within the curtilage of the building which, although not fixed to the building, forms part of the land and has done so since before 1st July 1948 (s. 1(5) of the Planning (Listed Buildings and Conservation Areas) Act 1990).

See 9-18 for the meaning of "curtilage", and 2-47 on the question of whether things form part of the land.

9-69 Listing has been applied not just to whole buildings but to parts of them—internal or external—and to things such as telephone kiosks. The process of listing is explained fully in the DETR's Guidance Note PPG 15: *Planning and the Historic Environment*. Whether a building will be listed by the DCMS depends upon a number of factors, including the age of the building, the type of building it is, and its rarity. Roughly 5% of listed buildings are listed as Grade I or Grade II*, the remainder being Grade II.

9-70 There is no legal requirement to notify the owner of a building that it is about to be listed, though the owner may be aware that this is so, and may seek to persuade the DCMS not to list it. If the local authority consider that a building which ought to be listed is in danger of demolition or alteration, they may serve a "building preservation notice", under s. 3 of the Act, and this has the effect of protecting the building for six months, during which time the building cannot be altered or demolished without listed building consent, and the DCMS has time to list the building.

9-71 Once a building is listed, it is an offence under s. 7 of the Act to demolish the building, or to alter it in a way which affects its character, without listed building consent. The maximum punishment is two years' imprisonment or an unlimited fine or both. But it is a defence (subject to certain conditions) to show that the works were urgently necessary. Applications for listed building consent go to the local authority, and must be publicised, so that the public have the opportunity to comment (s. 10 of the Act). Local authorities must generally notify English Heritage and other bodies concerned with conservation, so that they can comment, and local authorities must notify the DCMS if they propose to grant an application (s. 13). Consent, if granted, may be made subject to conditions, as planning permission may be (s. 16). If consent is refused, an appeal is possible.

See 1-20 for criminal law generally.

9-72 Local authorities have several powers which they can use to protect listed buildings. If a listed building is in urgent need of

These powers are specifically for listed buildings. See also 9-84 onwards for enforcement powers relating to planning generally.

repair, they may serve a notice under s. 54 of the Act, requiring the owner to carry out the repairs; failing which they may enter the land and carry out the repairs themselves, and recover the cost from the owner (s. 55). A different procedure can be used where a listed building has been unlawfully altered or partly demolished without consent: the local authority can serve a "listed building enforcement notice", requiring the building to be restored, or other remedial work to be carried out (s. 38).

See 12-20 for sources on listed buildings.

Conservation areas

9-73 By s. 69 of the Planning (Listed Buildings and Conservation Areas) Act 1990 local authorities have a duty to designate as conservation areas "areas of special architectural or historic interest the character or appearance of which it is desirable to preserve or enhance". In a conservation area, some special controls apply, with the aim of providing extra protection against inappropriate development. (See generally DETR Guidance Note PPG/15: *Planning and the Historic Environment*.) The procedure is designed for areas rather than specific buildings, but the procedures for listing specific buildings and designating conservation areas can be used together, and it is common to find listed buildings within a conservation area.

9-74 There is no statutory duty to consult before designating a conservation area, though in practice a local authority is likely to do so, in particular to give residents the opportunity to comment. Residents will be affected by the tighter planning control which a conservation area will bring. The size and shape of a conservation area are for the local authority to consider. Once an area has been designated as a conservation area, the local authority must from time to time consider how to preserve and enhance it (s. 71). In other words, designation of a conservation area is not just a one-off event: the local authority must follow up with further consideration and if appropriate further action.

See 9-33 and 9-75.

9-75 In a conservation area, the local authority are under a duty in exercising their planning powers—including the power to grant planning permission—to pay "special attention" to the "desirability of preserving or enhancing the character or appearance of that area" (s. 72 of the Act). What this provision actually means has been the subject of consideration by the courts. Does it mean that permission can be granted provided that the proposed development does not actually harm the conservation area, or that it can only be granted if it makes a positive contribution towards "preserving or enhancing" the area? The latter interpretation would make the provision more effective; but the courts incline towards the former view: development which does not harm a conservation area can be regarded as helping to preserve the character or appearance of the area.

The case of *South Lakeland District Council v. Secretary of State for the Environment* (1992) was concerned with the erection of a new house, within the curtilage of an existing house, in a conservation area. There was a dispute about the requirement in the planning legislation to consider whether the new house must positively contribute to the preservation or enhancement of the character or appearance of the conservation area, or whether it was enough that it did not harm the character and appearance of it.

The House of Lords (dealing with the case after a series of appeals) decided that the latter was the case, and that it was right to grant planning permission in this case.

Conservation areas

9-76 An application for planning permission in a conservation area must be publicised by the local authority, if it would affect the character or appearance of the area (s. 73). The rules on demolishing buildings in conservation areas are more stringent: special permission (known as "conservation area consent") must generally be obtained (s. 74). The fact that land is within a conservation area will mean that automatic permission is not granted as fully by the GPDO. And in exercising their power to give a direction under article 4, and so prevent the automatic permission granted by the GPDO, local authorities will often relate directions to conservation areas (though they are free to specify any area).

See 9-33 for directions under article 4 of the GPDO.

9-77 Special rules apply to trees in conservation areas: under s. 211 of the Town and Country Planning Act 1990, it is an offence to do anything which could be prohibited by a tree preservation order—that is, "cutting down, topping, lopping or uprooting, wilful damage or wilful destruction of trees". But it is a defence for a person to show that he obtained the consent of the local authority, or that he gave them written notice of what he intended to do, and waited six weeks before doing it. The point of this requirement is that the local authority then have time to consider the matter and make a tree preservation order, if they feel it is appropriate, in order to protect the tree.

See 10-20 onwards for tree preservation orders, and 10-21 for lopping and topping. The maximum punishment is the same as for breach of a tree preservation order.

9-78 There are exemptions from these provisions, and these are set out in Part III of the Town and Country Planning (Trees) Regulations 1999. They include:

- Trees which are already subject to a tree preservation order (and which therefore don't need extra protection).
- Felling, uprooting, topping or lopping by the local authority.
- Felling in accordance with the approval of the Forestry Commission.
- Cutting down or uprooting a tree if its diameter (at a height of 1.5 metres above ground level) is not more than 75mm, or, if the work is done to improve the growth of other trees, 100mm.

See 10-26 for local authorities' powers in relation to trees: without this exemption, it would be impossible for local authorities to use these powers.

See 10-34 onwards for forestry

9-79 Local authorities must keep a register, open to public inspection, of notices under s. 211 affecting trees in conservation areas (s. 214). If a tree is wrongly destroyed, the owner of the land is under a duty to plant a replacement, unless the local authority releases him from the duty (s. 213). The duty is enforced in the same way as the duty which applies where there is a tree preservation order.

See 12-20 for sources on conservation areas.

9-80 Control over outdoor advertisements is also stricter in conservation areas.

See 10-16 for advertisements in conservation areas.

Other special areas

Conservation areas are not the only areas in which the planning system is adjusted, so as to make development more difficult, in order to protect the environment; or less difficult, in order to encourage regeneration in run-down areas. Some other examples can be briefly mentioned. 9-81

Enterprise zones and simplified planning zones The DETR can create enterprise zones under the Local Government and Housing Act 1980, and the effect is to provide tax advantages and to remove some of the red tape associated with the planning system. Enterprise zones exist in a number of industrial towns in the Midlands and the North of England. Local authorities can also designate simplified planning zones ("SPZs") under the Town and Country Planning Act 1990 Act, and the effect is to grant planning permission for the types of development specified. SPZs have been designated in a number of inner city areas. 9-82

National Parks and areas of outstanding natural beauty. National Parks can be designated by the Countryside Agency under the National Parks and Access to the Countryside Act 1949. The DETR's Guidance Note PPG7: *The Countryside and the Rural Economy* lays down the policy that proposals for major development in National Parks should be looked at very carefully. National Parks are "article 1(5) land" and also "article 1(6) land" for the purposes of the GPDO, so the planning permission automatically granted by the GPDO does not apply as fully to national parks. The Countryside Agency can also designate areas of outstanding natural beauty, under s. 87 of the National Parks and Access to the Countryside Act 1949, and these areas are also "article 1(5) land". 9-83

See also 10-80 for National Parks.

See 9-33 for the meaning of "article 1(5) land" and "article 1(6) land".

Enforcement

In the language of the 1990 Act, a "breach of planning control" takes place where development is carried out without the necessary planning permission, or where there is a failure to comply with 9-84 planning conditions (s. 171(1)*(a)*). Following the changes made by the Planning and Compensation Act 1991, a range of weapons is available to local authorities to enforce the planning system. The main weapon is the enforcement notice (s. 172).

9-85 An enforcement notice must be served on the owner and occupier of the land in question. It must set out the alleged breach(es) of planning control and the steps which must be taken to put matters right, for example, ceasing some activity, or removing or alterting a building which has been put up without planning permission. The notice must also specify the time within which this is to be done (s. 173).

9-86 Owners and occupiers served with an enforcement notice can appeal to the DETR against it. This right can be exercised during the period (which must be at least 28 days) before the enforcement notice comes into effect. The appeal can be on a number of different grounds, including the following:

- That planning permission ought to be granted, or a planning condition discharged.
- That there was no breach of planning control.
- That the steps which have to be taken to comply with the enforcement notice are excessive, or the period allowed not long enough (s. 174).

9-87 Detailed rules for appeals are laid down in the Town and Country Planning (Enforcement Notices and Appeals) Regulations 1991. The DETR must hold an inquiry, if the local authority or the landowner wishes to have one. The DETR can dismiss an appeal, or can grant planning permission (with or without conditions) or alter planning conditions (s. 177). Subject to the possibility of an appeal, a failure to comply with an enforcement notice is an offence, the maximum punishment being a fine of £20,000 if the case is dealt with in a magstrates' court or an unlimited fine if it is dealt with in the Crown Court (s. 179). If the steps specified in an enforcement notice are not taken, the local authority can enter the land and carry out the work—for example, removing unlawful buildings—and can recover the cost from the landowner (s. 178).

If the local authority wish to bring a halt to the activity which is the subject of a enforcement notice, they can serve an additional notice, known as a "stop notice" (s. 183). The person concerned must comply, or he commits an offence for which the maximum punishment is a £20,000 fine (in a magistrates' court) or an unlimited fine (in the Crown Court) (s. 187). In limited circumstances, compensation may be payable to the person affected by a stop notice if it causes him loss and he is successful in an appeal against the enforcement notice (s. 186). 9-88

Though enforcement notices can be used where there is a breach of a planning condition, another sort of notice, known as a "breach of condition notice" may be used where the local authority is concerned with a breach of a planning condition (s. 187A). The procedure is designed to be more flexible. A breach of condition notice must be served on the person who is carrying out the development, or the person who is in control of the land. It must specify the steps to be taken in order to comply with the notice, and give a period of time (at least 28 days) for doing so. There is no right of appeal to the DETR, and at the end of the period the person concerned commits an offence if he has failed to comply with the notice, the maximum punishment being a level 3 fine (s. 187A). If there is a prosecution but the notice is still not complied with, there can be further prosecutions. 9-89

Time limits apply to enforcement notices and breach of condition notices. In the case of operational development, no action may be taken by the local authority more than four years after the operations were "substantially completed". In the case of a change of use which consists of a change to use as a single dwelling house, from any other use, the period is again four years. But for any other sort of material change of use, the period is 10 years (s. 171B). A landowner therefore does not have the possibility of enforcement action hanging over his head indefinitely: after these periods have expired, it is too late for the local authority to take action . 9-90

See 9-13 for the meaning of "operational development".

If a local authority is concerned about a possible breach of planning control but does not yet wish to go so far as to serve an enforcement notice or a breach of condition notice, it may serve a 9-91

Times limits for enforcement

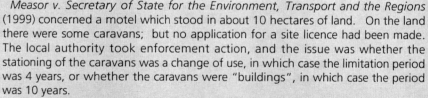

Measor v. Secretary of State for the Environment, Transport and the Regions (1999) concerned a motel which stood in about 10 hectares of land. On the land there were some caravans; but no application for a site licence had been made. The local authority took enforcement action, and the issue was whether the stationing of the caravans was a change of use, in which case the limitation period was 4 years, or whether the caravans were "buildings", in which case the period was 10 years.

The planning inspector decided that the caravans were not "buildings", and that the period was 4 years. (There was an appeal, and the court agreed.)

"planning contravention notice", under s. 171C of the 1990 Act. The notice can be served on the owner or occupier of the land, or any person who is carrying out operations on the land or using it for any purpose. The aim of the notice is to require information about what is happening on the land, and who is responsible for it, and a notice may also give a time and place at which the person concerned can (if they wish) make representations to the local authority about the notice and offer to apply for planning permission, to stop particular operations or activities, or to undertake remedial work on the land. Failing to give information or assistance required by a planning contravention notice is an offence, with a maximum of a level 3 fine (or a level 5 fine for giving false information) (s. 171D). A planning contravention notice is designed to put the local authority in touch with the person responsible for the activity which is causing concern, to give them information about it, and to provide an opportunity for problems to be resolved voluntarily. If that fails to put right any breach of planning control, an enforcement notice or a breach of condition notice may well follow.

9-92 Local authorities have powers to enter land, for the purposes of planning control, under ss. 196A, 196B and 196C. They also have a general power to apply to the courts for an injunction, to prevent a breach of the law, including breaches of the planning legislation, under s. 222 of the Local Government Act 1982.

See 3-29 for injunctions generally.

Assessment

Landowners do not have an unqualified right to develop their land. Minor development, such as porches and TV satellite dishes, is very often allowed, though it is still controlled by the law. More major development is dependent upon obtaining planning consent. An application, as it passes through the planning system, may have to be modified before it succeeds, and the grant of planning permission may be subject to conditions and obligations. 9-93

It is difficult to think of a better explanation for the purpose of the planning system than the single word "planning". The system exists to make, and put into effect, plans which balance the needs of the community and the interests of individual landowners. The key issue is not so much whether development should take place, but where it should be put. When the question of development arises, there is an understandable tendency to focus on the advantages and disadvantages to the owner of the land and his neighbours. These factors are important, but landowners need to take into account too, in supporting or opposing development, the policies of the local authority, embodied in the development plan, and of central government, as set out in Guidance Notes and other documents. 9-94

One big advantage of the plannig system is that it is open to input from the public. Landowners should take an interest in the development plan, because it its long-term significance. In relation to their own planning applications, or applications by neighbours which will affect them, they should not hesitate to make contact with the local authority staff, to discuss the issues informally. Leaflets and other publications issued by the local authority can also be very useful. The best way to influence a planning decision is to: 9-95

- Put forward clear reasons for or against the development, referring to the development plan and other policy issues as well as the merits or demerits of the application.

- Show a degree of flexibility.

9-96 Planning disputes can be legally complex, and the amounts at stake can be substantial, both because of the possible increases or decreases in the value of land and because of the costs which may be incurred. Landowners should recognise that there may well be a need to take professional advice.

Chapter 10

More regulation of land use

Introduction

This chapter explains a range of legal subjects, where the law regulates the way in which land is used. Landowners may be affected because they own the land in question, or because neighbouring land is subject to one of these forms of regulation. The list is not intended to be complete. Many more specialised forms of land use have their own forms of regulation. Landowners wishing to set up an aerodrome, a knacker's yard or a theatre will find that licensing requirements apply to these and many other activities—the requirements being in addition to planning permission for any "development" which may be involved. 10-0

Almost all the law explained in this chapter comes from Acts of Parliament. It is a mixture of civil and criminal law, since both have a rôle in ensuring that the requirements of the law are met. 10-1

See 9-13 onwards for the meaning of "development".

Building control

The system of building control lays down and enforces the technical requirements with which buildings must comply. The system is separate from, and additional to, the planning system. The law comes from the Building Act 1984, and regulations made under it, including the Building Regulations 1991, which have since been amended on various occasions. Apart from these national requirements, which apply to England and Wales, there are local 10-2

See chapter 9 for planning.

Acts (including Acts which apply to Inner London) in many areas which impose additional requirements.

See 1-1 for the meaning of "local Act".

10-3 The definition of "building" in s. 121 of the Act is very wide, and includes "any...structure or erection of whatever kind or nature". The Regulations, however, have a narrower definition, which in effect means buildings in the ordinary sense of the word, with walls and a roof.

10-4 The Regulations themselves do not set the detailed standards for buildings: this is done in a series of "Approved Documents"—documents which are approved by the DETR under s. 6 of the Act, and provided detailed guidance—and other sources, including British Standards. The advantage of setting the detailed requirements in this way is that the rules are easier to alter, and can also be expressed in less legalistic language. The Building Act 1984 imposes a few specific requirements, and other legislation impose a number of requirements. These include the following:

See 1-14 for codes of practice and similar documents.

- For buildings and extensions, there must be satisfactory provision for drainage (s. 21 of the Building Act).

- For residential property, there must be a wholesome water supply, whether mains water or a private supply (s. 25).

10-5 The approval of plans and the supervision of construction work is generally carried out by local authorities; though Part II of the Building Act allows inspectors to be appointed privately, and to carry out this function. The Act provides, in s. 35, that breach of the Building Regulations is generally an offence for which the maximum punishment is level 5 on the standard scale, with a further fine of up to £50 for each day on which the offence continues after conviction. However, there are provisions in the Act which allow a local authority to relax the requirements of the Building Regulations, and which allow an appeal to the DETR if the local authority refuse to relax them (ss. 8–10 and 39).

See 1-23 for the standard scale of fines.

10-6 Section 36 of the Buildings Act allows a local authority, as well as or in addition to other action, to serve a notice on the owner of the building, requiring her to remove or put right building work which does not comply with the Building Regulations. If the notice is not complied with, the local authority can take action itself, and recover the cost of doing so from the owner.

Cottingham v. Attey Bower & Jones (2000) was a case in which the buyers of some land were suing their own solicitors for failing to check that renovation work had been carried out in accordance with the Building Regulations.
The court decided that the solicitors had been negligent [see 4-58 for negligence]. Although 12 months had passed and it was too late for the local authority to serve a notice under s. 36, it was still possible that the local authority might apply for an injunction in relation to work which did not comply with the Building Regulations.

Building regulations

10-7 Section 76 of the Act gives local authorities the power to take rapid action where premises are in such a state that they are "prejudicial to health or a nuisance", and if acting under s. 80 of the Environmental Protection Act 1990 would result in unreasonable delay. The local authority can serve a notice on the owner of the premises giving warning that the local authority intend to do the necessary work to put matters right. Unless the owner serves a counter-notice, the local authority can, after nine days, proceed with the work.

See 4-30 for s. 80 of the Environmental Protection Act 1990 and local authorities' powers to deal with statutory nuisances.

10-8 Action can be taken under s. 77 if a building is dangerous. The local authority can serve a notice on the owner requiring him to carry out repairs. Failure to do so is an offence for which the maximum punishment is a level 1 fine; and the local authority can also do the necessary work and recover the cost from the owner. Emergency measures can be taken under s. 78, if needed, when a building is dangerous. A separate power, in s. 79, applies where a building is "by reason of its ruinous or dilapidated condition seriously detrimental to the amenities of the neighbourhood". The local authority can require the owner of the building to repair it or demolish it.

See 9-10 for the meaning of "amenity".

10-9 When a person wishes to demolish the whole or part of a building, he must generally give notice to the local authority of his intention (s. 80 of the Building Act 1984). Copies of the notice must be sent to the owners of adjacent buildings and to the utility companies. There are some exceptions, including a building which has a cubic content of not more than 1,750 cubic feet, and a

Contrast planning law on demolition: see 9-40 for a summary.

See 11-103 for utility company.

See also 6-47 onwards for rights of support from adjoining land.

See 12-21 for sources on building control.

greenhouse, conservatory, shed or prefabricated garage which forms part of a larger building. The purpose of the notice is to allow the local authority to regulate the demolition in various ways. These include requiring that adjacent buildings be shored up, removing materials, and removing or sealing drains or sewers (ss. 81 and 82).

Retaining walls

10-10 The Highways Act 1980 provides that the construction of retaining walls is subject to the approval by the local authority of the plans and specifications (s. 167). This requirement applies to any retaining wall which is not part of a permanent building and which is intended to serve as a support for earth or other material on one side of the wall only, if all or part of the retaining wall is to be within 4 yards of the street and at any point more than 4' 6" above the level of the ground at the boundary of the street nearest to the wall. (The provision thus applies to walls which may be in danger of collapsing on to the street, but not those which support the street.) Putting up a retaining wall without permission is an offence for which the maximum punishment is a level 3 fine.

See 5-63 for the meaning of "street" in the Highways Act 1980.

Advertisements

10-11 Control over the display of advertisements on land is related to planning law, but forms a separate system of control. By s. 55(5) of the Town and Country Planning Act 1990, the use of any external part of a building for the display of an advertisement is deemed to involve a material change of use—so on the face of it planning permission is needed for such advertisements. Planning permission may also be needed because operational development, or a change of use is involved, for example in the erection of a hoarding. But advertisements which are in accordance with the controls on advertising are deemed to have permission for any development involved (s. 222 of the 1990 Act). The effect of these rules is that where a landowner complies with the controls on advertising there is no need to worry about planning permission; but if the controls on advertising are not complied with, the landowner may be in trouble for breach of planning law, as well as breach of the advertising controls.

In *Great Yarmouth Borough Council v. Secretary of State for the Environment* (1997) the question arose of whether "advertisement" included an image projected by means of a beam of light on to the underside of a cloud.

The court's decision was that an advertisement did not have to consist of a physical object: a sign made by a beam of light could be an advertisement, and so the Regulations applied here.

What is an advertisement?

10-12 Most of the law on advertisements is contained in the Town and Country (Control of Advertisements) Regulations 1992, made by the DETR under the power in s. 220 of the Town and Country Planning Act 1990. The Regulations define what advertisements are covered, and when it is necessary to apply to the local authority for permission to display an advertisement. Also important are DETR PPG 19: *Outdoor Advertising Control*, and DETR Circular 5/92: *The Town and Country Planning (Control of Advertisements) Regulations 1992*.

See 9-5 onwards for DETR PPGs and Circulars.

10-13 The Regulations apply to a wide range of advertisements, including signs, placards, boards, notices, awnings, blinds, devices and representations, which are used to advertise something, or make an announcement or give a direction ("this way to the car boot sale"). Captive balloon advertisements are included in the definition, as are three-dimensional advertisements.

10-14 Having given a wide definition of "advertisement", the Regulations exempt some advertisements (reg. 3(2)). Schedule 2 lists advertisements to which the Regulations do not apply at all, provided they comply with certain conditions, some being "standard conditions", and some being set out in Schedule 2. The "standard conditions" include the requirements that the site be kept clean and tidy, that the advertisement be safe, that the owner of the site consents, and that the traffic signs are not obstructed. Within Schedule 2, there are many detailed conditions for particular sorts of advertisement, relating to such matters as the size, placing, visibility and purpose of the advertisements. Schedule 2 includes, among others, the following sort of advertisement:

- Balloon advertisements not more than 60 metres above ground level, for not more than 10 days a year.
- Advertisements on enclosed land, provided they are not readily visible from outside.
- Advertisements inside buildings, provided they are not illuminated.
- Notices relating to public elections.
- Official traffic signs.

10-15 Schedule 3 lists advertisements for which the local authority's consent is deemed to be granted, so that there is generally no need to apply for it. The consent is deemed to be subject to the standard conditions and detailed conditions set out in Schedule 3 itself (reg. 6). Schedule 3 includes the following advertisements:

- Signs identifying buildings, or giving warnings or directions about land or buildings.
- Nameplates and other signs relating to persons carrying on business at an address.
- Temporary signs relating to sale or letting of property.
- Signs for neighbourhood watch schemes.

10-16 The conditions in Schedules 2 and 3 are sometimes stricter if the advertisement is in a conservation area. Furthermore, the local authority can designate an area as an "area of special control" under

See 9-73 onwards for conservation areas.

the Regulations , whether or not it is already a conservation area (reg. 18). This tightens the restrictions on advertisements even more. Most of the advertisements in Schedule 2 are allowed, as are some in Schedule 3, and some with the express consent of the local authority.

10-17 If express consent for an advertisement is required, it can be granted subject to conditions, including (usually) a five-year time limit. When an application is refused by the local authority, there is a right of appeal to the DETR.

10-18 Displaying an advertisement in breach of the legislation is an offence for which the maximum punishment is a level 3 fine, and, if the offence continues, one-tenth of that amount for each day it continues (s. 224(3) of the Town and Country Planning Act 1990). Local authorities have a special power under s. 225 of the Act to remove or obliterate placards or posters which are displayed in breach of the legislation. This allows local authorities to deal promptly with fly-posting. But the power does not apply to advertisements in buildings to which the public have access; and, if the local authority know who is responsible for the advertisement, they must first give him notice that they intend to remove it.

For 12-20 for sources on advertising control.

Trees

10-19 Planning law takes notice of the need for trees as part of new developments. However, planting, felling and trimming trees does not require planning permission. Instead, trees have a separate form of protection, the tree preservation order. The system of making and enforcing tree preservation orders (which is in the hands of local authorities) is self-contained but linked to planning law—in particular, because trees in conservation areas are treated as though they were subject to tree preservation orders. The following paragraphs explain how the system works, and then go on to deal with powers which local authorities have, under separate legislation, enabling them to deal with trees and shrubs which are dangerous or in the way.

See 9-44 for s. 197 of the Town and Country Planning Act 1990

See 9-77 for trees in conservation areas.

Related subjects are forestry (see 10-34 onwards) and the protection of hedgerows (see 10-30 onwards).

10-20 *Tree preservation orders* The law is set out in ss. 198 - 214D of the Town and Country Planning Act 1990, and the Town and Country Planning (Trees) Regulations 1999. The DETR Circular 36/78, *Trees and Forestry*, contains detailed guidance on tree preservation orders. Under s. 198 of the 1990 Act, a tree preservation can be made by the local authority if it is "expedient in the interests of amenity" to do so. A local authority can act of its own accord, or when someone suggests that a tree needs protection. The Act does not define "tree", so that the word bears its ordinary meaning; but the DETR considers that a tree preservation order cannot relate to a bush or shrub, or to a hedge as such, though it can relate to a tree in a hedge (paragraph 44 of Circular 36/78). A tree preservation order can be made in relation to a single tree, or a group of trees, or an area of woodland.

See 9-10 for the meaning of "amenity".

10-21 The 1999 Regulations lay down, in Schedule 1, a model form for a tree preservation order, which the local authority can alter to suit the needs of particular cases. The order must specify the trees or woodland in question, and there must be a map showing their position. The order will generally forbid the "cutting down, topping, lopping, uprooting, wilful damage or wilful destruction" of the tree(s). Once an order has been made, it generally cannot take effect until it has been confirmed by the local authority (s. 199). However, the local authority may make an order which takes effect immediately, if they feel this is necessary, under s. 201.

Topping and lopping of trees

In *Unwin v. Hanson* (1891) the local authority, acting under the Highway Act 1835, obtained an order from the magistrates' court that some trees on Mr Unwin's land, near the highway, should be "pruned or lopped". Mr Unwin did not comply with the order and the local authority entered his land and cut the tops off two fir trees. Mr Unwin challenged their right to do so.

The court decided that the local authority was not entitled to cut the tops off the trees. "Lopping" meant cutting lateral branches, not cutting the tops off trees. "Topping" was the appropriate word to describe cutting the tops off.

10-22 Confirming a tree preservation order involves serving the order on the owners and occupiers of the land, and making a copy available for public inspection. Any objections or representations must then be made to the local authority, after which the local authority may confirm the order, with or without modifications.

See 1-47 for the meaning of "occupying" land.

(They might, for example, having considered objections and representations, feel that the order should include more trees, or fewer, or even that no order was necessary after all.) If the order is confirmed, the owners and occupiers of the land must be notified (regs. 2–7). Tree preservation orders can be varied and revoked later (regs. 8 and 9). There is a procedure for appeals, which can be dealt with by the DETR on the basis of written material (regs. 11–16). Tree preservation orders should appear on the register of local land charges.

See 1-67 for this register.

10-23 When a tree preservation order is in force, the activities forbidden by the order (generally, cutting down, lopping, topping etc) are an offence unless they are covered by an exception or the local authority grants consent. The exceptions are:

- Trees which are "dying or dead or have become dangerous" (s. 198(6)(a)).
- Trees which must be cut down, topped, lopped, etc to comply with an obligation in an Act, or to prevent or abate a nuisance (s. 198(6)(b)).
- Any exceptions written into a tree preservation order. One exception in the standard form of tree preservation order relates to fruit trees cultivated for fruit and growing in a garden or orchard; this enables the trees to be pruned without a breach of any tree preservation order covering them, though the pruning must be "in accordance with good horticultural practice".
- Trees which need to be cut down in order to implement a planning permission (e. g. trees standing on the site of a new building).

See 4-23 for the meaning of "abating" a nuisance.

The terms of a tree preservation order usually allow the local authority to consent to cutting down, topping, lopping etc; and they can thus be asked for consent where surgery to a tree becomes necessary, for example because a tree is too near a house. When consent is granted, it can be granted subject to conditions.

10-24 There are two offences which deal with breaches of tree preservation orders. The first applies where a person "cuts down, uproots or wilfully destroys a tree", or "wilfully damages, tops or lops a tree in such a manner as to be likely to destroy it". For this offence, the maximum punishment is a fine of £20,000 in the magistrates' court, or an unlimited fine in the Crown Court (s. 210(1)). In determining the size of the fine, the court must take into account any financial benefit resulting from the offence. So a landowner who gets rid of an inconvenient tree, in order to allow some profitable development, may have to pay a heavy price. There is also a less serious offence, which consists of other breaches of a tree preservation order (i.e. breaches which do not involve destroying the tree), the maximum fine being level 4 on the standard scale (s. 214(4)).

See 3-29 for injunctions.

10-25 Local authorities can obtain an injunction to prevent damage to a tree protected by a tree preservation order (s. 214A). In addition, s. 206 of the 1990 Act imposes a duty on the landowner to replace a tree which is covered by a tree preservation order and which is "removed, uprooted or destroyed" in breach of the order, or which is "removed, uprooted or destroyed or dies", when the tree is dying, or dead or dangerous—unless the tree is protected only because it is part of an area of woodland. The new tree becomes subject to the tree preservation order. If the landowner fails to comply with this obligation, the local authority may, after giving him notice of their intention, plant a new tree and recover the cost from him (s. 207).

See 12-20 for sources on tree preservation orders.

10-26 *Dangerous and overhanging trees* Local authorities have several powers enabling them to take action in relation to trees. Under s. 154 of the Highways Act 1980, which applies to hedges, trees and shrubs, a local authority may require the occupier of land to take action in two circumstances. First, they can do so where a hedge, tree or shrub overhangs a road to which the public has access,

> "so as to endanger or obstruct the passage of vehicles or pedestrians, or obstruct or interfere with the view of drivers of vehicles or the light from a public lamp".

10-27 Secondly, they can do so if a tree or shrub is dead, diseased or damaged and is likely to cause damage by falling on to a road or footpath to which the public has access. "Hedge, tree or shrub" is defined to include vegetation of any description, thus eliminating any argument, in this context, about what constitutes a "tree or shrub" ꕥ. A notice has to be served, specifying the work to be done. The person served with the notice can appeal to a magistrates' court. If she does not do the work, the local authority can do it, and recover the cost from her.

ꕥ Contrast the way in which the law works in relation to tree preservation orders: see 10-20.

10-28 Power is also given by the Local Government (Miscellaneous Provisions) Act 1976, s. 23, and this is essentially a power to make a tree safe if it appears likely to cause damage to persons or property. The power applies to trees on "any land", thus including all private as well as public property. The local authority can act in three different situations. The first is where it receives a request to make a tree safe from someone who is the owner or occupier of the land on which the tree is growing. The authority can carry out the work and recover the cost from the person in question (s. 23(2)).

10-29 The second situation is where a request to make a tree safe comes from a person who is the owner or occupier of neighbouring land. If the owner of the land on which the tree is growing cannot be found, the authority can proceed with the work and recover the cost from the person who made the request. But if the owner of the land can be found, the authority must (if they decide to take any action) proceed by serving a notice on that person requiring him to do the necessary work (s. 23(3)). If he fails to carry out the work, the authority can do so and recover the cost from him (s. 23(4)). The person concerned can appeal to the County Court against the notice, on one of four different grounds set out in s. 23(5). The final situation in which the local authority can act is where there is no request to make a tree safe, but a tree is likely to damage persons or property on land owned by the local authority itself.

Hedgerows

10-30 Since June 1997, hedgerows have enjoyed their own special form of protection, under the Hedgerows Regulations 1997, made under the power in s. 97(8) of the Environment Act 1995. The Regulations apply only to hedgerows which have a continuous length of at least

20 metres (or are shorter than that, but join other hedgerows) and which are in, or adjacent to:

- Common land.

- "Protected land" (meaning land which is a nature reserve, under s. 21 of the National Parks and Access to the Countryside Act 1949, or a site of special scientific interest under s. 28 of the Wildlife and Countryside Act 1981).

- Land used for agriculture or forestry or the breeding of horses, ponies and donkeys (reg. 3). ("Agriculture" is given a wide definition by the Regulations.)

See 10-65 for the meaning of "common land".

10-31 The Regulations do not apply to a hedge which forms the boundary of the curtilage of a dwelling-house, or which is within the curtilage. Where the Regulations apply, the owner of the land is free to carry out certain sorts of work, such as removing part of a hedge to form an access, or to carry out work for which planning permission has been granted (but most of the provisions of the General Permitted Development Order 1995 do not apply here). Work can also be done "for the proper management of the hedgerow", so that the landowner can trim or relay a hedgerow (reg. 6).

See 9-18 for the meaning of "curtilage".

See 9-31 onwards for the GPDO.

10-32 Otherwise, however, a landowner who wishes to remove a hedge must give notice to the local authority, who may either grant permission or serve a "hedge retention notice" (reg. 5). Such notices cannot be served in all cases, but only where the hedgerow is "important", which means that has existed for at least 30 years, and also satisfy detailed criteria set out in Schedule 1 to the Regulations (reg. 4). Schedule 1 is complicated, but it focuses on two sorts of test:

- Archaeology and history—whether, for example, the hedgerow marks the boundary of a parish or township which existed before 1850, or includes an archaeological feature or is within an archaeological site.

- Wildlife and landscape—whether the hedgerow contains certain numbers of various species of plants and trees.

10-33 A landowner can appeal to the DETR against the making of a hedgerow retention order (reg. 9). Removing a hedgerow in breach of the Regulations is an offence for which the maximum fine is the statutory maximum if the case is dealt with in a magistrates' court; or an unlimited fine in the Crown Court. The court must take into account any financial benefit which the landowner has obtained from removing the hedge (reg. 7). Where a hedgerow has been wrongly removed, the local authority may require the landowner to replace it, and if he fails to do so the local authority may carry out the work and recover the cost from the landowner (reg. 8). Local authorities also have the power to obtain an injunction to prevent a hedgerow being wrongly removed (reg. 11). Local authorities must keep records, open to the public, of notices received and issued by them, and the results of appeals (reg. 10).

See 1-20 onwards for criminal proceedings generally.

See 10-24 for a similar rule applying to tree preservation orders.

See 1-17 for the meaning of "injunction".

See 12-2 for sources on the Hedgerows Regulations.

Forestry

10-34 The Forestry Commission regulates forestry under the Forestry Act 1967, as amended by later Acts. The Act provides that a licence (i. e. permission) from the Forestry Commission is generally required for the felling of growing trees (s. 9). Planning permission is not required for the use of land for forestry (s. 55(2)(e) of the Town and Country Planning Act 1990).

See 9-13 onwards for the meaning of "development".

10-35 To the rule that a licence is required ss. 9 provides a number of exceptions, including the following:

- The felling of trees with a diameter of up to 8 centimetres, or, in coppices and underwoods, 15 centimetres.

- The felling of fruit trees or trees in an orchard, garden, churchyard or public open space.

See 10-21 for the meaning of "topping and lopping" trees.

- The topping or lopping of trees, or the trimming or laying of hedges.

- The felling of trees with a diameter of up to 10 centimetres in order to improve the growth of other trees.

- The felling of trees by the occupier of the land concerned, where the aggregate amount of wood (excluding felling for which no licence is required) is not more than 5 cubic metres in any quarter, or 2 cubic metres if the wood is sold.

See 4-23 for the meaning of "abating" a nuisance.

- Felling carried out for the prevention of danger or the abatement of a nuisance.

See 11-103 for statutory undertakers.

10-36 The Act, and regulations made under it, the Forestry (Exceptions from Restriction of Felling) Regulations 1979, also contain exemptions for felling by statutory undertakers and felling of elms suffering from Dutch elm disease.

10-37 Although the Forestry Act is not concerned only with commercial forestry operations, limited felling by landowners will very often fall within one of the exemptions mentioned above, so that there will generally be no need to obtain a licence. Where a licence is required, it may be granted subject to conditions about restocking the land with trees (s. 12). If the conditions are not complied with, the Commission has powers to enforce them (ss. 24–26). If a landowner wishes to fell a tree subject to a tree preservation order, the Forestry Commission must notify the local authority, and if the latter object the question of whether the tree can be felled must be referred to MAFF and dealt with under the planning legislation (s. 15). Compensation is generally payable if a licence to fell is refused (s. 11). Felling a tree without the necessary licence is an offence, the maximum punishment being a level 4 fine (s. 17). The Forestry Commission has power to require a person convicted of a s. 17 offence to restock his land (ss. 17A–17C). The Commission also has power, in certain circumstances, to direct the felling of trees (ss. 18–23).

See 12-2 for sources on forestry and the Forestry Commission.

Caravan sites and mobile home parks

10-38 Caravan sites and mobile home parks have their own legislation. The Caravan Sites and Control of Development Act 1960 regulates the use of land as a caravan site where the caravans are intended for human habitation. The Caravan Sites Act 1968 and the Mobile Homes Act 1983 are concerned with protecting the position of those who live in caravans. Though the legislation uses both "caravan" and "mobile home" there is no difference between the meaning of the two terms. However, the degree of protection which the law gives will depend upon the circumstances. The land on which a caravan stands within a caravan site is often called a "pitch", though this word is not used in the legislation.

10-39 *Caravan Sites and Control of Development Act 1960* An occupier of land must obtain a "site licence" from the local authority in order to use land as a caravan site. A caravan is defined widely in s. 29(1) of the Act, and means:

See 1-47 for the meaning of "occupying" land.

> "any structure designed or adapted for human habitation which is capable of being moved from one place to another (whether by being towed or by being transported on a motor vehicle or trailer) and any motor vehicle so designed or adapted, but does not include—
>
> (a) any railway rolling stock which is for the time being on rails forming part of a railway system, or
>
> (b) any tent."

In *Byrne v. Secretary of State for the Environment and Arun District Council* (1997) the question was whether a log cabin was technically a twin-unit caravan. This was important because it affected the enforcement period which applied, under planning law [see 9-90 for the 4- and 10-year periods].

The Planning Inspector (and the court, when the landowner appealed) decided that the log cabin was not a twin-unit caravan. It did not consist of only two separately-constructed sections; and it was not capable of being moved by road when assembled.

Twin-unit caravans

The definition has been modified by s. 13(1) of the Caravan Sites Act 1968 so as to include "twin-unit" caravans, and this means caravans which are composed of not more than two sections, intended to be assembled on site, and which are physically capable of being moved by road when assembled.

10-40 Conditions can be attached to a site licence. A single caravan may be enough to constitute a caravan site, but there are various exemptions from the need to apply for a licence, laid down in the First Schedule to the 1960 Act, and these include:

See 9-18 for the meaning of "curtilage".

- The use of land within the curtilage of a dwelling house if the use is incidental to the enjoyment of the dwelling. This would allow a householder to keep a caravan for use by guests, or for holiday letting—but not for use as an independent dwelling.
- The use of land for occasional stays by touring caravans. There must be only one caravan at a time, the stay must not be for more than 2 nights, and the land must not have been used in this way for more than 28 days in the preceding 12 months.
- The use of not more than 5 acres, for up to 3 caravans, provided that in the preceding 12 months there were caravans on the land for no more than 28 days.
- The use of land for up to five caravans by an organisation exempted by the DETR. (The DETR can grant exemptions to organisations whose objects "include the encouragement or promotion of recreational activities"—for example, the Caravan Club.)
- The use of agricultural land (or forestry land) to accommodate seasonal workers.
- The use of land which forms part of or adjoins a building site, to accommodate people employed on the site, provided that planning permission has been granted for work on the site.

10-41 In addition to the 1960 Act, planning law is relevant to caravan sites. Caravans and mobile homes are not usually "buildings": even if they are intended to stay in the same position indefinitely, and are connected to mains electricity and other services, they will generally not be permanently attached to the land for the purposes of planning law. Putting caravans on land will therefore not amount to a "building operation". But starting to use land as a caravan site may involve a change of use of the land, and so require planning permission; and work such as landscaping, or putting up buildings containing facilities such as showers or lavatories is likely to require planning permission on the ground that building operations are involved. Planning law, in the form of the General Permitted Development Order 1995, grants permission for the use of land as a caravan site in circumstances which almost exactly match the exemptions from the need for a site licence. So where there is no need for site licence, it is almost always the case that there is no need for planning permission for a change of use of the land.

See 2-47 on when things are attached to the land and therefore form part of it.

See 9-21 onwards for building and other operations.

See 9-31 onwards for the General Permitted Development Order ("GPDO").

10-42 Whether something is a caravan, a building or a "moveable dwelling" is vital, because it determines which area of the law regulates the use of the land. The position can be summarised as follows:

Table 7: caravans, buildings and moveable dwellings

Type of structure	Legislation regulating use of land
Buildings	Planning law for changes of use and building operations.
Caravans and mobile homes	Planning law for changes of use, and the Caravan Sites and Control of Development Act 1960
Moveable dwellings	Planning law for changes of use, and the Public Health Act 1936, s. 269.

See chapter 9 for planning law.

See 10-51 for "moveable dwellings".

10-43 This does not mean, however, that all the law applying to caravans, buildings etc, is in watertight compartments. In many cases, the law treats caravans and those who live in them in the same way as those who live in houses. This is true in particular of the protection given to caravan-dwellers: in addition to the Caravan Sites Act 1968 and the Mobile Homes Act 1983, the general law protects people living in caravans just as it protects people living in houses.

See for example 3-41 on burglary of caravans.

10-44 *Caravan Sites Act 1968* This Act (apart from introducing the concept of a twin-unit caravan) gives some protection to those who live in caravans. The 1968 Act applies only to what it calls "protected sites", meaning sites which require a site licence but where the conditions of the site licence or of planning permission do not confine the site to holiday use only, or to use at certain times of the year only. To put it another way, sites which are holiday sites, or which are open only at certain times of the year, because of conditions in the site licence or planning conditions, are not "protected sites", and the 1968 Act does not apply. On protected sites, the Act applies to those who have a "residential contract", meaning, by s. 1(1) :

> "any licence or contract ..... under which a person is entitled to station a caravan on a protected site and occupy it as his residence, or to occupy as his residence a caravan stationed on any such site".

So the Act applies both where a caravan-dweller brings her own caravan on to the site and where she lives in a caravan provided by the landowner. Although the Act uses the term "residential contract" a licence (permission) to occupy a caravan is included.

See 1-49 onwards for licences.

10-45 The 1968 Act, in s. 2, requires that if notice is required, under a residental contract, before a caravan-dweller leaves the caravan or the site, then at least four weeks' notice must be given. Section 3 then makes it an offence for the landowner himself to evict the occupier of the caravan, or to harass her. This means that the only way in which the landowner may make the caravan-dweller leave is (first) to end the residential agreement, and (secondly) and to obtain an eviction order from the court. The court can suspend an eviction order, under s. 4. In considering whether to do so, the court must take all the circumstances into account, and must have regard in particular to:

- Whether the occupier of the caravan has broken the residential contract.

◆ Whether the occupier has unreasonably refused an offer to renew the residential contract.

◆ Whether the occupier has made reasonable efforts to find other accommodation.

10-46 The court can suspend an eviction order for up to a year, and can impose conditions—a common condition will be that the occupier of the caravan must pay the rent. The period can be extended, or reduced or terminated by the court, on the application of the landowner or the occupier of the caravan. The landowner might thus apply to bring the eviction order into effect at an earlier date, if the occupier of the caravan has misbehaved; and the occupier of the caravan might apply to have the suspension of the order continued for a further period, if he has paid the rent and has been unable to find anywhere else to live. The suspension of the eviction order can thus be continued indefinitely, by means of repeated applications to the court, and the occupier can remain in the caravan. However the order cannot be suspended if there is no site licence; and if the site licence is about to end, the eviction order cannot be suspended beyond the end of the licence.

Caravan-dwellers are not covered by the Protection from Eviction Act 1977, because the 1968 Act protects them. However, the Criminal Law Act 1977 applies: see 8-94 onwards.

10-47 *Mobile Homes Act 1983* This Act extends, in certain circumstances, the protection given to caravan-dwellers. The Act applies to protected sites, though the definition of "protected " is slightly different from the definition in the 1968 Act; and the 1983 Act applies only to owner-occupiers who have a contract with the site owner entitling them to station a mobile home on the site and occupy it as their only or main residence. A range of situations will be outside the Act, including:

◆ Where there is no site licence.

◆ Where the site owner supplies the mobile home.

◆ Where the owner of the mobile home merely has permission to station the mobile home on the land, not a contract to do so.

- Where there is a contract but it says that the mobile home is not to be used as the occupier's only or main residence; for example, because the site for holiday use only.

10-48 If the Mobile Homes Act 1983 applies, the site owner must, within three months of the agreement, provide a written statement which sets out certain terms which the Act implies (i. e. writes in) for every agreement, and any express terms (i. e. terms devised by the parties themselves) and which is in the form laid down in regulations made by the DETR. The relevant regulations are the Mobile Homes (Written Statement) Regulations 1983.

10-49 The terms implied by the Act, which every agreement must contain, are set out in Part I of Schedule 1 to the Act. They include:

- The length of the agreement: the occupier of the mobile home can end the agreement by giving four weeks' notice in writing; but the owner of the site may end the agreement only by applying to the court and showing that the agreement has been breached by the occupier, or that it is reasonable for the agreement to be ended, or that the occuper has ceased to occupy the mobile home as his only or main residence; or that the mobile home is having a detrimental effect on the amenity of the site.

- The sale and gift of the mobile home: the occupier is entitled to sell the mobile home to a person approved by the site owner. The site owner can charge a commission of not more than 10% of the price. The percentage is fixed by the DETR under the Mobile Homes (Commission) Order 1983. The occupier can also give the mobile home to a member of his family approved by the site owner.

- Re-siting: if the agreement provides for re-siting, the new site must be broadly comparable to the old one, and the expense of moving must be borne by the site owner.

10-50 Other terms may be added by the court. The "matters" in respect of which terms may be added are set out in Part II of Schedule 1, and include such things as the amount payable by the occupier for the use of the site, the preservation of amenity, maintenance and repair of the mobile home and access by the site owner. Either the occupier of the mobile home or the site owner can apply to the court, within six months of the date of the agreement, for terms on these "matters" to be added.

See 12-21 for sources on caravan sites and mobile home parks.

Walker v. Badcock (1997) concerned a mobile home agreement, which was in a standard form approved by various industry bodies. The agreement allowed the "pitch fee" to be reviewed each year, to reflect various matters, including amounts spent by the site owner for the benefit of residents. The question arose of whether this included about £1,000 which the site owners had spent on trimming some trees on the site.

The court decided that this amount could be included. It also decided that there was no obligation on the site owners to consult residents before raising the pitch fee.

Calculating pitch fees

"Moveable dwellings"

10-51 The Public Health Act 1936, s. 269, controls the use of land for "moveable dwellings", which are defined as including:

> "any tent, any van, or other conveyance whether on wheels or not, and, subject as hereinafter provided, any shed or similar structure, being a tent, conveyance or structure which is used either regularly, or at certain seasons only, or intermittently, for human habitation:
>
> Provided that [the definition] does not include a structure to which building regulations apply".

See 10-2 onwards for the building regulations.

10-52 Until 1960, s. 269 applied to caravans; but by s. 30 of the Caravan Sites and Control of Development Act 1960, "caravans" as defined in s. 29(1) of the 1968 are no longer covered by the 1936 Act. Since the definition of "caravan" is wide, the 1936 Act now covers only tents and some other structures (but not caravans) used for human habitation

10-53 The 1936 Act provides that, without a licence from the local authority, land cannot be used as a site for a moveable dwelling for more than 42 consecutive days, or for a total of more than 60 days in any consecutive 12 months (s. 269(2)). (A tent or other structure which is not used for habitation, for example because it is used for storing materials, or as an office, etc is not subject to the 1936 Act.) Planning permission may be required for any material change of use involved.

See 12-2 for sources on moveable dwellings.

Public entertainments on land

10-54 Landowners may find that they wish to hold some sort of event to which the public at large will be invited, whether by payment or otherwise. The retail sale of alcohol generally requires a licence from the licensing justices (i. e. the local magistrates, exercising their powers to grant licences) under the Licensing Act 1964. But organisations which are "not carried on for purposes of private gain" can also obtain an "occasional permission" to sell drinks, under the Licensing (Occasional Permissions) Act 1983; and this allows permission to be obtained for the sale of drinks at social events, village fêtes and similar functions.

See 1-23 for the functions of magistrates' courts.

10-55 A licence from the local authority is required for "public dancing or music or any other public entertainment of a like kind", under s. 1 of and Schedule 1 to the Local Government (Miscellaneous Provisions) Act 1982. The exceptions include public religious worship, entertainments which take place wholly or mainly in the open air, and entertainments held in a "pleasure fair"—a pleasure fair being as defined in s. 75(2) of the Public Health Act 1961 as a place used for providing entertainments such as circuses, exhibitions of humans or animals, or merry-go-rounds. The effect of the 1982 Act can be extended, if the local authority adopts extra provisions in Schedule 1: the requirement for a licence then applies to a public musical entertainment held wholly or mainly in the open air, and on private land. But there are exemptions for a "garden fête, bazaar, sale of work, sporting or athletic event, exhibition, display or other function or event of a similar character...." or a "religious meeting or service".

Since these events will usually not last for more than a few days, planning permission will generally not be necessary: see 9-37 for the temporary use of land.

Keeping animals

10-56 The law goes to considerable lengths to protect animals, and there is a good deal of legislation on the subject. The following paragraphs deal with some of the requirements which apply. In some cases, there are general restrictions on the keeping of animals; in others the law regulates specific activities such as the use of land for breeding or for boarding. Keeping animals may of course give rise to other legal issues.

For example, noise and smells may mean that there is a nuisance (see 4-7 onwards); or planning permission may be required for a change of use (see 9-24 onwards).

10-57 Under the Dangerous Wild Animals Act 1976 (as amended) a licence from the local authority is required by any person wishing to keep "dangerous wild animals". These are listed in the Schedule to the Act, and include kangaroos, monkeys, apes, lions, tigers, bears and many other wild animals. A zoo needs its own licence, under the Zoo Licensing Act 1986. A pet shop requires a licence under the Pet Animals Act 1951. Keeping some animals may be prohibited indirectly, because there are restrictions on importing them or (for native wild animals) catching them—see for the Endangered Species (Import and Export) Act 1976 and Part I of the Wildlife and Countryside Act 1981, which makes it an offence to kill, injure or take any wild bird.

See 11-47 onwards for the protection of wild animals under the 1981 Act.

10-58 Under the Riding Establishments Act 1964 a licence is required from the local authority by a landowner who wishes to keep a "riding establishment"; and "keeping a riding establishment" means carrying on the business of keeping horses (including ponies, donkeys and mules) to let them out on hire, or use them in providing instruction in riding in return for payment (s. 1). Before the local authority can grant a licence they must consider a report from a veterinary surgeon or practitioner about the suitability of the premises and the condition of the premises and any horses there. In deciding whether to grant a licence, the local authority must have regard to a number of points, including (to summarise):

See 1-27 for the meaning of "premises".

- Whether the person applying appears suitable, and qualified by experience or otherwise, to hold a licence.

- Whether the horses will kept in good health, with proper accommodation and food, and fire precautions (s. 1(4)).

10-59 A licence may contain conditions, and some conditions are automatically included, by virtue of s. 1(4A). The automatic conditions include the following. A horse found by an "authorised officer" of the local authority to be in need of veterinary attention must not be returned to work until the holder of the licence has lodged with the local authority a veterinary certificate that the horse is fit. When working, horses must be under the supervision of a responsible person of at least 16; or, if the horse is hired out, the person hiring it must be competent to ride without supervision. The licence-holder must have insurance against injury, and must keep a register of horses aged 3 years or less (s. 1(4A)). Local authorities have power to inspect riding establishments; and the Act creates a number of offences designed to prevent ill-treatment to horses and ponies (ss. 2 and 3). The maximum punishment is a level 3 fine. A person who is convicted of an offence under the Act (or one of the other Acts concerned with the welfare of animals) may be disqualified from keeping a riding establishment (s. 4).

See 1-23 for the standard scale of fines.

10-60 The Animal Boarding Establishments Act 1963 applies only to dogs and cats, and not (despite its name) to animals generally (s. 5). Keeping an animal boarding establishment means looking after other people's dogs and cats, as a business, in any premises (including a private dwelling)(s. 5). The Act does not apply unless this is being done as a business. A licence from the local authority is required by any person who wishes to do so, and the local authority may take into account, in deciding whether to grant a licence, whether suitable accommodation will be provided, and other matters relevant to the welfare of the animals (s. 1). Failure to obtain a licence is an offence punishable with a level 2 fine or three months' imprisonment (s. 3). Local authorities have power to inspect animal boarding establishments, and there are provisions on disqualification which are similar to those in the Riding Establishments Act 1964 (ss. 2 and 3).

10-61 A landowner wishing to keep a "breeding establishment for dogs" will need to obtain a licence from the local authority, under the Breeding of Dogs Act 1973, as amended and strengthened by the

Breeding and Sale of Dogs (Welfare) Act 1999. A "breeding establishment for dogs" is any premises where a person carries on a business of breedings dogs for sale (whether by himself or someone else) (s. 4A of the 1973 Act). The Act makes it clear that a private dwelling is "premises" for these purposes (s. 4A(7)). The Act gives a detailed definition of what can constitute a business of breeding dogs. This will be so if a person keeps a bitch which gives birth to a litter of puppies, and four or more other litters are born during any twelve month period, to bitches kept by him at the premises or elsewhere, or kept by relatives at the premises, or kept anywhere by a person with whom he has a "breeding arrangement". A breeding arrangement is a contract by which the person concerned will receive one or more puppies if the bitch gives birth, or all or part of the proceeds of sale (s. 4A(2) to (4)).

The effect of this provision is that a licence may be required by a landowner even though some bitches are kept elsewhere, or are kept by others. However, the Act makes clear that a licence will *not* be required if no puppies are sold, apart from puppies from bitches kept by the landowner elsewhere (s. 4A(5)). 10-62

Other aspects of the legislation are similar to those explained above, in relation to riding establishments and animal boarding establishments. The local authority, must, however, arrange for an inspection and the making of a report before granting a licence (s. 1(2A) and (2B)). Conditions may be attached to the licence, for example, that the dogs are visited at suitable intervals, or that the bitches do not give birth to more than six litters of puppies each (s. 1(4)). Failure to obtain a licence is an offence which carries a level 4 fine or three months' imprisonment (s. 4) Local authorities may inspect licensed breeding establishments (s. 2). The Breeding of Dogs Act 1991 allows local authorities also to inspect premises not licensed under the 1973 Act, to see whether an offence is being committed. If a person is convicted of an offence under the Act, his licence may be cancelled, and he may be disqualified from keeping a breeding establishment or from keeping any dogs at all (s. 3(3)). 10-63

The 1993 Act also regulates the sale of dogs by a person who is licensed to keep a breeding establishment. Dogs can only be sold at the licensed breeding establishment or to a licensed pet shop. Puppies under eight weeks old can only be sold to licensed pet 10-64

See 10-57 for licensing of pet shops.

shops. Dogs cannot be sold to pet shops unless they were born at the breeding establishment and have a collar and tag giving the name of the name of the breeding establishment and any other details required by regulations (s. 8(1) of the 1999 Act). For breach of these requirements there is a maximum fine of level 4, or three months' imprisonment (s. 8(2)).

See 12-2 for sources on keeping animals.

Common land; town and village greens

10-65 A landowner may find that her land adjoins common land (sometimes known simply as a "common") or a town or village green; or she may even own part of a common or a green. In either case, the special rules which apply to these sorts of land are important. To understand the legal position, it is necessary to know a little about the history of land use in England and Wales.

See 10-74 for the meaning of "town and village greens".

10-66 *History* From early times, land was cleared and used for farming; and settlements were usually surrounded by untouched areas of forest, moorland or heath. Such land was known as "waste" land, meaning simply that it was uncultivated. Under the manorial system of agriculture, those who worked on the settlement would have the right to use parts of the cultivated land (which typically consisted of large open fields, divided into strips of land) and also some rights over the waste land. Depending on the nature of the waste land, it might provide grazing for cattle, sheep or pigs, or materials such as wood for building or burning. Shared rights to take things from land were (and are) known as rights of common. Land subject to such rights was accordingly "common land", or a "common". Villagers might, for example, each have the right to graze a certain number of animals on the waste land which belonged to the manor; and they would often also have rights of common over the cultivated land of the manor.

See 7-39 for rights of common.

10-67 The manorial system was gradually replaced by more efficient methods of cultivating land. This involved ending rights of common and turning the large open fields and the waste land into smaller units, which could then be owned and farmed separately.

"Enclosure" was the name given to this process, which was applied increasingly to waste land in order to produce more land for farming. At first, private Acts of Parliament were used to carry out schemes for enclosing land and sharing it out. Later, legislation established more streamlined procedures by which land could be enclosed.

See 1-2 for the meaning of "private Act".

10-68 During the nineteenth century it became apparent that common land was disappearing fast, as a result of enclosures. Because the land involved was generally open and unfenced, and generally subject to rights of common belonging to a number of different people, there was a tendency for it to be regarded as a public asset, which the public had a right to use for recreation. There was a particular demand for recreational land around the growing industrial cities. The legislation dealing with enclosures allowed common land to be set aside for public use, but in practice this was rarely done. The Commons Acts 1876 and 1899 changed the emphasis, by making sure that consideration was given to the question of public use when proposals for enclosure were made. Under these Acts, the public could be given access to land, and provision could be made for public rights of way, and the preservation of trees and any objects of historic importance.

10-69 *Regulation of commons* The 1876 Act is still in force; but the 1899 Act established a simpler procedure for regulating common land, which works as follows. District Councils can publish a draft scheme for an area of common land, following as closely as possible a model scheme set out in The Commons (Schemes) Regulations 1982. Public consultation follows, and the Council can then approve the scheme, with whatever modifications they think appropriate. When a scheme is in force, the Council has wide powers to make byelaws. These can regulate (for example) the way in which rights of common are exercised, the riding of horses, the holding of fairs, bathing, lighting fires, selling goods and putting up notices and advertisements. Several hundred schemes have been made under the 1899 Act. Fewer schemes have been made under the 1876 Act, which has been used very little since the early part of the twentieth century.

Commons (and other areas of open land) may also be regulated under local Acts—see 1-2.

10-70 Schemes under the Commons Acts can give the public a right of access to common land. But further attention was given to this question by the Law of Property Act 1925. Section 193 gives a public right of access for "air and exercise" to certain sorts of commons and waste land. In particular:

- Land which is a metropolitan common within the meaning of the Metropolitan Commons Acts 1866 to 1989.

- Manorial waste land or a common within a borough or urban district.

- Any other land subject to rights of common, if the owner declares by deed (which may be revocable or irrevocable, and which must be deposited with the DETR) that the land is subject to s. 193.

Public access under s. 193

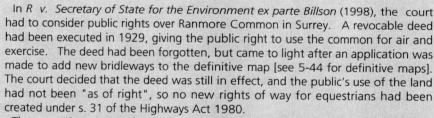

In *R v. Secretary of State for the Environment ex parte Billson* (1998), the court had to consider public rights over Ranmore Common in Surrey. A revocable deed had been executed in 1929, giving the public right to use the common for air and exercise. The deed had been forgotten, but came to light after an application was made to add new bridleways to the definitive map [see 5-44 for definitive maps]. The court decided that the deed was still in effect, and the public's use of the land had not been "as of right", so no new rights of way for equestrians had been created under s. 31 of the Highways Act 1980.

The court also expressed a view on two other points. First, use of the land to get from one place to another, rather than for air and exercise, could lead to the creation of a highway—though it could be difficult to distinguish between these two sorts of use [see 5-4 for dedication and acceptance of highways]. Secondly, the right to use the land for air and exercise, under s. 193, extended to use on horseback.

10-71 So not all common land is subject to public rights of access under s. 193. If there are such rights, they are subject to any scheme of regulation under the Commons Acts or other legislation (which may include a special Act of Parliament). Under s. 193, the DETR may impose conditions for the protection of the owner of the common. By s. 193(1)(c), the public has no right to drive vehicles, to camp, or to light fires on the land; and by s. 193(4) any person who does any of these things, or who fails to observe a condition imposed by the

DETR, commits an offence. Section 194 of the Law of Property Act 1925 applies to any land which is subject to rights of common, and forbids the erection of fences and buildings without the consent of the DETR.

10-72 Like other land, commons can be subject to highways, including footpaths and bridleways—in which case the public have the right to use these highways even if they do not have the right to use the land as a whole for air and exercise under s. 193.

See chapter 5 for highways.

10-73 *Registration of commons and greens* The Commons Registration Act 1965 was the result of a Royal Commission on common land. The Act was intended to be followed by legislation giving new rights of public access to common land, but this legislation was never passed. The purpose of the 1965 Act is to establish a register of common land, kept by local authorities, containing details of commons, town and village greens, rights of common over them, and the owners of the land. By s. 22(1), common land means land subject to rights of common and also waste land of a manor which is not subject to rights of common. The Act also gives a wide definition of "rights of common", to include not merely the rights referred to above but less commonly found rights which allow shared use of land.

But see 10-85 for the forthcoming "right to roam" legislation.

In the case of *R. v. Oxfordshire County Council, ex parte Sunningwell Parish Council* (1999) the question was whether some glebe land (i.e. land belonging to a parish church) should be registered as a village green, on the basis that it had been used for recreation "as of right" by the inhabitants of Sunningwell.

The House of Lords decided that such use had occurred, even though the inhabitants did not think of themselves as exercising a right, and even though the recreation was of an informal kind. The glebe land should therefore be registered under the Commons Registration Act 1965 as a village green.

Registration under the 1965 Act

10-74 A town or village green is land which has been set aside, under an Act, for the recreation of the inhabitants of any locality, or on which the inhabitants of a locality have a customary right to indulge in lawful sports and pastimes or on which they have done so, as of right for at least 20 years (s. 22(1)). The same land can be both a common and a town or village green, because it is (for example) subject both to grazing rights and to a customary right to use the land for

See 5-26 for the meaning of "as of right".

recreation. But the 1965 Act requires greens to be registered separately from common land.

10-75 The procedure laid down by the 1965 Act for registering common land and town and village greens was that between 1967 and 1970 applications for registration could be made to the County Council, or the County Council could act on its own initiative in putting land on the register (s. 2). Registration was at first only provisional, and there was a further period, until 1972, during which objections could be made (s. 4). In cases where the ownership of a town or village green was unknown, the County Council, after making enquiries, had to register themselves as the owner (s. 8). They could not do so if the ownership of common land was unknown, though they could take steps to look after the land (s. 9). The Act was supplemented by delegated legislation, including the Commons Registration (General) Regulations 1966.

10-76 Land can still become, or cease to be, a common or a town or village green, because the rights which make land a common or a green can be created or ended. But subject to that, once registration has become final the register is conclusive evidence of the entries shown on it: the person shown as the owner is legally the owner, and rights of common shown on the register are legally valid rights of common. In the same way, rights of common not shown on the register cease to exist; though this does not affect the application of ss. 193 and 194 of the Law of Property Act 1925 (s. 21(1)). If common land is registered under the Land Registration Act 1925, the ownership of the land is shown on the Land Register, rather than the commons register, the rights over the land being shown on the register of common land.

See 10-71 for the effect of ss. 193 and 194.

See 1-54 onwards for land registration.

Customary rights

Land known as "People's Park", at Sudbury in Suffolk, should have been registered as a town green under the Commons Registration Act 1965 because of customary rights to use the land for recreation. However People's Park was not registered. In the case of *R v. Suffolk County Council ex parte Speed* (1996) the court had to decide whether the customary rights had ceased to exist, because of the failure to register the land as a town green.

The court decided that this was not so: the customary rights did not come to an end because of the failure to register.

Disputes under the Act were referred to Commons Commissioners (s. 17). Resolving them has proved to be a long-drawn out affair, so that some disputes have still not been resolved, many years after the Act came into force. Meanwhile it was disovered that there was a flaw in the Commons Registration Act, in that, without the knowledge of the owners, some land which included houses had been placed on the register, and there was no way of removing the entries. The Common Land (Rectification of Registers) Act 1989 corrected this problem. 10-77

Apart from the protection given to common land by s. 193 of the Law of Property Act, and by any schemes which may apply to a common, s. 34 of the Road Traffic Act 1988 applies. And local authorities have power under s. 23 of the Caravan Sites and Control of Development Act 1960 to make an order forbidding the stationing of caravans on a common. 10-78

See 3-49 for s. 34 and motorised trespassing.

See 12-19 for sources on common land and rights over it

Public access

The public have a right of way on highways, including footpaths, bridleways and carriageways; they may also have a right of access to common land, under s. 193 of the Law of Property Act 1925, or to a town or village green; and there is a general right of access to ancient monumentss. In addition, it is always open to a landowner to give permission for visitors to come on to the land, with or without payment, and so the public may enjoy access to land by permission of bodies such as the National Trust. Some other ways in which the public may enjoy access to land can be mentioned briefly. 10-79

See chapter 5 for highways, 10-71 for s. 193, and 10-87 for ancient monuments

See 1-49 for licences.

Access orders and agreements Under Part V of the National Parks and Access to the Countryside Act 1949, local authorities may reach agreement with the owner of land for the public to have access, or may (with the approval of the DETR) make an order giving the public access. (Alternatively, the local authority can acquire land compulsorily, under s. 16.) These powers apply to "open land", meaning land which consists: 10-80

> "wholly or predominantly of mountain, moor, heath, down, cliff or foreshore (including any bank, barrier, dune, beach, flat or other land adjacent to the foreshore" (s. 60)

The definition was extended by s. 16 of the Countryside Act 1968, and now includes also woodlands, rivers and canals, and land adjacent to rivers and canals. Land fitting this description, whether or not it is within a National Park, can be made subject to public access.

See 9-83 for National Parks: the public do not automatically have access to land within a National Park.

10-81 The Second Schedule to the 1968 Act lists various activities which are prohibited within an area to which the public has access under the 1949 Act, including:

- Driving or riding any vehicle.
- Having a dog which is not under proper control.
- Lighting a fire.
- Causing damage to the land or to animals on it.
- Leaving litter.

10-82 The Act does not make it an offence to do these things; though they may amount to an offence under the general criminal law. But s. 60 of the Act provides that any person doing these things loses his right to be on the land, and so is a trespasser.

See for example 11-59 for criminal damage.

10-83 *Country parks* The Countryside Act 1968 allows local authorities to establish country parks on land which they own, or, by agreement, on someone else's land. Alternatively they may acquire land compulsorily in order to establish a country park (s. 7). The purpose of doing so is to improve opportunities for the enjoyment of the countryside by the public (s. 6). A right of public access—without charge—follows when a country park is established.

See 11-100 for compulsory purchase.

10-84 *The Countryside Access Regulations* Regulations made in 1994, the Countryside Access Regulations 1994, established a new basis for public access to land, following a European Regulation on agricultural, as part of the set-aside scheme. The owner or tenant of land could undertake for 5 years, running from 15 January in any given year, to set aside an area of his land, allow the public access to it, and to manage it in accordance with the requirements of the Schedule to the Regulations. In return MAFF would make an annual payment, known as "access aid". However, this scheme has been suspended: no new applications have been considered since 15 January 2000.

10-85 *The right to roam* The government elected in 1997 announced that it would legislate to provide a general public right of access to land. The Countryside and Rights of Way Bill, currently before Parliament, does this. Land to which the public will have access is known as "access land", and includes open land and registered common land.

10-86 *Other powers of local authorities* Powers exist under two Acts for local authorities to take over the care of certain sorts of land:

- The Town Gardens Protection Act 1863. (It is an offence to throw rubbish into such a garden.)
- The Open Spaces Act 1906.

See 12-19 for sources on public access to land.

Ancient monuments

10-87 The Ancient Monuments and Archaeological Areas Act 1979 (as amended by the National Heritage Act 1983) provides a system for protecting ancient monuments and areas of archaeological importance. Ancient monuments can be "scheduled"—put on a list kept by the DCMS. A "monument" is:

> "(a) any building, structure or work, whether above or below the surface of the land, and any cave or excavation;
>
> (b) any site comprising the remains of any such building, structure or work or of any cave or excavation;
>
> (c) any site comprising, or comprising the remains of, any vehicle, vessel, aircraft or other movable structure or part thereof which neither constitutes nor forms part of any work which is a monument within paragraph (a) above;

> and any machinery attached to a monument shall be regarded as part of the monument if it could not be detached without being dismantled." (s. 61(7))

So the definition is wide enough to take in a range of sites, from prehistoric sites to nineteenth century industrial archeology, including such things as the remains of boats. One class of building which cannot be scheduled is a dwelling-house, unless the occupant is merely a caretaker (s. 1(4)).

10-88 The tests used in deciding whether monuments should be scheduled are set out in the DETR PPG 16: *Archaeology and Planning*. They include such things as the age, rarity and condition of a monument. The DCMS must consult the Historic Buildings and Monuments Commission for England, now known as "English Heritage" (s. 1(3)). This body was set up by the National Heritage Act 1993, and has a duty to preserve ancient monuments and historic buildings (s. 33 of the 1983 Act).

For Planning Policy Guidance Notes see 9-5.

10-89 Once a monument has been scheduled, it is an offence to damage it (s. 28). It is also an offence to carry out any works which affect it, by damaging it, or repairing or altering it, unless scheduled monument consent has been granted (s. 2). "Works" which might damage an ancient monument could include such things as ploughing (in the case of a monument which formed part of a field) or altering a building. Regulations made under the Act, the Ancient Monuments (Applications for Scheduled Monument Consent) Regulations 1981 lay down the procedure for making of applications for consent. Consent for certain sorts of work have been granted by the Ancient Monuments (Class Consents) Order 1994, including agricultural, horticultural and forestry works which have been carried out in the previous 6 years. There is a general public right of access to ancient monuments; but access may be controlled by the DCMS or by the local authority (s. 19).

Depending on the nature of the work, planning permission may also be required: see 9-13 onwards.

10-90 The Act restricts the use of metal detectors on the sites of ancient monuments: using a metal detector is an offence punishable by a level 3 fine. It is also an offence for a person to take away from a site, without the written consent of English Heritage, any object discovered with a metal detector (s. 42).

And see 11-25 in relation to treasure.

See 12-21 for sources on ancient monuments.

Assessment

Some of the law explained above will be encountered by landowners because of the physical state of land, or its legal status—for example, because the land contains an ancient monument, or because it is common land. Some of it will be relevant only because of the landowner wishes to pursue a particular course, such as breeding dogs, opening a caravan site, or staging a public event of some sort. 10-91

The law is there to protect the public interest of different sorts, whether this is to do with the amenity of land, public health, or the use of land for recreational purposes. Although the law imposes some restrictions, it is not intended to prevent the reasonable use of land. 10-92

Landowners need to be aware of the law—and to bear in mind that breaking the rules is very often subject to criminal penalties, which can be severe. A particular example is breach of tree preservation orders, since the law allows fines to reflect the financial advantage of getting rid of inconvenient trees to a landowner who wishes to develop his land. Some of these areas of the law are of relatively recent origin. The rules concerning hedgerows, in particular, were only introduced in 1997, and the system may well undergo some changes before it settles down. The public right of access under the Countryside and Rights of Way Bill will be another new area of law for landowners to get to grips with; though only a minority will be affected. 10-93

The right approach in most cases will be to make contact with the local authority, which administers most of these areas of the law, to discuss any proposed action at an early stage. Guidance from the local authority can be very valuable. 10-94

Chapter 11

Miscellanea

Introduction

11-0 This chapter deals with a range of topics which do not fit comfortably in the preceding chapters. Some of these are essentially civil matters, such as the responsibility of landowners for the safety of those who come on to their land, or the ownership of valuable property found on land. Some are criminal—for example, poaching and vandalism.

11-1 The law explained comes mostly from statutes, though as in other areas of the law the courts have an important rôle to play in resolving disputes about the meaning of legislation.

Occupiers' liability

See 1-21 for the meaning of "tort", and 1-47 for the meaning of "occupying" land.

11-2 The law on occupiers' liability is part of the law of tort (civil wrongs). The law makes the occupiers of land responsible, subject to certain conditions, for the safety of those who come on to the land. Occupiers are regarded as owing a duty of care to people who come on to the land, and if they are in breach of the duty, by failing to take sufficient care, they may be liable to pay compensation for injuries or damage suffered by the person. Two Acts, both important to landowners, lay down the law. The Occupiers' Liability Act 1957 deals mainly with people who are invited on to land, while the Occupiers' Liability Act 1984 deals mainly with trespassers

See 8-9 for the position of landlord and tenant

11-3 Usually a landowner will also be the occupier of the land, but this is not always the case. The occupier may be someone other than the landowner, for example where the whole of the land is let. It may be that more than one person is an occupier of a given piece of land—or that different parts of the land are occupied by different people.

In a block of flats, the tenants will normally be the occupiers of the flats themselves; but the hallway and staircase may be owned and controlled by the landlord, and the landlord may thus be the occupier of those parts of the building. If so, and an accident occurs, through the landlord's breach of the duty of care, he will be liable to compensate the person injured.

But see 11-15 for how the liability may be excluded.

11-4 *Occupiers' Liability Act 1957* The 1957 Act is concerned with "visitors" to land. "Land", for the purposes of the Act, includes "moveable structures", and is thus a wider concept than fixtures—it would include such things as bouncy castles (s. 1(3)). "Visitors" includes both those who have been expressly invited on to the land, and those who have an implied invitation, for example members of the public going into a shop. The 1957 Act also covers people who come on to land in the exercise of a legal right, for example a statutory undertaker exercising a power to enter land (s. 1(6)). However, this does not include highways: though the public have a right to use a highway, the owner of the highway does not owe them the duty of care under the 1957 Act.

See 2-47 for the meaning of "fixture" and how fixtures form part of the land.

See 1-50 for the meaning of "express" and "implied" permission.

See 11-103 for statutory undertakers. The same applies to the police and officials with a power of entry.

See 5-0 onwards for the meaning of "highway".

11-5 The courts have been ready to regard children as being impliedly invited on to land where there is something on the land which attracts them and the landowner does not take steps to exclude them, by making sure that fences and gates are secure. The possibility of children coming on to land and being injured is thus one which an occupier of land should take particularly seriously.

In *Jolley v. Sutton London Borough Council* (2000) an old boat had been abandoned on land owned by Sutton LBC. Two boys decided that they would try to repair the boat, and propped it up so that they could get at the hull. The boat fell on one of the boys, who was seriously injured; and the question was whether the LBC was obliged to pay compensation under the Occupiers' Liability Act 1957, for breach of the duty of care. The LBC argued that although it was foreseeable that children would play with the boat, it was not foreseeable that this sort of accident would happen, so there was no breach of the duty of care.

The House of Lords decided that the LBC were liable to pay compensation: it was foreseeable that children would meddle with the boat and be injured, and it was well-known that children were ingenious in finding new ways of injuring themselves.

Occupiers' liability to children

See 3-12 onwards on this question.

See 11-11 onwards for the 1984 Act.

11-6 When a person is invited, expressly or implied, to come on to land, the invitation may restrict them to certain purposes, or to certain parts of the land. They must stay within the terms of the invitation, or they become trespassers. If this happens, the 1957 Act ceases to apply to them but the 1984 Act may apply. If a person comes on to land under a contract—for example, by paying an entrance fee for admission to a cinema, or garden open to the public, etc—the contract may make clear whether the occupier accepts liability for any injury or damage, but if nothing is said then the occupier may be deemed, as an implied term of the contract, to owe the visitor the duty of care under the 1957 Act (s. 5(1)).

11-7 The duty of care owed to visitors is defined in the Act as:

> "a duty to take such care as in all the circumstances of the case is reasonable to see that the visitor will be reasonably safe in using the premises for the purposes for which he is invited or permitted to be there (s. 2(2))".

Much will thus depend upon what the circumstances of the case are. But the Act gives two examples of visitors for whom more or less care may be required:

> "*(a)* an occupier must be prepared for children to be less careful than adults; and
>
> *(b)* an occuper may expect that a person, in the exercise of his calling, will appreciate and guard against any special risks ordinarily incident to it, so far as the occupier leaves him free to do so (s. 2(3))".

11-8 In the first case, the occupier will have to be more careful. In the second, she may generally be able to leave the visitor to look after himself. A specialist contractor called in to a repair a roof, for example, can be expected to know about the usual hazards of working on roofs. But if there is some special danger, not "ordinarily incident" to working on roofs, for example that a part of the roof is dangerously weak, and the occupier should have known this, then the occupier may be liable to pay compensation in the event of an accident.

11-9 An occupier of land may be able to discharge the duty of care by giving a warning, provided that in all the circumstances it is enough to enable the visitor to be reasonably safe (s. 2(4)*(a)*). There would then be no liability pay compensation in the event of an accident. In the example just given the occupier could warn the contractor about the weak area of roof, and the warning would on the face of it be enough to make sure that the occupier was not liable to pay compensation if there was an accident. The Act also provides that an occupier will normally not be liable where injury or damage is caused by a contractor (not an employee) working on the land, provided the occupier is acting reasonably in entrusting the work to the contractor (s. 2(4)*(b)*).

The 1957 Act applies both to bodily injury and damage to 11-10
property. A visitor who has an accident as a result of a breach by the occupier of the duty of care may claim compensation both for any injuries she has suffered and for any damage such as damage to her clothes or property which is broken.

Occupiers' Liability Act 1984 This Act lays down a lighter duty of 11-11
care, in relation to dangers on the land. This duty is owed by occupiers to trespassers, and also to some others such as those exercising a private (but not a public right) right of way. The Act says that the duty only arises in certain circumstances, namely where:

See chapter 5 for public rights of way and 6-33 for private rights of way.

> "*(a)* [the occupier] is aware of the danger or has reasonable grounds to believe that it exists;
>
> *(b)* he knows or has reasonable grounds to believe that the [person concerned] is in the vicinity of the danger concerned or that he may come into the vicinity of the danger ...; and
>
> *(c)* the risk is one against which, in all the circumstances of the case, he may reasonably be expected to offer some protection" (s. 1(3))".

If the duty arises, the occupier must take "such care as is 11-12
reasonable in all the circumstances to that the [person concerned] does not suffer injury .... by reason of the danger". Suppose that a landowner's neighbour has a right of way across her land, and sometimes uses it in the evening. The landowner digs a trench across the right of way. The neighbour falls into the trench one dark evening. The court is likely to conclude that the landowner (in the words of the Act) could reasonably be expected to offer some protection against the danger caused by the trench, either by covering it, or lighting it, or warning the neighbour. If that was the court's conclusion, the landowner would be liable to pay compensation to her neighbour. The same result would follow in relation to a trespasser whom the landowner knew was in the habit

of taking a short-cut over her land—the duty under the 1984 Act is also owed to trespassers. But no duty of care is owed in relation to risks which have been willingly accepted by the trespasser (s. 1(6)).

Injury to a trespasser

In the case of *Ratcliff v. McConnell* (1998) a student, who had been drinking, broke into a college's open-air swimming pool by climbing over the wall. He dived into the pool but struck his head on the bottom and suffered severe injuries.

The court decided that in the circumstances the student had willingly accepted the risk of injury, and s. 1(6) of the 1984 Act applied. The college was not liable to compensate him.

11-13 The 1984 Act applies only to injuries; but the common law (which, before the 1984 Act, applied to both injuries and damage suffered by trespassers) may allow compensation to be obtained for damage.

See 1-17 for the meaning of "common law".

11-14 *Negligence* The Occupiers' Liability Acts lay down duties of care which apply to an occupier of land. These duties cover part of the ground already covered by the law of negligence, so that the two torts overlap. The Acts, however, contain special rules which clarify the circumstances in which an occupier may be required to pay compensation to a person who suffers injury or damage as a result of an accident on his land. If a person is injured on land, and the accident is the fault of a person other than the occupier of the land, the tort of negligence allows a claim to be made against the person responsible.

See 4-59 on negligence.

11-15 *Excluding liability* As a general rule, a landowner can set the terms upon which people come on to her land, in that she can lay down the purposes for which they can come on to the land and the parts of the land they can visit. A landowner may also want to exclude liability for any accidents which occur to visitors. The two main methods for doing so are:

See 1-49 onwards for licences.

- Putting up a notice, either warning the person about particular dangers, or warning him in general terms that he comes on to the land at his own risk.

- If the person comes on to the land under a contract, making it a term of the contract that the occupier will not be responsible for any accidents.

Subject to several provisos, these methods will be effective to protect the occupier from liability. The first proviso is that, in the case of a warning notice dealing with a particular danger, the existence of the notice is not enough in itself—it must be sufficient in the circumstances to ensure that the person concerned is reasonably safe. This principle is to be found both in the Occupiers Liability Act 1957, in relation to "visitors" (s. 2(4)(*a*)) and in the 1984 Act in relation to other sorts of people who come on to land (s. 1(5)). 11-16

Secondly, the Unfair Contract Terms Act 1977 limits the extent to which any person (including landowners) can exclude liability by means of a term in a contract, or by putting up a notice. Despite its name, this Act does not apply only to contracts. The Act applies only to what it calls "business liability", meaning liability arising from something done in the course of business, or from the occupation of premises used for business purposes (s. 1(3)). "Business" has a wide meaning in this Act—by s. 14: 11-17

See 1-27 for the meaning of "premises".

> ""business" includes a profession and the activities of any government department or local or public authority".

The effect of the Act is to prevent people from limiting their liability for negligence, and "negligence" here includes liability under the Occupiers' Liability Act 1957 (s. 1(1)). There are two main rules in the Act on this point: 11-18

- A person can never exclude liability for death or injury resulting from negligence (s. 2(1)).

- For other sorts of loss or damage, a person can exclude liability only so far as it is reasonable to do so (s. 2(2)).

So, for example, the owner of a riding stable cannot prevent himself from being liable under the Occupiers' Liability Act 1957 (or under the tort of negligence) for death or injury, either by making this a term of the contract under which riders use the stable, or by 11-19 putting up a notice saying that he will not be responsible. Liability for other damage (particularly damage to property) can be restricted or excluded, but only if it is reasonable to do so.

11-20 To summarise, where the Unfair Contract Terms Act 1977 applies, a landowner can exclude liability for damage to property, if it is reasonable in the circumstances, but cannot exclude liability for death or injury. Where the Act does *not* apply, because there is no "business liability" (for example, to a private address where no business is being carried on) the landowner may be able to exclude liability by means of a term in a contract or by putting up a notice.

See 12-16 for sources on occupiers' liability.

Defective Premises Act 1972

11-21 An Act passed in 1972, the Defective Premises Act, imposes a duty on builders, and others involved, such as architects and subcontractors:

> "in connection with the provision of a dwelling (whether the dwelling is provided by the erection or by the conversion or enlargement of a building" (s. 1(1)).

The duty is to build in a workmanlike or professional manner, with proper materials, so that the dwelling will be fit for human habitation. The duty is owed to the person for whom the work is done, and to others who acquire an interest in the dwelling—in particular, later owners of it. If there is a breach of the duty, the person concerned can thus recover compensation. The Act applies only to the sorts of work specified; that is, certain work relating to dwellings. The Act would apply if a house was being split into flats, but not if an existing house or flat was being enlarged by a loft conversion, because there were be no "provision of a dwelling" in that case.

11-22 The right to seek compensation under the Act lasts for six years from the date when the work is done; unless corrective work is done, in which case the six years run from the date of that work (s. 1(5)). The Act does not apply where there is an "approved scheme" which gives rights in respect of any defects in building work (s. 2).

"Approved" means approved by the DETR, and one scheme which was approved by the Department was the National House-Building Council ("NHBC") scheme, which applied to many new houses. The approval process was phased out in 1979, so that the Defective Premises Act now applies to new houses built under the NHBC scheme, just as it does to other new houses. The original owner of a new house, or someone who has bought the house from the original owner, may be able to claim compensation for building defects, either under the 1972 Act or the NHBC scheme, subject to the relevant time limits (under the NHBC scheme a claim may be possible for up to 10 years).

See 12-16 for sources on the Defective Premises Act 1972.

Finding things on land

11-23

If something valuable is found on land by someone other than the occupier of the land, the question may arise of whether the finder or the occupier of the land has a better right to it. The courts have taken the view that generally the finder has the better right; but if any of three conditions apply, the occupier has the better right. This is so where:

See 1-47 for the meaning of "occupying" land.

- The finder was trespassing.
- The property is buried in, or in some other way attached to, the land.
- The occupier has shown an intention to exercise control over the land and things found on it. Some land—for example, a park open to the public—would probably be subject to a relatively light degree of control. Other land—for example, a shop—would usually be subject to a much higher degree of control. In the first case, the owner of the park would be unlikely to have a better claim than member of the public finding something valuable; in the latter case, the shop probably would.

See chapter 3 for trespassing.

See 2-47 for fixtures.

Ownership of objects found.

In *Waverley Borough Council v. Fletcher* (1995) Mr Fletcher used a metal detector in a public park, and found a medieval gold brooch, buried about 9 inches below the surface. The coroner's court decided that the brooch was not treasure trove, and so did not belong to the Crown [see 1-70 for coroner's courts]. The question then was whether Mr Fletcher had a better right to the brooch than the Council.

The Court of Appeal decided that the Borough Council were the owners of the brooch, because it had been found under the land, and also because Mr Fletcher was trespassing in digging up the ground, since he was going beyond what members of the public were entitled to do in the park.

11-24 Subject to the Treasure Act 1996, these rules settle disputes between the finder and the occupier of the land about who owns property found on the land. The true owner of the property, however, has a better claim than either the finder or the occupier of the land; though it may be clear, especially in the case of a very ancient object, that there is no realistic prospect of tracing the true owner's descendants, who may have inherited his property.

11-25 The Treasure Act 1996 lays down special rules for certain sorts of property found on land. It replaces the old law on "treasure trove". The Act provides that treasure consists of objects at least 300 years old which are either coins or which have a gold or silver content of at least 10 per cent, and other objects found with those objects. The DCMS has power under the Act to extend the definition in the Act so that it applies to objects at least 200 years old (s. 1). Unless the true owner or his descendants can be traced, treasure generally belongs to the Crown (s. 4).

See 1-72 for the meaning of "the Crown".

11-26 When a person finds an object which he believes may be treasure, he must notify the coroner for that area, within 14 days (s. 8). The coroner has the task of holding an inquest to determine whether the object is in fact treasure. Whether an object was buried with a view to being found later is no longer relevant to the question of whether it treasure, though it was relevant under the law before the Treasure Act. If the object is treasure, the DCMS, on behalf of the Crown, may decide what is to happen to it (s. 6). The object may be returned to the finder or some other person (bearing in mind the law explained above as to who has the best claim to property found on land); or it may be transferred to a museum, in which case the DCMS must decide whether a reward should be paid by the museum, and if so how much and to whom (s. 10).

11-27 The DCMS is required by the Act to prepare a code of practice setting out, in particular, the principles to be followed in deciding what should be done with treasure belonging to the Crown (s. 11). The DCMS has published a code, entitled *Treasure Act 1996: Code of Practice*.

See 12-21 for sources on archaeology and related subjects.

Control of dogs

11-28 Various pieces of legislation have addressed the question of dogs which are dangerous or not under proper control. Under the Dogs Act 1871, a magistrates' court can take action if a dog is dangerous or is not kept under proper control. The magistrates' court can order the dog to be kept under control by the owner, or to be destroyed (s. 2). Failure to comply with an order to keep a dog under control is an offence for which the owner is liable to a level 3 fine, this being laid down by the Dangerous Dogs Act 1989, which also allows the court in making an order to disqualify the owner from keeping dogs in the future.

See 1-23 for the standard scale of fines.

11-29 The Dogs Act 1906 adds to the 1871 Act by providing that where a dog is proved to have injured cattle or poultry, or chased sheep, it may be dealt with as a dangerous dog under the 1871 Act (s. 1). The 1906 Act also allows the police to seize stray dogs (s. 3(1)). If the dog has a collar with the owner's name on the police must notify the owner; but if the dog is not collected within seven days, and the expenses of the police paid, it may be sold or destroyed (s. 3(2) to (4)). The police must keep a register of dogs seized under the 1906 Act (s. 3(6). Local authorities also have a rôle to play in relation to stray dogs: they must appoint an officer to deal with strays (Environmental Protection Act 1990, s. 149(1)). When a stray is found in a public place or any other place it must if possible be seized and detained (s. 149(3)). The owner must be notified, if the dog has a collar, and may be sold or destroyed after seven days, if the owner

For the position under the civil law, where dogs worry livestock, see 3-63.

See 11-33 on collars for dogs.

has not collected it and paid the local authority's expenses (s. 149(5) and the Environmental Protection (Stray Dogs) Regulations 1992). Like the police, the local authority must keep a register of dogs seized.

11-30 Any member of the public who takes possession of a stray dog must either return it to its owner or hand it in to the police or the local authority. There is also a procedure by which dogs handed to the local authority may be claimed by the finder (Environmental Protection Act 1990, s. 150).

11-31 The Dangerous Dogs Act 1991, which has been amended by the Dangerous Dogs (Amendment) Act 1997, imposes restrictions in relation to certain breeds of aggressive dog. It also makes it an offence by the owner or person in control of any dog, if the dog is "dangerously out of control" in a public place (s. 3(1)). (The law is different from the law under the Dogs Act 1871, because under that Act there is no offence until a magistrates' court has made an order directing that a dog be kept under control.) A "public place" is:

See 11-28 for the 1871 Act.

> "any street, road or other place (whether or not enclosed) to which the public have or are permitted to have access whether for payment or otherwise and includes the common parts of a building containing two or more separate dwellings" (s. 10(2)).

The last part of the definition means that, for example, the hallway, staircases and corridors in a block of flats are a "public place", even though the public at large do not in fact have access to such places.

Dangerous dogs

In *D.P.P. v. Fellowes* (1993) Mr Fellowes was prosecuted for having a dog which was dangerously out of control in a public place and which had injured someone. The incident had happened on a garden path; and it was argued that this was a "public place" because the public had an implied invitation to use the path in order to call at the house [See 3-12.]

The court's decision was that the garden path was not a "public place", since members of the public were able to use it not in their capacity as members of the public, but only as visitors to the house. Fellowes therefore could not be convicted of the offence.

11-32 If a dog which is "dangerously out of control" injures somebody, this is an aggravated (i. e. more serious) offence by the owner or the person in charge of the dog. Under s. 3(3), it is also an offence if a dog enters any place which is not a public place but where it is not allowed to go, and while there it injures somebody, or there are grounds for a reasonable fear that it will do so. The offences under s. 3(1) and (3) are subject to a maximum fine of level 5 on the standard scale, or six months' imprisonment. For the aggravated offence under s. 3(1), the maximum fine is the statutory maximum.

11-33 An Order made under the Animal Health Act 1981 s. 13, the Control of Dogs Order 1992, requires that while on a highway or in some other public place a dog must wear a collar inscribed with the name and address of the owner, or with these details on a plate or badge attached to the collar. There are exceptions for packs of hounds, sheep dogs, police dogs, guide dogs and others. The owner or the person in charge of a dog who causes or permits it to be on a highway or any other public place without a collar is guilty of an offence, and the maximum fine is level 5 (s. 75 of the Animal Health Act 1981). The Control of Dogs Order also provides that a dog which should be wearing a collar, but which is not doing so, may be treated as a stray under the Dogs Act 1906 or the Environmental Protection Act 1990.

11-34 The Dogs (Protection of Livestock) Act 1953 deals with dogs which worry livestock on agricultural land. "Livestock" here means cattle, sheep, goats, pigs, horses and domestic poultry; while "agricultural land" includes (in addition to farm land) market gardens, allotments, nursery grounds and orchards (s. 3(1)). "Worrying" has a special meaning:

See also 3-63 for the civil law on dogs worrying livestock.

- Attacking livestock.
- Chasing livestock in such a way as may reasonably be expected to cause injury or suffering, abortion or loss of production.
- In the case of sheep, being in a field containing sheep and not being on a lead or under close control (s. 1(2)).

11-35 There are exceptions for police dogs, sheep dogs and others. Subject to these exceptions, the owner of the dog, and the person in charge of it if different, commits an offence, the maximum fine being

See 12-2 for sources on dogs and animal law generally.

level 3 on the standard scale. A prosecution can only be brought by the police, or the owner of the land or the livestock (s. 2). If a dog is found on land and appears to have been worrying livestock, and no-one present admits to being the owner of the dog or in charge of it, the police may seize it and deal with it under the Dogs Act 1906.

Pests

11-36 Under the Prevention of Damage by Pests Act 1949, occupiers of land (apart from agricultural land) must notify the local authority if rats or mice are to be found on the land in "substantial numbers". Failure to give notice is an offence punishable by a level 1 on the standard scale (s. 3). The local authority (whether or not as a result of receiving a notice) can require the owner or occupier of land to take steps to destroy the rats or mice. There is a right of appeal under the Public Health Act 1936; but, subject to that, failure to carry out the specified steps is an offence punishable with a level 3 fine; and the local authority may carry out the necessary work at the expense of the owner or occupier of the land (s. 5). Landowners wishing to control rats, mice and other pests need to be aware of a number of different rules, spread across different Acts, about the methods which can be used:

11-37 *Poisoning* Under the Protection of Animals Act 1911, s. 8, there is a general ban on putting down "any poison, or any fluid or edible matter (not being sown seed or grain) which has been rendered poisonous". The maximum fine is level 4 on the standard scale. It is a defence for a person accused of an offence to show that:

> "...the poison was placed ... for the purpose of destroying insects and other invertebrates, rats, mice or other small ground vermin, where such is found to be necessary in the interests of public health, agriculture, or the preservation of other animals, domestic or wild, or for the purpose of manuring the land, and that he took all reasonable precautions to prevent injury thereby to dogs, cats, fowls, or other domestic animals or birds."

The defence does not apply where there is a breach of the Animals (Cruel Poisons) Act 1962, and the regulations made under it, the

Animals (Cruel Poisons) Regulations 1963. The Regulations forbid the use of phosphorus and a poison known as "red squill" for all animals, and strychnine for all animals apart from moles. The use of poisonous gas in rabbit holes is permitted (Damage by Rabbits Act 1939, s. 4).

Special rules apply in relation to grey squirrels and coypus: under s. 19 of the Agriculture (Miscellaneous Provisions) Act 1972 an Order can be made specifying a poison for use against these animals, and the power has been used to make the Grey Squirrels (Warfarin) Order 1973, specifying Warfarin. Use of this poison in accordance with the Order is a defence to a prosecution under the Protection of Animals Act 1911. 11-38

There is a also a general ban in the Game Act 1831, s. 3, on the use of poison to kill game. "Game" here includes hares (but not rabbits) pheasants, partridges, grouse and other game birds. Deliberately spreading myxomatosis is an offence under s. 12 of the Pests Act 1954, as amended. The maximum punishment is a level 1 fine. 11-39

Trapping Traps used for taking animals must be approved, in accordance with the Spring Traps Approval Order 1995, made under s. 8 of the Pests Act 1954. Using a trap other than an approved trap is an offence punishable with a level 3 fine. Under s. 9 of the same Act, a trap for rabbits or hares may generally only be used in a rabbit hole. Traps set for rabbits or hares must be inspected at least once a day between sunrise and sunset (s. 10 of the Protection of Animals Act 1911). 11-40

See 12-2 for sources on pests.

Poaching

Wild animals do not belong to anyone until they have been caught or killed; and the Theft Act 1968 makes clear that a wild animal cannot be stolen by a person unless it has first been caught by someone else (s. 4(2)). For this reason, poaching—trespassing on land and taking game or fish—does not amount to theft. Instead, there is a range of different offences, mostly under old Acts, which apply. 11-41

See 2-50for the ownership of wild animals, and 11-57 for theft.

11-42 Poaching by night is dealt with by the Night Poaching Act 1828, by s. 1 of which it is an offence to take game (the definition of which includes hares, pheasants, partridges and grouse) or rabbits by night, or trespass with any "gun, net, engine or other instrument, for the purpose of taking or destroying game", the maximum punishment being a level 3 fine. It is thus not necessary to show that any game has been taken in order to prove the offence. In relation to poaching in the daytime, it is an offence under s. 30 of the Game Act 1831 to trespass in pursuit of game (which is defined, and is similar to the definition in the 1828 Act) and also woodcock, snipe and rabbits. The offence consists of trespassing with the intention of taking any of these animals. Whether this can be proved will depend upon the circumstances, but possession of a gun or other equipment for taking wild animals (though not mentioned in the Act) will be powerful evidence. The maximum punishment for this offence is a level 3 fine, or, if five or more persons are involved, level 5. The Act contains other offences which apply to those who sell or buy game unlawfully.

11-43 The Poaching Prevention Act 1862, s. 2, creates three separate offences: firstly going on to land in search or pursuit of game, secondly using certain articles (guns, nets, snares, traps and other devices of a kind used for the killing and taking of game), and thirdly being an accessory (in other words an accomplice) to such activities. The maximum punishment is a level 3 fine. This Act overlaps with the Night Poaching Act 1828 and the Game Act 1831; but it also contains powers enabling the police to stop and search any person suspected of coming from land where he was poaching.

11-44 Deer are covered by the Deer Act 1991, which applies to deer of any species (s. 16). It is an offence under s. 1(1) to enter any land as a trespasser "in search or pursuit of any deer with the intention of taking, killing or injuring it"; and under s. 1(2), while on land as a trespasser, to take, kill or injure any deer or attempt to do so, to search for or pursue deer, or to remove the carcase of any deer. The maximum punishment for these offences is a level 4 fine or three months' imprisonment; but if more than one deer is involved, the maximum fine is calculated as if there were a separate offence for each deer (s. 9). Any "authorised person" (meaning the owner of the land, or any person authorised by him) may require a person suspected of committing an offence to give his name and leave the land immediately—failure to do so being an offence. Other offences under the Deer Act deal with the taking of deer during their close seasons (which are set out in Schedule 1 to the Act); the taking of deer by night; and the use of traps, snares and baits (ss. 2, 3 and 4).

In relation to fish, it is an offence under Schedule 1 to the Theft Act 1968 to take or destroy, or attempt to do so, any fish in private water or water where there is a private right of fishing. It is not necessary to prove that the person fishing intended to keep the fish: taking them with the intention of returning them to the water alive is just as much "taking" for the purposes of the Act. The offence takes two forms. If the offence is committed at night, the maximum punishment for the offence is a level 3 fine, or three months' imprisonment; if it is committed during the day, by angling, the maximum is a level 1 fine. The Schedule gives the power of arrest not just to the police but to any person who suspects with reasonable cause that someone is committing the more serious offence; so this power applies to any fishing which took place at night and any fishing during the day otherwise than by angling (e. g. with nets or chemicals). 11-45

See 2-57 onwards and 7-40 for fishing rights generally.

Salmon are the subject of the Salmon Act 1986. Poaching of salmon is covered by the Theft Act 1968; but the Salmon Act contains an offence of "handling salmon in suspicious circumstances" (s. 32). A person is guilty of this offence if, at a time when he believes, or has reasonable cause to believe the salmon was taken unlawfully he receives it, or "undertakes or assists in its retention, removal or disposal by or for the benefit of another person". The offence can be dealt with before a magistrates' court, where the maximum punishment is three months' imprisonment or the statututory maximum fine; or by the Crown Court, which can impose up to two years' imprisonment or an unlimited fine or both. The seriousness of the punishment reflects the potentially lucrative nature of dealing in unlawfully-taken salmon. 11-46

See 1-20 onwards for the criminal courts.

Protection of wildlife

See 11-53 for badgers.

11-47 Many wild animals, birds and plants enjoy legal protection which varies according to the species involved. The main Act is the Wildlife and Countryside Act 1981, though badgers have their own legislation.

11-48 *Animals* The animals listed in Schedule 5 to the 1981 Act must not be killed, injured or captured; and it is also an offence for a person to be in possession of a live or dead animal unless he can show that the animal was not killed or captured in breach of the Act; and an offence is committed by damaging or destroying a place where an animal shelters, or disturbing it in such a place (s. 9(1)–(5)). Depending upon the circumstances, the maximum punishment may be a fine up to level 5 (s. 21).

11-49 The many species listed in Schedule 5 include adders, newts and toads, butterflies and other insects, bats and otters. There are some exceptions. An offence is not committed by anything done within a dwelling-house, though the position is different in relation to bats (s. 10(2)). It is not an offence to capture an injured wild animal in order to treat it, or to kill a wild animal which is so disabled that there is no reasonable chance of its recovering (s. 10(3)(a) and (b)). And it is not an offence if a person can show that what he did was "the incidental result of a lawful operation and could not reasonably have been avoided"—though the position is again different in relation to bats (s. 10(3)(c)).

11-50 In order for a person to avoid committing an offence where bats are involved—for example, where bats are living in a loft, and building work is likely to disturb them—English Nature (formerly the Nature Conservancy Council) must first be consulted and given the opportunity to advise (s. 10(5)).

11-51 A further defence is provided by s. 10(4): an "authorised person" can kill a wild animal listed in the Schedule if he shows that it was "necessary for the purpose of preventing serious damage to livestock, foodstuffs for livestock, crops, vegetables, fruit, growing timber or any other form of property or to fisheries". An "authorised person" is the owner or occupier of the land in question, or someone authorised by them, or a person authorised by the Environment

Agency or certain other official bodies (s. 27(1)). In addition, a licence is required from the DETR or (depending on what is involved) another official body (s. 16).

Even when killing or capturing a wild animal is lawful, there are 11-52
some restrictions on the methods which can be used. Some apply to all animals, including self-locking snares, decoys, bows, cross-bows and explosives (s. 11(1)). Others apply only to certain species: for the animals listed in Schedule 6, including badgers, bats, hedgehogs, otters, dolphins and porpoises, the methods which are banned include traps, snares, poisons, electric shocks, decoys, and dazzling lights (s. 11(2)). Even where snares are allowed, they must be inspected once a day if they are likely to cause injury (s. 11(3)).

Badgers are protected by the Protection of Badgers Act 1992, 11-53
which consolidated several earlier Acts. This makes it an offence to capture, injure or kill a badger (s. 1); to cruelly ill-treat a badger (s. 2); to intefere with badger setts (s. 3); or to possess or sell a live badger (s. 4). There are exceptions from these offences, some of which are broadly similar to those in the Wildlife and Countryside Act 1981; and there is a special defence of obstructing the entrance to a sett for the purpose of fox-hunting (s. 8). The maximum penalties for offences under the 1992 Act are fines up to level 5 and six months' imprisonment (s. 12). Equipment used in the course of offences may be forfeited, and dogs may be destroyed or otherwise disposed of, and their owners banned from keeping dogs (ss. 12 and 13).

See 1-1 for the meaning of "consolidating Act".

In the case of *Good v. Director of Public Prosecutions* (2000) some men were prosecuted under s. 3 of the Protection of Badgers Act 1992. The evidence was that they had been digging in an area which was an active badger sett. They had not, however, actually dug into the tunnels and chambers made by the badgers. The question was whether this was sufficient for them to be guilty of the offence.

The court decided that it was not. Because s. 3 created a criminal offence, it had to be read in a narrower sense rather than a wider one, if the meaning was not clear. By that test, the soil above the badgers' tunnels and chambers was not a "badger sett". The men were therefore not guilty of an offence.

Protection of badgers

Birds Under the Wildlife and Countryside Act 1981 it is an 11-54
offence to kill, injure or capture a wild bird or to damage or destroy

its nest or eggs (s. 1(1)). It is also an offence to have possession of a wild bird, alive or dead, or an egg or a part of a wild bird, if the bird was captured or killed unlawfully (s. 1(2)). The expression "wild bird" does not include one bred in captivity, or poultry or a game bird (s. 27(1)). A higher degree of protection is applied to the birds listed in Schedule 1 to the Act, which embraces about 85 species, including birds such as curlews, eagles, grebes, swans and many others. A few species are protected only during the close season, but otherwise it is an offence to disturb these birds when nesting, or to disturb their young while they are still dependent. For Schedule 1 birds, the maximum fine is level 5, and for others it is level 3 (s. 21).

11-55 Schedule 2 lists birds which can be caught or taken without committing an offence. The first Part of the Schedule contains birds such as duck, geese and woodcock, which may be killed or taken outside their close seasons. (The Schedule does not include birds reared for sport, such as pheasants, which are not wild birds at all for the purposes of the Act.) The second Part of the Schedule contained birds regarded as pests, such as crows and pigeons, which could be killed by "authorised persons", which included the owner or occupier of the land. To comply with European legislation, however, this part of the Schedule was repealed, and any person wishing to kill birds of these species must apply to the DETR for a licence.

11-56 *Plants* The Wildlife and Countryside Act 1981 makes it an offence to pick, uproot or destroy any of the wild plants listed in Schedule 8 (s. 13(1)). Schedule 8 includes about 170 species of wild plants. It is a defence for a person to show that what he did was "the incidental result of a lawful operation, and could not reasonably have been avoided" (s. 13(3)).

Theft and criminal damage of land

11-57 Theft means dishonestly taking property with the intention of permanently depriving the owner of it. Most offences involve personal property, rather than land. The Theft Act 1968 makes clear that land can be stolen, but only in three circumstances:

- Where a person such as a trustee or liquidator is responsible for disposing of land, and appropriates the land or anything forming part of it.
- Where a person is not in possession of the land and causes something to be "severed" (i. e. separated) from it.
- Where a tenant is in possession of land and he takes any fixture, or structure let with the land (s. 4(2)).

A person cannot legally steal land just by taking adverse possession of it.

11-58 There is a separate rule for mushrooms (and any other fungi) and flowers, fruit and foliage growing wild on someone else's land: picking these things, if they are growing wild, is not theft unless it is done for reward or for sale or for some other commercial purpose. (But even if picking does not amount to theft, it may still be an offence under the Wildlife and Countryside Act 1981.) Theft is subject to a maximum punishment of seven years' imprisonment.

11-59 Under the Criminal Damage Act 1971 it is an offence to damage property, and property includes land (s. 10). This is what most people would refer to as vandalism. There are provisions similar to those in the Theft Act 1968 which deal with wild animals and mushrooms etc growing wild. Breaking something on land, or writing graffiti, or dumping rubbish on land, would thus amount to criminal damage of the land (s. 1). The maximum punishment is 10 years' imprisonment; and there is a more serious offence of damaging property with intent to endanger life, for which the maximum is life imprisonment (s. 3). Where damage is caused by fire, the offence (which is otherwise the same) is known as arson.

11-60 It is a defence for a person accused of causing criminal damage to prove that:

See 2-47 on fixtures and fittings.

See 1-47 for the meaning of "possessing" land.

See chapter 8 for the law on leases and tenancies, and 2-47 for fixtures.

See 2-67 for the meaning of "adverse possession".

See 11-56 for this Act.

And see 11-82 onwards on dumping.

Criminal damage

In the case of *Chamberlain v. Lindon* (1998) there was a dispute about a right of way over some land belonging to Mr Chamberlain. The land was used by his neighbour, Mr Lindon, to gain access to his own land, but in a way which Mr Chamberlain did not consider lawful. Mr Chamberlain put up a wall, to prevent the use of the land in this way. After correspondence, Mr Lindon demolished the wall. He was prosecuted for causing criminal damage. His defence was that he believed that it was necessary to demolish the wall, to protect his right of way.

The court decided that Mr Lindon was entitled to act in this way: he genuinely believed that he was protecting his right of way. There was an immediate need to remove the wall, to avoid any suggestion that Mr Lindon was acquiescing to the obstruction.

(The court added that criminal proceedings were inappropriate, since this was essentially a civil matter. It did not decide who was right or wrong about the right of way as a matter of civil law.)

- He honestly believed that the owner of the property had consented, or that he would have consented if he had known about it.

- He damaged the property in order to protect property of his own, or a right in property, and honestly believed that the property or right was in immediate need of protection and that the action he took was reasonable in all the circumstances (s. 5(2)).

See 12-24 for sources on criminal law.

Pollution

11-61 A concern for the environment has long been reflected in many areas of the law, including planning law and the law of nuisance. But "environmental law" is now a large and complex subject in its own right, the subject of international agreements and European Union legislation, and a rapidly increasing amount of law within the United Kingdom. The following paragraphs look briefly at the law on pollution of the air, land and water.

See chapter 9 for planning and chapter 4 for nuisance.

11-62 *Air pollution* The Clean Air Act 1993, which consolidated earlier legislation on air pollution, contains a range of provisions on air pollution. Part I of the Act is concerned with emissions of dark smoke; and Part II with smoke, grit, dust and fumes. These provisions are mainly relevant to non-domestic premises.

See 1-1 for the meaning of "consolidating Act".

11-63 Part III deals with smoke control areas. Local authorities have power to decide whether their area or part of it is a smoke control area (s. 18). They take this step by making an order; and the order may include exemptions, including exemptions for particular types of building or types of fireplace. Where an order is in force, no smoke may be emitted from any chimney in the area, and if smoke is emitted, the occupier of the building is guilty of an offence, for which the maximum punishment is a level 3 fine on the standard scale (s. 20).

11-64 No offence is committed, however, by a person who uses only "authorised fuel", even though some smoke may in fact be produced. This means fuel declared in regulations to be authorised fuel, the relevant regulations being the Smoke Control Areas (Authorised Fuels) Regulations 1991, as amended by later regulations. Where a smoke control order is in force, it is generally an offence to buy or sell unauthorised solid fuel (s. 23). In addition, no offence is committed by a person using a fireplace of a class exempted by the DETR under Smoke Control (Exempted Fireplaces) Orders (s. 21).

11-65 A landowner concerned about emitting smoke from a chimney will thus need to consider whether the provisions of the Clean Air Act 1993 on dark smoke, grit etc apply. If not, the next question will be whether the area is a smoke control area; if so, landowners must generally use only authorised fuel or exempted fireplaces, which are designed so as to minimise the amount of smoke emitted.

11-66 The burning of stubble is dealt with specifically by the Crop Residues (Restrictions on Burning) Regulations 1993, under s. 152 of the Environmental Protection Act 1990 which now restrict the burning of "crop residues". They apply to the activities of persons engaged in agriculture, on agricultural land and cover cereal straw and stubble and some other crop residues. There are some exemptions, which include burning crop residues for disease control and the burning of straw stack remains (i. e. the remains of stacks of straw) and broken bales; but the precautions set out in Schedule 2 to the Regulations must be followed. There are also regulations which regulate the burning of heather and grass, namely the Heather and Grass etc (Burning) Regulations 1986 (which cover the burning of bracken and gorse).

11-67 *Pollution of land* The Environmental Protection Act 1990, s. 33, as amended by the Environment Act 1995, is concerned with "controlled waste". "Waste" is defined in s. 75 of and Schedule 2B to the 1990 Act and means in effect any substance or object which the holder discards or intends or is required to discard. The term "controlled waste" is defined in s. 75, and includes "household, industrial and commercial waste", each of which has its own definition. "Household waste", for example, means waste from domestic property (including caravans), residential homes, schools, universities and hospitals (s. 75(5)). Some substances are excluded from the definition of "controlled waste", chiefly because they are dealt with under other legislation, and this includes sewage from domestic premises.

11-68 Section 33 of the Act creates three offences. People must not, without a waste management licence, deposit controlled waste in or on land. (The offence applies to a landowner's own land, just as it does to any other land.) They must not "treat, keep or dispose of" controlled waste without a waste management licence. They must not "treat, keep or dispose of" controlled waste—whether or not they have a licence—in such a way as to cause pollution of the environment. These are serious offences: the maximum punishment is 6 months' imprisonment or a £20,000 fine in a magistrates' court, or an unlimited fine and two years'imprisonment in the Crown Court (s. 33(8)). It is a defence for a person prosecuted under s. 33 to prove that he "took all reasonable precautions and exercised all due diligence to avoid the commission of the offence" (s. 33(7)).

See 1-20 onwards for criminal law generally

11-69 There are some exceptions, however. Under s. 33(2), the offence does not apply "..in relation to household waste from a domestic property which is treated, kept or disposed of within the curtilage of the dwelling by or with the permission of the occupier of the dwelling". A householder could thus deposit a broken washing machine in a corner of her garden without committing an offence; but she could not do so in a field or other land which was not

See 9-18 for the meaning of "curtilage" and 1-47 for the meaning of "occupying" land.

considered to be part of the "curtilage" of the house. Regulations can also be made under s. 33(3) to create more exemptions, and the DETR has made the Waste Management Licensing Regulations 1994 using this power. The exemptions (which are from the first two of the three offences mentioned above) are listed in Schedule 3 to the Regulations. Many are specialised, and relate to particular industries, but the following are also included:

- Spreading waste soil, wood, bark or other plant matter in forests, woodlands, gardens, landscaped areas and similar places (para. 7).

- Burning wood, bark or other plant matter in forests, woodlands, gardens, sports grounds, landscaped areas and similar places, or burning wood from demolition work, provided the total does not exceed 10 tonnes in 24 hours (para. 30).

- Burying a dead domestic pet at domestic premises where it lived (para. 37)

Even where there is an exemption, an "establishment or undertaking" must register, generally with the local authority (reg 18 of the 1994 Regulations).

In short, the law now tightly controls the disposal of waste. Householders may find that in some cases they can deposit waste within the curtilages of their house; but otherwise there is no general exemption which allows members of the public to dispose of waste by burning or burying it, even where this may seem harmless. Instead, the waste must be entrusted to an operator with a waste management licence, such as the local authority itself. 11-70

The planning legislation also has something to say about the deposit of waste: there is a material change of use, so development requiring planning permission, if waste is deposited on land in a way which increases the area of land used for depositing waste or brings the height of the deposit above the level of surrounding land (s. 55(3)(b) of the Town and Country Planning Act 1990). 11-71

Apart from laying down penalties for depositing waste without a licence, the Environmental Protection Act 1990, as amended by the 11-72

See 9-13 onwards for the meaning of "development".

Environment Act 1995, sets up a system for identifying and cleaning up contaminated land. The provisions are in Part IIA (ss. 78A–78YC) of the 1990 Act and they finally came into force on 1 April 2000. Section 78YA requires the DETR to issue guidance about the working of the law. Guidance has been issued in DETR Circular 02/2000: *Contaminated Land*.

11-73 Under the new system, "contaminated land" means land which appears to the local authority to be in such condition, by reason of substances in, on or under the land, that significant harm is being or may be caused, or controlled waters polluted. "Harm" means harm to the health of living organisms, or other interference with ecological systems, or damage to property (s. 78A(2) and (4)). Local authorities must take steps to identify contaminated land within their area. If the land appears to be in a serious condition, they may designate the site as a "special site" (s. 78A(3) and s. 78C). While the local authority has the duty of enforcing the Act in relation to contaminated land generally, enforcement in relation to special sites is a matter for the Environment Agency. When they have identified contaminated land, the local authority must inform the owner and occupier of the land, the Environment Agency, and any person who appears to be responsible for the contamination (referred to in the Act as "appropriate person")(s. 78B and 78C). This may be the current owner or occupier, or a previous owner or occupier, depending upon the circumstances. However, the rule is subject to the proviso that if the person who caused contamination cannot be found, the current owner or occupier of the land is an "appropriate person" (s. 78F).

See 11-78 for the meaning of "controlled waters".

11-74 The local authority (or, for special sites, the Environment Agency) have a duty to serve "remediation notices" on "appropriate persons", specifying the work which must be done on the site and the time allowed (s. 78E(1)). All persons affected by a remediation notice must first be consulted (s. 78H). The work which is required to be done must be reasonable having regard to the seriousness of the harm and the cost of remediation (s. 78E(4)). The "appropriate person" may be a former owner of the land, for example a company which has sold off an old industrial site, on which new housing has been built. In such cases, the Act requires the new owner to consent to the work by the appropriate person, but he or she must be consulted first, and the Act gives a right to compensation (s. 78G). In some cases, the local authority (or the Environment Agency) may take action itself, in which case it must not serve a remediation notice (ss. 78N and 78H(5)).

A person served with a remediation notice may appeal against it. If the notice was served by a local authority, the appeal is dealt with by a magistrates' court; if by the Environment Agency, by the DETR (s. 78L). Subject to an appeal, it is an offence to fail to comply with a remediation notice without reasonable excuse. The maximum fine is level 5 on the standard scale, with one-tenth of that amount for each day the offence continues after conviction; but if the land is industrial, trade or business premises, the figures are £20,000 and £2,000 per day (s. 78M). 11-75

If the local authority (or the Environment Agency) carries out remediation work, it can recover the cost (s. 78P). Local authorities must keep a register of remediation notices and other information under the Act (s. 78R). 11-76

The sections inserted into the Environmental Protection Act 1990 provide a framework They are supplemented by regulations, the Contaminated Land (England) Regulations 2000. The provisions on contaminated land will be very important to those owning or buying land on sites which may be contaminated, especially because the owner or occupier may be required to pay for the cost of "remediation", if the person who caused the contamination cannot be found. This may be because the contamination was caused long ago, or because it is recent but was caused by a company which has since ceased to exist. 11-77

Pollution of waterways Part III of the Water Resources Act 1991 is concerned with pollution of "controlled waters". "Controlled waters" means territorial and coastal waters, inland freshwaters (including lakes, ponds, rivers and watercourses) and waters contained in underground strata. However, lakes and ponds are only included if they drain into another watercourse. Public sewers and drains which drain into them, are not included. 11-78

Section 85 of the Act creates a number of different offences which apply to controlled waters, including: 11-79

- Causing or knowingly permitting any poisonous, noxious or polluting matter or any solid waste matter to drain into them (s. 85(1).

- Causing or knowingly permitting any trade effluent or sewage effluent to be discharged into them (s. 85(3).

- Causing or knowingly permitting any matter to enter inland freshwaters, so as to impede the proper flow of the waters and aggravate pollution due to other causes (s. 85(5)).

See also 2-59 for the obstruction of waterways.

The maximum punishment is a fine of £20,000 or three months' imprisonment in a magistrates' court, or two years' imprisonment in the Crown Court (s. 85(6)).

11-80 Part VII of the Water Resources Act 1991 contains a range of powers for use by the Environment Agency in combatting water pollution. In particular, the Agency can carry out anti-pollution works, or require others to carry them out (ss. 161 and 161A). Failing to comply with a notice to carry out works is an offence, the maximum punishment being the same as under s. 85.

See 12-22 for sources on environmental law.

Rubbish

11-81 The law approaches the question of rubbish in several different ways. In addition to the system which controls the disposal of waste (explained under the last heading) there are separate areas of the law which deal with dumping and with litter. Landowners may find that old cars or other debris is dumped on their land; their land may be subject to controls on litter, though this will be the exception rather than the rule.

See 11-85 for litter.

11-82 *Dumping* The Refuse Disposal (Amenity) Act 1978, s. 2(1), creates an offence of unauthorised dumping, which may take two forms. The offence is committed by "any person who, without lawful authority:

> "*(a)* abandons on any land in the open air, or on any other land forming part of a highway, a motor vehicle or anything which forms part of a motor vehicle and was removed from it in the course of dismantling it on the land; or
>
> (b) abandons on any such land any thing other than a motor vehicle, being a thing which he has brought on to the land for the purpose of abandoning it there."

It is important to note that a "motor vehicle", as defined in s. 11 of the Act, includes trailers, and "any chassis or body", with or without wheels, from a vehicle or trailer. Otherwise, parts of motor vehicles can only form the subject of an offence if abandoned in the course of dismantling the vehicle on the land in question, or brought on to the land to be abandoned there. The offence also applies to anything other than a motor vehicle, if it has been brought on to the land in order to be abandoned. The offence is punishable with a level 4 fine, or imprisonment for up to three months, and can be used to deal with "fly-tipping" and other forms of dumping.

11-83 Sections 3 and 4 of the Act impose a duty on local authorities to remove motor vehicles—but not other things—which have been abandoned on land. The Removal and Disposal of Vehicles Regulations 1986 (and since amended on several occasions) supplement the provisions of the Act. The procedure is for the local authority to give notice to the occupier of the land. If it appears that the motor vehicle should be destroyed, a notice to that effect must be fixed to it. The local authority may recover their costs from the person responsible for the abandoned vehicle. The Removal, Storage and Disposal of Vehicles (Prescribed Sums and Charges) Regulations 1989—also since amended on several occasions—deal with the amounts which can be charged by the local authority.

See 1-47 onwards for the meaning of "occupying" land.

11-84 Another set of provisions, ss. 99–103 of the Road Traffic Regulation Act 1984, is aimed specifically at vehicles which are parked on highways and other roads to which the public have access. These apply if the vehicle:

- Is contravening a statutory prohibition, for example parking restrictions.
- Is causing an obstruction or danger.

◆ Appears to have been abandoned.

Depending on the circumstances, the police or the local authority may be able to remove the vehicle. Some regulations, the Removal and Disposal of Vehicles Regulations 1986, supplement the Act.

11-85 *Litter* The law is now contained in Part IV of the Environmental Protection Act 1990. It is an offence to drop litter in places which come within s. 87, and these include:

◆ Any "public open space", meaning any place in the open air to which the public have access without payment (including any place with is covered but open on one side) (s. 87(4)).

◆ Highways maintainable at the public expense.

◆ Crown land to which the public have access without payment.

◆ Land within "litter control areas".

See 5-14 for the meaning of "highway maintainable at the public expense."

See 1-72 for the meaning of "the Crown".

11-86 For an area to be a "litter control area", the type of area must first be prescribed in delegated legislation under s. 90(1). The DETR has accordingly made the Litter Control Areas Order 1991 (since amended) which prescribes various sorts of land, including public car parks, markets, caravan sites, beaches and some public-access land. Local authorities, which are responsible for administering this Part of the Act, under s. 86, can now designate areas of land of this sort and makes them litter control areas, where dropping litter will be an offence.

What is "litter"?

In *Westminster City Council v. Riding* (1995) the question arose of whether some black plastic refuse sacks, and some empty cartons, which had been deposited on the highway, were "litter".

The court decided that trade and commercial waste were capable of being "litter" for the purposes of the Part IV of the Environmental Protection Act 1990. (Mr Riding was found not guilty of the offence, for a different reason.)

11-87 Under s. 88, there is a fixed penalty notice procedure, which enables people to be fined for dropping litter. Section 89(1) imposes a duty on local authorities to keep highways and certain other land clear of litter and refuse, so far as practicable; and other persons are also made responsible for litter—Crown bodies are responsible for Crown land, for example, and the occupier of land in a litter control area is made responsible for that land. Section 89(2) makes local authorities responsible for keeping highways clean, as far as practicable. DETR has the power to publish a code of practice under s. 89(7) giving guidance on the duties in s. 89(1) and (2), and has duly published a *Code of Practice on Litter and Refuse*. The Act also contains, in s. 91, a procedure by which members of the public can initiate action to clear up litter. Where a highway, or land in a litter control area, or land of certain other types appears to be defaced by litter or refuse, any person can apply to a magistrates' court for an order against a local authority or other person who has a duty under s. 89(1) or (2) in relation to the land. Five days' notice must first be given, so that the person concerned has an opportunity to clear up the land (s. 91(5)). Failing that, the magistrates may make an order, known as a "litter abatement order", requiring the person concerned to clear the land of litter (s. 91(6)). Failing to comply with an order is an offence, for which the maximum punishment is a level 4 fine, with an additional one-twentieth of that amount for each day on which the offence continues. Local authorities must keep a public register of litter control areas (s. 95).

See 1-14 on codes of practice and similar documents.

11-88 Abandoned supermarket and luggage trolleys are a special problem in some areas. If local authorities chose to adopt the provisions of s. 99 of and Schedule 4 to the Environmental Protection Act 1990 they can collect abandoned trolleys and return them to their owners, charging a fee for doing so.

See 1-16 for the adoption of provisions by local authorities.

11-89 Local authorities have a power under s. 5(1) of the Litter Act 1983 to put litter bins in any "street or public place". (They also have power to do this under s. 185 of the Highways Act 1980.) They must make arrangement for the regular emptying and cleansing of litter bins, and as an alternative may put up signs about the leaving of litter (s. 5(2) and (4)).

See 12-22 for sources on environmental law.

Dwellings and public health

See chapter 4 for nuisance and 4-27 onwards for statutory nuisances.

11-90 Some activities on land can interfere with the health or comfort of neighbours or the general public, and the law on nuisances—particularly statutory nuisances—deals with these. The following paragraphs deal with legislation which is similar, but is concerned with the health and comfort of people in houses and other dwellings, rather than neighbours or the public.

11-91 *Overcrowding of dwellings* The Housing Act 1985 imposes limits on the numbers of people who may occupy a dwelling (meaning a house, flat or other living accommodation). The test (which is complicated) consists of two parts. For each part of the test, the rooms to be taken into account are bedrooms and living rooms. Firstly there is a "room standard", the question being whether persons of opposite sexes (excluding those under 10 years old and those living as man and wife) must share a room (s. 325). Secondly there is a "space standard", and here the number of persons permitted is whichever is the less according to two tables. The first table lays down numbers of persons in relation to numbers of rooms (3 for 2 rooms, 5 for 3 rooms, 7.5 for 4 rooms, and so on) while the second table lays down the total number of persons for rooms of a certain size (s. 326).

Over-crowding

The case of *Islington London Borough Council v. Rogers* (1999) concerned a house which contained 10 bedrooms. These were let to young people, who shared the kitchen and living room and bathrooms. Was the house in "multiple occupation" for the purposes of the law on overcrowding?

The court's decision was that the house was in multiple occupation, because there was no connection between the young people. Occupation by students was in different category, however: students sharing accommodation would usually be regarded as forming a single household.

See 1-47 onwards for the meaning of "occupying" land.

11-92 The occupier of the dwelling commits an offence if the above limits are exceeded; though there are exceptions for visiting members of the family, and the local authority can be asked to relax the limits in exceptional circumstances (ss. 329 and 330). Landlords must summarise the law on overcrowding in the rent book which they must provide to their tenants in certain circumstances. They must also report overcrowding to the local authority, failure to do so being an offence (s. 333). These rules apply where there is a single household; other provisions of the Housing Act govern the situation where a dwelling is in "multiple occupation", i. e. occupied by persons who do not form a single household (ss. 358 -364).

See 8-81 for rent books.

11-93 *Fitness for human habitation* The Housing Act 1985, in s. 604, lays down that a dwelling-house is fit for human habitation unless, in the opinion of the local authority, it fails to meet various tests, and is therefore not reasonably suitable for occcupation. The tests include:

- Structural stability.
- Freedom from serious disrepair.
- Freedom from dampness prejudicial to health.
- Provision of light, heating, and ventilation; water supply; drains.
- Facilities for the preparation of food.
- Facilities for washing; lavatory.

11-94 In relation to flats the same tests apply, and there are also others relating to the surrounding building. Under s. 189 of the Housing Act 1985, if a dwelling is not fit for human habitation, the local authority can serve a "repair notice". The notice must be served on the person who is in control of the dwelling, and anyone else with an interest in it, and must set out the work to be done. A repair notice can also be served where the local authority consider that substantial repairs are needed, even though the dwelling is not unfit for human habitation (s. 190). A person who is served with a repair notice can appeal to the county court (s. 191).

11-95 If a repair notice is not complied with, the local authority can carry out the necessary work themselves and recover the costs from the person in control of the dwelling (s. 193). Where a dwelling

See 12-2 for sources on public health.

cannot be repaired at reasonable cost, the local authority can make a "closing order", to prevent it being lived in, or a demolition order (ss. 264–269). The local authority must take into account guidelines from DETR in considering whether to take action.

Protecting amenity

See 1-27 for the meaning of "amenity".

11-96 Local authorities have several powers which are concerned with the amenity of land. Under s. 215 of the Town and Country Planning Act 1990, if it appears that the amenity of the area is adversely affected by the condition of land, they can serve a notice on the owner and occupier of the land requiring him to take steps to put matters right within a specified time. Whether land is in a bad enough condition to justify action will depend in part on the nature of the immediate area; but in an attractive residential area, for example, action might be justified if land was badly overgrown and strewn with refuse. The owner and occupier of the land can appeal to a magistrates' court against the notice on one of a number of grounds, including the ground that the condition of the land does not adversely affect the amenity of the area; but, subject to an appeal it is an offence punishable with a level 3 fine not to comply with the order (ss. 216 and 217). If necessary, the local authority can carry out the work and recover the cost from the landowner (s. 217).

11-97 The National Parks and Access to the Countryside Act 1949, s. 89, allows a local authority to carry out work on land which is "derelict, neglected or unsightly". The local authority could use the power (for example) to clear up rubbish, and plant trees or shrubs. But the permission of the owner is necessary, and the cost of doing the work falls on the local authority.

For powers to deal with litter, see 11-85 onwards.

11-98 Under the Public Health Act 1961, ss. 17–37, local authorities can repair drains, and remove accumulations of rubbish in the open air if "seriously detrimental to the amenities of the neighbourhood", after first serving notice on the owner and occupier of the land.

11-99 More generally, Part III of the Leasehold Reform, Housing and Urban Development Act 1993 created a body known as the Urban

Regeneration Agency, which works to secure the reclamation of land which is contaminated or derelict. And the Derelict Land Act 1982 allows grants to be made for reclaiming derelict, neglected or unsightly land.

See 12-20 and 12-22 for sources on amenity.

Compulsory purchase

11-100 Local authorities may need to acquire land compulsorily, for roads or other public purposes, as may government departments and other bodies, including statutory undertakers. Powers to acquire land compulsorily are found in many different Acts. In planning legislation, for example, local authorities have a general power to acquire land compulsorily, if authorised to do so by the DETR, where the land:

See 11-103 for the meaning of "statutory undertaker".

> "(a) is suitable for and required in order to secure the carrying out of development, redevelopment or improvement; or
>
> (b) is required for a purpose which it is necessary to achieve in the intersts of the proper planning of an area in which the land is situated" (Town and Country Planning Act 1990, s. 226(1)).

11-101 The DETR itself has a power to acquire land compulsorily (s. 228). Other powers are provided for more specific purposes; for example, the DETR can authorise a local authority to acquire a listed building, if it appears that reasonable steps are not being taken to preserve the building (s. 47 of the Planning (Listed Buildings and Conservation Areas) Act 1990). While the powers themselves are contained in different Acts, the procedure for acquiring land compulsorily is largely standarised.

See 9-66 for listed buildings. For other examples of compulsory purchase, see 2-61 and 10-80.

11-102 The Acquisition of Land Act 1981 lays down the procedure for making a compulsory purchase order. Generally, the order must be submitted to the appropriate government department; objections from the owner of the land, and a public enquiry, may follow. The owner of the land must be compensated, and the basis for compensation, under the Land Compensation Act 1961, is the market value of the land, assuming a willing buyer and a willing seller; and the acquiring body must also pay for any damage caused. The 1961

Act contains detailed rules for the valuation of land being acquired compulsorily. If there is a dispute as to the amount of compensation payable, the Lands Tribunal will resolve it. The process of transferring land to the body acquiring it is governed by the Compulsory Purchase Act 1965.

See 12-2 for sources on compulsory purchase.

Statutory undertakers

11-103 *Powers of statutory undertakers* The term "statutory undertaker" is generally used of private companies which undertake some major project with the assistance of statutory powers. The project may be a one-off (such as the Channel Tunnel) or one which is repeated (such as the construction and operation of telecommunications networks of different sorts, or in different areas). The most significant statutory undertakers are the privatised utility companies, responsible for gas, electricity, water, and telecommunications. Statutory undertakers are not dependent upon negotiating for the rights and property which they may require, but can exercise their powers so as to acquire them, and this enables them to lay the necessary pipes, cables and other apparatus, either underground or over the surface. Planning permission is generally not required for this work, because it is deemed not to be "development" (s. 55(2)(c) of the Town and Country Planning Act 1990). Landowners may find that they already have pipes, cables etc on or under their land, or that they receive notice from one of the utility companies that they will be laid. In some cases, landowners have a right to the installation of a supply—for example, water companies can (subject to some exemptions)be required to provide a supply of water to premises.

See 9-13 onwards for the meaning of "development".

See also 6-52 for easements which allow pipes and cables to be laid across land.

11-104 The utility companies operate under their own legislation, and each has its own regulatory body, which has responsibility for seeing that they act properly and maintain a proper standard. The position can be summarised as follows:

Table 8: Utility regulators

Sector	Regulatory body	Main legislation
Gas	OFGEM (formerly OFGAS)	Gas Act 1986 (amended by the Gas Act 1995 and the Utilities Act 2000)
Electricity	OFGEM (formerly OFFER)	Electricity Act 1989 (amended by the Utilities Act 2000)
Water	OFWAT	Water Industry Act 1991
Tele-communications	OFTEL	Telecommunications Act 1984

These Acts contain wide powers allowing the utility companies to install equipment on and under land. But there are also safeguards built into the legislation; and the utility companies, like other statutory undertakers, are expected to pay scrupulous attention to the legislation and to act responsibly and fairly in exercising their statutory powers. Rights of entry on to private property are strictly controlled. Apart from the above Acts, the Rights of Entry (Gas and Electricity Boards) Act 1954 lays down further safeguards for landowners in relation to some powers of the gas and electricity companies. The different Acts work in different ways; but in many cases the utility company must either obtain the consent of the landowner or apply to a court in order to obtain an order confirming what it wishes to do. In some cases where a right to place equipment on land is exercised, the landowner may have a right to make a charge for the grant of a "wayleave", as it is sometimes known—in other words permission for the use his land. 11-105

The New Roads and Street Works Act 1991 Part III of this Act is intended to minimise the disruption caused by street works. 11-106

Statutory undertakers who wish to carry out work must give notice to the local authority, who keep a register of street works, and who may give directions as to the timing of the work. The Act is supplemented by the Street Works (Registers, Notices, Directions and Designations) Regulations 1992, which have been amended on several occasions, and by several codes of practice issued by the DETR.

See 12-12 for sources on statutory undertakers and their powers.

Assessment

11-107 Of the different subjects dealt with in this chapter, two will be particularly important for many landowners, especially because the law is not obvious. First is the question of occupiers' liability. Landowners will generally be responsible for the safety of all the people who come on to their land, including (though to a lesser extent) trespassers. Landowners should think carefully about whether there is a risk of injury or damage, and be prepared to take action or at least to give warnings of the danger. It is particularly important to guard against the risk of injury to children, since they may be treated by the law as having implied permission to come on to land, rather than trespassers, and so require more care from the owner of the land.

11-108 Secondly, the law is now increasingly concerned to protect the environment by regulating the disposal of waste. There are restrictions on what landowners can dispose of on their own land, as well as controls over dumping and litter. Penalties can be severe. The law on contaminated land will be extremely important for those thinking of buying property, since they may run the risk of having to remedy contamination at their own expense. Specialist firms now offer advice on whether there is a risk of contamination.

Chapter 12

More information

Introduction

This chapter gives details of sources of further information about the topics dealt with in the preceding chapters, for readers who wish to research further into the law. 12-0

The "Notes and Queries" pages linked to the text can be found at http://www.barsby.com, and these contain much further information and also links to many sites where more can be found. 12-1

General sources

Printed copies of Acts of Parliament and delegated legislation are available from HMSO. These often amend earlier legislation; and to legislation in its amended, up to date form it is almost always necessary to look at publications such as text books (often loose-leaf) produced for lawyers and other professionals, or *Halsbury's Statutes.* The latter is a series of volumes setting out the text of Acts, with notes, subject by subject. Replacement volumes are issued, to keep the whole work up to date. A separate publication, *Halsbury's Laws of England*, aims to explain what the law is, subject by subject in a series of volumes. It deals both with judge-made law and legislation. Replacement volumes are issued to keep the series up to date. 12-2

Many public libraries hold a copy of *Stone's Justices Manual*, in three volumes, which contains up to date legislation and other materials; though this is geared to the work of magistrates' courts and so is concerned mainly with the criminal law. Another 12-3 indispensible practitioner's work is *Current Law*, published monthly, which gives brief details of changes to the law.

12-4 Government bodies also produce much material about the law, from consultation papers on proposals for legal reforms to codes of practice and guides to the law. Other public bodies, including local authorities, also produce leaflets and guides for the public, and these can provide useful summaries of the law and guides to how legal procedures work. See for example the leaflets produced by the Land Registry.

12-5 The decisions of courts and tribunals are reported in many different series of law reports. These are of course selective: only cases which decide questions of law are reported. Larger public libraries may have one of the two main series, which deal with the law as a whole, the Weekly Law Reports and the All England Law Reports (abbreviated to "W.L.R." and "All E.R."—a full list of abbreviations for law reports is set out in *Current Law*).

12-6 In civil cases, the legal aid scheme has been replaced by the Community Legal Service, launched in April 2000. The Scheme is based on local networks of advisers, including solicitors, Citizens' Advice Bureaux and others, providing assistance at different levels. Some private-sector organisations also provide advice services for their members, including the Country Landowners' Association and the Consumers' Association.

12-7 The following paragraphs give details of some legal textbooks and other materials which deal with the areas of law covered in this book. The list is not intended to be exhaustive, and omits most practitioners' books. The prices given are recent published prices. Most are paperbacks, but some are hardbacks and some loose-leaf publications (and so more up to date than the date of publication might suggest).

Land law generally

12-8 Books on land law deal with the general principles of the law, rather than its practical effect. They deal with many of the topics covered in this book—leases and tenancies, licences, easements, restrictive covenants, adverse possession of land, and so on. Some examples: *Megarry and Wade: the Law of Real Property*, by R. Megarry and W. Wade (Sweet & Maxwell, 1999, ISBN 04214744602, £60); *Land Law*, by Patrick J. Dalton (Financial Times, 1999, ISBN 0273614231, £26.99); *Textbook on Land Law*, by Judith-Anne Mackenzie and Mary Philips (Blackstone Press, 1999, ISBN 1854318756, £17.95).

There are several books which conveniently set out the relevant legislation on land law, selectively and in up to date form, though with little commentary—in particular *Butterworths Property Law Handbook* (Butterworths, 1998, ISBN 0406905223, £40). 12-9

Specific aspects of land law

Though the above books deal with such topics as easements, leases and registered conveyancing, their treatment can be quite brief, leaving a full treatment to works such as those mentioned below. 12-10

Leases and tenancies On leases and tenancies generally, many books are available, including *Practical Approach to Landlord and Tenant Law*, by Simon Garner (Blackstone Press, 1998, ISBN 185431761X, £19.95), and *Principles of Landlord and Tenant*, by John Rhys Morris (Cavendish, 1999, ISBN 1859413846, £21.95). There are also specialised books on different sorts of leases, such as business and commercial tenancies, and aspects of the law such as forfeiture and enfranchisement—for example *Leasehold Enfranchisement* by David Clarke and Andrew Wells (Jordans, 1999, ISBN 0853084262, £2.50). 12-11

Easements The practitioners' guide to easements is *Gale on the Law of Easements*, by Jonathan Gaunt and Paul Morgan (Sweet and Maxwell, 1996, ISBN 0421444703, £150). Another detailed work of reference is *Boundaries and Easements*, by Colin Sara (Sweet & Maxwell, 1996, ISBN 0421537906, £125). There are also books on specific sorts of easement, including *Rights of Way*, by Simon Blackford (CLT Professional, 1999, ISBN 1858111668, £24); *Rights of Light and How to Deal with Them*, by John Anstey (RICS Publishing, 12-12

1998, ISBN 0854068546, £13); *Pipes, Mains, Cables and Sewers*, by Dr H. W. Wilkinson (Financial Times, 1996, ISBN 075200 1906, £38.50).

12-13 *Boundaries* See *Boundaries and Easements*, by Colin Sara, mentioned above, and *Boundaries, Walls and Fences*, by Trevor M.Aldridge (Sweet & Maxwell, 1997, ISBN 0752004131, £39). On party walls, see *Party Walls and What to Do With Them*, by John Anstey (RICS Books, 1998, ISBN 0854069070, £15) and *Party Wall etc Act: the New Law*, by Jill Alexander (Northumbria Law Press, 1997, ISBN 1873298277, £16.50)

12-14 *Restrictive covenants* The available books include *Restrictive Covenants Affecting Freehold Land*, by George L. Newsom (Sweet & Maxwell, 1998, ISBN 0421600802, £115) and *Land Covenants* by Ernest H. Scammell (Butterworths Law, 1996, ISBN 0406081514, £102). Material published by the Lands Tribunal is also valuable—the address of the Tribunal is 48 Chancery Lane, London WC2A 1JR.

12-15 *Conveyancing* The practitioner's book on transferring land and interests in it, under the system of land registration, is *Law and Practice of Registered Conveyancing*, by Theodore B. F. Ruoff and other authors (Sweet & Maxwell, 1991, ISBN 0421440600, £255). There are many shorter books, on registered and unregistered conveyancing, some dealing with specific aspects of conveyancing such as the sale of flats or business property.

Tort

12-16 Books on tort deal with the civil wrongs covered in this book—trespass, private and public nuisance, negligence, occupiers' liability, and liability under the Animals Act 1971, as well as others not directly relevant to landowners. Some examples: *Street on Torts*, by Margaret Brazier and John Murphy (Butterworths Law, 1999, ISBN 0406981036, £28.95) and *Winfield and Jolowicz on Tort*, by W. V. H. Rogers (Sweet & Maxwell, 1998, ISBN 042158730X, £29).

12-17 On nuisance,specifically, there is *Nuisances*, by Gordon Wignall (Sweet & Maxwell, 1998, ISBN 0752004751, £49) and *Statutory Nuisance: Law and Practice*, by McCracken and other authors

(Butterworth Law, 2000, ISBN 0406926735, £50). The law on animals, including civil liability for them, in dealt with in a number of books, including *Animal Law* by Palmer (Jordans, 2000, ISBN 072190820, £29.95).

Roads and paths; public access

Highway Law, by S. J. Sauvain, Q. C. (Sweet & Maxwell,1997, ISBN 0421044500, £90) is the practitioners' guide to the law, and includes detailed discussion of the process of dedication and acceptance and also the procedures under the National Parks and Access to the Countryside Act 1949 and the Countryside Act 1968. See also *Public Rights of Way*, by Sydenham (Jordans, 2000, ISBN 0853085706, £40). The books mentioned above on easements cover private rights of way. 12-18

The law relating to private roads is covered in *Private Roads: The Legal Framework*, by A. W. and C. Barsby (A. W. & C. Barsby, 1997, ISBN 0952162539, £35). Public access to land is covered in books such as *Countryside Law*, by J. F. Garner and B. L. Jones (Shaw & Sons, 1997, ISBN 0721910629, £19.95). This book also deals with common land, as does *Manorial Law* by A. W. and C. Barsby (A. W. & C. Barsby, 1996, ISBN 0952165 2 0, £49.95) and *The Law of the Manor* by Christopher Jessel (Barry Rose Law Publishers, 1998, ISBN 1872328849, £88). The Countryside and Rights of Way Bill is likely to be the subject of new guides to the law, in relation to its public access provisions. 12-19

Planning and related subjects

Among a range of general guides are *A Practical Approach to Planning Law* by Victor Moore (Blackstone Press, 1997, ISBN 1854316850, £19.95) and *Planning Law and Procedure* by R. M. C. Duxbury (Butterworths law, 1999, ISBN 0406993742, £20,95). Books on 12-20 planning law deal with trees and advertisements as well as planning law in the narrow sense.

12-21 On aspects of planning law and related areas of law, see: *Listed Buildings, Conservation Areas and Monuments*, by Charles Mynors (Sweet & Maxwell, 1999, ISBN 0752004409, £95) and also *Heritage Law and Practice* by G. Campbell (Palladian, 2000, ISBN 1902558278, £48); *Caravan Sites and Mobile Home Parks: The Legal Framework*, by A. W. & C. Barsby (A. W. & C. Barsby, 1995, ISBN 0 9521625 1 2, £25); *The Building Regulations Explained and Illustrated*, by Vincent Powell-Smith (Blackwell Science, 1999, 0632050691, £29.50). And on advertising note the DETR's booklet, *Outdoor Advertisements and Signs—A Guide for Advertisers.*

Environmental law

12-22 Environment Law is now generally treated as a legal subject in its own right, with many guides, among which are *Environment Law* by Richard Burnett-Hall (Sweet & Maxwell, ISBN 0421594101, £40) and *Environmental Law* by David Woodley, Q.C. (Oxford University Press, 1997, ISBN 0198260083, £95).

12-23 The new legislation on hedgerows is dealt with in several guides by the DETR—there is a free leaflet, *The Hedgerows Regulations: Your Questions Answered*; and also a fuller guide, *The Hedgerows Regulations 1997: A Guide to the Law and Good Practice* (£5.50). On contaminated land see, for example, *Guide to Contaminated Land* by Trevor Hellawell (Blackstone Press, 2000, ISBN 1841741426, £22). On water, see *Water and Drainage Law* by John Bates (Sweet & Maxwell, 1990, ISBN 0421387009, £255).

Criminal law; public law

12-24 Guides to criminal law include *Blackstone's Criminal Practice* (Blackstone Press, 2000, ISBN 1841741000, £110) and *Criminal Law* by

J. C. Smith and Brian Hogan (Butterworths Law, 1999, ISBN 0406983836, £28.95). These deal with the property offences mentioned in this book, such as burglary, and other serious offences such as public nuisance. Not every criminal offence is mentioned, since there are very large numbers of minor offences. Many of the latter, however, are covered briefly in *Stone's Justices Manual*—see above. There are books on specific spects of criminal law. Note particularly *Harrassment Law and Practice* by Tim Lawson-Cruttenden and Neil Addison, (Blackstone Press, 1998, ISBN 1854318349, £24.95).

Public law—the terms "constitutional law" and "administrative law" are also used, in relation to much the same area of law—is relevant to this book because it is concerned with the way in which public bodies such as local authorities behave, especially when they use the powers given to them by legislation, including the power to make byelaws. Books include *Administrative law*, by Carl Emery (Sweet & Maxwell, 1998, ISBN 042160005, £19.95) and *Constitutional and Administrative Law*, by Alex Carroll (Financial Times, 1999, ISBN 0273644351, £23.99). 12-25

This area of the law is concerned with public bodies and a few private ones which perform public functions; but *not* with statutory undertakers. The use of legal powers by private bodies is subject to the principle that the powers should be exercised responsibly and fairly, the the purposes for which they were given; the law is explained briefly in books on the interpretation of statutes, such as *Statutory Interpretation* by F. A. R. Bennion (Butterworths Law, 1997, ISBN 0406021260, £187). 12-26

Appendix

Relating law and facts

The table below is intended to help readers relate the law to the facts. The first column lists the subjects of possible problems—in other words, what someone might, if asked to explain very briefly, say a particular problem was about. The second column tries to indicate some of the legal issues to which such a problem might give rise, with references to the relevant parts of the text.

The table gives only an initial indication of what may be relevant, and doesn't cover all possible types of problem or dispute. But it should help to bring out the way in which a problem may give rise to different legal issues.

Table 9: relating law and facts

Subject	Possible legal issues
Access to land	Can access be obtained from a public highway? → 5-11 (but note 9-19). Can access be obtained over private land (e. g. a private road or drive)? → 6-33. Are the public entitled to access generally? → 10-79. Can access be obtained from neighbouring land, for repairs or maintenance? → 2-31, 6-50 and 7-2.
Animals	Are animals straying on to land and causing annoyance or damage? → 3-10. (See also 3-61 for cattle straying on to highways.) Is planning consent or other permission necessary for keeping animals? → 9-24, 10-56. See also Noise, below.
Boundaries	Is the position of a boundary in dispute? → 2-10. Who can (or must) maintain a wall or fence along a boundary? → 2-18, and see 2-73. Is planning permission required for a wall or fence? → 9-35, and see also 10-30 on removing hedges.

Table 9: relating law and facts

Subject	Possible legal issues
Building	Will planning permission be required? → 9-13; also 9-47, and note 9-73 onwards for conservation areas and other special areas. Will listed building consent be necessary? → 9-71. Will consent under the Building Regulations be required? → 10-2. Is the land subject to a restriction which will allow neighbours to prevent development? → 7-13. Is a neighbour's consent required for building on or near the boundary?→ 2-28 and 2-36. Will building restrict a neighbour's right to a light? → 6-43.
Dangers on land	Might a lawful visitor be able to claim compensation for being injured? → 11-4; and see 11-11 for injuries to trespassers. Is there a risk of injury to people using a highway? → 4-25. See also Trees, below.
Demolition	Is planning permission required? → 9-23. See also 9-71 on listed buildings. Is consent under the Building Regulations required? →10-9. Will demolition remove support from neighbouring buildings? → 6-47. Can the local authority demolish a building which was put up without planning permission, or is dangerous? → 9-87, 10-6.
Land which is derelict, waste land	Can the local authority take steps to improve the land? → 11-96. Can action be taken if land is a health hazard? → 4-30. And see Ownership, below.
Neighbours	Can action be taken against noise and other anti-social activities by neighbours? → 4-5. Can a landowner exert influence over development on neighbouring land? → 9-52; also 7-13 and 6-35 if a private right of way is required. See also Boundaries, above.
Ownership of land	How can members of the public find out who owns land? → 1-63. Can a person claim land where the true owner is unknown? → 2-67; note also 1-44.
Parking	Is there a right to park on a public road? → 5-10. Can a right to park on some-one else's land be acquired over a period of time? → 6-40. What action can be taken against people who park unlawfully? → 3-29, 3-38, 3-49.

Table 9: relating law and facts

Subject	Possible legal issues
People coming on to land	Are they trespassing, or do they have a legal right to come on to the land? → 3-11. Can continued trespassing, over the years, create legal rights? → 5-22, 6-15. Can they acquire rights if allowed to come on to land? → 7-46.
Pipes, cables, etc	How does the law provide for pipes, cables, etc to be laid under and over land? → 11-103, 6-52.
Roads and paths	How can the public find out whether a road or path is subject to a public right of way? → 5-63. Can footpaths be closed or diverted? → 5-53.
Squatters	Has a person, by taking possession of land for at least 12 years, acquired a right to it? → 2-67. What protection do squatters have against direct action by the owner of the land? → 3-9, 8-88, 8-94.
Trees, shrubs, etc	Protection: is a tree subject to a tree preservation order? → 10-20. Or is it in a conservation area? → 9-77. Is Forestry Commission consent for felling required? → 10-34. Can trees or other vegetation overhanging the boundary of land be trimmed? → 4-22. Is a tree dangerous and in need of felling? → 10-26. See also 4-27 for trees which injure users of the highway.
Water	Can action be taking when water drains on to land from neighbouring land? → 4-14, 6-5. Does a landowner have the right to use water flowing on her land, or to sink a well to extract water? → 2-52; see also 6-46 for taking water from neighbouring land. See also Pipes, cables, etc, above.

Table of Authorities

1. Acts of Parliament

2. Delegated legislation

3. Cases

4. Other material

Index

Note

There is no separate glossary. Where a word or phrase has a special meaning, the Index entry starts with a reference to the paragraph where the meaning is explained.

A

B

D

E

F

G

K

L

M

N

O

P

R

S

T

U

V

W

Y

Z